*C*ompleting
a
*Q*ualitative
Project

For *Anselm Strauss* (1916–1996),
who taught us by example
to write, to mentor, and
to collaborate

Question: Who's the audience for this book?

Hutchinson: The world. At large.

———————•◆•———————

Participants in the group discussion for
Completing a Qualitative Project

From Left:

Front row (kneeling): Katharyn A. May, Judith Wuest, Sally Ambler Hutchinson, Janice M. Morse, Marjorie A. Muecke

Middle row (standing): Rita Schreiber, Holly Skodol Wilson, Judith E. Hupcey, Margarete J. Sandelowski, Joan L. Bottorff, Sally Thorne

Back row: Dauna Crooks, Janice M. Swanson, Judy R. Norris, Joy L. Johnson, Martha Ann Carey, Phyllis Noerager Stern, Juliene G. Lipson, Joyceen S. Boyle

Completing a Qualitative Project

Details and Dialogue

edited by

Janice M. Morse, PhD, FAAN

Professor, Faculty of Nursing
Director, International Institute of Qualitative Methodology
University of Alberta

Adjunct Professor, School of Nursing
The Pennsylvania State University

SAGE Publications
International Educational and Professional Publisher
Thousand Oaks   London   New Delhi

For information:

SAGE Publications, Inc.
2455 Teller Road
Thousand Oaks, California 91320
E-mail: order@sagepub.com

SAGE Publications Ltd.
6 Bonhill Street
London EC2A 4PU
United Kingdom

SAGE Publications India Pvt. Ltd.
M-32 Market
Greater Kailash I
New Delhi 110 048 India

Printed in the United States of America

Library of Congress Cataloging-in-Publication Data

Completing a qualitative project: Details and dialogue/
    editor, Janice M. Morse.
        p. cm.
    Includes bibliographical references and indexes.
    ISBN 0-7619-0600-2 (cloth: acid-free paper).—
    ISBN 0-7619-0601-0 (pbk.: acid-free paper)
    1. Nursing—Research. 2. Nursing—Authorship.
    I. Morse, Janice M.
    RT81.5.C656 1997   97-4679
    610.73′072—dc21

This book is printed on acid-free paper.

97 98 99 00 01 02 03 10 9 8 7 6 5 4 3 2 1

Acquiring Editor:	Daniel T. Ruth
Editorial Assistant:	Jessica Crawford
Production Editor:	Sanford Robinson
Production Assistant:	Denise Santoyo
Book Designer/Typesetter:	Janelle LeMaster
Cover Designer:	Candice Harman
Print Buyer:	Anna Chin

Contents

Preface

May: I think that those of us who do qualitative work are always
        vulnerable to guilt-by-association phenomena—the methods
        are soft, therefore your science is soft. In some ways, we need
        to work a little harder to make sure we have some hard edges
        in how we describe our work.

May is right. There are a lot of "loose edges" in qualitative inquiry;
a lot of questions that remain unanswered. This book is intended to
address those unaddressed issues in qualitative research that occur
after data analysis, or what to do once the analysis is finished.
Qualitative methods books are unusually silent about issues of how
one presents or publishes qualitative work, how one determines the
usefulness of qualitative findings to clinicians, how one "publicizes"
the work, or how qualitative research results in changes in policy.
Qualitative methodologists have been unusually silent on how one
recognizes quality qualitative work, on issues of generalizability, and
on how one actually implements the findings of a qualitative study.

Due to the lack of such discussion, the potential of qualitative work
is not being realized. Qualitative work will not be fully legitimized
until these issues are fully addressed and explicated. It is hoped that
this book will provide beginning discussion on such topics and provide
preliminary guidelines, so that the power and the usefulness of qualitative research will be recognized. And with increased use and in-

creased confidence, qualitative research will earn its rightful position in knowledge development.

Lipson: I want some real critique—hard line critique. Where am I just
           so basic that it doesn't say anything? Have I missed critical pieces
           of literature? And do you have any examples that I can put in
           here?

Lipson's quote (above) captures the essence of this book, and preparing this book was an interesting process. After a chapter was negotiated with a potential author, she often called to complain that she "could not find literature" on the selected topic. In this sense, it indicated the vast gaps that exist in the qualitative literature.

Filling this gap was a difficult but rewarding task. Again, after the authors had prepared a first draft of their chapters, we met for a two-day think tank to discuss the work, to brainstorm about the dilemmas and the issues, and to combine our joint expertise to seek solutions to apparently unsolvable problems.

I have followed our custom of putting dialogues from this think tank between chapters. You will notice they are getting longer. It's interesting that the original intent in using dialogues with our first book *(Qualitative Nursing Research: A Contemporary Dialogue)* was to make the book less dry. To my astonishment, we found that these quotes were read, enjoyed, and sometimes even cited. The same thing happened with the second book *(Critical Issues in Qualitative Research Methods)*, so we have continued the tradition and have extended the dialogues to include "Advice" and what Sally Hutchinson dubbed a "Dead Dog Section," or unfortunate stories of what went unexpectedly wrong—airing our dirty laundry, so to speak. Maybe, in the future, we should forget about writing chapters and simply present our book as a series of transcribed wisdom and witticisms. It would sell just as well, be equally useful, be more fun to read, and be much less work for everyone, except the poor editor. And it would be *very* qualitative.

Those who attended the two-day seminar were Katharyn May (University of British Columbia), Janice Swanson (Samuel Merritt College), Joan Bottorff (University of British Columbia), Margarete Sandelowski (University of North Carolina, Chapel Hill), Sally

Thorne (University of British Columbia), Martha Ann Carey (U.S. Department of Health and Human Services), Joy Johnson (University of British Columbia), Rita Schreiber (University of Victoria), Judy Norris (University of Alberta), Joyceen Boyle (Medical College of Georgia), Sally Hutchinson (University of Florida, Jacksonville), Juliene Lipson (University of California, San Francisco), Marjorie Muecke (Ford Foundation), Dauna Crooks (McMaster University), Judith Wuest (University of New Brunswick), Judith Hupcey (The Pennsylvania State University), Phyllis Stern (University of Indiana), Holly Wilson (University of California, San Francisco), Janice Morse (The Pennsylvania State University and the University of Alberta), and Dan Ruth (Sage Publications).

We thank Katharyn May, Director, School of Nursing, University of British Columbia, for hosting this event. She, along with her team —Joan Bottorff and Joy Johnson—made the arrangements so it could all happen. We thank Sue Dolan and Anna Lombard, our editors at Penn State. And, most of all, we thank Dan Ruth, Editor, Sage Publications, who provided answers to many dumb questions, and whose presence and support throughout the project was much appreciated.

Recognizing the Power
of Qualitative Research

Janice M. Morse

Boyle: There a lot of things that we are talking about in this book that
         ordinarily we don't talk about. They are almost considered
         things that we don't talk about.

There is no doubt that qualitative research is underrated, underval-
ued, and undersung. Perhaps this has happened because we have been
so preoccupied with methods—worrying about how to *do* qualitative
research—that we have forgotten to examine the product. We have
ignored how useful qualitative methods are for understanding what is
"going on," how information gained from qualitative research fits into
the Greater Scheme of Things, and, the ultimate test, what qualitative
findings actually contribute to knowledge. We have forgotten to
consider what would happen to knowledge development in the social
sciences if we did not have qualitative methods. On the other hand,
maybe this silence about the power of qualitative methods is due to
the fact that we are unsure of the contribution of qualitative research

ourselves, and dodging these issues is really symptomatic of keeping our heads in the sand. We really do not know how to respond to Cochrane's (1972, pp. 20-21; see also Sackett, Haynes, Guyatt, & Tugwell, 1991, p. 360) accusation that qualitative research is not more than mere opinion. We do not know how to respond to the charge that qualitative research has no validity, is not generalizable, and must be tested quantitatively before it can be considered useful and usable. We have been intimidated by the sheer volume of the chorus from other side of the debate, by the articulate, complex, and persuasive arguments denouncing or questioning qualitative work. These arguments have been backed by influential philosophers and statisticians, but not always by common sense. Qualitative researchers have had little to cite to reinforce their position. The result has been a weighty silence in which qualitative researchers, outvoted on funding committees and crushed by the democratic process of a committee's vote, traditionally have been forced to concede.

But slowly and inevitably, subtle changes have been occurring. Qualitative research is slowly gaining acceptance. More and more, granting agencies are asking for proposals to include a "qualitative component." More and more, the NIH is looking kindly upon qualitative proposals; more and more, qualitative research is finding its way into journals that usually only publish quantitative research; and more and more, qualitative methods are becoming an established part of graduate courses in research methods and even a required course in their own right. And, most important, a flood of qualitative methods texts are swamping the market, albeit still sidestepping the issues described above.

Of interest, most of these qualitative books consist of methodological instructions and end once they have described *methods*. Although these books may include a section of "standards" for evaluating the conduct of qualitative work (e.g., describing an audit trail), they do not discuss how to evaluate the end product or how to implement the findings. And it is this gap that this book is all about. Therefore, it is time, as Boyle notes, to speak about the unspoken and to address the nitty-gritty issues that previously we have tried to dodge.

Of course, as far as I can tell, I do not think discussing these issues (or not stressing the virtues of qualitative research) has stopped anyone from doing the research. How would I know? I don't. But I do know that the lack of appreciation of these issues by others has led to difficulties in getting the research published, difficulties in getting the research funded, and, for some, even difficulties in obtaining tenure and promotion. And the failure to think these issues through has led to misconceptions that even qualitative researchers themselves have bought into. For example, as late as 1995, Morse and Field wrote: "If qualitative research is to fulfill one of its important functions, these theories should be significant enough and polished enough for subsequent quantitative testing" (p. 10). Now, with the enlightenment of this volume, please correct your copy: TEAR OUT THE PAGE!!!!

"Speaking about the unspoken" was not easy. There were few guidelines for authors to follow. Each problem had to be thought through and then carefully argued in a first draft. These were circulated to all authors. We met for two days and discussed and debated these issues. Then, when some agreement had been reached, authors refined their chapters, rewrote, and created principles or guidelines for each problem encountered.

In this sense, this book is a landmark.

The first section of the book addresses issues in dissemination of qualitative research methods. In her chapter, Boyle discusses how to maximize the numbers of publications arising from a research project or dissertation without falling into the trap of duplicate publication. She has important advice for doctoral students who must prepare for an academic position after graduation. She talks about the significance of preparing oneself for the race down the tenure track and suggests that some of the pressure may be eased by beginning publishing while in the doctoral program. Coauthoring with one's adviser may be tricky when it comes to assigning authorship credits. A major contribution of Boyle's chapter is the development of guidelines for student-faculty collaboration.

Completing a research project is more than closing a book. In her chapter, Lipson writes of the delicate relationships between the researcher and the participants at the completion of the project. Although the intent of the researcher may be to close the relationship, this goal may not be shared by the participants who wish to continue the relationship.

When writing or disseminating research, it is often necessary for the researcher to protect participants' anonymity and confidentiality.

These issues also are clearly presented in Lipson's chapter, with pragmatic information about how to change details when writing so that the participants' confidentiality is maintained and research integrity is not jeopardized.

The presentation of qualitative research is always an art because of the difficulty of compressing descriptive information without losing the rich description and essence of the message. Wilson and Hutchinson present important, pragmatic information necessary to prepare a readable and attractive qualitative proposal presentation. On the other hand, Norris's chapter addresses innovative and exciting alternative ways to convey the essence of a qualitative research project. It is refreshing that the form of qualitative research need not always mimic the traditional quantitative research report. The development of alternative modes of representation is an area that will develop tremendously in the future.

Many authors have struggled with standards for critiquing qualitative research. Thorne presents refreshingly new criteria that enable the reader to evaluate the theoretical, epistemological, and technical quality of research proposals. Her criteria of epistemological integrity (moral defensibility), representative credibility (disciplinary relevance), analytic logic (pragmatic obligation), and interpretive authority (contextual awareness and probable truth) are innovative and important dimensions for evaluating research.

Receiving criticism and reviewers' reports on one's research is always a painful experience. One's research article often emanates from several years of focused research, and often it appears that the reviewers' responses are trivial and condemning. Stern notes that the "rage of rejection," while a normal response, must be overcome to use the criticism constructively, to revise and resubmit the article. If the rage engulfs the researcher, in essence the criticism will bury the research, and all of the previous work will be lost. In her humorous and encouraging way, Stern legitimizes the rage and provides encouragement to use it constructively.

Hupcey extends Stern's chapter by suggesting five strategies to respond to such criticism: (a) Correct the original work (that is, the reviewers were right, there was an error); (b) justify the original work (that is, expand the original work so that the criticism is no longer valid); (c) diffuse the criticism (in essence, ignore it or deflect it); (d) counterattack (to make the debate more general); and (e) simply ignore the criticism. She outlines pragmatic suggestions for using each of these strategies and important advice about how to actually respond.

The next section includes chapters that address the use or evaluation of qualitative research projects. In other words, they address issues on how to think about completed qualitative research projects, what to do with these qualitative research projects when applying them to practice, or how to extend the qualitative research project within one's own research program. Morse argues that theory derived from qualitative research is different than theory developed for quantitative research. Qualitatively derived theory is more solid than quantitative theory. Qualitative theory has been "tested" in the process of development and therefore is more representative of reality and involves less conjecture than quantitatively derived theory. Because of this important fact, qualitative theory may move directly toward implementation. In fact, "testing" of qualitatively derived theory does not test the theory per se; at best, it tests components of the theory. This has important ramifications for the evaluation of qualitative research and its role in knowledge development. It was considered previously that because qualitative research was so context bound, it was not generalizable, and this was not its purpose; however, it is now evident that qualitative research is generalizable according to its level of abstractness.

Expanding on the notion of generalizability, Johnson develops nine suggestions to be considered when determining the generalizability of a qualitative project. She advises us not to define generalizability too narrowly but to carefully analyze the context from which the theory has arisen and to be clear about the goal of the inquiry. Sandelowski addresses the issue of programmatic research in qualitative inquiry. Given the unstructured, exploratory, and undetermined nature of qualitative inquiry, how can researchers predict or plan with sequential studies? Building an area of inquiry is important, not only for the researcher's career development but also for the development of substantive areas in research.

Bottorff explores the linkage between qualitative and quantitative research. When one is doing sequential or simultaneous triangulation, what is the relationship between the qualitative and the quantitative study? She explores various types of qualitative methodology and looks at the use the qualitative base has in the subsequent quantitative research project. Although qualitative research may stand on its own, this chapter provides important information about the usefulness of qualitative research to quantitative inquiry.

The next two chapters, by Swanson, Durham, and Albright and by Wuest and Merritt-Gray, address the relationship between qualitative research and the participants in clinical use or participatory action research. The chapter by Swanson et al. extends from Johnson's chapter on generalizability to show that clinical use is not only possible but an important end result of qualitative research.

The final chapter in this section, by Schreiber, Crooks, and Stern, develops methods of synthesizing qualitative research results. They have identified three purposes of qualitative analysis: theory building, theory explication, and theory description. They clearly illustrate the important role that qualitative meta-analysis performs in lifting the results to formal theory, and it is this process that brings real strength to qualitative inquiry.

The final three chapters look at the political application of qualitative research. May provides pragmatic hints on how one prepares one's findings for release to the press, and gives important advice on how to interact with reporters. Carey explores the role of qualitative research in policy development at the national level, and Muecke delineates qualitative research at the international level, in particular for developing countries.

Taken as a whole, this book is intended not only to demonstrate or guide the researcher about "what to do" when one finishes a research project but also to show the strengths and significance of the use and application of qualitative research. This is an area that is in dire need of development. Only by addressing such issues will qualitative research become significant in its own right. Although qualitative research methods predate quantitative research methods, they have been relatively ignored in the last 30 years. The development of our methods is lagging behind those of quantitative research, but together we can work to explicate and fully comprehend what we do. Again, as May noted,

I think that those of us who do qualitative work are always vulnerable to guilt by association phenomena—the methods are soft, therefore, your science is soft. In some ways, we need to work a little harder to make sure that we have some hard edges on how we describe our work.

References

Cochrane, A. L. (1972). *Effectiveness and efficiency*. London: Abingdon, Berks, Burgess.
Morse, J. M., & Field, P. A. (1995). *Qualitative research methods for health professionals* (2nd ed.). Thousand Oaks, CA: Sage.
Sackett, D. L., Haynes, R. B., Guyatt, G. H., & Tugwell, P. (1991). *Clinical epidemiology* (2nd ed.). Boston: Little Brown.

Dialogue: On Terminating a Project

Lipson: But what do you do with participants who *will not* terminate? Like Middle Eastern immigrants. Whether the study is over or not, they are your friend forever, and they keep calling, and they expect favors, and, you know, now I have a new bird because—

Stern: Ah huh.

Lipson: I think that a lot of cultures are like that. Termination does not mean the same thing. "Termination" is basically a culturally devised concept. "A research study" is a culturally devised concept, where you start, come to an end and you it write up. And you come to the end, and the dance doesn't end because one of the partners won't quit dancing, when the partner is from a cultural group which—

May: They still hear music.

Lipson: Yes! You can't even get out the door at the end of the interview because they keep you there, and you keep drinking tea, and—

Morse: But then there is another problem when the researcher can't stop. You think you have finished your study, it's wonderful, and you write it up—you publish it. Then you walk down the street two years later and see your participant—a burn patient or someone—and they are doing so marvelously, and you think, "Gee, I've go to write this now!"

Thorne: I think we have to think more about the dance metaphor. Maybe the music is always there, but some of us don't hear it. [laughter]

CHAPTER

Writing It Up
Dissecting the Dissertation

Joyceen S. Boyle

In this chapter I will discuss issues about when and how to publish
research findings from a dissertation. For example, should one
publish from a dissertation research project while it is in progress
instead of later when it is completed? I will argue that, for a number
reasons, publications should be generated from a qualitative dissertation while the project is ongoing. The assumptions underlying this
assertion are that there are sufficient data for two or more substantive
publications, and that when more than one publication is generated,
the publications are not overlapping or repetitive. These assumptions
are important and are sometimes overlooked in the rush to publish.

A second issue involves the form or kind of publications that are
produced from the ongoing or completed dissertation: monographs,

AUTHOR'S NOTE: I wish to thank Jim A. Ferrell, M. Katherine Maeve, and Suzanne
Pursley-Crotteau, who read and commented on several drafts of this manuscript.

book chapters, or articles? There are different ways to go about publishing, depending on your academic discipline. What is the best way to expand knowledge in your discipline? How do you split a comprehensive qualitative study into several articles and still retain the holistic integrity of the research project? Embedded in these issues and assumptions are concerns about duplicate publications, authorship, and successful attainment of tenure within an academic setting. I will consider these issues and questions in the following sections of this chapter.

Early Publications

Entering a doctoral program is a significant investment in one's career that consumes several years and a considerable amount of money. If you are going to spend years doing something and spend thousands of dollars to accomplish a goal, you want to carefully plan and to go about it in such a way that you can be assured of success. It is important to establish the habit, early in your career, of submitting papers for publication. Most experienced faculty would agree with Downs (1992), who observed that "the immediate concern of most students is to pass a course with an acceptable grade" (p. 131). Graduate students, especially those in doctoral programs, should look ahead and carefully build their careers over a span of several years. Publishing is a prerequisite to success in an academic career. One of the most important ways to measure success in academe is the award of tenure, an acknowledgment by your peers that you have contributed to the advancement of knowledge in your field. Tenure is seldom granted at major institutions unless the faculty member can demonstrate a consistent number of publications from research-related activities. Although the actual number and quality of publications required may differ by institution, the sooner the publication process begins during an academic career, the more likely the faculty member will be successful in her or his career. Therefore, the process of publishing should begin in graduate school, usually from the dissertation project, for two very compelling, yet quite different reasons. The first deals with the general nature of scientific knowledge and the second reason is more practical as it involves the establishment of a successful career and the achievement of tenure within an academic setting.

The Generation and Sharing of Knowledge

The first argument in support of early publications from a piece of research stems from the nature of scientific knowledge and can be understood through a brief discussion of how we create and share knowledge. Regardless of whether we are talking about quantitative or qualitative paradigms or some other way of knowing, most philosophers of science agree that new knowledge is created by building upon what we already know. Scientific inquiry proceeds in a rather predictable manner and it occurs in the context of other research. For example, if you have the answer to a compelling scientific question, or if you have generated new knowledge about a topic of interest, you can be relatively certain that it is only a matter of time before someone else will discover the answer to that question or will generate similar knowledge about the same topic. Even in qualitative research, where the answers to questions are not as cut and dried as they are in quantitative studies, similar findings eventually will be generated by others. In many scientific investigations, numerous researchers are pursuing a range of similar inquiries. No matter how creative you are, how well you write, or the compelling nature of your findings, if you do not publish the results of your research in a timely manner, someone else will beat you to it.

A fascinating example of how new knowledge was discovered and shared with others was provided by James Watson in *The Double Helix* (1968). As graduate students, Watson and his colleague Francis Crick were trying to understand and explain the structure of DNA. The well-known researcher Linus Pauling and his associates were working on the same problem. Not only did Watson and Crick have to come up with the right explanation, they had to get their results into print before Pauling published his findings. Pauling was working from theoretical knowledge of the field, while Watson and Crick had roentgenographic data from an associate's radiological measurements. The story, as Watson tells it, was filled with exciting yet somewhat frantic efforts to explain DNA, write up the results, and submit for publication. Watson knew that he had only days, maybe a few weeks at the most, to beat Pauling to a publication. Most of us do not have that kind of pressure, but delaying publications can sometimes place a new scholar in a disadvantageous position.

Any research study, including a dissertation project, is a search for information or answers to puzzling questions. If you have new information, you must inform your colleagues through publications before someone else does. The study is not completed until you have the published article in hand and your colleagues all over the world have access to it. In qualitative research, we seldom encounter cliffhangers like the search for DNA. However, there are topics that are "hot" or popular and that generate a great deal of interest, sometimes even controversy. It is usually the case that we do not know much about these topics, and new and/or additional knowledge would help us understand more about a phenomenon or an aspect of human behavior. Frequently, these same topical areas are defined by funding agencies as priorities for funding. It stands to reason that articles generated from such research may be published relatively quickly because editors recognize that results need to be disseminated.

A recent example of such popularity has been the focus on women with HIV disease. Five or six years ago, research studies about women with HIV disease were scarce, probably because most everyone assumed that women were not at high risk. Now, in just a few years, research findings about HIV and women are beginning to proliferate in the literature, and it will be more difficult to find publication sources for this topic because knowledge has become more commonplace. Many of the gaps in our understanding have been filled in or bridged with new findings.

If you are conducting a study on a new area of interest, it is important to publish the results as quickly as possible. Presentations are also important and can lead the way to publications. You not only share your ideas but also receive input and comments from your colleagues. Often you have the opportunity to meet others who are working in your field. The problem arises if the new scholar continues to travel around the country, attending conferences and presenting the same research over and over. The time, money, and effort go into presentations rather than publications. Many dissertations take at least four years to complete, even longer if the graduate student is pursuing her or his studies on a part-time basis. Some doctoral students choose to go directly into postdoctoral studies; in such a case, previous publications will strengthen the postdoctoral application. A trend that is becoming common in many disciplines is for the new doctoral graduate to take a nonacademic position (industry, business, clinical, or other) and not publish from her or his dissertation study at all—an interruption and abrupt end to scientific inquiry. Even when a new graduate accepts an academic appointment, the length of time between the completion of the dissertation and publication after employment by a university is much too long. If you have a great idea for your research, you can be certain that other investigators have the same great idea. Someone else will submit similar findings for publication and by the time our hypothetical graduate student has completed the dissertation, settled into a faculty position, and then written up the findings, most of what we need to know about the topic will have been published by other researchers.

The Tenure Time Bomb

Expanding the field of knowledge and exploring the frontiers of science are lofty, yet still appropriate goals for researchers; we should not lose sight of them. However, on a more personal level, it is important for your academic success to have as many "substantive" publications as early as possible in your academic career. I use the term *substantive* to imply that the article has something worthwhile to report and that it is published in a reputable, peer-reviewed journal. It is extremely important to submit articles to journals that are recognized and acknowledged in your discipline. The journal should have name recognition by your peers and have a reputation as a "research journal," that is, one that publishes reports of scientific studies. Publishing in a source—a journal, a newsletter, or whatever—that no one recognizes or can find is worse than not publishing at all. It implies the study was not worthwhile and it gives the impression that the author does not have the ability to discriminate among publication sources. Most of my colleagues call these publications *throwaways*, meaning just what the term implies, you might as well throw the manuscript away. Once it is published, you cannot "take it back" and publish it again in a more respectable journal.

The expectation for substantive publications over a number of years is a fairly standard criteria for success and tenure in all scientific fields. Suppose that a graduate student completes her or his dissertation or postdoctoral studies and, within a month or two, she (or he) accepts an appointment at a university in another state. This, of course, results in a major geographic relocation that sometimes involves a spouse and her or his career opportunities, children, the purchase of a new house, different schools for the children, and so on. It is a major readjustment process that takes a great deal of time and energy. The new position also takes a great deal of time and high levels of energy. In any new academic environment, there are new colleagues to meet, new classes that require extensive preparation, new readings and new lectures to prepare. In the health professions, there are new clinical facilities that must be explored and new personnel to meet as well as different organizational structures that take time to get to know. All of these many factors deplete energy and require time that could be used in writing activities. Many faculty are more comfortable spending their time and energy in teaching activities and attending meetings than in conducting research and writing. The research activities, *most often the writing*, are pushed aside while other tasks are accomplished; always the excuse is that there is no time for writing. Because faculty typically have seven years to attain tenure, it is easy to assume that everything else in addition to writing should be done first as the deadlines for classes, examinations, meetings, and so on come around quickly.

In addition, it is easy to underestimate the amount of time that is needed to write well. Most of us can remember at least once in our academic career when we sat down at night to write a paper that was due the next day. I hope that last-minute approach to writing has changed because good writing takes tremendous amounts of time. Many of us "learn" to write when we are in graduate school, especially when we are writing up our dissertation findings. I believe that good writing is a skill that can be learned like other skills, and practice is the activity that helps the most. However, it is true that some individuals have better backgrounds and preparation for writing than others. The novice writer needs much more time than the experienced writer as those exquisite writing skills take years of practice to develop and refine. Anyone who needs a little assistance can hire someone to edit a completed manuscript. Moreover, being able to write well usually means the author has the ability to think both conceptually and critically, skills that are necessary when writing up qualitative studies. These skills take even longer to develop and the process seems a little more "painful." No one else can do it for you.

With good luck, but even more with persistence and work, the new faculty member might complete two articles during the first year of an academic appointment. These articles probably will take another two or three years before they are published. Some journals have a review time of six months or longer. Others have a backlog of articles already accepted and waiting for publication. Furthermore, many articles are not accepted on their first submission. Even if one or perhaps both of them are accepted on first submission, it will be "pending revisions," and the rewriting and the second round of reviews (and more writing) still could take another year or more. Publication is a very time-consuming process.

A common scenario is that an article is rejected but at least the reviewers have provided helpful critique and feedback. So our new faculty member must revise the article and look for another journal that seems a likely source for the second submission. Many novice authors require time (and psychological counseling) to recover from the first editor's rejection and, in particular, the reviewers' critical comments (see Stern, this volume). Although that last sentence is based on evidence that is anecdotal and fragmented (my experiences and those of my colleagues), some reviewers' comments are quite devastating. Sometimes the author is too involved, too close to the article; therefore any suggestions for change and improvements are easily resented. The best advice that I can offer is not to take reviewers' comments as a personal affront. After all, it was a blind review. Tell your colleagues about the rejection and repeat all of the nasty comments. Your colleagues can relate to what you are going through because it has happened to everyone, including them. They will be pleased with the opportunity to share their war stories with you so that you will feel better. Develop a thick skin and begin work on the article again *as soon as possible*. Do not put it away in a drawer for more than a couple of weeks. Ask for advice from your colleagues about where to try for a second submission, as this may save you some time. I have a personal rule that a "rejected" article must be resubmitted to another publication source within one month after the rejection.

The pressure to conduct research and to publish builds in academe. During that first year as a new faculty member, a major effort must be undertaken to start another research project, and this by necessity involves a search for funding. The line of inquiry or the research topic should be continued from the dissertation research. Some faculty begin an ill-advised attempt to start anew on a topic that is not related to their previous research. Even worse, some novice faculty announce that they are going to "switch" methods—having done a quantitative dissertation, now they intend to do qualitative research. If a faculty member of any vintage (novice or expert) wishes to make such a radical change in research skills and critical thinking ability, she or he should apply for postdoctoral studies. The way to learn to do research is the time-tested way, by working with an expert who is doing that kind of research. You cannot learn to be a qualitative researcher by reading a book or taking a class. The choice of a dissertation topic and the appropriate method implies a serious commitment. Choose a topic that is interesting and compelling because you will spend the remainder of your academic career reading, writing, and thinking about it. It is important that there be a connection or relationship between the dissertation and the skills and knowledge learned while conducting it and the subsequent research that follows the dissertation. This continuity decreases the start-up time that is required for a new project. The likelihood of successful grant funding depends to some extent on previous work of the principal investigator, and this includes publications. Still, even when you know what you are doing and how to do it, starting another research project, receiving human assurance approval, gaining access to agencies and recruiting participants, and then actually conducting the research involves a tremendous amount of time and attention. Then comes the very difficult part of a qualitative study—writing it up. It is likely to be a long time between the start of the project and the first publication. Remember that all of this occurs while our new faculty member is writing two new manuscripts from her or his dissertation and coping with a new job, new colleagues and agencies, new friends, and sometimes with disgruntled family members who wish they were back home.

Criteria surrounding publications vary by institution and by the profession or discipline. In the health professions, frequently the expectation is that within two years following her or his academic appointment, the new faculty member should have at least three publications in print. The third and fourth year of an academic appointment are critical in terms of productivity. Consistency of publications is also important; more than one year cannot go by without publications. The only way to have publications coming out each year is to write and submit two or more articles each academic year. Plan for these activities in a determined manner by meeting your own deadlines. It is a constant juggling act as productive faculty are always conducting research, writing, revising, and publishing, all at any one time.

Sometime during the sixth year of university employment, a "pretenure" review occurs. But, by the time this takes place, it is too late to worry about a publication track record and it is certainly too late to begin frantically writing. No matter how many articles are in press (*accepted* for publication), what really counts are the articles that have been consistently published over the years. Expectations for publications vary somewhat by academic discipline, by institution, and by region in the United States. Most commonly in many of the health and social sciences, research-based articles that have been published in refereed journals are the publications that receive the most credit during a tenure review. Some disciplines might value scholarly books. Of course, by the time the tenure review is scheduled, the *prolific* author has numerous research articles, several nonresearch publications, a few book chapters, and maybe a book as well. Publications of all kinds (articles, monographs, and/or scholarly books) provide evidence that the faculty member can think conceptually, work independently, and create knowledge that has been disseminated to professional colleagues. Research-based articles in recognized journals are frequently given the most credit in a tenure review because they have been peer-reviewed prior to publication.

The point that I am arguing should be clear. A new faculty member who begins an academic career without any publications may have difficulty earning tenure at a major academic institution. This may vary, of course, with the expectations of any given institution as some have more rigorous tenure criteria than others. While creating knowledge is a wonderful goal and we all should strive for it, obtaining tenure has immediate rewards (both personal and professional) that make the arguments very compelling for publishing as early as possible in an academic career.

Planning for Publications During the Dissertation

Anyone serious about an academic career should conduct her or his dissertation in such a way that several publications can be generated from it. Doctoral students should include a time line for publications in their plans for completing their dissertations. I hope they can structure their research project and doctoral education in such a manner that they will have one or two publications when they apply for an academic position. Presentations at research conferences are an excellent way to begin on a publication. Evidence of presentations, and especially of publications, places a faculty applicant in a stronger position than other candidates who have not attempted to disseminate their research findings. Often faculty applicants who have published can command a higher salary for the very reason that they already have a track record of publications.

The arguments for publishing during the dissertation process rest on the assumption that the dissertation is a substantive piece of work and that there can be three or more articles generated from it. Doctoral students and/or novice scholars should acknowledge very early in their careers that research activities must become a way of life. There are no compelling reasons to conduct a research project in such a hurry that only one "thin" article can be generated from it. If you are willing to spend a year or more collecting the data, make certain that you collect a sufficient amount to generate several articles. I hesitate to place a number (two, three, or more) on possible publications from a dissertation because there are many variations in dissertations that result in different kinds of publications. However, no one can afford to publish only one article per research project because the start-up time of any study is too intensive and demanding and the analysis and writing activities that lead to successful publications are too involved and time-consuming.

It is common to encounter doctoral students who say they do not want to do a "quick and dirty" dissertation, yet they want to finish their dissertation in three years. This attitude means that they will not have sufficient time during their dissertation research to investigate serendipitous findings, to pursue a piece of intriguing data, or to answer questions that arise during the collection and analysis of data. In some cases, it may be that the research participants are interviewed only one time with a broad array of questions, without follow-up with more rounds of interviews. With only one round of interviews, it is not possible to attain what is known as theoretical saturation. We say that the data are "not thick" (as in "thick description") or "not saturated"—meaning thin. These are the kind of dissertations that produce only one "thinly spread" article. It may be difficult to get that one article published because the lack of rigor will be apparent to the journal editor and the reviewers. Thus it is important to allow sufficient time during doctoral education to make certain that you learn all you need to know about research and that you do a solid, appropriate study from which you can generate several articles.

Breaking Up the Dissertation

The subject of early or "dissertation-in-progress" publications may focus on an innovation in the method or on other related topics. After the literature review has been completed, an article might be generated that deals with the "state of the science" in terms of what is known about the research topic. Remember that this type of article should be a synthesis of known knowledge, not just an annotated bibliography. Although such articles may not be viewed by everyone as "real" research publications, they clearly demonstrate that the author can write well enough to have her or his work accepted for publication. One suggestion is to pick a topic or idea that you like or the one that interests you the most in your research; start where your passion is and you are more likely to be successful on that first try. Having articles accepted for publication during doctoral studies implies that the author is gaining experience in writing and thinking as well as in submitting and revising articles; all of these skills are necessary in the successful application for tenure and in academe in general.

There are no firm rules for dividing up a dissertation into smaller publishable articles. There are some commonsense guidelines that suggest each article should be substantive and "complete" within its pages. And, of course, the article should not duplicate previous publications, but other than those parameters, it is a matter of your own judgment. Obviously some dissertations are tighter, more compact than others. Several of the new faculty at my institution have told me that there is a trend toward smaller, thinner dissertations. If so, I have not heard about it and my initial reaction would be to ask, "Why?" followed closely by, "How many articles can you publish from it?" Some kinds of dissertations may have more potential for several studies than other kinds. For example, a grounded theory study that focuses on a select social process may not be as amenable to "breaking up" as other kinds of studies. It would seem that the generation of articles, including the number of them, the topics they address, and the particular way that data will be collected all need to be considered from the beginning of the study. If the researcher simply assumes that the publications will consist of a literature review, a "methods" article, and an article about the findings, such an approach may leave the author vulnerable to charges of "duplicate publications," which is the practice of publishing what is essentially the same article in different journals. In this case, the duplication occurs through sequential or segmented publications.

Instead, potential authors should be alert for serendipitous findings and be ready to follow intriguing leads in data collection and analysis. Plan carefully to make certain sufficient data are gathered to write an expanded or in-depth discussion of selected topics. Perhaps some examples from my own experiences would be helpful in explaining how ideas for articles can develop during the dissertation project. During my dissertation research (Boyle, 1982), I used a Family Health Calendar Recording (FHCR) to describe illness episodes over a month's time that occurred in members of my sample ($N = 132$) as well as how the illnesses were managed by the individuals and family members. In my actual dissertation, I devoted approximately two paragraphs of the discussion to "emotionally derived" illnesses, those emotional upsets that were associated with an illness. There were not very many of them and I noted that nearly all them occurred among women and were attributed to anger or crying—emotional upsets that followed episodes of domestic violence. However, in the field notes that I had taken during other stages of my research, I had recorded numerous instances of abusive behavior and/or narratives about domestic violence. Some of these observations and experiences were described in my dissertation when they added appropriate contextual information. I later pulled out these serendipitous findings from the FHCR as well as my notes on domestic violence from my field journal; then I wrote an article about women's health and the ideology underlying male-female relationships in a Latin society (Boyle, 1985a). I also wrote a chapter on the trials and tribulations of using an FHCR and how to avoid or at least partially solve the problems that I had encountered (Boyle, 1985b). The focus on illness behavior was a major thrust of my dissertation research and it was apparent in the literature review and in the methodology. The "reconceptualization" or refocus on women's health from a feminist perspective represented something new. Nothing appeared in my literature review that would have indicated that topic was of particular interest in my research. To me, this is an example of how an investigator "pushes" the analysis, refocusing or reconceptualizing the data. The idea that the qualitative dissertation follows a predictable track and never deviates should be questioned. A good substantive dissertation ought to provide the researcher with sufficient data to analyze and publish for a number of years. Those publications may take quite a different direction than the one described in the dissertation proposal.

Many qualitative dissertations represent a significant amount (years) of work, and it is nearly impossible to present them as one integrated "whole." In attempting to write up the dissertation as an integrated "whole," authors often conclude to their dismay that the richness, as well as compelling stories about their participants, have been eliminated. Several years ago, Dr. Jana Lauderdale and I submitted an article titled "Infant Relinquishment Through Adoption" to *IMAGE: The Journal of Nursing Scholarship*. The original manuscript was some 27 pages in length and represented the major findings from Dr. Lauderdale's dissertation (Lauderdale, 1992). At the time of submission, we asked the reviewers for suggestions about how to "cut it down," or shorten the manuscript. In retrospect, I would advise other authors in a similar situation to do their own cutting or seek help from a colleague before they submit such a lengthy manuscript. Reviewers are likely to comment, "too wordy" or "too long," and let it go at that. Anyway, "in the goodness of time" (a quote from Donna Diers, the journal editor at that time), we received the manuscript in the mail asking us to make some revisions including shortening the article and then to resubmit it. Dr. Lauderdale and I completed the revisions, shortening the article considerably, and resubmitted it to the same journal. The new editor, Dr. Henry, eventually instructed us that the journal would publish the manuscript if we could cut it down to about 12 pages, including figures and references. Dr. Lauderdale tackled the "first cut" and managed to get the manuscript down to 15 pages before throwing up her hands in frustration. I then took over and cut out more and more and more. Finally, we had a manuscript that was 14 pages in length including references and one figure; it was subsequently published (Lauderdale & Boyle, 1994). We were not totally pleased with the results; we judged the article to be only the "bare bones," a mere sketch of fascinating and interesting findings that were included in the original dissertation (Lauderdale, 1992). But we had spent almost two years writing and revising the article, so we concluded that we were too invested with the journal to turn elsewhere at that point. The published article generated a significant number of letters to the editor, and several readers wrote directly to us. A few of them were very critical because, in their opinions, we had not presented an adequate review of the literature! We thought we had done well to condense, cut, and delete some six pages of the original literature review into three brief paragraphs so that we could present the findings in an understandable manner. Dr. Lauderdale and I are convinced that we could easily write two or three articles from the material that we deleted from the first draft. Such a situation always presents a dilemma and challenge for qualitative researchers as it is nearly impossible to present a "coherent whole" from a good qualitative dissertation in only 12 pages. It is always a good idea to search out those journals that accept manuscripts of 15 pages or more if you are trying to write about several difficult concepts that must be linked together in a "coherent whole."

Researchers within the health sciences may be at more of an advantage than other academicians because we have more choices, or more variety, in publication sources. We can orient our research articles so that they emphasize research, application to clinical practice, or even educational strategies. Not only is the focus different for each of the articles, the audience that reads each article will vary also. There is an obvious advantage of publishing research findings in clinical journals. If you want to make changes in practice then it makes sense to publish in journals that practitioners read, and many of them do not read the "mainline" research journals.

Student-Faculty Authorship

There is no agreement on acceptable criteria or guidelines for student-faculty authorship. Whose names appear on a paper and in what order (first, second, or even third author) involve decisions that frequently are discipline specific and sometimes also vary by region and type of institution. The most important point is that a discussion of the issues surrounding authorship should begin early in the student-faculty relationship and continue throughout the educational process and longer if the joint authorship continues. It is much more pleasant to talk about publications and student-faculty responsibilities at the beginning of the dissertation rather after the first article has appeared in print and one or more of the authors is offended and/or angry.

Generally, there are several advantages to student-faculty publications, but there are also many *devastating* pitfalls. Doctoral (or master's) students and their faculty should consider the possibility of coauthoring articles whether they are from the dissertation or developed from papers originally submitted for course assignments by the student. The academic milieu in most institutions recognizes and encourages both single and dual authorship, and there are advantages for both faculty member and student if they can work together on manuscripts. Most seasoned academicians have published numerous articles that were coauthored with students. In fact, at most institutions, writing and coauthoring articles with students is a clear expectation for faculty. Faculty are hired to teach students, and teaching, at least at the graduate level, includes research and writing. Mentorship of students is valued and can be demonstrated by joint publications with students.

In offering advice for beginning researchers, Byrne, Kangas, and Warren (1996) suggested that the connection between an experienced and a novice researcher is enhanced when mentoring includes joint publications. This association increases collaboration and support in the research process; writing for publication is more successful if one of the authors has some expertise and experience. Yet it is a process that is fraught with potential problems. In the best of all worlds, a doctoral student will want to begin publishing with her or his mentor about the second year of a doctoral program. This is approximately the time that graduate students have chosen their research topics and their dissertation advisers. When faculty members agree to coauthor papers with students, authorship (who does what and whose name goes first), as well as an explicit description of responsibilities and deadlines, should be spelled out clearly. Some faculty are very comfortable in saying to students, "If I am going to spend a lot of time helping you, then I want my name on any publication from this endeavor." Many faculty are comfortable with being second author on a manuscript based on the student's ideas or research. But there are those advisers who want their names to appear first. It is always a good idea to have all details in writing and clearly understood by both the faculty member and the student before any writing begins or at least at the first draft. If we are talking about publishing a paper from a course assignment, usually faculty need to read a first draft to ascertain if there are some ideas that can be developed into a publishable paper. It is also important to talk about what will happen if the agreed-upon writing does not occur as planned. Incorporating the "writing agreement" into objectives for an independent study or a research practicum is one approach, and the student's attainment of mutually agreed-upon objectives determines the grade in the course. This process helps the student remain focused and assures that the faculty adviser will carry out her or his responsibilities as well. In addition, it ensures the publications are completed or at least close to completion before the student graduates and leaves the academic environment. More doctorally prepared graduates are going into nonacademic positions where the "pressure" to publish is not as intense as it is in an academic environment. So the former student, although promising to "write it up," gets more and more involved in activities on the job and pushes the writing aside. That leaves the faculty member in a dilemma. She or he can decide to drop the project and forget about it. The faculty member can also do the writing— harassing the former student to do as much as possible. When that situation occurs, a faculty member (who has done the majority of the writing) can renegotiate for first authorship, acknowledging that the "ideas" belonged to the second author. Some faculty are not comfortable usurping the student's first authorship and so they submit the article with the student's name as first author. It is a judgment call and is always a bit awkward because the student has not followed through on her or his commitments.

Most important, any success in student-faculty publications provides a feeling of accomplishment that should lead to an increased emphasis on writing for publication. Doctoral students who are writing on their own initiative, and not collaborating with a faculty mentor, can ask a wide assortment of persons for help and guidance.

Usually, faculty members are willing to read manuscripts and provide direction for revisions or suggestions about submissions to journals. Their help and assistance should always be acknowledged in a brief sentence or two that accompanies the manuscript.

A very controversial topic involves the order of names, usually whose name should be first on a manuscript. Because the subject of this chapter is about "writing up the dissertation," the discussion of "authorship" will be limited to the questions that might arise from student-faculty publication of articles that come from the student's dissertation. Procedures, or what is commonly acknowledged as acceptable, in one discipline might be inappropriate in another. So keep in mind that the ground rules are not clear, and sometimes the boundaries or the "rules" can be overlooked, quite unintentionally. Sometimes the boundaries involve good "academic manners"; at other times, when they involve professional ethics, the issues are serious and there is no excuse for not knowing the "rules."

We have all heard the horror stories that circulate in academe. Someone did all of the work and yet another name appears on the manuscript, or one name appears first and that person did not contribute as much as the person whose name is listed second. Most of the stories involve a faculty member or "other" claiming recognition for something (an idea or a piece of writing) that belongs to someone else, usually a student. No doubt, there are instances when this has happened. It is also important to acknowledge that students can and occasionally do take advantage of faculty and overstep the bounds that govern research activities and publications.

In any discussion of authorship, the concept of "intellectual property" or "intellectual authorship" must be considered and acknowledged. Whose ideas are discussed in the manuscript? If a graduate student is working on a faculty member's grant or under the auspices of a faculty member's research project, then any work that student does (and this includes publications) must carry the name of the mentor or the principal investigator. It does not matter whether the student wrote the proposal (under the umbrella of a faculty member's grant), collected and analyzed all of the data, and then wrote every word in the manuscript. The faculty member's name must appear on that article. A general rule of thumb is that the faculty member "owns" the "intellectual property," or the ideas, in the grant proposal and that faculty member must always receive appropriate recognition. This usually means that the faculty member's name appears first on all publications from the grant or that she or he is acknowledged in some way as the primary author. It does not matter who collected the data, who analyzed the data, or who wrote the manuscript—intellectual property, or who "owns" the idea, takes precedence over all other factors. Sometimes students do not understand this very important "rule" or principle in research activities.

If the student is completing a dissertation that is a part of a faculty member's funded research project, the faculty member, as the principal investigator, is under an obligation to publish the data. Further successful grant funding is tied to publications generated from that project. It is extremely problematic if a student fails to follow through and does not publish from either a thesis or a dissertation that was conducted when the student was participating in her or his mentor's research. Students are sometimes in a position to be exploited, yet in the circumstances just described, the mentor has been placed in a very awkward position. Most faculty try reasoning, cajoling, threatening, in that order, to motivate the student to write up her or his findings. If those methods do not produce results, then the faculty member can go ahead reluctantly and publish from the student's research. The student's contribution should be acknowledged by showing her or his name as second author. The principle of intellectual property as well as the faculty member's academic reputation must be considered. If the original research was a funded project, the intellectual property rights belong to the faculty member and she or he has an obligation to publish the research. It is a political reality that whoever gets the money must publish; it is an academic ethic that the principal investigator "owns" the ideas in the grant and she or he has the right and obligation to publish them.

If the publication comes from the student's dissertation and the original ideas belong to her or him, then the guidelines about the order of names on a manuscript are not as clear. The faculty member must be very clear with students about expectations for publications. A common scenario begins with the faculty member and student discussing the potential manuscript and clarifying the expectations. Usually the student chooses what to publish from the dissertation, and the shape of the manuscript must be discussed in great detail by the faculty member and student. Usually the student writes the first draft. The faculty member invests a great deal of time editing, rewriting, revising, and providing direction. Sometimes the faculty member and student may choose to do the writing together, sharing the ideas and discussing them as they write them out. This procedure works well in some cases and not in others; sometimes the faculty member's and student's writing styles do not mesh. In most cases the writing and rewriting continues until the faculty member is satisfied with the manuscript. Usually it is the faculty member who makes the final decision about the choice of journal for submission. Most often, the faculty member does the final editing and her or his name is placed on the manuscript as the second author. A word of caution is appropriate here. The process just described is not the only way to approach student-faculty authorship; many faculty and students develop a process that works for them.

If a student is working on her or his dissertation and the chairperson has not discussed writing a joint publication, then the student should take the initiative and discuss writing plans with the mentor. The most important thing is that the plans for writing are explicit and clear to both faculty member and student, and the details discussed and agreed upon by both parties. It may be helpful to put the details into writing and develop a time line for all activities. The relationship between the dissertation adviser and the graduate student usually lasts for several years and can be rather intense. Most dissertation advisers spend a great deal of time—many, many hours—helping students with their research. If the student publishes from her or his research with another member of the supervisory committee without the prior knowledge and consent of the major adviser, there probably will be serious ramifications. Quite possibly the student will need to find another adviser if the dissertation is still in progress. If this situation occurs after the dissertation has been completed, there will be potential problems between the adviser and the committee member. Clearly the committee member has infringed on the adviser's working relationship with the student. Sometimes students can be excused because they are naive, but a faculty member is not allowed to have this excuse; such behavior is unethical. Articles that involve two faculty (the major adviser and a committee member) and a student are relatively rare. That situation could be fraught with problems. Again, if the agreement among faculty members and student is clear and everyone knows and understands their exact responsibilities and all involved are punctual about commitments, such a writing project could be successful.

What about the student simply publishing solo from her or his research? If the dissertation is ongoing, the major adviser's scholarly reputation is involved and she or he will want to approve any manuscripts that evolve from the study. This is particularly true because the dissertation is not a completed piece of work and is still under the direction of the faculty member. The situation could get a little sticky if the adviser has not been informed from the beginning that the student plans to publish during the dissertation.

The most common situation is that the doctoral student does not publish until the dissertation has been completed. After graduate students have completed their dissertations to the satisfaction of their advisers and committees, the students must live with their own triumphs and mistakes. They can write up their dissertations and publish them independently of their dissertation advisers, if that's what they want to do. When faculty have strong feelings about this procedure, it is up to them to tell their former students what they believe about student-faculty publications. Some faculty will argue that the time and effort they have spent on a dissertation research project (advising, reading, editing, and so on) entitles them to authorship (not just an acknowledgment) on any publication. Other faculty are even more emphatic about publications and tell their students that if the students do not publish after a certain length of time—say, two years—then the faculty member will publish the study for them. Again, it is a matter of being clear about expectations from the beginning of the project and the relationship. Regardless of authorship, the role and guidance of the faculty adviser should always be acknowledged on all publications. It is a matter of good manners and academic protocol to acknowledge the role of the faculty adviser in the acknowledgments section if the faculty member's name does not appear on the manuscript. Even when the adviser has had little to do with a dissertation (which occasionally *does* happen, I am sorry to admit), the adviser's role should still be mentioned in the acknowledgments section.

Sometimes after a student has completed the dissertation and accepted an academic position, she or he will ask their former chairperson to read a manuscript from the dissertation and provide feedback. It is clear (and mutually agreeable) that only the former student's name will appear on the manuscript. The new author will, it is hoped, follow the mentor's advice for revising the manuscript. When it is submitted for publication, there should always be an acknowledgment of the mentor's time and efforts—always, always, always. The rules are not explicit, but the faculty mentor has spent a considerable amount of time and effort, not only with the dissertation but in reviewing the manuscript and providing suggestions. A short acknowledgment is the appropriate way to recognize this type of help and expertise. It costs the former student nothing and goes a long way in expressing appreciation to the mentor for the hours of assistance that she or he has provided.

The same "rules" or considerations that apply to written publications also apply to presentations. Intellectual authorship must be taken into account and all persons who have contributed to the study should be acknowledged for their help and assistance. Authorship and the order in which names appear on presentations or posters must be discussed and agreement must be reached before the abstract is submitted for presentation. In both presentations and publications, the ground rules may vary depending on individual circumstances as well as the discipline involved.

A major point in this chapter is that by the time the PhD is awarded and the new doctorally prepared individual is looking for an academic position, she or he should have at least one publication on her or his vita. The outdated notion that you wait until you have a faculty position before you begin to write up your dissertation for publication is antiquated and harmful to success in an academic career. There are some academic institutions that only "count" or consider publications for the tenure review that have been published after the faculty member was employed by that particular institution. Even under such circumstances, experience with publishing before formal employment will enhance the faculty member's abilities to write and publish. Counting publications postemployment reinforces the argument that a dissertation should be in such depth as to enable the researcher to publish numerous articles from it. It is also one more reason that potential faculty should ask many specific questions about promotion and tenure at any university before accepting an academic position.

To sum up this discussion of student-faculty authorship, it will be helpful to briefly reiterate two major points. In qualitative research, the analysis always involves ideas and/or conceptualizations that ideally evolve and develop from both the faculty mentor and the student. Writing up a qualitative dissertation is an important part of the analysis, and the faculty member is involved in the project in quite a different way than in a quantitative project. The contributions of the faculty member to a qualitative dissertation should be significant. Those contributions should lead to publications that reflect student-faculty authorship. Second, if the faculty adviser of a qualitative dissertation is not an author on a publication, then her or his role should be acknowledged in the acknowledgments section along with any other person who has been influential in helping with the manuscript or the research that preceded it. Table 2.1 suggests "manners" or guidelines for student-faculty authorship.

Avoiding Duplicate Publications

I have been emphatic in the previous sections of this chapter in encouraging novice scholars—those completing dissertations—to publish early results from their research, and to write publications while the study is in process. Whenever I have expressed these convictions in conversations with colleagues, someone usually points out that I am encouraging duplicate publications, which was mentioned above, and is defined by the American Psychological Association (1994) as the simultaneous or subsequent publication of the same article or major elements of an article such as methods, discussion, conclusions, graphics, or other illustrative material. The concern is "that duplicate publication distorts the knowledge base by making it appear there is more information available than really exists" (p. 295).

Most of the discussion and concern that exists within the nursing profession about duplicate publications has arisen from quantitative studies. Blanchett, Flanagin, and Young (1995) recently published a study about duplicate publications in nursing. They sampled all articles published in a four-year time period by 77 authors originally published in three consecutive issues of the journal *Nursing Research*. That particular journal tends to publish primarily quantitative nursing studies. Blanchett et al. (1995) classified 28% of the articles they reviewed as duplicate publications. However, qualitative studies by their very nature are different than quantitative studies and are more

Table 2.1 Guidelines for Student-Faculty Authorship

Circumstances	Faculty Responsibilities	Student Responsibilities
Student writes paper for a class.	Faculty member reads paper; talks with student about revising and submitting paper for publication.	Student agrees to work on paper. Makes appointments with faculty member to continue dialogue.
	Acknowledges and signs form for Independent Study. Writes memo to the student acknowledging that faculty member will read, critique, and otherwise provide feedback on each draft of paper. Confirms date for completion of paper. Agrees in writing to authorship agreement. Lists potential journals for submission.	Writes objectives for Independent Study. Objectives include the following information: (a) dates for each draft of the paper, (b) date paper will be completed, (c) authorship agreement (student first author, faculty member second).
	All authors read and approve the final version including the sequence of authors.	
Student asks faculty member to be dissertation adviser.	Faculty member agrees to chair dissertation committee. Asks student to develop time line for dissertation research including one article prior to completion of dissertation.	Student develops time line for proposal and article from dissertation research.
Article from student's dissertation research.	Asks student to develop Independent Study proposal or similar agreement for writing activities. Makes suggestions about form article should take, that is, "state of the science," methods article, or data based. Suggests name of journal for article submission.	Student makes decision on focus of article.

Student prepares Independent Study or other agreement with objectives that include (a) description/focus of article; (b) time lines for all drafts and completed article, which includes the review, revisions, and writing responsibilities of faculty member as well as student writing responsibilities; and (c) authorship. |
| | Shares her/his philosophy on student-faculty authorship. Usual arrangement is that student's name appears first on all articles generated from dissertation. | |
| | All authors read and approve the final version of the manuscript including the sequence of authors. | |

(continued)

Table 2.1 Continued

Circumstances	Faculty Responsibilities	Student Responsibilities
Dissertation research conducted by student under the auspices of faculty member's funded research.	Faculty member very clear that publications must result from all research. States clearly who will be first author and what procedures will be employed if student fails to write up articles. Faculty member reviews and signs proposal. Faculty member reads and critiques manuscript, providing feedback. Follows procedures above. All authors read and approve the final version of manuscript including the sequence of authors.	Student approaches faculty member to chair dissertation. Student makes choice at this point. May choose another dissertation chair. Student develops writing proposal that includes the following information: (a) dates for each draft of the papers, (b) dates papers will be completed, (c) authorship arrangement on each paper, and (d) responsibilities of student and faculty member. Student conducts dissertation research and meets obligations for writing, which usually include major responsibility for "good" first draft and subsequent revisions.
Student fails to write up articles from dissertation research completed under auspices of faculty grant.	When student fails to write up article as agreed upon, faculty member must assume responsibility for publication process. Faculty member writes up articles, acknowledging student contribution in acknowledgment section and listing her- or himself as single author. Or faculty member may include student's name as second author.	

amenable to publication of several articles from each study. According to Blanchett et al. (1995), the most common type of duplication publication is so-called "salami slicing," or segmented publications. They define segmented research as "research articles in which related aspects of the same study were published separately (for example, separate methods articles or reports of different subsamples)" (p. 52).

A substantive qualitative study can be planned and conducted in such a way as to yield several articles that present new and useful information, without duplication. Methods and designs used in qualitative studies are not as cut and dried as they are in quantitative research. Even more interesting, both the methods and the designs used by qualitative researchers currently are undergoing a renaissance and change. Like it or not, there is much more to current qualitative research than ethnography, grounded theory, and phenomenology. Probably each design was used differently as it was adapted by numerous disciplines, changing considerably from the original way it was used. In addition, the postmodern influences on all qualitative methods have been profound. The incorporation of philosophy into research methods, especially phenomenology, is still an ongoing process. In addition to the changes brought about by postmodernism, qualitative researchers are trying numerous variations that are yielding intriguing results; just recall the growth of focus groups in both qualitative and quantitative studies. Feminist research, action research, participatory research, critical research, and other approaches should convince us that all qualitative methods are undergoing considerable change. Another example of something new is narrative method, often using a life history approach to offer something new in both design and method. Furthermore, the analyses used in a narrative account are different than the usual comparative analyses for qualitative data. There is a need for expanded discussions of these newer designs and methods; usually, they are described only briefly in research articles. An in-depth description of an innovative method with or without the results achieved is not a duplicate publication.

It is often possible to conduct a secondary analysis or to reanalyze qualitative data. Thorne (1994) has written about the contributions of secondary analysis and how an investigator might offer an analytic expansion or a different interpretation of original data. A secondary analysis is not a duplicate publication. In qualitative research, one cannot assume that the method or analysis that was described in the first publication is exactly the same in a second publication that has used the same data set. Other procedures, such as amplified sampling and cross-validation, might have been employed, and these procedures alone (or together) would yield a different kind of data or answer other questions. To further illustrate this important point, some researchers (myself included) often publish from an ongoing study and then try something a little different in the approach to data collection—group interviews or another round of different questions, for example. It is the same study, but the method has taken "another turn"; sometimes not only the method but the topic changes as well. It stands to reason that the theory generated will be different also.

Often qualitative studies are longitudinal in nature and the data generated are so rich that there is more than an adequate amount to write a second substantive article. Thus, in any two articles from the same qualitative study, the methods may be different, the topics might have changed, and so will the nature and amount of data. This kind of "sequential" publication is not duplicative or overlapping. However, if there is any doubt whatsoever about the possibility of duplication, it is important to consult the journal editor. All prior publications from the study should be noted and should be referenced appropriately (American Psychological Association, 1994).

Where and How to Go About Publishing

The well-rounded scholar publishes in a variety of journals and books. In some academic institutions, research-based publications in refereed journals are the only publications that are evaluated for award of tenure. In other words, these are the "real" publications; the other kinds of publications are secondary. This means that the beginning scholar should concentrate on writing research-based articles and submitting them for publication in refereed journals. Sometimes new scholars inquire about the choice of a journal for submission of an article. A good choice might be those journals that actively solicit qualitative studies and, of equal importance, have reviewers who understand qualitative research. Look or ask for information about the length of the review process and "in press" time. Those factors need consideration if you want an article to be published within the next 12 or 18 months. Some journals may have a "backlog" of publications, and even if your article is accepted, it may be one or more years before it is published and available to your colleagues. Journals whose issues are topic oriented may be highly competitive and your article may be rejected due to the high level of competition. On the other hand, the reviews are turned around quickly (simply because they are all reviewed for that particular "topic" issue); the reviews can be helpful and provide good feedback. If you receive a rejection, keep trying. Make the revisions that the reviewers suggest and try another journal. A novice scholar should be cautious about submitting an article to one of the more prestigious journals as competition can be formidable. An article from a qualitative study should not be submitted to a journal that does not publish qualitative studies or have reviewers with expertise in qualitative methods. It wastes time and effort and sometimes can be a demoralizing experience.

In some instances, there may be alternatives to publishing research-based journal articles. Although not all academic institutions have exact criteria about what constitutes a research publication, there is a prevailing notion that books or book chapters are "synthesized" knowledge, not "new" knowledge. In other words, the author is taking "known" information and presenting it in a new or more under-standable way. At the Medical College of Georgia, where I am employed, books or book chapters are considered an "educational activity" and their publication meets educational criteria for tenure. Most faculty teach sufficient numbers of classes and/or participate in other related educational activities that we easily meet educational criteria for tenure. It is the scholarship criteria that provoke the most concern. Other institutions or especially other disciplines within the social sciences may view books or book chapters as evidence of scholarship and encourage new faculty to become involved in such projects. And it is possible under some circumstances to publish research findings in a book or a book chapter. All of these possibilities should be thoroughly investigated when a faculty candidate interviews for an academic position. For example, a scholar who bases her or his scholarship on theory or ethics and publishes "theoretical" articles should carefully evaluate an institution's tenure and promotion criteria as they relate to "research" and "research publications." Those same scholars will want to engage in some very frank discussions before signing a contract with the institution.

In my experience, books or even book chapters take a tremendous amount of time and effort. If you spend a year or more writing a book and then it is rejected by a publisher, you will be in a terrible dilemma. As previously suggested, there are certain academic settings where there is little recognition for textbooks, and the efforts that writing a book require may be misdirected or at least not given the amount of credit that they deserve. Although it can be argued that the well-rounded scholar does write books or book chapters, these activities should come later in a career or at least after several research articles are in print. New scholars should make a deliberate choice to publish dissertation results in research journals because journal articles are considered the appropriate source of research findings that advance knowledge in the profession. Journal articles are peer-reviewed or found acceptable by your colleagues prior to publication. The publications from a dissertation are the first step to obtaining grant monies, and all universities and disciplines appreciate scholars who can generate extramural funds.

I have argued in this chapter that publications should be generated while the qualitative dissertation is ongoing. Qualitative dissertations yield sufficient data and provide opportunities for serendipitous findings; therefore, duplicate publications should not be a problem for the qualitative scholar who wishes to get a head start on an academic career. Publications early in an academic career are now the norm and should be encouraged by student-faculty authorship. The relationship between students and academic mentors should be amicable and trusting and set the stage for open negotiations about authorship and publications. A qualitative dissertation provides a doctoral student with opportunities to publish several articles that make contributions to the state of the science, innovation in methods, and generation of theory.

References

American Psychological Association. (1994). *Publication manual of the American Psychological Association* (4th ed.). Washington, DC: American Psychological Association.

Blanchett, S. S., Flanagin, A., & Young, R. K. (1995). Duplicate publication in the nursing literature. *IMAGE: Journal of Nursing Scholarship, 27,* 51-56.

Boyle, J. S. (1982). Dimensions of illness behavior among urban Maya (Doctoral dissertation, University of Utah, 1982). *Dissertation Abstracts International, 43,* 9495B.

Boyle, J. S. (1985a). Ideology and illness experiences of women in Guatemala. *Health Care for Women International, 6*(1-3), 73-86.

Boyle, J. S. (1985b). Use of the family health calendar and interview schedules to study health and illness. In M. Leininger (Ed.), *Qualitative research methods in nursing* (pp. 217-235). Orlando, FL: Grune & Stratton.

Byrne, M. M., Kangas, S. K., & Warren, N. (1996). Advice for beginning nurse researchers. *IMAGE: Journal of Nursing Scholarship, 28*, 165-167.

Downs, F. S. (1992). Faculty-student publication. *Nursing Research, 41*, 131.

Lauderdale, J. L. (1992). The unbroken cord: The experience of infant relinquishment through adoption (Doctoral dissertation, University of Utah, 1992). *Dissertation Abstracts International, 92*, 26185.

Lauderdale, J. L., & Boyle, J. S. (1994). Infant relinquishment through adoption. *IMAGE: Journal of Nursing Scholarship, 26*, 213-217.

Thorne, S. (1994). Secondary analysis in qualitative research: Issues and implications. In J. M. Morse (Ed.), *Critical Issues in qualitative research methods* (pp. 263-279). Thousand Oaks, CA: Sage.

Watson, J. D. (1968). *The double helix.* New York: Atheneum.

Dialogue: What Do I Publish?

Muecke: What kind of book, or monograph that is a research report, should you publish? You know—a solid, one-piece report?—or should it be a collection?

Stern: I really disagree. I sit on the university promotion tenure committee, and we had representation from health and social science, and education and you name it. And every school wanted *articles*. The sciences wanted more writing—but they all wanted refereed articles.

Muecke: And, they didn't want books?

Stern: Books were OK if they were best sellers. But they were downgraded.

Muecke: What about history? What about political science? Anthropology?

May: I think there may be some disciplinary and regional differences. Historians, social sciences, such as the history of women, don't get promoted without one solid book. And articles are not considered as important.

The Politics of Publishing
Protecting Participants' Confidentiality

Juliene G. Lipson

I don't know how many papers have been written about us because we
don't usually get copies . . . we didn't know this information would go
into books and disclose our privacy . . . I fear your writings would hurt
the feelings of village people if they could read; they will certainly hurt
our great-great grandchildren who will read.

U. Pandey (1992, p. 3)

In "Ethics and Ethnography" (Lipson, 1993), I cited this 1992 open
letter from a North Indian villager to readers of the *Anthropology
Newsletter* as an example of unintentional harm from publishing field
research. Ethnographers studying remote tribal or village groups often
assumed that distance, geographic isolation, and/or social change over
time were adequate to safeguard informants, and that the individuals
or groups they studied would not be reading their reports. Their

publications usually were unconstrained by their fear of exposing informants' identities or village or by informants' opinions of their interpretations.

Given that many qualitative studies are now done in urban settings, sometimes within walking distance of the researcher's institution, we can no longer assume that we can thoroughly mask the identities of our informants or institutions. The explosive increase of electronic information resources such as the Internet and World Wide Web allows access to reports that previously may have been hidden away in obscure journals or library corners. Even if we do not "member check" our findings with informants, they usually are able to access our reports. Feminist and postmodernist researchers have inspired many researchers to form collaborative relationships with informants, and many participants expect to see, alter, or censor a researcher's report.

In this chapter, I address issues related to protection of the identity of participants in qualitative research, including a review of ethical conventions and potential harms, an outline of threats to anonymity and confidentiality, and suggestions for disguising identities. The last section discusses issues related to validity.

Conventions Regarding Ethics

Although institutional review boards (IRBs) vary in how they interpret federal guidelines on protection of human subjects, most insist on confidentiality and protection of privacy and/or anonymity. Sieber (1992) delineates the differences between these concepts:

> Privacy refers to *persons* and to their interest in controlling the access of others to themselves. Confidentiality is an extension of the concept of privacy; it refers to *data* (some record about the person, such as notes or a videotape of the person) and to how data are to be handled in keeping with subjects' interest in controlling the access of others to information about themselves. Ideally, confidentiality is handled in an informed consent agreement between researcher and subject; the agreement states what may be done with private information that the subject conveys to the researcher. . . . Anonymity means that the names and other unique identifiers (e.g., Social Security number, address) of subjects are never attached to the data or even known to the researcher. (pp. 44-45)

Breach of privacy, confidentiality, or anonymity can hurt research participants in minor or major ways. Such techniques as assigning code numbers or removing names from tape transcriptions are not foolproof means of protection in qualitative research. Cassell (1980) points out that "the majority of harms and benefits of fieldwork are less immediate, measurable, and serious than the harms associated with other research modes" (p. 34), such as side effects or physical damage that could result from biomedical research. Nevertheless, harm can occur. Potential harm associated with qualitative research includes embarrassment, psychological distress, divulging of information that affects relationships, or a tarnished reputation or spoiled identity. In short, potential harm to participants is different when insights about human experiences and lives, not statistical findings, are the goals of a study, when "researchers and subjects" become friends and collaborators, and when rich narratives or life history segments, rather than tables, are published as findings.

Privacy/Confidentiality/Anonymity Issues

The Ethical Issues: How Can People Be Hurt?

How are people hurt when researchers divulge their identities or when publication invades their privacy? Larossa, Bennett, and Gelles (1981) suggest that the two major risks in qualitative research are public exposure and self-exposure, "more specifically, the difficulty of masking identities and the problem of seeing one's personal life scrutinized and objectified" (p. 309). Punch (1986) notes that

> a harmonious relationship in the field may come unstuck at the moment of writing and impending publication when the researcher's material appears in cold print. The subjects of research suddenly see themselves summarized and interpreted in ways that may grate with their own partial perspective on the natural setting. When the research bargain includes an implicit or explicit obligation to consult with the group or institution on publication, then severe differences of opinion may arise. (p. 24)

Some problems with others' recognition of informants in print include their feelings (of betrayal or embarrassment), damage to reputations, interference with personal or family relationships, and sometimes endangerment.

Feelings. In qualitative studies using long-term participant observation or interviews of the same informants over time, the researcher and participants form relationships, blurring the boundaries between researcher and friend. When interactions are natural and informal, even when "reminded," informants easily "forget" that they are participating in a study. They often reveal things to a "friend" that they would not reveal to a researcher (Lipson, 1993). Hansen (1976) described the dilemmas in her dual role as anthropologist and friend with respect to what people willingly shared and what they unintentionally revealed. Despite her efforts to change names and edit out material that might identify informants to those who knew them, people still saw themselves behind the "veneer" of her editing and recognized other people they knew. Thus publication may lead to feelings of betrayal or embarrassment through seeing in print things informants may have said very casually.

In very small groups, it is almost impossible to maintain informants' anonymity. Harrell-Bond's (1976) dilemma stemmed from the fact that the number of professionals she studied in Sierra Leone was very small. Almost everyone who read the case studies and verbatim accounts in her first research record, despite her care to conceal individual identities, could recognize who was involved. In her final write-up for publication, she had to discard much rich illustrative material to preserve the privacy of her informants.

Reputation. Recognizability in print can damage informants' reputations, especially if the information revealed involves past or current situations that are embarrassing, potentially stigmatizing, or illegal. Larossa et al. (1981) described a family study in a small town in which the characteristics of one family were so unique that it was quickly identified by friends and neighbors. Family relationships were damaged because of historical information that was divulged in print and read by family members who had not been privy to such history. There were threats of lawsuits. Punch (1986) also pointed out that "contemporary researchers can face the formidable hazards of the law" (p. 18). Even the title of a study can inadvertently hurt a participant's reputation should it include a stigmatized group. Picture, for example, signing a consent form to participate in a focus group in which the title includes HIV/AIDS. Participants might well feel very uncomfortable before and during the group, wondering whether other members identify them as HIV positive or negative and being concerned about the accuracy and effect of such identification.

In my research with Afghan refugees in the United States, I have learned that the desire to maintain a good reputation is an extremely strong social force. In this community, gossip and rumors are rife, and everybody knows a lot about each other, even if they do not know each other personally. People work hard to enhance their own reputations, sometimes by tearing down the reputations of others. I have seen incidents in which rumors were used as weapons to mar the reputation of someone who had slighted another. As a researcher, I must go to extra lengths to keep from identifying individuals or families when I am portraying incidents or characteristics that could be construed as negative, so as not to contribute additional harm.

Endangerment. Most of the attention to ethics in qualitative research focuses on avoiding danger to informants, which is particularly important when informants are undocumented or engage in illegal or stigmatizing activities. Endangerment could include harassment, arrest, imprisonment, attack by "enemies," or deportation. Even informants who normally would not be considered vulnerable because of their legal status or activities may be subjected to questioning or surveillance should their opinions or activities be disapproved of by the government, such as a political group or people who use marijuana for medicinal purposes. Qualitative researchers are cautioned to keep our informants anonymous, sometimes by not even knowing their real names and obtaining verbal rather that written consent, in case our records should be subpoenaed. In some cases, the researcher is endangered, such as a doctoral student who had studied the radical animal rights movement and refused to divulge his sources; he was jailed on the grounds of "withholding evidence of criminal activity" (K. May, personal communication, 1996).

It is not just publication or the possibility of subpoenaed research records that can endanger informants, however. Verbal information can also be a problem, such as among Afghan refugees who use verbal information in complex ways, including using it to punish others. An informant described the following example, which subsequently appeared in the newspaper; however, it could easily have been revealed in my research. The S. family was waiting for their asylum hearing in California. Other Afghans had advised them previously that their chances for asylum would be improved if they proclaimed that they came directly from Pakistan, and that they should not mention spending a few intervening years in Germany. Later, the S. family refused to have their daughter engaged to the son of another family who had helped them. Angered, the other family told the U.S. Immigration and Naturalization Service about Mr. S's "lie," which led to his imprisonment and threat of deportation (Lipson & Omidian, 1997). I mention this incident to show that even experienced qualitative researchers may not realize the dangers for other people in the study group, and we must be alert to sometimes very subtle ways that field research might endanger people.

Threats to Anonymity and Confidentiality

The risks and potential harm from identification of informants are complex and differ depending on who or what is being studied. Is the research focused on a group, an institution, or individuals who share an experience? How vulnerable is the population? What are informants' own desires with regard to anonymity?

Institution, Group, or Agency

A unique institution or group may be easy to identify, even when the location is disguised. For example, how many Torticollis Support Groups are there in the United States? We must ask ourselves whether identification of the group or agency will cause harm, either to the group or to individuals who are part of it. For some readers, guessing the identity of an institution, agency, or specific group is a challenge, like solving a puzzle. It may be relatively easy to identify a setting when the researcher's institution is mentioned because the demands of the academic year may not allow for researchers to study a group or agency at a distance. An agency can be threatened indirectly via its services to a stigmatized group or clients who engage in illegal activities. Care to mask individual identities of those who use the services of such an agency will protect the clients but does little to protect the agency from potential harm, such as providing health services to undocumented immigrants in the wake of new prohibitive legislation.

Identification of Individuals

Regarding potential identification of individuals, we should ask ourselves whether the participants desire strict anonymity, do not care one way or another, or want themselves explicitly identified. Is the topic of the study stigmatizing, potentially embarrassing, or relatively neutral? What potential harm can come from identification of the individual or publication of some details that are attributed to him or her? What happens when researcher and participant disagree about potential identification? And how does the passage of time affect these issues?

Some of these issues are illustrated in my research on Jews for Jesus (1990). On completion of my dissertation in 1978, I gave two copies to the group. After they were circulated throughout the membership, the copies were put away in the leader's house and not seen again. Members had recognized each other easily and were concerned about recognition by family members and others who knew the group, even though nearly four years had passed since I had completed data collection. Because members were evangelists who shared their stories with many people, including strangers, I was surprised by their sensitivity to identification, even though the abbreviated life histories used pseudonyms and omitted clear identifying material.

Vulnerable Populations or Public Figures

Masking individual or group identities ranges from absolutely critical to relatively unimportant. It is critical when the study focuses on people who have had stigmatizing life experiences, like women who used drugs during pregnancy or lesbians in recovery from alcohol addiction (Bolla, 1996; Hall, 1992). Vulnerable populations are easily subject to harm through the divulging of information that marginalizes or stigmatizes them. Having "a history" can keep people from getting certain jobs, health insurance, running for office, and so on. Rita Schreiber (1996) points out that vulnerable subpopulations in urban areas may resemble small rural populations in their lack of privacy. For example, the researcher interested in studying treatment issues for people with schizophrenia in an urban area must acknowledge that potential participants are likely to know each other as well as knowing most providers, treatment centers, and hospitals—the psychiatric/mental health community can be a very small world, indeed.

In contrast to those whose anonymity must be guarded, some public figures do not mind being identified or specifically request that their names be mentioned. In Sally Hutchinson's rescue squad study, for example, an informant she had interviewed and observed over a few years became very annoyed when he did not find himself clearly depicted in her publications (Hutchinson, 1996). A related issue is informants who identify themselves by "telling friends, relatives, and sometimes strangers about their participation in a particular study" (Larossa et al., 1981, p. 311). Members of Jews for Jesus, for example, ranged from desiring anonymity to wanting their names in print. I didn't consider the members to be especially vulnerable (except to the group's enemies in the Jewish community) because the group used "making the news" to advance its evangelism. My dissertation used pseudonyms for everyone, including the highly visible and recognizable leader, but he insisted on use of his real name in the book because he was a public figure and had been named in other books about him and/or Jews for Jesus.

Writing for Publication

In studies of people who share a specific life circumstance or condition, such as cancer or single motherhood, I think that it is easier to maintain anonymity than it is in studies of groups, communities, or institutions. It may be impossible to disguise a unique group, like Jews for Jesus, which began in the San Francisco Bay Area early in 1970. By the time I completed data gathering in 1972, it had achieved nationwide notoriety and would have been easily identifiable no matter how I might have attempted to disguise it.

Table 3.1 Techniques to Resolve Issues of Privacy, Confidentiality, and Anonymity

Issue	Technique
Privacy (Researcher does not violate control of others' access to the self of the participant; participant maintains control.)	Avoid stigmatized term in consent form for focus groups. Delay publication. Seek the approval of participants before publication. Increase the number of participants. Know the field or seek consultation to make a reasonable judgment on what is considered private in the research context.
Confidentiality (Researcher handles data according to participant's desire to control access to information about self and prior consent form.)	Omit potentially damaging details. Use pseudonyms or code numbers. Remove identifying material from transcriptions. Do not send raw data over the Internet. Change demographic data not central to "the story." Recruit participants from different geographic locations. Participants help construct own story to provide adequate protection.
Anonymity (Unique identifiers are not attached to the data or known to researcher.)	Ask participant for pseudonym, don't record real name. Obtain verbal, not signed consent. Exclude background people from videotaping to prevent inadvertent identification. Create composite identities. Remove unique identifiers attached to data.

What are some common ways of disguising identities of individuals or groups? Qualitative researchers use a variety of means, including delaying publication, omitting potentially identifying information, skirting the issue, creating new identities, and disguising the setting (Table 3.1).

Delaying Publication

Waiting several years may allow publication of a study that would have been too sensitive to publish earlier. An issue that garnered considerable media attention at the time of the writing later may have died down or been forgotten. Punch (1986) was constrained, for a number of years, from publishing his study of an elite private school in England. I'm not sure if he ever was able to publish his study in its entirety, but he finally did publish a thoughtful methodological monograph outlining his difficulties and many ethical issues that other researchers have encountered in field research.

When I learned of the sensitivity of some members of Jews for Jesus about potential recognition and their concerns about family embarrassment because relationships were mentioned in life histories, I petitioned to delay publication of the abstract in *Dissertation Abstracts International*. I was allowed only a one-year delay during which I hoped to keep the dissertation out of the hands of the curious and angry. I did publish an article on ethnic identity and rituals that described members only in the aggregate. However, when invited to publish the dissertation ten years later, I discussed the issue of confidentiality with the leader of Jews for Jesus, who agreed that the use of pseudonyms and the passing of a decade were sufficient to mask individual identities and keep members' histories from public scrutiny. Most had moved from San Francisco and some were no longer associated with the organization. I then published it as a historical piece with an update chapter (Lipson, 1990).

Unfortunately, in recent years, it may have become more difficult to delay publication in light of how the rules have changed. The doctoral student must complete her or his dissertation, and it goes into the library, where sophisticated technology makes it widely available. When the threat of tenure review is looming, the assistant professor cannot afford to leave his or her findings unpublished. University IRBs expect submission of adverse events from research, including names of participants, and some funders, particularly drug companies, reserve the right to examine research records. NIH expects a final report for its funding and such reports are available to the public.

Omitting or Changing Details

It is a fairly common practice, when attempting to disguise an institution or group, to omit potentially identifying but unimportant details. For example, Malone's (1995) ethnographic study of "heavy users" of emergency care provided enough detail to clearly depict the day-to-day workings of two hospital emergency departments, but she could have been describing urban emergency departments anywhere.

Had the locations been identified, certain major "characters" might have been identifiable; they were identifiable clearly to staff of those institutions. When I use quotes or incidents to illustrate themes in writing up my research, I often change demographic details that have little or no bearing on the story, such as geographic origin, occupation, age, appearance, or even gender, to enhance anonymity. I do not change descriptors if they are vital to the story line; for example, place of birth and area where one was raised are essential pieces of information in studies of immigrants or refugees. In one of my immigrant studies, for example, I observed a slightly "illegal" but fairly common activity in which an informant had engaged. In describing this activity in a publication, I changed the gender because the activity was not gender specific. In another example, I was a participant in a friend's dissertation survey of intra- and interethnic marriages. I was uncomfortable knowing that the investigator could identify me and read about my husband's and my perceptions of our marital and sexual relationships, so I deliberately altered our occupations. To be careful of validity, I chose different professions that required graduate degrees and supported a similar lifestyle. In this way, I altered information that was inconsequential to the study but preserved my relative anonymity.

Masking or Creating New Identities

In contrast to studies of groups or institutions, it may be easier to mask the identities of individuals who have been interviewed on a particular topic. The process of analysis, even in narrative studies, rarely ends up with whole people being described. Even when a short life history provides the context of the phenomenon of interest, identification can be impeded by separating demographic information from segments of experience. Except in rural or small town areas, where people know each other for many years, including many unique details about each other, it is relatively easy to mask identities to all except the participant or someone who knows him or her very well.

The two studies of vulnerable populations mentioned earlier successfully masked the identities of the women informants yet were peppered with rich and gripping life history segments—Hall's (1992) study of lesbians in recovery from alcohol and Bolla's (1996) study of women who used drugs while pregnant. The women informants might weil recognize their own words but few others were likely to. Hall asked her participants for first names only, then immediately chose a pseudonym for each woman so that she thought about the woman by that name right from the beginning. She began interviews by suggesting that women not talk about criminal behavior unless it was completely in the past or the case was closed legally. With the IRB, she negotiated giving immediate cash payment for interviews rather than university-issued checks that would be sent several weeks later; thus she needed no Social Security numbers and also prevented potential problems from someone else opening the woman's mail and demanding an explanation about a university check.

Bolla's (1996) recruitment flyers posted in various locations asked potential interviewees not to leave their real names on her answering machine. She deleted details on anything that might compromise anonymity such as by changing potentially identifiable specific occupations to a general description of the work situation—for example, "a professional woman whose work required frequent meetings over lunch and cocktails." She kept no real names or phone numbers, asked for verbal rather than signed consent, and asked participants to contact her if they wanted a summary of the findings.

In the Afghan study, I have used identity disintegration and synthesis—mixing and matching—to protect people whose ethnic community thrives on gossip, rumors, and stories. I've observed that when Afghans first meet each other, they spend considerable time placing each other in social context by asking about each other's family background and former circumstances. Afghans know a great deal about each other—some of the information is accurate, some not—even when they do not know each other personally. Therefore, informants would have been identifiable were it not for my creative identity development. In instances where an experience is common to many people, with one person describing it particularly well, I might place the experience and/or quotes in another identity, which may be created by combining two to three other people. In other words, the person is fictional, but the experiences are not. When I ask key informants to review a manuscript for accuracy and suggestions before submission, they sometimes puzzle about who the person is. They may say that they know her but just can't quite place her (who may have been a "him" in real life). This is also a check on validity.

However, if a story has circulated widely through the Afghan community or was written up in the newspaper, I do not change its shape because it has become part of community lore, even though the protagonist is known in the community. In Afghan culture, stories are a very important part of interpersonal communication. For example, several Afghans illustrated the power of family shame in telling about the incident of a young woman who killed herself by jumping off a bridge because her father had behaved in a shameful manner. Such key stories illustrate cultural themes and typical situations blown large by the acculturative stress experienced by many Afghans. Other stories illustrate important values, such as the story of Nahid, a heroic nurse who was killed by fundamentalists in Pakistan because she insisted, despite a strong warning, on going to the hospital because her patients needed her. Thus, while community members know the identity of the protagonists of such stories, I feel comfortable mentioning them in print because they have become public knowledge.

Geographic Considerations

Generalizing about geographic setting is often used to mask identities in a large and diverse country, but it may be tricky. We read that a study was done in a generic institution in a "large West Coast city." However, the doctoral student or faculty researcher employed at the University of Washington or California makes it fairly easy to guess that the study was not conducted 2,000 miles away. It is easier to preserve confidentiality by interviewing individuals recruited from more than one geographic setting. For example, Preston (1994) interviewed informants in 24 states, sometimes driving between 100 and 300 hundred miles a day, in his superb study of hearing children of deaf parents. Had he stayed in one geographic location, the highly cohesive deaf community with its reliance on frequent face-to-face contact would have significantly increased the potential for identifying informants and their families.

Electronic issues. Recent exponential growth in the use of electronic media and cyberspace poses new dangers to confidentiality. My dissertation students and I are now enjoying the ease of international communication afforded by E-mail. Rather than depending on slow or undependable mail or expensive fax transmission (which can be read by others), these researchers in Ecuador, Botswana, and Japan have sent sample interviews or observational notes for perusal by, and for further guidance from, their committee members. What about potential interception? I recently realized that I have been saving some messages from colleagues or forwarding such messages to others with little thought about the confidentiality ramifications. This medium is too new to have generated research guidelines to address a host of new ethical and methodological issues, such as recruitment of participants or surveys conducted over the Web, identifiers that could be traced to specific participants, those who lurk in electronic support groups for people with specific conditions and record the discussion as data, and so on. A good rule is to E-mail only what you would not regret seeing in a newspaper.

Validity Issues

Does leaving out rich descriptive material to mask identities hurt the validity of a study? Does one maintain the validity of the study by changing part of the story? There is a historical take on this issue, and qualitative researchers have changed their views on this issue over time. Twenty years ago, qualitative researchers were torn between their "scientific" goals and their desire to protect their informants. Hansen (1976) changed all the names and edited out material that might identify an informant to those who knew him, but she was afraid that "too radical a change would have resulted in data that were not, in fact, representative of the reality I observed" (p. 133). Harrell-Bond (1976) discarded much rich illustrative material because "the rights of privacy had to take precedence over the claims of science for well-documented data" (p. 119). Davis (1991) illustrates this issue in writing up "rich cases" for teaching ethics, pointing out the conflict between advancing knowledge through "thick description" that allows for true psychological empathy and depicts the complexity of reality, on the one hand, and protecting patient anonymity on the other. She describes as a powerful paradox the "very details that needed to be falsified were just those that gave the cases their integrity and usefulness" (p. 12).

Many qualitative researchers reframe the "representation of reality" issue in acknowledging that our observations are screened through our own perceptions, experiences, and personalities anyway. Our "data" are not collected in a vacuum but co-created through interactions with informants that we ourselves help shape. And our informants must be protected to our best ability if this is what they desire. I reframe *science* and *rigor* to mean research that reaches and teaches readers something about the meat of the experiences of my informants; the work gives my informants voice and strikes a chord of recognition. I am gratified when a reader says, "I can see my family in your article, you really got it down," or "It made me cry." Sandelowski (1994) expresses this "truth value" much more eloquently: "The Quintessential qualitative piece . . . is both representative and evocative; it tells an interesting and true story, it provides a sense of understanding and sometimes even personal recognition, and it conveys some movement and tension—something going on" (p. 59).

If the writing does all this, how much does it matter if the details are changed to protect the innocent? I use the following general guideline when thinking about how to mask identities: *How much do the changes really matter in the overall story?* For example, if I was exploring the experience of living with a specific chronic disease, I could add or subtract a decade for an adult, but I wouldn't change an adult to a child. I could change the person's ethnic group unless there were significant health care access or racism issues or cultural ways of coping with the illness. I certainly would not change the chronic disease itself and probably would not change the informant's gender. Am I playing fast and loose with the data? Can my work be trusted?

Validity issues vary somewhat with the study topic and methodological style. As mentioned earlier, it may be easier to more flexibly disguise the identity of informants in interviews around a specific life situation than in a study based on life histories. My dissertation summarized 7 of the 27 life histories of members of Jews for Jesus to illustrate different family patterns, previous lifestyles, and paths into the movement. Mixing and matching their lives would have ruined their cohesive and rich stories, and would have been of questionable validity.

These ideas may sound like heresy to beginning researchers. In the meeting that preceded publication of this book, the chapter authors engaged in lively debate about "creating identities." Some were silent (I don't know what they were thinking). One said, "I took a deep breath when I read this but then I realized that I do it too," and Katharyn May (personal communication, 1996) said:

How can you be shocked? How can you not do composites? Because my work has attracted media attention, I have disciplined myself to erase the original informant so that I can't, even by accident, construct the right name on live radio. It is true to the data but I do my best to make sure that it is not trackable to the person because I can't control what happens when someone else takes my work.

I would never suggest such fast-and-loose treatment of "data" in the absence of sufficient knowledge and experience with the group or phenomena. The researcher has to know what is important and what is not important before making changes to disguise people. Ten years of research with Afghans has deepened my understanding of this community to the point that I am rarely surprised by individual stories of trauma, cultural conflict in the United States, or problems resulting from poor English or limited job opportunities. (Fortunately, I am still surprised by how the community is changing.) So I feel fairly safe mixing and matching to protect informants.

A significant issue is researcher honesty. Does the publication acknowledge the creation of composite identities? Some authors openly state that they created composite pictures and the reasons for doing so, while others simply don't mention it. If techniques to mask identities are not made explicit, readers will assume that the researcher is describing real people. To whom are our reputations as researchers most important—qualitative peers who agree that protecting informants is more important than exact journalistic accuracy, or hard scientists and lay readers who criticize such research as unethical falsification akin to fiction or, more kindly, simply ask, "How can anybody know that what you are saying is accurate?"

On another note, what do we mean by *validity* anyway? Whose truth are we seeking? Are we constrained by quantoid definitions of validity or their recent qualitative reinterpretations? Postmodernist and feminist writing supports the importance of voice over slavish obsession with "exact depictions of reality" and certainly has assuaged my guilt about protecting identities through various means (I'm a product of my generation). Richardson (1994) suggests that we are fortunate to be working in a postmodern climate characterized by *"doubt* that any method or theory, discourse or genre, tradition or novelty, has a universal and general claim as the 'right' or privileged form of communication." Arguing that language does not "reflect social reality, but produces meaning, creates social reality," she suggests that current forms of writing like "the narrative of the self" and other evocative representations "see through and beyond sociological naturalisms, such as ethnographic fictional representations or poetic representations" (p. 521).

Sandelowski's (1994) exploration of the kinship between art and science —their mutual beginnings in the creative act, the search for truth and ways of illuminating reality—holds an important lesson in questions about validity. Her research with infertile couples interpreted their experience through sociology and fiction

> because a strict scientific description would have been less true to the emotional content of their experiences and to my response to their stories. Admitting that the kinship between art and science is not a failing, but rather a directive to develop the kinds of imaginative and critical skills we associate with artists. (p. 61)

Finally, Silva, Sorrell, and Sorrell (1995) broaden Carper's (1978) "patterns of knowing" to include the "in-between," which "reveals itself through nonlinear meditative thinking that moves in all directions and depths" (Silva et al., 1995, p. 3) in light of the idea that "virtual worlds and environments raise profound ontological questions about what is reality, what is meaning, and what is being" (p.12). As Judy Norris (this volume) points out, some human experiences may be depicted better through art or dance than through words.

Conclusions

To end where we began: How does one write up a study so that informants' friends and families, and other folks, will not know who is who and still maintain the validity of the study? Major ethical issues arise from the tension between "science" and the protection of informants. Hansen (1976) noted that as long as the precise identity of individuals is disguised, the publication of confidential data is necessary for "the greater good of scientific understanding and thereby of humanity" (p. 133). As Punch (1986, p. 42) noted, some academics argue that sociologists should be concerned with documenting abuses in public and business life. In research that is designed to expose people and institutions, some feel that conventions with regard to privacy, harm, and confidentiality should be waived when an institution is seen to be evading its public accountability. He asks whether public figures can claim the same rights of privacy as ordinary citizens.

There are no easy or right answers for these complex issues. Each research situation is different, and ethical dilemmas around identifying participants might arise suddenly at any point in a study's progression. Because of the emerging character of any qualitative study, such issues come up spontaneously and may surprise the researcher. Are there ways in which the researcher can prepare for such issues? General guidelines include maintaining the ongoing participation of informants' anticipating issues throughout the study, and being reflexive and flexible.

A number of authors suggest that researchers make decisions in collaboration with their informants on what and how to publish. In other words, if informants coauthor their own reports, they have some choice and control over public exposure that goes beyond simply being asked to check for accuracy or being asked how they want their lives or situations portrayed publicly.

Qualitative researchers need to maintain their reflexivity throughout a study, including deciding what and where to publish and for what purpose. At each step, we should examine our decisions about what we record and our own effects on the research process. We should train ourselves and our students to look inside ourselves at each point in the research process as if we were in the shoes of the informants, to ask, "If this were me, what would I worry about? What might scare or embarrass me? What would happen if that were in print?" After publication, we must keep our eyes open for unwitting or unintentional harm for the purpose of damage control (if possible).

Part of reflexivity is clarifying one's own reasons for doing and publishing the research. For example, are you doing the study for the purpose of "exposure for the purpose of social change" or do your own ethics preclude publishing findings that could reflect badly on a particular group or even slightly expose the identity of informants? Clarification of one's own values and reasons for doing the research may well result in a decision that one cannot publish the findings. Many qualitative researchers have a file drawer of unpublished interesting data that they think might result in some kind of harm to participants. They regret that the time and effort put into the study will not lead to its dissemination. However, flexibility might mean writing a methodology piece, à la Punch, or using the data in teaching new researchers.

Overall, each researcher must address issues of privacy, confidentiality, and anonymity in the whole research process—from recruiting participants to publication. Although the general guidelines suggested in this chapter may help qualitative researchers to think through these issues, we also need to consider how the ethical principle of "do no harm" applies to the specific characteristics and demands of each specific research project.

References

Bolla, C. (1996). —I'm not a monster!" Lived experiences of pregnant addicted women. Unpublished doctoral dissertation, University of California, San Francisco.

Carper, B. (1978). Fundamental patterns of knowing in nursing. *Advances in Nursing Science, 1,* 13-23.

Cassell, J. (1980). Ethical principles for conducting fieldwork. *American Anthropologist, 82,* 28-41.

Davis, D. (1991). Rich cases: The ethics of thick description. *Hastings Center Report, 21*(4), 12-17.

Hall, J. (1992). *Lesbians' experiences with alcohol problems: A critical ethnographic study of problemization, help seeking and recovery problems.* Unpublished doctoral dissertation, University of California, San Francisco.

Hansen, J. (1976). The anthropologist in the field: Scientist, friend, and voyeur. In M.A. Rynkiewich & J. P. Spradley (Eds.), *Ethics and anthropology: Dilemmas in field-work* (pp. 123-134). New York: John Wiley.

Harrell-Bond, B. (1976). Studying elites: Some special problems. In M. A. Rynkiewich & J. P. Spradley (Eds.), *Ethics and anthropology: Dilemmas in fieldwork* (pp. 110-121). New York: John Wiley.

Hutchinson, S. (1996, August 30). [Discussion]. Qualitative Research Symposium, Vancouver.

Larossa, R., Bennett, L., & Gelles, R. (1981). Ethical dilemmas in qualitative family research. *Journal of Marriage and the Family, 43,* 303-313.

Lipson, J. G. (1990). *Jews for Jesus: An anthropological study.* New York: AMS Press.

Lipson, J. G. (1993). Ethics and intervention in ethnography. In J. Morse (Ed.), *Critical issues in qualitative research* (pp. 333-355). Newbury Park, CA: Sage.

Lipson, J. G., & Omidian, P. (1997e). "We don't know the rules": Afghan refugee issues in the U.S. social environment. *Western Journal of Nursing Research, 19,* 110-126.

Malone, R. (1995). *The Almshouse revisited: Heavy users of emergency services.* Unpublished doctoral dissertation, University of California, San Francisco.

Pandey, U. (1992 , May). "Would you like to listen or not?" [Letter]. *Anthropology Newsletter,* p. 3 (Correspondence section).

Preston, P. (1994). *Mother father deaf.* Cambridge, MA: Harvard University Press.

Punch, M. (1986). *The politics and ethics of fieldwork.* Beverly Hills, CA: Sage.

Richardson, L. (1994). Writing: A method of inquiry. In N. Denzin & Y. Lincoln (Eds.), *Handbook of qualitative research* (pp. 516-529). Thousand Oaks, CA: Sage.

Sandelowski, M. (1994). The proof is in the pottery: Toward a poetic for qualitative inquiry. In J. Morse (Ed.), *Critical issues in qualitative research* (pp. 46-63). Thousand Oaks, CA: Sage.

Schreiber, R. (1996, August 30). [Discussion]. Qualitative Research Symposium, Vancouver.

Sieber, J. E. (1992). *Planning ethically responsible research.* Newbury Park, CA: Sage.

Silva, M., Sorrell, J., & Sorrell, C. (1995). From Carper's patterns of knowing to ways of being: An ontological philosophical shift in nursing. *Advances in Nursing Science, 18,* 1-13.

Dialogue: Coauthorship

Morse: I want to separate this discussion into "most work" and "ideas" because work can be very pedestrian and it can be very enlightening. But much of it can be assigned to an RA [research assistant], or someone who can be paid to do it. So I think that unless we separate this discussion into ideas and work for attribution—

Lipson: But there is a whole range of faculty who insist that they are always on their students' work. *I do badly because* I don't push myself. I don't insist—

Sandelowski: It brings up the questions of what's "authorship." In the science domain, we do almost have this expectation that there are certain constituents that are going to get "on there," but they haven't really done anything. Authorship means that you "author" something, and nothing else. And the other thing that I see happening now, too, is that faculty are taking credit for student work. It's a part of your vita to show what a good mentor you are. It's theses and dissertations and work that you have copublished with the student. I think that is a whole chapter in itself that should be addressed in future methods books—the ethics and politics of this kind of coauthorship.

Stern: At our school it's a point in your favor that you—

Sandelowski: Yes, it is. And—

Stern: And it's a point in your favor that you are helping the student get published.

Sandelowski: But the idea is that's what you are hired to do. You are the teacher.

Stern: But your name on it helps it get published. Your editing of the work helps get it published. And I tell students up front that if I'm doing a lot of work with the analysis—

Sandelowski: But your name shouldn't [help get it published]. It's a blind review!

Morse: This is how I see it: it is my responsibility to be teaching them how to do research. I don't know how to teach how to do research except to teach them how to think— which involves getting into their data and doing their thinking for them, at least by example, for a number of times. And that has to be acknowledged [in authorship] because in qualitative research the thinking is the strength of the study. The level of conceptualization is what makes the study. And if that is left to the student, then nothing is going to happen—the student is not going to learn. Now whether that contribution is worthy of first or second authorship, who knows? The rest is technician stuff. But it's good manners and it's polite for ideas to be acknowledged. How can they take your conceptualization of their data and pretend it's theirs? That is immoral. And how can you step back and not teach them how to do it, when that is your role as a faculty member?

May: Having done an awful lot of that preliminary work with the dissertation, the thinking does not stop with the dissertation. If the first couple of articles are regurgitations or a shorter version of the dissertation, by and large those papers are difficult to get published because the work continues. And I have had to work on manuscripts. When I have done some text moving, and I have reorganized text and pushed it around, and I have had to step back and say, "My God, I have just rewritten their work, I need to be sure that that's OK with them." Because the analysis is in the writing. The analysis is not anywhere else. So every time you write it, you should be taking it a step further. And that can happen with students with their dissertations. It can happen with new faculty at the point of getting articles published. But it also happens when you try to get something published when you are established in your career, and it also happens when someone says, "There are concepts hanging out here in space, link it to the scheme or get rid of it!" And after you get angry, you think, "Well, hell, they're absolutely right!"

Morse: We must remember, though, that there are advisers who never have anything to do with the dissertation—and they have no right to put their name on the work as author.

Stern: Up front, when students ask me to be their adviser, up front, I say, "On at least one publication, I want to be second author."

Morse: You don't say "depending on contribution?" or whatever?

Stern: Oh, well—I never take on first author.

Morse: So the principle should be "according to contribution" and that
            should be ideas, theoretical contribution—

Hutchinson: Jan, I can't see that. I had the same thing happen with a
            student. I had one student, and I totally did a grounded theory
            on it [the data] myself. Did the whole lit. review, wrote the
            entire article, and I could *not* put my name first. And I did the
            whole entire thing—because it was her original stuff. The data
            were hers. And I just couldn't do it. Some people do. But I
            couldn't.

Morse: Well, let's list all the norms: There is another norm that says,
            "OK, student, write this up, you can be first author, but if I don't
            see it in a year, I'll take it, and I'll be first author!"

Stern: Well, yes, that's another problem. What do you do with a stu-
            dent who doesn't write up the work?

Morse: Or what do you do with a student who is so ashamed of a
            rejection slip, she hides it and doesn't tell you? [laughter]

Boyle: Or what do you do with a student who writes it, puts your name
            on it, and submits it, and you don't see it?

Thorne: I don't disagree with anything that has been said, but at the same
            time I think the student ought to have some ownership over
            what they do, and not to feel indentured to the faculty who
            hasn't contributed, and also to have some freedom to depart
            from what their supervisor thought that they contributed—

Wilson: It's their intellectual property, too.

Hutchinson: If you have a qualitative analysis seminar, and you are bandy-
            ing ideas about and if somebody did a tape on that, which I
            doubt, and did a content analysis of people who came up with
            ideas, it does not really matter who came up with the ideas, it's
            your job—

Stern: Yes, it's your job.

Morse: But I have trouble with that. I think ideas are associated with
            people, and a student has no right to take an idea from a seminar

and put it in an article or a thesis and couch it as their idea. I think that is a moral issue.

May: I'm not sure that I agree on that one, because in the heat of analysis I can look across the table, and I know exactly what that student is thinking; I've just gotten to the same place, I'm faster to say it because I do this for a living. So I think we each have to find our position of comfort with that. But I would agree with you that I think it is improper conduct for a young academic to not, at a minimum, acknowledge the contributions, somewhere —the decision is not to put authorship on it, but to say in the acknowledgment, "I want to thank . . ." I would agree with you that it must be in the acknowledgment, but we all have to find our level of comfort with that.

CHAPTER

Presenting Qualitative Research Up Close
Visual Literacy in Poster Presentations

Holly Skodol Wilson
Sally Ambler Hutchinson

A nurse scientist who had completed a powerful phenomenological study related to the experience of surgery among men who had been sexually abused in childhood presented a poster session to report it at an important regional research conference. He learned later that his poster was seen as disorganized and carelessly constructed. Consequently, either his presentation failed to attract the attention of the audience or his research tended to be discounted based on the poor form in which it was communicated.

* * *

A team of senior qualitative scientists traveled from the United States to Bogotá, Colombia, to present their collaborative work on "living with dementia" at an international qualitative research meeting. They had planned their poster presentation to rely substantially on the videotapes they had filmed and edited to communicate their ethologic findings. Not only could the setting for the poster presentation not accommodate the technology for reasons as fundamental as the inaccessibility of proper electrical outlets and equipment suitable for U.S. video playback, but the conference venue was prone to approximately six hours of electrical "blackout" each day that could not be predicted. Technology did indeed fail, and the researchers had no backup plan for presenting their poster session.

* * *

A qualitative research team with noteworthy talent in designing and producing slides and transparencies using contemporary computer software packages generated a superbly attractive poster reporting their research on the use of traditional Chinese herbs and remedies to treat pain and depression. Their poster addressed all the conventional guidelines for effective poster presentations, and they had run "spell-check" to proofread their work. Regrettably, despite their visually attractive creation, their interesting research topic, and the credibility of the grounded theory they had discovered, they had included a very noticeable grammatical error on almost all of their display panels, confusing "there" with "their." This error became a major distraction to an otherwise fine study.

* * *

Research conducted in the naturalistic/interpretive paradigm (often called "qualitative research") has earned respect in the scientific community for its potential to illuminate personal meanings, explain human experience, present richly detailed "stories," achieve understanding, generate theory about processes that are shifting over time, explain variation as well as patterns and themes, and preserve historical, cultural, and contextual conditions (Wilson & Hutchinson, 1991). Sandelowski (1994) has added to this list the notion that qualitative research reports are aesthetically and intellectually satisfying "stories" that appeal to your mind's eye—your sense of style and craftsmanship—teach you something important, and also touch your heart.

We qualitative investigators have traditionally preferred the research monograph over the page-limited, refereed, scientific journal article for portraying the richness and the density of our interpretive and insight-generating discoveries. We have come to believe that capturing the rigor of our method as well as the complexities of our findings within a 17-page journal manuscript in the interest of parsimony often sacrifices too much of the detail of what we have learned. Consequently, searching the literature for reports of qualitative studies reveals both classic and contemporary monographs such as Whyte's *Street Corner Society: The Social Structure of an Italian Slum* (1914), Glaser and Strauss's *Awareness of Dying* (1965), Wilson's *Deinstitutionalized Residential Care for Schizophrenics: The Soteria House Approach* (1982), Hutchinson's *Hidden Dimensions of Watchful Readiness: Survival Practices of Rescue Workers* (1986), Kayser-Jones's *Old, Alone, and Neglected: Care of the Aged in Scotland and the United States* (1981), Benner's *From Novice to Expert: Excellence and Power in Clinical Nursing Practice* (1984), and Morse and Johnson's *The Illness Experience: Dimensions of Suffering* (1991), to name but a few.

If the constraints of a page-limited article pose barriers to reporting qualitative work through the scientific journal medium, the research poster looms as an even greater challenge for the qualitative researcher because posters are by definition concise and visual rather than richly detailed and dependent on language. Yet the potential value of presenting an effective poster session is sufficiently promising that qualitative researchers must engage this challenge and craft an appropriate rendition of poster pragmatics befitting studies conducted in the naturalistic/interpretive paradigm.

Sandelowski (1994) set the standard for reporting and disseminating qualitative research, naming it a *poetic*. We must be able to make science out of biography, make theory from life stories, reveal secrets of the heart, claim rigor as well as imagination, resound with the experience of others, be faithful to the subject, be true to our participants, and tell an aesthetically and intellectually satisfying story. This chapter takes up the gauntlet to achieve a poetic in poster presentations. We will examine strategies to avoid errors exemplified by the beginning vignettes and explore the pragmatics of how to bring visual literacy to poster sessions that effectively present qualitative inquiry.

The Value of Presenting Qualitative Research Up Close

Knowledge and insights discovered through qualitative research can make a difference only if investigators report them to others through publication of research monographs, scientific journal articles, talks at professional meetings, and poster presentations (Wilson & Hutchinson, 1996). A poster is a means of summarizing and communicating research in a primarily visual format (Kleinbeck, 1988; Ryan, 1989; Sexton, 1984; Sherbinski & Stroup, 1992). Although visual elements predominate in posters, language complements and expands on the visual message. As Sharf (1995) aptly points out, "Visual art with its elements of aesthetics, economy of statement and individualized expression, conveys information and points of view in emphatic and convincing ways" (p. 72). In so doing, posters are characterized as possessing dynamics that constitute a unique rhetorical type. The rhetorical dynamics include word and image, the literal and the symbolic, personal experience and political agenda, and distance and proximity (Sharf, 1995). Stylistically, posters can range from literal to symbolic, realistic to fantastic, with juxtapositions that assist the viewer in comprehending the researched problem and yet transcend it as well (Sharf, 1995). Sharf, for example, comments on a set of posters created by breast cancer survivors to convey varying reactions to the experience. She characterizes the posters as "the inward gaze and the outreach to others . . . blended in seamless and clever ways, so that the impact of both dimensions are experienced simultaneously by the viewer . . . the visual tension between proximity and distance echoes the interplay between the personal and the political" (p. 73). Sharf emphasizes that certain meanings in the posters she explicates are intended to be understood when viewing the poster from afar, for example, the messages portrayed in the "Spread the Word" poster, which was designed as a joint effort of the Office of Cancer Communications and the National Black Leadership Initiative on Cancer as part of "the art series of cancer prevention posters." Sharf describes this poster as employing form over content by depicting ageless, featureless women in a stylized image of African women dressed in sumptuous colors of turquoise, gold, green, and red telling each other about regular mammograms starting at 50. They are indeed "spreading the word."

Polly Strand, whom Sharf (1995) describes as a breast cancer survivor with three daughters, who is herself the daughter of a woman whom she describes as "dying a horrible death from treatment of breast cancer" (p. 75), created a poster image of a red scar with black stitches standing out on her chest and "up close" printing of insistent political messages urging today's mothers to take a strong political stand in support of financial support for breast cancer prevention.

The work of artist/model Matuschka in her bare-chested self-photograph titled "Beauty out of Damage" (August 15, 1993), which appeared on the front cover of the *New York Times Magazine*, brought the taboo image of mastectomy to the general public and raised funds for breast cancer advocacy. In another more introspective and personal poster, writer/poet Deena Metzger was photographed with a tree tattooed on her own mastectomy scar in the hope of challenging viewers to look beyond the wound as stigma, to resee it as a symbol of healing, regeneration, and vitality. It is this notion of reframing poster presentations as artistic rhetoric that qualitative researchers must embrace if we are to use the poster session as a medium for presenting qualitative research up close and as a poetic for qualitative inquiry.

However, as indicated in the vignettes that began this chapter, "A good poster display cannot rescue a bad idea, but a poor one can easily sink the best idea—as well as the viewers' impression of the author" (Bushy, 1991, p. 11). In short, a poster, as well as the presenter's execution of it, informs the viewer as much about the researcher as about the information presented (Bushy, 1991). Careful design, visual literacy, and meticulous proofreading and editing can help avoid the unfortunate scenario described in this chapter's first vignette. Bushy (1991) reminds us that posters are often the only opportunity some researchers have to make a first and lasting impression. Based on principles drawn from photography, art, education, computer science, and even marketing, most authorities concur that effective posters should be concise, eye-catching, appealing, informative, unified, and interactive with the viewers. These qualities are relatively easily achieved when one can report quantitative research findings in colorful pie charts and bar graphs. They are more challenging to achieve when findings consist of stories, concepts, description, explanation, and grounded theories. In her chapter "Meaning Through Form: Alternative Modes of Knowledge Representation," Norris (this volume) points out that "it is important to distinguish between nondiscursive forms that *express* meaning and discursive forms that *state it.*" She views this distinction as the difference between *showing* and *telling.* Most qualitative research posters must accomplish both.

Purposes for Posters

Posters are often used as an early phase in the research dissemination process prior to presenting a completed study in a formal paper or published article or book. Such a purpose is particularly relevant to theory-generating qualitative research that is viewed as ever becoming, ever extending, and ever densifying. In-progress presentations can provide immediate, face-to-face feedback to investigators by stimulating detailed discussions with audiences who are pursuing similar lines of research or who are struggling with comparable methodological concerns. At one such session during the American Psychiatric Association's annual scientific session in 1995, Wilson presented preliminary findings from the qualitative phase of an instrument development study that identified conceptual domains for the meaning of Quality of Life (QOL) among ethnically diverse advanced AIDS patients (PLWAs). In his interactions with the investigators, a psychiatrist audience member made a cogent argument for attempting to collect some indicators of personality traits to address the question of how to explain how some PLWAs sustain their QOL while others are unable to do so. His suggestion influenced additional data collection and another analytic direction.

Audiences for posters can seek clarification as well as offer criticism and ideas to investigators. Like an art "installation," poster presentations are not complete until viewers experience and interact with them. Viewers move at their own pace as they examine poster displays.

Both viewers and poster presenters can be enriched and informed by virtue of the interactive experience effective posters can inspire. Another particular value to qualitative researchers is the opportunity interactive poster sessions offer for what Lincoln and Guba (1985) term *peer review*. Legitimate claims to credibility (validity) and dependability (reliability) for findings generated through qualitative research are enhanced by both *member checks* in which investigators seek confirming feedback from study participants themselves and *peer review* in which findings are presented and discussed with professional peers who attend scientific meetings and bring their expertise and research experience to bear on the study at hand. Such exchanges in an informal setting are rarely possible during a timed paper presentation at a scientific meeting. Although letters to the editor in professional journals do represent a means for audiences to communicate with investigators who publish their research, both the time lag and the limited space detract from the broad-ranging discussions that can occur during a poster session.

The Poster Presentation Process: Pragmatic Strategies

Presenting your research in a scientific poster session will be more effective if you proceed through a three-phase decision process: prepresentation, presentation, and postpresentation. In so doing, poster sessions are more akin to craftsmanship than the creation of works of art. Yet, despite the deliberate process described here, it is possible to incorporate a leap of imagination while proceeding through the step-by-step set of decisions involved in crafting an effective research poster. Originality, novelty, freshness, and creativity often represent the very elements that distinguish an outstanding and memorable poster that attracts viewers from across a crowded hall from all those posters that can be easily overlooked. Poster presentations must be visually dynamic to gain viewers' attention and then must be sufficiently informative to engage the passersby in broader discussion. Posters must be designed as "sight bites" (May, personal communication, 1996) that draw viewers into interaction with the poster presenter and textual materials, using nonlinear, graphic textual strategies.[1]

The Prepresentation Phase

Targeting your audience. Preparation for presentation of a research poster begins as long as six months to a full year prior to the date of a scientific or professional meeting that you have targeted. The choice of one meeting over another requires that you identify the audience you wish to reach with your in-progress or completed prepublication research. If your intent is to encourage others to extend your work cross-culturally, you may begin your search with international research meetings, such as the International Congress of Nursing, scheduled for Canada in 1997; the Japan Academy of Nursing Science International Research Conferences, held in Kobe in 1995; the Qualitative Research Conference sponsored by Curtin University in Fremantle, Western Australia, also held in 1995; or the International Qualitative Health Research Conference, held in Bournemouth, England, in 1996.

If, on the other hand, you seek discussion with peers who are conducting research similar to yours with your population or addressing your phenomena of concern, it makes sense to identify a regional or national specialty or scientific meeting that includes poster presentation sessions.

Still another audience eager to learn about qualitative research with clinical relevance is the cadre of practitioners in nursing, medicine, social work, and psychology who strive to base their clinical work on research findings. If you as a qualitative researcher are interested in the perceived clinical "grab" and utility of your discoveries and insights, seek an institute, symposium, conference, or professional forum such as a Sigma Theta Tau research day or an association of clinicians such as the Association of Nurses in AIDS Care (ANAC) meeting that is likely to attract practitioners who might use your qualitative findings in their clinical work or in clinical intervention studies.

Obtaining official guidelines. Once you have identified an audience and targeted a conference or meeting, it is crucial to obtain the specific official guidelines for poster presentations, which will at minimum outline the dimensions and type of expected poster displays (including details as specific as whether easels and bulletin boards or simply tables will be provided for your poster or whether you must bring your own). Other information that you should obtain is the accessibility of power for audiovisual and other technologies and the location of the poster display area. Sherbinski and Stroup (1992) urge nurse presenters to get very specific information such as on the amount and type of display space available. They emphasize that the size and type of poster display possible will be determined by whether you have a 6-foot booth with a wall backboard or a 4-foot table. They also urge that you be certain to check what times during the conference, meeting, or convention posters will be on display because most poster sessions require that investigators be present to answer questions and engage in discussion of their work. The time for displaying posters at a scientific meeting is usually a half day or a full day with specifications about when the author(s) will be present (Coulston & Stivers, 1993). If detailed information about these issues is unclear or unavailable, you are at risk for creating the scenario described in the second vignette that began this chapter. Consequently, it makes sense for a prospective poster presenter to take an active role in seeking out requisite information from the conference planners (McDaniel, Bach, & Poole, 1993). This recommendation is especially relevant to qualitative researchers, who may intend to attempt a less conventional poster representation of their work, although it applies to all poster presenters.

Crafting an abstract and deciding on a title. Most research posters are reviewed for acceptance by a panel of referees based on a 100- to 200-word abstract that you must write and submit. Brevity and precision are the hallmarks of a well-written abstract as well as of a well-organized poster display (Coulston & Stivers, 1993). In some cases, poster abstracts are reprinted in a conference syllabus or book, and conference attendees make decisions about which posters to visit based on reading the abstracts in the conference book. Think carefully about what to include in your abstract and how to write it.

Typical components of a study abstract include

- the title, the investigators, and their affiliations;
- funding sources for the research;
- the study purpose and questions;

- a description of the sample;
- a brief rendering of the data collection and analysis methods;
- and, most important, the study's preliminary findings and their implications.

Make your title active in voice, yet informative of the type of study you've conducted. Most experts suggest that you include the major study problem or process on which you've focused and a description of the participants whose narratives provided your textual data. Titles usually should be limited to approximately 10 words and when printed on your poster should be large enough to be read easily at a distance of 10 feet. From as early as deciding on a title, begin to think about principles of visual literacy and apply them to the plan for your poster. Your primary aim in a poster design must be "to attract attention among a sea of posters competing for viewers' time, and then to enable the viewer to decide rapidly whether the poster is relevant or interesting" (Forsyth & Waller, 1995, p. 83). Edit a title like "A Cross-Sectional Descriptive Study of Spiritual Mediators of Anxiety, Hope and Quality of Life in African American Men and Women With HIV Infection" to a more succinct, active form such as "Spirituality Affects Quality of Life for African Americans Living With HIV." Keep your abstract clear, concise, direct, vivid, stimulating, and informative. Remember that language can corrupt thought and that bored writers produce bored readers. But, also, begin entertaining ideas about how to achieve the properties of a successful abstract and still retain the human interest of your research. The text of your abstract should be considered carefully and rigorously edited. The review panel's decision to select your poster for inclusion at the conference, meeting, or convention will be based on it. Craft a substantive, lean, and direct presentation of your conclusions. Avoid overly detailed literature citations and elaborate discussions of methodology.

An annotated bibliography and copies of your interview guides can be shared with viewers as handouts during your poster display. McDaniel et al. (1993) remind poster presenters to be sure to put your name, address, and phone number on the handouts you distribute or attach your business card, which should include an E-mail address and fax number.

Designing a poster based on principles of visual literacy. Forsyth and Waller (1995) emphasize the importance of what they term "visual literacy skills" if health care researchers are to communicate effectively with professional as well as lay audiences who have increasing visual sophistication. Although full mastery of visual literacy requires a long apprenticeship in graphic and print design, contemporary desktop publishing computer software has, in their words, "put great design power into inexperienced hands" (p. 80). Good visual design has one straightforward aim—to ease communication so that the flow of information from presenter to viewer is easy and enjoyable and both are free to concentrate on the content of the presentation.

The primary visual elements of a poster presentation include (a) the text, (b) the materials and layout, and (c) the illustrations and/or graphs. All must be crafted so as to provide a clear visual structure to your material that is first and foremost suited to your audience. Every choice you make about your poster's design—from selecting the type font, the color scheme, the illustrations and graphics, the layout, and the adjunctive materials—can contribute to the clarity of your poster's message if made with savvy and care. Effective posters make what viewers describe as an unambiguous and immediate statement, drawing viewers to look at your poster up close despite multiple competing stimuli. Yet, once your paper has attracted viewers, it can make use of diverse arrangements of text, different sized boxes or columns, and various typefaces and colors to engage the audience in both the expressive and the informative elements of the text.

The text content. Deciding what essential information to include in your poster presentation is the initial challenge. The text, like the abstract, should be vivid, concise, error-free, and logically organized. If you neglect to allow sufficient lead time to rigorously proofread the copy for your poster, you risk the scenario depicted in the third vignette that began this chapter. Typically, posters include the same information that appeared in your abstract. Forsyth and Waller (1995) emphasize that the visual structure of essential elements must be such that the viewer who is not likely to study the poster in detail can pick out the key components. They suggest that the IMRDA (introduction, method, results, discussion approach) may be specified by conference planners as the poster structure. However, more informative section titles often contribute to what's called "eye appeal."

Whatever stylistic structure you select, at minimum a poster should show, as well as tell, a project's entire story in a visually appealing and effective way. The content customarily includes a title, the study aims and conclusions, and then methods, results, and discussion. These elements should be organized so that headings guide the viewer to the major points. Viewers should be able to answer the following questions about your poster as a result of its design (Forsyth & Waller, 1995):

• Where can I find out what it's about?
• Where do I find the take-home message?
• Where do I begin reading?
• How far through am I?

The text design. Design choices begin with something as basic as decisions about fonts (Forsyth & Waller, 1995). *Font* refers to typefaces and styles. Font choice has an impact on the "personality" of a poster. Type size and leading (the space between lines) can also affect the light or heavy feel of a panel and its legibility. Experts recommend that posters use no more than two font types in a poster. Sans serif fonts like Helvetica have the clarity and emphasis useful for titles and headings. Serif fonts like Times Roman have small tails or "serifs" on the ends of letters that aid the reader by visually linking adjacent letters. Consequently, serif fonts are preferred by some for longer blocks of text but categorically avoided by others (Ryan, 1989) (see Figure 4.1).

Typographic experience has yielded a few other font design guidelines. For example, guidelines published by Forsyth and Waller (1995) are summarized in the Box 4.1.

The materials and layout. McDaniel et al. (1993) echo most others in emphasizing that cost and time are influential when planning the materials and layout for your poster. Box 4.2 summarizes some crucial information for decisions about materials and layout. The most common material for a poster is a foam-backed plastic board or large sheets of poster board.

Normal Left Justification

The use of font styles and line justification can enhance or detract from the message or the information you are trying to convey. The tone of the text can change from dramatic to light-hearted by changing the font.

Italic Setting

The use of font styles and line justification can enhance or detract from the message or the information you are trying to convey. The tone of the text can change from dramatic to light-hearted by changing the font.

Centered Justification

The use of font styles and line justification can enhance or detract from the message or the information you are trying to convey. The tone of the text can change from dramatic to light-hearted by changing the font.

All Capitals

THE USE OF FONT STYLES AND LINE JUSTIFICATION CAN ENHANCE OR DETRACT FROM THE MESSAGE OR THE INFORMATION YOU ARE TRYING TO CONVEY. THE TONE OF THE TEXT CAN CHANGE FROM DRAMATIC TO LIGHT-HEARTED BY CHANGING THE FONT.

Inappropriate Personality Font

The use of font styles and line justification can enhance or detract from the message or the information you are trying to convey. The tone of the text can change from dramatic to light-hearted by changing the font.

Full Justification

The use of font styles and line justification can enhance or detract from the message or the information you are trying to convey. The tone of the text can change from dramatic to light-hearted by changing the font.

Figure 4.1: Font and Format Comparisons

Box 4.1.   FONT DESIGN GUIDELINES

Use uppercase letters to stand alone at the beginning of a sentence; don't set entire words in all capitals.

• If you need emphasis, use boldface or color, not capitalization or underlining.

• Use italic text sparingly for single words and Latin names. The legibility of italic text tends to be low. The same guideline applies to use of calligraphy.

• Smooth scanning along lines of text is enhanced by keeping line length to 50-70 characters per line (including spaces and punctuation).

• Avoid varying the starting position of lines in the body of text because shorter lines can interrupt scanning and the eye of the viewer can have difficulty locating the start of the next line.

• Centering titles is fine but avoid centering lines in the body of text.

Use of color is an important consideration. A muted but distinctive background wash such as taupe or blue-grey is suggested to unify the poster elements and distinguish your poster from others. Colorful heads and subheadings are also encouraged. Brightly colored icons or symbols can highlight major concepts and add poster eye appeal. Color experts discourage the use of pastels and light colors on a light background and the use of dark colors on a dark background. Be wary of a poster design that consists of many monochrome, laser-printed, 8½- by 11-inch sheets of densely typed text, taped on separate pieces of colored art paper. The resulting impression is one of separate islands of information overload—each demanding equal attention. Not only does the viewer's eye become aware of the edges and the haphazard arrangement, but often the text is too small and too much to be read from any farther away than a few feet (Forsyth & Waller, 1995). Use your imagination by making some panels larger and others smaller. Consider arrows or some designation that will serve as directions for your viewer. Put the most important message in the

---

Box 4.2. LAYOUT GUIDELINES

- The typical size for a table poster is 3 by 6 feet; a wall-mounted poster is 4 by 8 feet; and a tripod or easel poster is usually 2 by 3 feet.

- Professional display boards with an aluminum frame and cloth surface range from $500 for a tabletop model to $3,500 for a complete backdrop with display tables. Costs of professional graphic art services were quoted at approximately $100/hour (in 1996).

- Access to color laser-quality printers and computer-generated graphics can conserve the cost of engaging a commercial graphic artist.

- Poster board, the most common material for a research poster, and the Velcro to attach panels to the board can be purchased at moderate cost from artists' supply stores, university bookstores, and office supply companies.

---

center of your poster at eye level or higher. Highlight key points with visual techniques like colored bullets. Keep your format lean and uncluttered. Lettering on posters must be viewed from 3 to 4 feet and thus should be in at least 16- to 18-point type. The visual schema of a grounded theory study readily lends itself to graphic presentation. The ethnographer, phenomenologist, narrative analyst, and investigator emphasizing other modes of qualitative inquiry must be inventive and imaginative to determine how to tell a visual story.

Because we (Wilson and Hutchinson) must often transport our research posters in the passenger cabin on international flights and carry the poster through international airports to clear customs, we have elected to place transportability near the top of our list of considerations in selecting poster materials and choosing a design. Consequently, instead of the most common format—printed display sections that are arranged on a poster board—we have (with Holzemer) prepared a cream and blue, professionally printed research poster on a 4- by 6-foot laminated single panel that can be rolled into a cardboard tube for transporting it and that weighs little or nothing. This particular format cost $125.00 and requires that a backboard or wall be present at the conference so that the laminated rectangular single panel can be tacked up. We realize that, in emphasizing portability, our poster can be viewed as "flat" when compared with three-dimensional displays.

We also carry handouts of bibliographic literature, interview guides, and focus group topics as well as copies of our abstract and business cards in a briefcase. Such a briefcase can also accommodate about 12 separate panels or "spreads" that themselves also can be laminated individually and mounted on a poster board as an alternative, although less portable, poster design. Our decision to use a professionally printed and laminated panel also sacrifices the flexibility that Lippman and Ponton (1989) encourage. They argue that because poster sessions often are used to report research in progress, a design that makes it possible to add to the poster once the study is completed or to make changes based on feedback from conference participants is worth considering. This property is especially noteworthy for qualitative research, which by nature continues to be reshaped with additional data. Authorities urge that an effective poster is one that is done with style, simplicity, orderliness, and sincerity. We add to this list creativity and visual literacy. The layout should not confuse clutter and a jumbled, overwhelming amount of content with artistic expression in the context of a poster presentation. Make every word tell a story.

Morra (1984) has summarized 20 advertising principles for poster presentations that serve as a useful checklist for effectiveness. (See Box 4.3.)

Art, illustrations, and graphics. Colorful pie and bar graphs are regularly used to report quantitative research findings in poster presentations. They break up the text and contribute "eye appeal." They certainly can become components of qualitative research posters as well and are effective in summarizing demographic information. But because qualitative research often discovers concepts and themes, symbols and photographs as well as carefully selected quotes (nongraphics) can be used to communicate the essence of meanings that your study has surfaced. Figure 4.2 illustrates a research poster that has employed the guidelines for effective poster design, while Figure 4.3

Box 4.3. POSTER CHECKLIST

1. Less is better. Don't try to say too much.
2. Bigger is better. Don't crowd your exhibit.
3. Put the most important message at eye level.
4. Write to one person (often a stranger) using active verbs.
5. Use short sentences, short paragraphs, and short words.
6. Write headlines with brief, colorful nouns and vigorous active verbs.
7. Five times as many viewers read headlines as read text copy.
8. Headlines (panel titles) with 10 or fewer words get more readers than those with more.
9. Headlines that promise the reader a benefit, contain news or offer helpful information attract above average readership.
10. Use the largest type possible. Headlines must be read from across the room. Text must be seen from three to five feet away.
11. Avoid using all capital letters to present text.
12. Keep columns three to four inches wide. Longer lines are harder to read.
13. Darker (blue or green) type on lighter (white or cream) background is easier to read than white type on a dark background.
14. Use color for emphasis but limit colors to one or two.
15. Help your readers with arrows, bullets, or other marks.
16. Set a key paragraph in boldface type for attention.
17. Use subheads every two to three inches.
18. Photos are better than drawings.
19. Write a caption for every graph or illustration. People read text under illustrations.
20. If you present unrelated ideas, number them and put them in a list. (Morra, 1984)

offers a hypothetical illustration of a poster on the same study that fails.

In the research poster depicted in Figure 4.2, which was based on an analysis of interview data focused on awareness contexts in early probable Alzheimer's disease, Hutchinson, Leger-Krall, and Wilson (in press) selected brief, pithy quotations to illustrate the differences between open, closed, suspected, and pretense awareness contexts. An example illustrating open awareness was the straightforward statement, "I need help"; an example of closed awareness, "I am not like the others." An example of suspected awareness was the statement, "My brain feels like it shut down"; an example of pretense, "I feel trembly but I smush it down." Each of these brief, vivid quotations was accompanied by a computer-generated symbol representing the awareness context being explained. Each of the four contexts was displayed on a different color spread. Figure 4.3 portrays unrelated islands of text overload using an uninteresting black-and-white color scheme.

A poster is said to be worth a thousand words if it is effective. Colleagues in nursing, medicine, and dietetics have all published authoritative articles on how to make one that works. All urge that photos, tables, graphs, and other visually appealing elements replace lengthy, detailed narratives whenever possible. This recommendation poses a particular challenge for the qualitative researcher attempting to report narrative textual data.

Experts concur that it is wise to seek the advice of local medical illustration departments in hospitals and universities and also to invite your colleagues to critique your poster before finalizing it and presenting it at a regional, national, or international meeting. At the University of California, San Francisco's Department of Community Health Systems, faculty members are encouraged to display posters about their research on a designated hall bulletin board, not only to obtain feedback about the poster's effectiveness but also to keep students, faculty, and visitors informed about in-progress research.

The Presentation Phase

If you have attended to the many details of the prepresentation phase of a poster, the presentation phase should be smooth and straightforward. All of the authorities we consulted in preparing this chapter (Gregg & Pierce, 1994; Miracle & King, 1994; Vogelsang, 1994) agreed that it's essential that you assume that anything that can

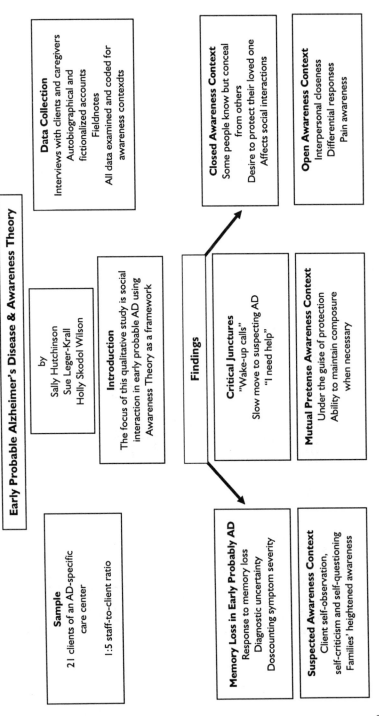

Early Probable Alzheimer's Disease & Awareness Theory

by
Sally Hutchinson
Sue Leger-Krall
Holly Skodol Wilson

Introduction
The focus of this qualitative study is social interaction in early probable AD using Awareness Theory as a framework

Data Collection
Interviews with clients and caregivers
Autobiographical and fictionalized accounts
Fieldnotes
All data examined and coded for awareness contexdts

Sample
21 clients of an AD-specific care center
1:5 staff-to-client ratio

Findings

Critical Junctures
"Wake-up calls"
Slow move to suspecting AD
"I need help"

Mutual Pretense Awareness Context
Under the guise of protection
Ability to maintain composure when necessary

Closed Awareness Context
Some people know but conceal from others
Desire to protect their loved one
Affects social interactions

Open Awareness Context
Interpersonal closeness
Differential responses
Pain awareness

Memory Loss in Early Probably AD
Response to memory loss
Diagnostic uncertainty
Doscounting symptom severity

Suspected Awareness Context
Client self-observation, self-criticism and self-questioning
Families' heightened awareness

Figure 4.2: Example of More Effective Poster Design

Early Probable Alzheimer's Disease & Awareness Theory
Sally A. Hutchinson, Sue Leger-Krall, and Holy Skodol Wilson

Abstract
The focus of this qualitative study is on social interaction in early probable Alzheimer's Disease. Glaser and Strauss's Awareness Context theory is used as a framework for the analysis of data from 14 probable AD clients, 1 autobiographical account, 14 family caregiver, 1 family caregiver focus group and over 500 pages of field notes.

Purpose
The purpose of this research was to use the substantive theory of Awareness Context to illuminate social interactional issues of early AD. This use of this theory and application of its data is called emergent fit. The emergent fit mode "allows the researcher...to expand personal work by exploring in depth...a small part of a larger phenomenon."

Setting and Sample
The primary site for clients was an AD specific day care center in a large southeaster city. The program maintained an average of 21 clients who represented all stages of AD; there were 66% women, 29% African Americans 64% Caucasians and 7% Hispanics. Staff-patient ratio was 1:5. Inclusion criteria was probable AD based on family report, clinical record or presence in care facility.

Data Collection and Analysis
Data collection involved interviews with clients and care-givers. We had both original and retrospective accounts. All interview data, the autobiography, fictionalized account and the field notes were examined for data that yielded information on awareness contexts. Data were coded and analyzed to fit the awareness context theory...

Findings
Memory loss in early probable AD
Diagnostic uncertainty: People were aware of memory loss but as a diagnosis of probable AD. Physicians offered literature but no actual dialogue of events. Discounting symptom severity: When clients were examined by a physician memory loss was noted as part of aging and misdiagnosed. Attributing memory loss to age, normalized and minimized probable AD symptoms

Findings
Critical Junctures
A shift from lack of awareness to suspecting of disease, occurred at different speeds of each client. Some patients experienced "wake up calls" about their condition. Closed awareness context Some people know of their disease but conceal it from others.
The concealing of status affect social interactions with kin, friends and co-workers.

Findings
Suspected awareness context
Client self-observation, self-criticism, and self-questioning: the client begin to self-evaluate the situation. Clients confirm or invalidate their suspicions. Families 'heightened awareness: Families become suspicious of clients behavior.
Multiple Pretense Awareness Context
Patient and family both know of the disease and it's care.

Discussion
Awareness is central to interaction. Awareness Context Theory provides a perspective on social interaction in AD, probably the most stigmatized and feared of the elderly.
Independent assessments of clients' and families' awareness contexts are important so health care providers can be informed of the responses to AD.
Understanding the wishes of those involved is essential for client centered care.

Figure 4.3: Example of Poorly Designed Poster With Spelling and Other Errors

go wrong, will. They tell us to anticipate the worst-case scenario when planning the materials to bring to a poster presentation session. They urge that we bring our own hammer, pushpins, thumbtacks, heavy-duty stapler, masking tape, glue, extra slide projector lightbulb and extension cord, and copies of all the handouts. Biancuzzo (1994) in her piece on posters about clinical innovation stresses the importance of bringing all the necessary materials for erecting a poster, and urges that you take a checklist to remind yourself of the date, time, and location for poster presentations. She also recommends that you keep track of other information for displaying posters including the name of the poster session, contact person and his or her phone number, and what the conference organizers will provide ranging from tables and backdrops to extension cords and power outlets. Her list of essentials includes a place to put the business cards of others interested in your work as well as your own business cards. She also encourages poster presenters to bring pages of stick-on mailing labels so colleagues who are interested in additional information about your work can receive it. Biancuzzo (1994) encourages poster presenters to anticipate questions and then to write viewers' questions down on a notepad.

Authorities also agree that you should arrive at least a half hour before the session is scheduled to begin; we suggest that you allow an hour. Morra (1984) has written the definitive article on both a schedule for producing a poster and tips on presenting it. Lippman and Ponton (1989) suggest that arriving early is absolutely necessary so that you can locate the building, find a convenient parking space, select a desirable location if one has not been preassigned, and exhibit your poster from the conference registration period onward. Arriving early also gives you time to troubleshoot.

The Postpresentation Phase

The most important way to gauge the effectiveness of your poster is to take note of the people who stop to look at it and engage you in discussion. You also can invite viewers to complete a brief, simple evaluation that contains questions that will stimulate responses from the audience about their perceptions of your work. After your poster session has been concluded, it's a good idea to note the interest of viewers in other posters on display. Figure out which were successful and why.

Lynch and Woolgar (1988) emphasize that visual representations in science require not only the crafting of resemblances but also the task of plumbing the depths of a phenomenon. Qualitative researchers have available the full range of literary devices and artistic conventions when preparing visual and graphic representations for rigorous, convincing, and defensible poster presentations. Strunk and White (1979) leave us with a word on style that is particularly apropos for qualitative researchers: "Style not only reveals the spirit of a (wo)man; it reveals his/her identity as surely as would fingerprints" (p. 68). Leave the mark of your fingerprints, identity, and visual literacy on the qualitative research poster presentations you create. Try for an up-close research poetic.

Note

1. See also Norris (this volume) for examples of visual/graphic textual presentation strategies in her chapter "Meaning Through Form."

References

Beauty out of damage. (1993, August 15). *New York Times Magazine*, p. 1.

Benner, P. E. (1984). *From novice to expert: Excellence and power in clinical nursing practice*. Menlo Park, CA: Addison-Wesley.

Biancuzzo, M. (1994). Developing a poster about a clinical innovation. Part 1: Ideas and abstracts. *Clinical Nurse Specialist, 8*(3), 153-155.

Bushy, A. (1991). A rating scale to evaluate research posters. *Nurse Educator, 16*(1), 11-15.

Coulston, A. M., & Stivers, M. (1993). A poster worth a thousand words: How to design effective poster session displays. *Journal of the American Dietetic Association, 93*(8), 865-866.

Forsyth, R., & Waller, A. (1995). Making your point: Principles of visual design for computer aided slide and poster production. *Archives of Disease in Childhood, 72*(1), 80-84.

Glaser, B. G., & Strauss, A. L. (1965). *Awareness of dying*. Chicago: Aldine.

Gregg, M. M., & Pierce, L. L. (1994). Developing a poster presentation. *Rehabilitation Nursing, 19*(2), 107-109.

Hutchinson, S. A. (1986). *Hidden dimensions of watchful readiness: Survival practices of rescue workers*. Washington, DC: University Press of America.

Hutchinson, S. A., Leger-Krall, S., & Wilson, H. S. (in press). Early probable Alzheimer's disease and awareness context theory. *Social Science and Medicine*.

Kayser-Jones, J. (1981). *Old, alone, and neglected: Care of the aged in Scotland and the United States*. Berkeley: University of California Press.

Kleinbeck, S. V. (1988). Poster sessions bring research to the OR. *AORNJ, 47,* 1299-1304.

Lincoln, Y. S., & Guba, E. G. (1985). *Naturalistic inquiry.* Beverly Hills, CA: Sage.

Lippman, D. T., & Ponton, K. S. (1989). Designing a research poster with impact. *Western Journal of Nursing Research, 11*(4), 477-485.

Lynch, M., & Woolgar, S. (1988). Introduction: Sociological orientations to representational practice in science. *Human Studies, 11,* 99-116.

McDaniel, R. W., Bach, C. A., & Poole, M. J. (1993). Poster update: Getting their attention. *Nursing Research, 42*(5), 302-304.

Miracle, V. A., & King, K. C. (1994). Presenting research: Effective paper presentations and impressive poster presentations. *Applied Nursing Research, 7*(3), 147-157.

Morra, M. E. (1984). How to plan and carry out your poster session. *Oncology Nursing Forum, 11*(2), 52-57.

Morse, J., & Johnson, J. L. (1991). *The illness experience: Dimensions of suffering.* Newbury Park, CA: Sage.

Ryan, N. M. (1989). Developing and presenting a research poster. *Applied Nursing Research, 2*(1), 52-55.

Sandelowski, M. (1994). The proof is in the pottery: Toward a poetic for qualitative inquiry. In J. Morse (Ed.), *Critical issues in qualitative research* (pp. 46-63). Thousand Oaks, CA: Sage.

Sexton, D. L. (1984). Presentation of research findings: The poster session. *Nursing Research, 33,* 374-375.

Sharf, B. F. (1995). Poster art as women's rhetoric: Raising awareness about breast cancer. *Literature and Medicine, 14*(1), 72-86.

Sherbinski, L. A., & Stroup, D. R. (1992). Developing a poster for disseminating research findings. *Journal of the American Association of Nurse Anesthetists, 60*(6), 567-571.

Strunk, W., Jr., & White, E. B. (1979). *The elements of style.* New York: Macmillan.

Vogelsang, J. (1994). Guidelines for developing a research poster presentation. *Journal of Post Anesthesia Nursing, 9*(2), 126-128.

Whyte, W. F. (1914). *Street corner society: The social structure of an Italian slum* (2nd ed.). Chicago: University of Chicago Press.

Wilson, H. S. (1982). *Deinstitutionalized residential care for schizophrenics: The Soteria House approach.* New York: Grune & Stratton.

Wilson, H. S., & Hutchinson, S. A. (1991). Triangulation of qualitative methods: Heideggerian hermeneutics and grounded theory. *Qualitative Health Research, 1*(2), 263-276.

Wilson, H. S., & Hutchinson, S. A. (1996). Methodological mistakes and grounded theory research. *Nursing Research, 45*(2), 122-124.

Dialogue: Other Ways to Do Things

Muecke: When reading this [Norris's chapter], I thought back to a student who almost didn't make it through her master's because she didn't "think" in a normal, logical sequence that you could put a master's thesis into. She couldn't; she was a poet. She was brilliant! And what she studied was nonverbal physician-patient communication, and she analyzed videotapes. The work was unprecedented. Nobody could do it. And she worked at a choreography. She did not know how to capture this, except as a choreography, and she had great sheets of papers all over the office floor. She composed her own way to describe all of this, and then said, "How do I put this into a master's thesis?"

Boyle: Well, APA format, of course! [laughter]

Muecke: Well, we struggled and struggled with this. And then she started writing poetry about it. Ultimately that was the thesis that I wanted. She caved in to the rest of the committee and the power of academia, and finally just wrote a descriptive kind of narrative. And this was a tremendous loss to nursing. Tremendous! We are creatures of our culture! We have to be very careful of how our culture is squelching some of these new ways of knowing and being.

CHAPTER 5

Meaning Through Form

Alternative Modes of Knowledge Representation

Judy R. Norris

The centrepiece of the show is a large installation in the centre of the gallery, where almost 12 metres of Johnson and Johnson muslin bandages are stitched together. A letter from the artist to his parents, interspersed with transcripts of Harrison's interviews, covers the exterior. The piece leads you into a dim maze of acrylic paint. Inside in the darkness, angry men loom clutching bats, rocks and razors. You're surrounded, and the sense of an imminent beating is real.

Charles Mandel (1996, p. C14)

In this 1996 gallery exhibition, Spencer J. Harrison, a Canadian artist, used various forms of installation art to disseminate his learnings from 30 interviews with gay and lesbian people on their experience of being gay-bashed. His intent was not to portray violent acts but to provide a vicarious learning experience so that others can "understand what it's like to carry that stuff around on a day-to-day basis and how that affects your personal identity" (Mandel, 1996, p. C14). The enduring meanings that result from an encounter with art like Harrison's are not evident immediately but evolve through repeated encounters (Stake, 1994) as participants relive, interpret, and reflect upon the experience. It is "not the primary exposure to a work of art, but rather the secondary contemplation, which evokes genuine understanding" (Rubin, 1991, p. 49).

In the last decade, growing numbers of qualitative researchers have been seeking ways to overcome the limitations of traditional print forms for research dissemination. Many of us are experimenting with forms that expand our capacity to privilege multiple voices and realities, and to present knowledge for which we do not yet have adequate words or that cannot be experienced directly (Eisner, 1985; Rosario, 1991). As is evident in the example above, art forms allow us to provide vicarious, situated learning experiences for our audience, inviting their involvement in dynamic interpretive evolution of our texts.

In this chapter, I will offer a sampling of some artistic forms and textual strategies that researchers have used to transform knowledge, and I will consider some issues regarding the use of alternative forms: Will our audience comprehend and give credence to knowledge presented in forms other than traditional text? What about the potential for ambiguous or wholly unintended interpretations? How can research presented in artistic forms be useful for practice disciplines? How will we recognize quality? Can anyone use artistic forms, or are skill and aptitude necessary? How can nonprint forms come to count toward a publication record? What about the problems of distributing and cataloguing film, music, dance, or other performance modes? Will this devalue our academic currency at a time when qualitative research is finally gaining assent in a still-quantitative world?

I have a postmodern agenda; by this I mean that I intend to raise some questions about traditional and alternative forms for representing knowledge from research. Postmodernism encourages us to examine our need for imposing order and structure (Flax, 1987), and the way that our structuralist orientation leads us to think in competitive false dualisms like quantitative/qualitative, science/art, objective/

subjective, "normal" science/new paradigm science (Hlynka, 1991). Postmodernism celebrates diversity and plurality; multiple voices, perspectives, truths, and meanings; tolerance for paradox, contradictions, and ambiguity; and the blurring of boundaries between research and everyday life. Unlike Kuhn's (1970) concept of "paradigm shift" in which one paradigm eventually replaces another, postmodernism "insists on the co-existence, juxtaposition, and interaction of multiple paradigms" (Hlynka, 1991, p. 28).

Postmodern research tends to feature dialogue, self-disclosure, and process rather than goals such as theory generation or direct applications for practice (Shotter, 1992; Tyler, 1986). As the nature of all knowledge is considered to be transient, partial, provisional, situated, and constructed, new understandings are reported in open-ended instructive accounts that contain no "story of stories" and no "synthesizing allegory." "At best, we make do with a collection of indexical anecdotes or telling particulars with which to portend that larger unity beyond explicit textualization" (Tyler, 1986, p. 131).

The postmodern perspective is useful for providing a means to function within the real world of conflicting paradigms (Hlynka, 1991) and for taking a standpoint outside the current canon. My intent will be to provoke awareness about artful forms for representing knowledge, and to encourage the reader to notice how our current structures work against these forms being taken seriously as ways of knowing.

The Way We Write Up Our Research

For centuries, writing has been divided into separate domains: literature—aligned with art and culture, and concerned with nonutilitarian aesthetic values (Clifford, 1986)—and scientific writing for which there "was the belief that its words were objective, precise, unambiguous, noncontextual, nonmetaphoric . . . 'transparent' — simply reflecting, like a clear pane of glass, an objective 'reality' " (Richardson, 1995a, p. 203). Many of us were drawn to qualitative research as we came to realize how much life was squeezed out of human experience when we attempted to make sense of it in a numeric, noncontextual way. But even though qualitative methods gave us a way to write about the lives of our participants in context—to provide for our audience "the surprise of a recognizable person"

(Miller, 1994)—most of us (who needed to graduate or publish) have continued to write qualitative research reports that resemble the traditional forms of the scientific paradigm. Of the various efforts to legitimize qualitative research by making it look more like conventional science (Sandelowski, 1995), I believe that this practice may have the most pernicious consequences.

Insistence on traditional research writing genres has been less vehement in certain disciplines, such as education and the humanities, than in some of the health disciplines; a case in point is nursing with its recent past as a somewhat self-conscious newcomer to academia. As was the situation in numerous other disciplines, many nurse researchers had been socialized in positivistic methods, but this legacy does not account for the decades-long display of oppressed group behavior evidenced by the inordinate emphasis placed on structure, techniques, and method as a way for nursing to "prove its scientific merit within academia" (Lowenberg, 1993, p. 62). Sandelowski (1993) cautions that although we have progressed to a greater understanding of what constitutes rigor, we are still in danger of making a fetish of technique at the expense of the inherently artful nature of qualitative work:

> It is as if, in our quasi-militaristic zeal to neutralize bias and to defend our projects against threats to validity, we were more preoccupied with building fortifications against attack than with creating the evocative, true-to-life, and meaningful portraits, stories, and landscapes of human experience that constitute the best test of rigor in qualitative work. (p. 1)

Only recently have nurse researchers begun to venture into the use of nontraditional forms of research inquiry and writing, and this is in some part due to those who have brought these ideas back to us from their travels within the cultures of other disciplines. (See Sandelowski, 1994.)

Another deterrent to risking the use of more artful writing forms is that the more "personal" (as opposed to "academic") forms of writing, for example, autobiography, narrative, and qualitative reports where the author uses the active voice and is present in the text as "I,"[1] have been linked with "the feminine" and sometimes dismissed as " 'soft,' 'idiosyncratic,' 'undertherorized,' 'individualistic,' even 'narcissistic' " (Miller, 1994, p. 505). Women especially may be hesitant to transgress academic orthodoxy in this area; women's research work has been devalued for such things as interdisciplinary or team research; applied, practical, or action-oriented research; the nature of the topic; questioning the notion of objectivity; or work that challenges the status quo such as societal power distributions (Caplan, 1994). For those who endure hostilities of this nature, conformance to traditional writing formats may seem a very minor concession.

Richardson (1994b), however, would see this as an abdication of our responsibility to our audience: To use a mechanistic model of writing intended for quantitative research is discordant with the experience of doing qualitative research and, also, it is likely to produce a boring text that people won't read. This is not an inconsequential point:

> Unlike quantitative work, which can carry its meaning in its tables and summaries, qualitative work depends upon people's reading it. Just as a piece of literature is not equivalent to its "plot summary," qualitative research is not contained in its abstracts. Qualitative research has to be read, not scanned; its meaning is in the reading. (p. 517)

Qualitative researchers wishing to break free of the confines of scientific writing structures have a groundswell of support and precedent,[2] indeed, a directive (Sandelowski, 1994), to acquire artful ways to "capture and keep" our informants' experience, even as we understand that this is, of course, impossible; all we can hope for is a repertoire of ways to simulate, represent, reference, and reconstruct experience (Donmoyer & Yennie-Donmoyer, 1995).

I will now focus on the principal topic of this chapter: knowledge representation that uses art forms such as poetry, fiction, painting, tapestry, sculpture, dance, music, theater, film, photography, installation art, and textual strategies.

Artistic Forms of Representation

Free at last? Free to break every convention?
Free not to write? Not to speak?
Free to dance, hum, fingerpaint the sociological?

Laurel Richardson (1995b, p. 192)

Although he had been writing about knowledge transformation using art forms since the 1970s, Elliot Eisner's celebrated 1993 presidential address to the American Educational Research Association (AERA)[3] was considered to be an event that enlivened the interest in artistic modes of knowledge representation that was already growing among some educational researchers. Since then, in addition to increasing numbers and varieties of artistic presentations at subsequent AERA conferences, a 1996 qualitative research conference was organized around this theme,[4] and also that year, an AERA Special Interest Group (SIG), "Arts-Based Approaches to Educational Research," was formed.[5]

Form[6]

Life is incoherent unless we give it form.

Susanne K. Langer (1957, p. 27)

The thrust of Eisner's 1993 address was that using forms other than language and numbers affords us the opportunity to understand the world in other ways. "The selection of a form through which the world is to be represented not only influences what we can say, it also influences what we are likely to experience" (Eisner, 1991a, p. 8). Form, as Eisner (1985) tells us, is usually thought of as a noun—"the products made by both artists and scientists" (p. 27)—but thinking of the word as a verb helps us to recognize that knowledge is made, or *formed*. When through our research we have come to understand something about a phenomenon, we choose some medium to carry the experience (Dewey, 1934), to give it public form, thus *making* it into something else:

> One feature of a medium is that it mediates and anything that mediates changes what it conveys; the map is not the territory and text is not the event. We learn to write and to draw, to dance and to sing, in order to *re*-present the world as we know it. (Eisner, 1991a, p. 27)

Not just any form will do; the form must be integral to the work, and arise from it. As Tyler (1986) notes, "Questions of form are not prior, the form itself should emerge" (p. 127). Form carries the experience "not as vehicles carry goods but as a mother carries a baby when the baby is part of her own organism" (Dewey, 1934, p. 118). Form is not superimposed, or merely associated with a work, it is *of* it.

When examining form, it is important to distinguish between nondiscursive forms that *express* meaning and discursive forms that *state* it, that is, the difference between showing and telling. Phenix (1964) writes:

> Alfred North Whitehead and Susanne Langer have defined the contrast between the discursive and nondiscursive by means of the concept of *presentational immediacy*. In the discursive forms meanings unfold in sequential argument. In the nondiscursive forms meanings are presented in a unitary vision, i.e., in direct or immediate insight. In the former, meaning is attained at the end of a demonstration (whether explicit or implicit), while in the latter, meaning is grasped all at once, as an immediate presentation. (p. 82)

Expressive forms *are* the experience, and they can't be translated: "There is no verbal equivalent for Bach's *Mass in B Minor*" (Eisner, 1991a, p. 235).

For Dewey (1934), "Science states meanings; art expresses them" (p. 84). Eisner (1991a) likens Dewey's "stated meaning" to Langer's notion of *representational* symbols, and "expressed meaning" as *presentational* symbols. Representational symbols are transparent because we're so used to them that we ignore the form, "we move through them to their referents" (p. 31). Presentational symbols, on the other hand, are opaque; we obtain their meaning directly.[7] This distinction will take on additional meaning when we consider various forms of theater.

Texts

In popular usage, the term *text* denotes written words, but as we consider other forms of representation, it will be helpful to think about texts more broadly. For instance, a garden can be thought of as a text, as can a family, a chess match, and, indeed, life.

For Clandinin and Connelly (1994), inquiry starts with experience and, through various methods, field texts (data) are created to represent chosen aspects of that experience. All field texts are interpretive, having been selected, and shaped, by researcher relationships to participant stories: "A field note is not simply a field note; a photograph is not simply a photograph; an oral history is not simply an oral history. What is told, as well as the meaning of what is told, is shaped by the relationship" (p. 419). The field texts, which tend to be descriptive, particular, and close to the experience, cannot be left to speak for themselves; the researcher must interpret them further, transforming them into research texts (Clandinin & Connelly, 1994).

Research texts are some form of performance or artifact presented to an audience for the purpose of telling about our learnings. Blumenfeld-Jones (1995) uses Paul Ricoeur's work to help us understand how dance is text:

> He [Ricoeur] takes text to be the paradigmatic case for interpretation and he takes the interpretive processes for understanding text to be the paradigmatic processes for interpreting meaningful action. Dance can be taken as a meaningful action which can be treated as a text. (pp. 394-395)

In theater, "performance text" is considered to be that which is experienced by a spectator or listener (Törnqvist, 1991).

These texts are dynamic artifacts that have evolved from an object for interpretation to a transformed communicative object. If we have refrained from instructing our audience on what meaning is to be taken from our artifact, which extinguishes the aesthetic effect (Iser, 1978), then the text functions "as a happening and the experience of the reader . . . is activated by this happening" (p. 22). The message of a text "is transmitted in two ways, in that the reader 'receives' it by composing it" (p. 21). Thus our audience transforms our texts again (and again), participating in the creation of a virtual text:

> It must inevitably be virtual in character, as it cannot be reduced to the reality of the text or to the subjectivity of the reader, and it is from this virtuality that it derives its dynamism. As the reader passes through the various perspectives offered by the text and relates the different views and patterns to one another he sets the work in motion, and so sets himself in motion, too. (p. 21)

Art Encounter as a Way of Knowing

> It is the function of art to reorganize experience so it is perceived freshly. At the very least, the painting, the poem, or the play cleanses a familiar

scene washing away the film of habit and dust collected over time so that it is seen anew.

Madeleine Grumet (1988, p. 81)

There are a number of reasons some of us may experience discomfort with the notion that experiential knowledge from an encounter with art is a legitimate way of knowing. As Eisner (1985) points out, in Western culture "we do not typically associate the aesthetic with knowing. The arts, with which the aesthetic is most closely associated, is a matter of the heart. Science is thought to provide the most direct route to knowledge" (p. 24). Further, appreciation of art forms is diminished by the belief that we *search for* knowledge (through science), rather than construct it:

> If there were greater appreciation for the extent to which knowledge is constructed—something made—there might be a greater likelihood that its aesthetic dimensions would be appreciated. To make knowledge is to cast the scientist in the role of an artist or a craftsperson, someone who shapes materials and ideas. (p. 32)

Few of us were socialized in ways of learning that were remotely participatory, were artistic, or included an emotional component. Typically, like May (1991), by the age of 5 we had probably "learned what counts as legitimate school knowledge, experienced the disjuncture between authentic and artificial experience, and realized that aesthetic interests and expression in school most often are undesirable, if not punishable" (pp. 140-141). Primary school is also where we learned to sever our minds from our bodies. The educational system required that we become alienated and disconnected from our emotions and our bodies;[8] we learned early to face the front, to stop wiggling, and even to delay trips to the bathroom in conformance to the belief that our physicality must be managed so that learning can take place (Stinson, 1995). If we went on to engage in scientific discourse, we learned to transcend our bodies, to represent ourselves as entirely as mind (Brodkey & Fine, 1988)—disembodied knowledge expressed in disembodied language. So, sensual art encounters in a research context may seem somewhat embarrassing, perhaps pretentious or ostentatious, and, further, may evoke feelings of inadequacy if we think we can't understand it.[9]

Art Education

As our minds have come to be disassociated from our bodies and emotions, so too has art become discrete from our everyday lives. Once seen as an essential and functional part of the fabric of society, in Western culture the arts are now a separate, specialized, hierarchical, and multidisciplinary overlay associated with high culture (Anderson, 1995). Unlike some societies, where children learn about art as seamlessly as they acquire their language, in Western culture art education is considered a luxury and is taught haphazardly in schools, if it is taught at all.

Elliot Eisner (1992) points out that the time and expertise allocated to a field of study indicates what is considered important, and determines the kinds of skills that children will have the opportunity to acquire. As a consequence, many of us who were deprived of an adequate art education[10] are aesthetically illiterate; to the degree that we lack the ability to perceive the subtleties and complexities of form, we are variously unable to access aesthetic modes of knowing (Eisner, 1985). Artistic training is "the education of feeling" as typical schooling is the "education of thought" (Langer, 1953, p. 401); if we missed this instruction, we may experience degrees of discomfort with artistic expression or, unaware of the skill, ability, and cognition required, might "conceive of the arts as the discharge of affect" or "as a consequence of emotion finding its release in a material" (Eisner, 1991b, p. 38).[11] Maxine Greene (1996) would see the remedy for this situation as obvious: "Teaching people to paint teaches them how to be present to paintings."

Qualitative Research Skills and the Arts

Eisner (1991b) maintains that "all so-called abstract knowledge depends upon the ability to relate language to images" (p. 41); we notice qualities (such as time and space) to which we assign imagistic words (for example, *infinity*). However,

> to the extent to which our imagination is impoverished, the meaning of these terms also will be. Imagination is fed by perception and perception by sensibility and sensibility by artistic cultivation. With refined sensibility, the scope of perception is enlarged. With enlarged perception, the resources that feed our imaginative life are increased. (pp. 41-42)

Enlarged perception, a skill of utmost importance to qualitative researchers, is developed with effort and experience over time. "Seeing, rather than mere looking, requires an enlightened eye" (Eisner, 1991a, p. 1).

Art education, and indulging our innate longing for artistic expression, develops our capacity to perceive more amply, improves our tolerance for ambiguity, and sparks our creativity.[12] Further, the arts hone our proficiency in "qualitative thinking." McCutcheon (1991) observed that experiencing opera calls for multidimensional qualitative thinking:

> One of these dimensions is epistemological, where I wonder, What is this thing? Another is ontological, which asks, What is the meaning of this thing in the world? Ethics and moral issues enter here. Yet a third is cosmological, where I wonder, What is the meaning of this in the broader order of things? (p. 164)

Once we are open to the idea of using nontraditional forms to disseminate our research learnings, we can choose among forms we think can do the best job of bringing our audience to a place conducive to understanding. "How else can we represent heat other than to tell the temperature?" (Eisner, 1996).

Our most elegant work surely will be with the art forms we love and are good at, but if we can add new forms to our repertoire, we open more avenues to understanding, thus increasing the kinds of questions we can ask. Skill and aptitude do count; if a researcher does not have the skills to use a form, the content will not emerge: "Representation requires the skills needed to treat a material so that it functions as a medium, something that mediates content" (Eisner, 1993, p. 9). But those willing to acquire the requisite skills will become better qualitative researchers in the process. In the next section, I will provide some examples of how others have used artistic forms.

Examples of Artistic Forms

Experimental Writing

Poetry. In a 1992 chapter, sociologist and poet Laurel Richardson relates the process and life-changing consequences of having constructed a poetic representation, "Louisa May's Story of Her Life," from interview data. In addition to the departure from traditional academic prose, Richardson's poem transgressed the norms of sociological writing by leaving out expected demographic data and by using only Louisa May's words and style of speaking rather than paraphrasing or using her words as exemplars. The intense reactions to the poem by diverse audiences allowed her to gain insight into the familiar. At a sociological convention, she experienced "the hold of positivism" when asked to "prove" Louisa May existed by producing the transcript, "as if transcripts were real" (Richardson, 1992, p. 135). She experienced a new level of engagement with the informant: "Louisa May moved into my psychic interior in a way that no interviewee of mine ever had. She moved in the way poetry does. She's not yet moved out" (p. 133).[13]

Fiction. The novel *Crazy February* (Wilson, 1974) is based on field experience with the Mayan people of Chamula in the mountains of southeastern Mexico. The author had no plans to write a novel about Indian Mexico but, wanting to sharpen his observation skills, he apprenticed in fieldwork with an anthropologist and in exchange gave back the data he had collected. The issue of "raw" versus "cooked" data often arises where data are represented verbatim. Wilson explains the controversy:

> Some people believe ethnographic novels are comparable to fieldnotes—the data themselves in their original, unanalyzed form. Though I can see the reason for the analogy, I still disagree with it. Good fieldnotes record raw experience. For the time being, the anthropologist squelches his desire to interpret, and he writes down everything he can see or remember. Good ethnographic fiction also presents experience raw, without generalization. But in building the story, in selecting to tell *this* because it is important and not to tell *that* because it seems trivial, the novelist is analyzing his material. Between the raw and the cooked, both ethnographies and ethnographic novels belong in the processed pot. (p. 1)[14]

Performance

Performing science. Paget (1995) took a published research article about physician-patient talk to the stage, where it was performed almost verbatim. The work tells the story of how a cancer patient was on three occasions given a medical diagnosis of depression because her cancer was a censored topic between herself and the physician. The performance "intends an experience. In fact, theater is a vehicle for the recovery of experience and for the play of emotion and imagination so typically suppressed in the production of social science texts" (pp. 235-236). Performing the text engaged the research audience in a different way, bringing the experience to the present and providing "textured characters" and dimensions that couldn't be communicated in writing.

Through techniques of systematic introspection, Ellis and Bochner (1992) created dialogue to present a personal account of the lived experience of an abortion. Readers follow the couple on a journey, gaining a sense of what the experience must have been like for them. The narrative is written as a script with the intention that it be performed so an audience

> is subjected to much more than words: they see facial expressions, movements, and gestures; they hear the tones, intonations, and inflections of the actors' voices; and they can feel the passion of the performers. The audience is moved away from the universal and forced to deal with the concrete. (p. 80)[15]

Dance. To the nondancer, it seems plausible that an understanding of concepts could somehow be choreographed (or improvised) and danced, but because Western culture is nondance, we may believe we could not understand it (Blumenfeld-Jones, 1995). In his 1995 presentation at AERA,[16] Blumenfeld-Jones, dancer and philosopher of education, performed, through improvisational expressionist dance and spoken text, important teachings about how to look at dance as a mode of research representation and about the myth that words (unlike other forms) are transparent, that is, directly naming reality and requiring no interpretation. He did not mime these ideas (as nondancers might expect) but extracted their essences and presented them in a condensed form: "I sought to persuade, not through rational discourse but through a weaving of argument, motion, and repetition of words and phrases" (p. 396).

To help us understand how to access the mode of dance when it is used as a form of research representation, Blumenfeld-Jones explains that the meaningful action of dance can be thought of as a text, the dance act as writing, and the dance journey as having a narrative in which the audience participates. "The motion itself must be the meaning rather than laying theatrical acting over general culturally acclaimed motion" (p. 394).[17] Although only certain kinds of research will be appropriate to dance representation,[18] and relatively few able to use this form, it can be useful as an adjunct to other forms as well as in the development of ideas,[19] where it can "extend, energize, and bring out previously unseen aspects of the objects of our interest" (p. 400).

Theater. Actor Anna Devere Smith interviewed around 200 people who had experienced the Los Angeles riots that erupted on April 29, 1992. From these data she developed a documentary play *Twilight* (and companion book *Twilight: Los Angeles, 1992*) in collaboration with four others of various races who functioned as dramaturges. The play, which uses the verbatim words of selected informants, was performed for the community as a call to action: "I performed it at a time when the community had not yet resolved the problems. I wanted to be a part of their examination of the problems" (Smith, 1994, p. xxxiv).

In a 1995 article, Jim Mienczakowski describes the process of constructing ethnographic narratives into two full-length plays. The first, *Syncing Out Loud: A Journey into Illness*, reflects schizophrenics' experiences of psychosis and treatment regimens, and the second, *Busting: The Challenge of the Drought Spirit*, was a study of a detox center. *Busting* used nonfictionalized verbatim narrative validated by informants (health consumers and health professionals) at every stage from initial scripting to postperformance reworks. The plays were performed in the research settings, for health professionals, health consumers, educators, and students, and for target audiences in clinical and community settings. The scripts were made available at performances of the plays, and audiences were invited to comment and thus contribute to the data; the representations were "renegotiated with every performance, their validity . . . reconfirmed and recontextualized by each successive audience." Mienczakowski (1995) states:

> As ethnodrama is written in a public voice and is translated into performance in an accessible and unassuming form, its agendas are instantly open to interpretation by nonacademics as well as by the academy. To

ensure reflexive interest from target groups, the performance aspects of ethnodrama depend on the process being a mode of high-profile ethnography that embraces media coverage and public debate . . . the ethnodrama report-process provokes response rather than passively awaits it. (p. 368)[20]

Readers Theater. Readers Theater, sometimes called Theater of the Mind, or Theater of the Imagination, is a presentational art form where two or more interpreters perform an oral reading so as to create vivid images of characters and scenes that will play out primarily in the minds of the readers and their audience (Coger & White, 1967; Tanner, 1993). There are similarities between Readers Theater and a play, but in a stage play, there is a fourth wall between actors and audience: The audience looks in at the actors, but the actors do not look out and engage the audience as interpreters do in Readers Theater. Actors in plays strive to *become* their character, while interpreters merely provide a suggestion without losing their own identities. For this reason, Readers Theater is a *presentational* rather than *representational* form; "the emphasis is on stylization rather than realism" (Donmoyer & Yennie-Donmoyer, 1995, p. 406).

Readers Theater is particularly useful for illuminating tensions. Jean Konzal (1995) used the form as a vehicle for a drama about a school conflict between parents who were old-time residents and those who were newcomers to an old New England town. A companion script examines a related issue, "Is common ground between educators and parents possible?" (p. 54). Konzal intends to stage the script as a way to engage parents and educators in dialogue. Each audience member will bring another, different level of interpretation to the performance and the ensuing dialogue. Interpreters have described performing Readers Theater as a situated learning experience: "I [was] situated to understanding her perspective, her emotional reactions . . . by my having taken on her character" (Donmoyer & Yennie-Donmoyer, 1995, p. 421).[21]

Music. The researcher psychologist/musician Helen Kivnick writes songs as a way of presenting an essence, or a story, from data.[22] As a singer, she had always chosen material (and as an audience member remembered material) that presented an important idea, and that did so in a way that caused it to reverberate, thereby involving singer and audience in continuing to think about the content of the lyrics. As a qualitative researcher, she wanted to find a form that would allow her to engage other people in her research findings with the same intensity with which she experienced the messages of powerful songs. Further, it was important to her to disseminate research findings (at least the kernels of findings) beyond a scholarly audience. Presenting findings in songs has become one way to accomplish these goals (Kivnick, personal E-mail communication, September 12, 1996). Helen explains that

> ten years of work on the importance of singing in contemporary black life in South Africa thoroughly convinced me of the many different kinds of power associated with singing. Singing together transforms a collection of people into an integrated, effective group. Singing actively involves an audience member in ideas for which he/she might otherwise remain a passive observer. Singing a chorus essentially requires audience members to experiment with making the song's words (and ideas) their own, prompting increased attention both during the actual singing, and also later, as audience members find phrases or whole verses repeating inside their heads. Singing is an informal, painless way to transmit information that might never be received if the intended recipient had to commit the resources (time, energy, money) to procuring a written article or book and then reading it. Over the years I have discovered that my students and audience members for various kinds of professional presentations retain and integrate ideas I have conveyed in songs far more powerfully than they do with ideas I convey in conventional verbal form.

Christine Jonas-Simpson is a nurse who uses music in her research and practice not as music therapy, not as entertainment, but guided by the theory of human becoming (Parse, 1995) as a unique way of living the art of nursing. With the goal of enhancing quality of life from the person's perspective, Christine lives true presence with persons through music (Jonas, 1994b, 1995). In her practice, she is with persons as they create their own musical expressions of life, and has extended the use of music to her research. In a descriptive exploratory study (Jonas, 1994a), Christine wrote interpretive music for each of the research themes to enhance deeper understanding, but currently she is with research participants as they create their *own* musical expressions of lived experience. Christine presents her research using narrative, musical notation and by playing the musical expressions that were composed by the participants. She believes that music speaks the unspeakable and will push the boundaries of our knowing and understanding about lived experiences of health (Jonas-Simpson, in press). Through enhanced understanding, nursing practice is transformed, as new paths are illuminated for enhancing quality of life from the person's perspective.

Visual/Graphic Textual Strategies

Print forms are so dominant in our culture that we scarcely notice our expectation that narrative text be presented in a linear and sequential way, or that these characteristics lead us to attend in a certain way (Gibson, 1996). Texts are fundamentally transformed when authors use nonlinear and graphic ways to add dimensions to their work. Sophisticated word processing and desktop publishing software now make it easy to alter the appearance of a text, but the use of textual strategies is not new. In 1894, as an example, Valéry (1972) structured the text of *Leonardo* using columns with different fonts and sizes; the left column containing the primary text is wider with larger type than the right, which contains supplementary material or asides. Derrida (1974) furnishes another example with *Glas;* here the reader is continuously surprised by varying arrangements of text, different size columns, text boxes, and differing typefaces. In the classic "Stabat Mater," Julia Kristeva (1983) uses irregular columns and boldface to differentiate the text of an essay on maternal symbols from her personal reflections on motherhood. The structure of the text is an embodiment of this dialogical juxtaposition. The personal narrative "weaves in and out of the analytical text, which sometimes becomes the sole text when the left-hand text disappears or, occasionally, mimics the right-hand 'voice' . . . words, images, ideas cross over from one column to the other" (Edelstein, 1992, pp. 30-31).

There are numerous recent examples of textual presentation strategies. In a book by Bennington and Derrida (1991) (a biographical exposition of Jacques Derrida's thought), the text is split horizontally: Bennington's text fills the top two thirds of the page while the bottom, in smaller typeface, is Derrida's commentary on Bennington's text. Brian Fawcett also used horizontally split text. In *Cambodia* (1986), stories are featured on the top part of the page, and on the bottom third are essays written as a subtext to the stories. Another Fawcett (1994) book, the part-fiction, part-essay *Gender Wars*, uses red, black, and gray-shaded text arranged in many configurations.

Marilyn Urion (1995, 1996), who has employed visual/graphic textual strategies in two recent journal articles, cautions that not all journals are receptive to working with authors to achieve the textual effects they want. She believes, however, that if there is good reason to use textual strategies, authors should push for what they need, developing a working relationship with supportive editors who will fight the requisite battles at journals where standard textual characteristics have been specified.

The Issues

There are consequences inherent in any form; each constrains while offering unique possibilities. The use of nontraditional forms, however, is still considered experimental, and the academy has a few questions, some of which will be addressed below.

Ambiguity and Unintended Interpretations

There is no question that artistic forms give rise to heightened ambiguity, and that there is some risk for what Eisner (1991a, 1996) calls "the Rorschach syndrome" (the interpretation can be anything). But no form can eliminate ambiguity or determine the interpretation of a text because it is impossible to predict how a reader will respond to it—misreadings are inevitable (Tyler, 1986).

Art forms can be used like a decree to say "this means that"—no optional interpretation is invited. Toni Vezeau (1994) provides an example where literature was used in a teaching situation not to evoke but to state meaning: "The reader remains an outsider to the story. There can be little engagement when the meaning is predetermined" (p. 166). Carolyn Ellis's aim is to offer a text that allows her audience to experience the experience, one that is "primarily concerned with evocation rather than 'true representation'" and where "learning about" has to do with "participating with rather than describing for" (Ellis, 1993, p. 726).

We can acknowledge and work with ambiguity (Sandelowski, 1994). As Ellis (1993) suggests: "Acknowledging a potential for optional readings gives readers license to take part in an experience that can reveal to them not only how it was for me (the author), but how it could be or once was for them" (p. 726).

Elitism

If we are to invite our audience in, we must offer texts (in whatever form) that are understandable. Traditional research texts have for the most part been exclusionary, that is, comprehensible only by the educated elite. This is changing in response to criticism and demand for accountability for the use of public funds; some funding agencies now direct that research be explained in a language understood by the nonscientific public. With art-based forms, it would seem that elitism would not be an issue, but this has not always been the case. Wolf (1992) provides an example:

> Experimental ethnography so obscure that native speakers of English with a Ph.D. in anthropology find it difficult to understand is written for a small elite made up primarily of first-world academics with literary inclinations. The message of exclusion that attaches to some of these texts contradicts the ostensible purpose of experimental ethnography, to find better ways of conveying some aspect of the experiences of another community. (p. 138)

Knowledge for Practice

Donmoyer (1990) has argued that for practice disciplines "concerned with individuals, not aggregates, research can never be generalizable" (p. 182) in the traditional sense; it can serve only as a heuristic. He suggests that an experiential knowledge perspective provides a way to think about generalizability in the context of research use. Using a modification of Piaget's schema theory, and the notion of vicarious experience through case studies, Donmoyer demonstrates how the research consumer can access unique situations, individuals, experiences, and vantage points that would be otherwise unattainable. In just this way, research understandings represented in art forms offer exceptional opportunities for health professionals to enlarge their repertoire of usable personal knowledge for practice.[23]

How Will We Know Quality?

The value of research is determined in critical examination by the relevant scientific community (Mishler, 1990). But how are we qualified to critique qualitative research represented in artistic forms? At the personal level, we are able to decide if a work is believable, is satisfying, and appeals to our hearts (Sandelowski, 1994). For private appreciation, the only qualification we need is our response. As Langer (1953) explains, "The criterion of good art is its power to command one's contemplation and reveal a feeling that one recognizes as real, with the same 'click of recognition' with which an artist knows that a form is true" (p. 405). But public discourse is required where research is concerned; we need the contribution of competent critics from many theoretical perspectives to build a body of knowledge in this field. For this to happen, it will be necessary to develop connoisseurship among ourselves as scholars and researchers (Belland, 1991; Belland, Duncan, & Deckman, 1991).

Oldfather and West (1994) explored the similar discomforts of being inducted into the cultures of both jazz and qualitative research. Newcomers must become accustomed to "ambiguities, unexpected freedoms, and new ways of thinking . . . [they] may search for the sheet music, or the instructions, and finding none, may be quite uncomfortable until they develop an intuitive sense of the guiding deep structures" (p. 23). Similarly, as newcomers to the evaluation of research represented in artful forms, we may feel awkward but, with practice, we'll improve our ability to notice, experience, and appreciate subtle qualities. This is connoisseurship, a private activity that may be given a public presence through criticism (Eisner, 1991a). "Criticism is an art of saying useful things about complex and subtle objects and events so that others less sophisticated, or sophisticated in different ways, can see and understand what they did not see and understand before" (p. 3).

At this time, researchers have only just begun to use artistic forms to transform knowledge from research, so few of us have had the opportunity to become connoisseurs, and only a handful of critics have emerged. Eventually, through public dialogue among knowledgeable critics, we will gain insight about the nature of excellence in this specialized area.

The Academy

Serious deliberation is under way in some disciplines about whether alternative representations of knowledge should be sanctioned by the academy. In education, for example, the 1993 AERA Annual Meeting featured several sessions that employed "experimental formats," including theater, dance, and musical performance. This gave rise to the inevitable question, "Is it research?" to which program chair Robert Donmoyer (1993) responded, "Neither substance nor form should be prematurely dismissed because it does not fit outmoded, no longer defensible conceptions of what research is and what research ought to be" (p. 41). These events inspired a discussion forum at the 1994 meeting titled, "Yes, But Is It Research?" and a 1996 sequel where the discussants considered a more focused question: "Should a novel count as a dissertation in education?" Howard Gardner took the position that although we can learn much from a novel, one shouldn't get a degree for it. A dissertation should be citable, abstractable, and a contribution to a discipline: "You can't ask what the argument of art is." Elliot Eisner countered that the purpose of research is to enlarge understanding, and the novel can do this very well by developing our awareness; "images larger than life inform us in special ways." He pointed out that if we agree that we can learn a lot from a novel, then the issue is that the form doesn't fit current academic structures. We can open the possibility for an intellectual climate where this kind of contribution is not excluded, and work out the ways to do this. He suggested, for example, that there could be an epilogue to the novel where the analysis is explained (Donmoyer, Eisner, & Gardner, 1996).

Another structural obstacle is that, in the current system, nonprint forms do not count toward a publication record or promotion in the same way that a book or article does, although reward and recognition for creative work may come from other sources. Researchers who opt to spend precious time developing expertise with art forms need to be aware of this risk.

There is the perception that it is difficult to catalog, reproduce, and distribute forms such as music, film, dance, scripts, or performance art. Libraries already catalogue many forms of media, and with the advent of multimedia technology, and the Internet—especially the World Wide Web (WWW)—access to nonprint forms has become easier to attain than ever before. Art forms of all kinds are now distributed inexpensively by video and CD-ROM, and are available in various ways on the Internet. Using a WWW browser, one can visit the Louvre, hear a recording of Florence Nightingale's voice, and, to use an example of a work cited in this chapter, order the video of Blumenfeld-Jones's 1995 AERA dance performance from his Web site. With demand, indexing services will select more nonprint materials, and this will improve access. It would seem that even now, cataloging, reproducing, and distribution of art forms is a minor issue that can be resolved through structural change.

Finally, there is the fear that endorsing the work of researcher-artists will devalue our academic currency at a time when qualitative research is finally gaining acceptance in a still-quantitative world. Krieger (1991) has already addressed this:

> By writing to fit in, or to blend, with what has been done in a field or a discipline, we contribute to a general climate of fear concerning what might happen were our individual subjectivities to be given more room. What would happen were the world truly to be seen according to multiple and different points of view? (p. 33)

Conclusion

The intent of this chapter was to consider some theory, opinions, and issues surrounding the use of alternative forms of knowledge representation and to offer a sampling of publicly accessible work in which researchers have used artistic forms and alternative textual strategies. My aim was not to deprecate traditional forms of research representation but to promote awareness and dialogue about how we might provide a plenitude of pathways to knowledge for our audience. Following Eisner, I have proposed that engaging the arts, and learning from knowledgeable critics, improves our sensibility, develops our ability to perceive more amply, and enlarges our repertoire of experience. These are essential conceptual tools for the *researcher as instrument*. And that would seem to be reason enough.

Notes

1. See Behar (1994) for a discussion of "personally engaged scholarship."

2. Readers looking for a way into the immense literature on nontraditional writing genres might start with Richardson's (1994b) review of "experimental representations" (and evocative forms) and Richardson's (1995b) recommended readings (pp. 201-203). The following are examples of specific forms: autobiographical writing (Grumet, 1988), memoir (Zinsser, 1987), life writing (Kadar, 1992), biography (Bateson, 1990; Edel, 1984/1959; Heilbrun, 1988), narrative (Clandinin & Connelly, 1994; Coles, 1989; Connelly & Clandinin, 1987), and the annual series of volumes edited by Josselson and Lieblich (1993-1996). Also see Carolyn Ellis's and Carol Ronai's work with personal narrative (e.g., Ellis, 1993, 1995; Ronai, 1992, 1995).

3. The address is published as Eisner (1993). See Phillips (1995) for a dissenting opinion on some of the points.

4. This conference was the 1996 Conference on Qualitative Research in Education, "Improvisations and Deep Structures: Alternative Forms of Data Representation," held on January 4-6, 1996, in Athens, Georgia. Proceedings will be available on-line. http//www.coe.uga.edu/quig/proceedings/.html

5. Information about this SIG can be accessed from the AERA home page: http:// aera.net

The SIG has a discussion forum for those interested in arts-based research. To subscribe, send E-mail to maiser@fis.utoronto.ca, and in the body of the note say: subscribe babette Yourfirstname Yourlastname.

6. There are many meanings of the word *form*, and we need to consider at least two of them. Most commonly we use the term in the structural sense, such as jazz is a form of music; ballet is a form of dance; a sonnet is a form in poetry. But when we speak of a work of art as being "an expressive form somewhat like a symbol" (Langer, 1957, p. 127) that can carry our understandings from research, we mean something more abstract than choosing a shape; here we use the term in the artistic sense to include the relationship of all the factors that constitute the whole. In Langer's (1957) definition: "The artistic form is a perceptual unity of something seen, heard, or imagined—that is, the configuration, or *Gestalt*, of an experience" (p. 165).

7. Langer (1969) cautions that some presentational symbols are "merely proxy for discourse," for example, a graph. These express facts that can be verbalized, unlike artistic symbols that "are untranslateable; their sense is bound to the particular form which it has taken" (p. 260).

8. Phillip Corrigan (1988) points to the "volumes of educational theory (however radical) that never mentions bodies" (p. 153).

9. To understand art, the only qualification we need is responsiveness, but intellectualizing can get in the way. Susanne Langer (1953) explains:

If, for instance, a reader of poetry believes that he does not "understand" a poem unless he can paraphrase it in prose, and that the poet's true or false opinions are what make the poem good or bad, he will read it as a piece of discourse, and his perception of poetic form and poetic feeling are likely to be frustrated. He may be naturally quite sensitive and responsive to literature, but anything he identifies as "poetry" will seem incomprehensible or else fallacious to him. His intellectual attitude, fostered by a theoretical conviction, stands in the way of his responsiveness. (p. 396)

10. For a review of literature addressing the importance of the arts in every child's education, see Darby and Catterall (1994).

11. Langer (1969) wrote that artists express their *knowledge* about human feelings, not their own actual feelings (see p. 26): "Art is the articulation, not the stimulation or catharsis, of feeling; and the height of technique is simply the highest power of this sensuous revelation and wordless abstraction" (p. 107).

12. Some companies offer art-based sabbaticals to workers in the belief that there will be creative payoff in areas unrelated to art. Hallmark Cards rotates workers through "artist's heaven," where for three months they can do whatever they want to regenerate their creative spirits. One metal engraver who chose to work in ceramics said, "It's given me an opportunity to get back to thinking wild, crazy things" (Glass, 1996, p. B9).

13. See also Richardson (1994a). For another example of data transformed into original poetry, see Euswas (1993). For an example of original poetry used to explicate a theoretic structure, see Hodnicki, Horner, and Simmons (1993).

14. For another example of fiction, see Gerla (1995); for a discussion of issues around the use of fiction as an experimental text (and another example), see the informative book by Wolf (1992). For a related form, "faction" (creative nonfiction, literary tales), from an ethnographic perspective, see Agar (1995).

15. For a script (in the form of dialogue) in which the authors tell a story about how they do performance science, see McCall and Becker (1990).

16. The intact script of this presentation may be read in the cited article, and the video of this performance may be ordered at this Web address: http://seamonkey.ed.asu.edu/dbj/dance.html

17. Holly Wilson drew my attention to the long-standing debate about whether dance should be "about something" or about motion itself ("pure," abstract, or nonreferential dance). Although Blumenfeld-Jones agrees with the "pure dance" position that dance must not re-present reality as a kind of signing, he is of the opinion that all dance is ultimately about something. Even if the choreographer does not intend to illustrate something, the attention of the audience is directed to make sense of the elements presented (dance, set, title, costumes, music) in a particular way. He believes that to say that dance is not "about" something is no more correct "than thinking that Jackson Pollock's canvases were not about something, even his canvases that do not have representational meanings. As I experience the drips and splashes of color and rhythms of the colors I have an immediate, sensual, physical experience which leaves me different when I step outside into nature. I see nature differently. I see humanly made environments differently. I see color differently. I am changed. As I relate to these environments and objects I relate differently through my experience with his painting." (D. S. Blumenfeld-Jones, personal communication, November 15, 1996)

18. Choreographer George Balanchine once remarked that "it is still not possible to depict a mother-in-law in a dance" (this statement appears in Cohen, 1965, p. 97, cited in Gardner, 1985, p. 224).

19. Susan Stinson, dancer, choreographer, and scholar, believes as Albert Einstein did that the words of a theory may be a late form after visual and kinesthetic images (Stinson, 1995). She tells her students, "If you can't draw it or make a three-dimensional model of it or dance it, you probably don't understand it" (p. 51). "Knowing in the bones" is authentic learning.

20. For another example of ethnographic drama, and the story of how it was constructed, see Richardson (1995b).

21. For another example of research presented as Readers Theater, see Clark et al. (1996).

22. See Kivnick's song "Hang On" about the concept of psychosocial legacy, which appears in Kivnick (1996). Only the lyrics appear in that article; for the music, contact Helen Kivnick (kivni001@maroon.tc.umn.edu).

23. Art, as Langer (1957) reminds us, does not generalize. Although both science and art tend constantly toward abstraction, "science moves from general denotation to precise abstraction; art, from precise abstraction to vital connotation, without the aid of generality" (p. 180). "A work of art is and remains specific. It is 'this,' and not 'this kind'; unique instead of exemplary" (p. 177). It is this specificity that can inform practice.

References

Agar, M. (1995). Literary journalism as ethnography. In J. Van Maanen (Ed.), *Representation in ethnography* (pp. 112-129). Thousand Oaks, CA: Sage.

Anderson, T. (1995). Rediscovering the connection between the arts: Introduction to the Symposium on Interdisciplinary Arts Education. *Arts Education Policy Review, 96*(4), 10-12.

Bateson, M. C. (1990). *Composing a life.* New York: Plume.

Behar, R. (1994, June 29). Dare we say "I"? Bringing the personal into scholarship. *Chronicle of Higher Education,* pp. B1-B3.

Belland, J. C. (1991). Developing connoisseurship in educational technology. In D. Hlynka & J. C. Belland (Eds.), *Paradigms regained: The uses of illuminative, semiotic and post-modern criticism as modes of inquiry in educational technology* (pp. 23-35). Englewood Cliffs, NJ: Educational Technology Publications.

Belland, J. C., Duncan, J. K., & Deckman, M. (1991). Criticism as methodology for research in educational technology. In D. Hlynka & J. C. Belland (Eds.), *Paradigms regained: The uses of illuminative, semiotic and post-modern criticism as modes of inquiry in educational technology* (pp. 151-164). Englewood Cliffs, NJ: Educational Technology Publications.

Bennington, G., & Derrida, J. (1991). *Jacques Derrida.* Chicago: University of Chicago Press.

Blumenfeld-Jones, D. S. (1995). Dance as a mode of research representation. *Qualitative Inquiry, 1*(4), 391-401.

Brodkey, L., & Fine, M. (1988). Presence of mind in the absence of body. *Journal of Education, 170*(3), 84-99.

Caplan, P. J. (1994). *Lifting a ton of feathers: A woman's guide for surviving in the academic world.* Toronto: University of Toronto Press.

Clandinin, D. J., & Connelly, F. M. (1994). Personal experience methods. In N. K. Denzin & Y. S. Lincoln (Eds.), *Handbook of qualitative research* (pp. 413-427). Thousand Oaks, CA: Sage.

Clark, C., Moss, P. A., Goering, S., Herter, R., Lamar, B., Leonard, D., Robbins, S., Russell, M., Templin, M., & Wascha, K. (1996). Collaboration as dialogue: Teachers and researchers engaged in conversation and professional development. *American Educational Research Journal, 33*(1), 193-231.

Clifford, J. (1986). Introduction: Partial truths. In J. Clifford & G. E. Marcus (Eds.), *Writing culture: The poetics and politics of ethnography* (pp. 1-26). Berkeley: University of California Press.

Coger, L. I., & White, M. R. (1967). *Readers Theatre handbook.* Glenview, IL: Scott, Foresman.

Cohen, S. J. (Ed.). (1965). *The modern dance.* Middleton, CT: Wesleyan University Press.

Coles, R. (1989). *The call of stories: Teaching and moral imagination.* Boston: Houghton Mifflin.

Connelly, F. M., & Clandinin, D. J. (1987). On narrative method, biography and narrative unities in the study of teaching. *Journal of Educational Thought, 21*(3), 130-139.

Corrigan, P. (1988). The making of the boy: Meditations on what grammar school did, with, to, and for my body. *Journal of Education, 170*(3), 142-161.

Darby, J. T., & Catterall, J. S. (1994). The fourth R: The arts and learning. *Teachers College Record, 96*(2), 299-328.

Derrida, J. (1974). *Glas.* Paris: Éditions Galilée.

Dewey, J. (1934). *Art as experience.* New York: Capricorn.

Donmoyer, R. (1990). Generalizability and the single-case study. In E. Eisner & A. Peshkin (Eds.), *Qualitative research in education: The continuing debate* (pp. 175-200). New York: Teachers College Press.

Donmoyer, R. (1993). Yes, but is it research? *Educational Researcher, 22*(3), 41.

Donmoyer, R., Eisner, E., & Gardner, H. (1996, April 8). *Yes, but is it research? The conversation continues: Should a novel count as a dissertation in education?* Panel discussion at the 1996 Annual Meeting of the American Educational Research Association, New York. (Cassette Recording No. RA6-5.25). Chicago: Teach 'em.

Donmoyer, R., & Yennie-Donmoyer, J. (1995). Data as drama: Reflections on the use of Readers Theater as a mode of qualitative data display. *Qualitative Inquiry, 1*(4), 402-428.

Edel, L. (1984). *Writing lives.* New York: Norton. (Original work published 1959)

Edelstein, M. (1992). Metaphor, meta-narrative, and mater-narrative in Kristeva's "Stabat Mater." In D. R. Crownfield (Ed.), *Body/text in Julia Kristeva: Religion, women, and psychoanalysis* (pp. 27-52). Albany: State University of New York Press.

Eisner, E. (1985). Aesthetic modes of knowing. In E. Eisner (Ed.), *Yearbook of the National Society for the Study of Education: 84. Learning and teaching the ways of knowing. Part II* (pp. 23-36). Chicago: University of Chicago Press.

Eisner, E. W. (1991a). *The enlightened eye: Qualitative inquiry and the enhancement of educational practice.* New York: Macmillan.

Eisner, E. W. (1991b). What the arts taught me about education. In G. Willis & W. H. Schubert (Eds.), *Reflections from the heart of educational inquiry* (pp. 34-48). Albany: State University of New York Press.

Eisner, E. W. (1992). The misunderstood role of the arts in human development. *Phi Delta Kappan, 73*(8), 591-595.

Eisner, E. W. (1993). Forms of understanding and the future of educational research. *Educational Researcher, 22*(7), 5-11.

Eisner, E. W. (1996, January 4-6). *The promise and perils of new forms of data representation.* Keynote address to the Conference on Qualitative Research in Education, "Improvisations and Deep Structures: Alternative Forms of Data Representation," Athens, GA.

Ellis, C. (1993). There are survivors. *Sociological Quarterly, 34*(4), 711-730.

Ellis, C. (1995). *Final negotiations.* Philadelphia: Temple University Press.

Ellis, C., & Bochner, A. P. (1992). Telling and performing personal stories: The constraints of choice in abortion. In C. Ellis & M. G. Flaherty (Eds.), *Investigating subjectivity: Research on lived experience* (pp. 79-101). Newbury Park, CA: Sage.

Euswas, P. (1993). The actualized caring moment: A grounded theory of caring in nursing practice. In D. A. Gaut (Ed.), *A global agenda for caring* (Pub. No. 15-2518, pp. 309-326). New York: National League for Nursing Press.

Fawcett, B. (1986). *Cambodia: A book for people who find television too slow*. Vancouver, Canada: Talonbooks.

Fawcett, B. (1994). *Gender wars: A novel and some conversation about sex and gender*. Toronto, Canada: Somerville House.

Flax, J. (1987). Postmodernism and gender relations in feminist theory. *Signs, 12*(4), 621-643.

Gardner, H. (1985). *Frames of mind: The theory of multiple intelligences*. New York: Basic Books.

Gerla, J. P. (1995). An uncommon friendship: Ethnographic fiction around finance equity in Texas. *Qualitative Inquiry, 1*(2), 168-188.

Gibson, S. B. (1996). Is all coherence gone? The role of narrative in web design. *Interpersonal Computing and Technology: An Electronic Journal for the 21st Century, 4*(2), 7-26 [Online serial]. Available E-mail: LISTSERV@LISTSERV. GEORGETOWN.EDU Message: Get GIBSON IPCTV4N2

Glass, D. (1996, June 10). Hallmark nurtures worker creativity. *Globe and Mail*, p. B9.

Greene, M. (1996, January 4-6). *Art, imagination, and the capture of meanings*. Final keynote address to the Conference on Qualitative Research in Education, "Improvisations and Deep Structures: Alternative Forms of Data Representation," Athens, GA.

Grumet, M. R. (1988). *Bitter milk: Women and teaching*. Amherst: University of Massachusetts Press.

Heilbrun, C. G. (1988). *Writing a woman's life*. New York: Ballantine.

Hlynka, D. (1991). Postmodern excursions into educational technology. *Educational Technology, 31*(6), 27-30.

Hodnicki, D. R., Horner, S. D., & Simmons, S. J. (1993). The Sea of Life: A metaphorical vehicle for theory explication. *Nursing Science Quarterly, 6*(1), 25-27.

Iser, W. (1978). *The act of reading: A theory of aesthetic response*. Baltimore: Johns Hopkins University Press.

Jonas, C. M. (1994a, October). *The experience of being in an unfamiliar place for persons whose community is the street*. Paper presented at the Annual International Qualitative Nursing Research Colloquium: Research Related to the Human Becoming Theory, Marcella Niehoff School of Nursing, Loyola University, Chicago.

Jonas, C. M. (1994b). True presence through music. *Nursing Science Quarterly, 7*(3), 102-103.

Jonas, C. M. (1995). True presence through music for persons living their dying. In R. R. Parse (Ed.), *Illuminations: The human becoming theory in practice and research* (pp. 97-104) (Pub. No. 15-2670). New York: National League for Nursing Press.

Jonas-Simpson, C. M. (in press). Parse's research method through music. *Nursing Science Quarterly*.

Josselson, R., & Leiblich, A. (Eds.). (1993-1996). *The narrative study of lives* (Vols. 1-4). Newbury Park, CA: Sage.

Kadar, M. (Ed.). (1992). *Essays on life writing: From genre to critical practice*. Toronto, Canada: University of Toronto Press.

Kivnick, H. Q. (1996). Remembering and being remembered: The reciprocity of psychosocial legacy. *Generations: Journal of the American Society on Aging, 20*(3), 49-53.

Konzal, J. L. (1995). *Our changing town, our changing school: Is common ground possible?* Unpublished EdD Thesis, University of Pittsburgh.

Krieger, S. (1991). *Social science and the self: Personal essays on an art form*. New Brunswick, NJ: Rutgers University Press.

Kristeva, J. (1983). *Histoires d'amour*. Paris: Éditions Denoël.

Kuhn, T. (1970). *The structure of scientific revolutions*. Chicago: University of Chicago Press.

Langer, S. K. (1953). *Feeling and form*. New York: Scribner.

Langer, S. K. (1957). *Problems of art*. New York: Scribner.

Langer, S. K. (1969). *Philosophy in a new key* (3rd ed.). Cambridge, MA: Harvard University Press.

Lowenberg, J. S. (1993). Interpretive research methodology: Broadening the dialogue. *Advances in Nursing Science, 16*(2), 57-69.

Mandel, C. (1996, February 3). Harrison's art explores fears behind gay-bashing. *Globe and Mail*, p. C14.

May, W. T. (1991). The arts and curriculum as lingering. In G. Willis & W. H. Schubert (Eds.), *Reflections from the heart of educational inquiry* (pp. 140-152). Albany: State University of New York Press.

McCall, M. M., & Becker, H. S. (1990). Performance science. *Social Problems, 37*(1), 117-135.

McCutcheon, G. (1991). Curriculum and *The Magic Flute*. In G. Willis & W. H. Schubert (Eds.), *Reflections from the heart of educational inquiry* (pp. 161-167). Albany: State University of New York Press.

Mienczakowski, J. (1995). The theater of ethnography: The reconstruction of ethnography into theater with emancipatory potential. *Qualitative Inquiry, 1*(3), 360-375.

Miller, J. L. (1994). "The surprise of a recognizable person" as troubling presence in educational research and writing. *Curriculum Inquiry, 24*(4), 503-512.

Mishler, E. G. (1990). Validation in inquiry-guided research: The role of exemplars in narrative studies. *Harvard Educational Review, 60*(4), 415-442.

Oldfather, P., & West, J. (1994). Qualitative research as jazz. *Educational Researcher, 23*(8), 22-26.

Paget, M. A. (1995). Performing the text. In J. Van Maanen (Ed.), *Representation in ethnography* (pp. 222-244). Thousand Oaks, CA: Sage.

Parse, R. R. (1995). *Illuminations: The human becoming theory in practice and research*. New York: National League for Nursing Press.

Phenix, P. H. (1964). *Realms of meaning*. New York: McGraw-Hill.

Phillips, D. C. (1995). Art as research, research as art. *Educational Theory, 45*(1), 71-84.

Richardson, L. (1992). The consequences of poetic representation: Writing the other, rewriting the self. In C. Ellis & M. G. Flaherty (Eds.), *Investigating subjectivity: Research on lived experience* (pp. 125-137). Newbury Park, CA: Sage.

Richardson, L. (1994a). Nine poems: Marriage and the family. *Journal of Contemporary Ethnography, 23*(1), 3-13.

Richardson, L. (1994b). Writing: A method of inquiry. In N. K. Denzin & Y. S. Lincoln (Eds.), *Handbook of qualitative research* (pp. 516-529). Thousand Oaks, CA: Sage.

Richardson, L. (1995a). Narrative and sociology. In J. Van Maanen (Ed.), *Representation in ethnography* (pp. 198-221). Thousand Oaks, CA: Sage.

Richardson, L. (1995b). Writing-stories: Co-authoring "The Sea Monster," a writing-story. *Qualitative Inquiry, 1*(2), 189-203.

Ronai, C. R. (1992). The reflexive self through narrative: A night in the life of an erotic dancer/researcher. In C. Ellis & M. G. Flaherty (Eds.), *Investigating subjectivity: Research on lived experience* (pp. 102-124). Newbury Park, CA: Sage.

Ronai, C. R. (1995). Multiple reflections of child sex abuse: An argument for a layered account. *Journal of Contemporary Ethnography, 23*(4), 395-426.

Rosario, J. (1991). On thinking as a sacred act, Coltrane jazz, the inaccessible, and curriculum. In G. Willis & W. H. Schubert (Eds.), *Reflections from the heart of educational inquiry: Understanding curriculum and teaching through the arts* (pp. 174-181). Albany: SUNY Press.

Rubin, L. (1991). The arts and an artistic curriculum. In G. Willis & W. H. Schubert (Eds.), *Reflections from the heart of educational inquiry* (pp. 49-59). Albany: State University of New York Press.

Sandelowski, M. (1993). Rigor or rigor mortis: The problem of rigor in qualitative research revisited. *Advances in Nursing Science, 16*(2), 1-8.

Sandelowski, M. (1994). The proof is in the pottery: Toward a poetic for qualitative inquiry. In J. M. Morse (Ed.), *Critical issues in qualitative research methods* (pp. 46-63). Thousand Oaks, CA: Sage.

Sandelowski, M. (1995). On the aesthetics of qualitative research. *IMAGE: Journal of Nursing Scholarship, 27*(3), 205-209.

Shotter, J. (1992). "Getting in touch": The meta-methodology of a postmodern science of mental life. In S. Kvale (Ed.), *Psychology and postmodernism* (pp. 58-73). London: Sage.

Smith, A. D. (1994). *Twilight: Los Angeles, 1992.* New York: Doubleday.

Stake, R. E. (1994). Case studies. In N. K. Denzin & Y. S. Lincoln (Eds.), *Handbook of qualitative research* (pp. 236-247). Thousand Oaks, CA: Sage.

Stinson, S. W. (1995). Body of knowledge. *Educational Theory, 45*(1), 43-54.

Tanner, F. A. (1993). *Readers Theater fundamentals: A cumulative approach to theory and activities* (2nd ed.). Topeka, KS: Clark.

Törnqvist, E. (1991). *Transposing drama: Studies in representation.* London: Macmillan Education.

Tyler, S. A. (1986). Post-modern ethnography: From document of the occult to occult document. In J. Clifford & G. E. Marcus (Eds.), *Writing culture: The poetics and politics of ethnography* (pp. 122-140). Berkeley: University of California Press.

Urion, M. (1995). Public Text/Private Text: Making visible the voices that shape our social conscience. *Computers and Composition, 12*(1), 3-13.

Urion, M. V. (1996). Wall working. *Frontiers, 16*(1), 77-86.

Valéry, P. (1972). *Leonardo Poe Mallarmé* (M. Cowley & J. R. Lawler, Trans.). Princeton, NJ: Princeton University Press.

Vezeau, T. M. (1994). Narrative inquiry in nursing. In P. L. Chinn & J. Watson (Eds.), *Art and aesthetics in nursing* (pp. 163-188). New York: National League for Nursing Press.

Wilson, C. (1974). *Crazy February: Death and life in the Mayan highlands of Mexico.* Berkeley: University of California Press.

Wolf, M. (1992). *A thrice-told tale.* Stanford, CA: Stanford University Press.

Zinsser, W. (1987). *Inventing the truth: The art and craft of memoir.* Boston: Houghton Mifflin.

Dialogue: On "Helping" or Working With Students

Hutchinson: It was wonderful to hear you people say yesterday that authoring with students is positive, because I have been told that I am authoring too much with students, and it's not positive—students should do their own work. And I think it's hard because some of the people I am working with aren't researchers and don't understand the traditions. And so, I was told, "You make their work yours. You do too much of their work for them."

Wilson: I've seen the flip side of it on our faculty, too. A senior faculty member authors a lot with students, and then when her review comes up, and she is being reviewed by other senior faculty, the question comes up, "Isn't this *really* [students'] work?" And they think she is just on for administrative purposes and because it's courtesy, and she's their mentor, so it works against her, but not because they were saying she was doing their work, but because her name was going on these postdoc students' work.

Boyle: Do you know, when I applied for tenure the last time—having earned it numerous times in my life—I was surprised to see that in a period of maybe four or five years, I had only one or two publications that just had my single name on. All the others were students first, and I was second. And I thought, "Oh, Lord!" But fortunately, I have a very supportive dean, who said, "Oh, wonderful! This is exactly what we hired you to do! It will be great for our doctoral program, you will help our students learn to write"—blah, blah, blah. "This is exactly what you should be doing!" So, my portfolio went up with that kind of a note on it. "This is a professor who is working with doctoral students, who is helping them learn to write, is actively involved in research, mentors students . . ."

Stern: I think in some way it's location-specific.

Schreiber: Yes, but it is up to the person to find out what the rules are in that location—you could be operating under false assumptions.

Boyle: Yes, and those are very hidden rules!

The Art (and Science) of Critiquing Qualitative Research

Sally Thorne

Despite the enthusiastic claims of its adherents that qualitative research is the key to accessing subjective realities, the products of qualitative inquiries are not inevitably accurate, relevant, or even socially responsible. Although qualitative methods privilege species of knowledge that are grounded in the everyday life of those who may be closest to a phenomenon under study, it does not follow that the knowledge they generate is any more or less credible than knowledge derived from range of alternative sources. We now have a considerable body of theory that guides us in distinguishing properly from improperly conducted qualitative research. In most instances, this literature presupposes that weak qualitative research is due to weak or ambiguous methodology, and that flaws are a product of an incomplete shift from a quantitative to a qualitative philosophical orientation (Burns, 1989; Leininger, 1994). Indeed, much of the "bad" qualitative research that has appeared in the social and health science literature reflects epistemological confusion and the inappropriate application of quantitative quality measures to an entirely distinct epistemological enterprise.

In this chapter, existing sources of insight about the evaluation of qualitative research efforts will be extended to include a more theoretical examination of how we can understand and judge quality within the constraints of our qualitative traditions, and how we might distinguish mediocrity from excellence. A synthesis of accepted approaches to credibility will establish ways in which qualitative research scholars have translated the mandate of the quantitative "holy trinity" of reliability, validity, generalizability (Kvale, 1995) into a more compatible philosophical orientation. It will provide a basis from which to appreciate the difficulties associated with articulating a methodological "gold standard" within qualitative research. Processes elevating evaluation into a more comprehensive critique also will be explored so that guiding principles can be extracted. From this foundation, two recent trends within qualitative inquiry will be examined for their complicating influence on the determination of quality within qualitative research. The first of these, the influence of an emancipatory thrust within postmodern health research, has had a considerable influence on the issues inherent in a normative approach to inquiry. The ways in which quality criteria change when an emancipatory perspective is inserted into a qualitative research tradition will therefore be probed. The second trend reflects an increasingly persistent call to the poetic within qualitative research, the artistry within the science. This trend is equally fascinating in that it holds similarly compelling implications for reexamining quality measures within our research. In examining these two twists to the already complex issue of critiquing qualitative research, an embryonic approach to the challenge of capturing the artistry and the science of critique will emerge.

Critique and Evaluation: Quality Processing

Leininger's (1968, 1994) classic attempts to distinguish critique from evaluation suggest that critique is the product of a review by someone of recognized authority rather than a matter of comparison against some general standard. It considers a piece of work not against evaluative standards but against the critic's "areas of expertise, intellectual astuteness, and philosophical commitments" (Leininger, 1994, p. 98). However, assuming that critique can be examined apart from the stature of the individual critic, a more salient approach might be to recognize the solid theoretical strength that evaluation per se is directed toward, and to consider critique as its extension rather than an alternative. From this angle, critique of qualitative research blends knowledge of the evaluative criteria of qualitative research with a solid foundation in the disciplinary domain for which the knowledge is claimed. Just as the wine connoisseur must command an intimate knowledge of the technology and the artistry of wine making to appreciate subtle distinctions that would escape a mere wine drinker, an expert critique of qualitative research demands broad knowledge of the substantive field into which the research attempts to gain acceptance (Parse, Coyne, & Smith, 1985).

Despite its focus on the stature of the critic rather than the breadth and soundness of his or her ideas, Leininger's perspective effectively orients us to a kind of evaluation that extends beyond adherence to a set of external standards for methodology and toward a more grounded appreciation for the nature of the knowledge toward which the methods are applied. The importance of extending traditional evaluation into the domain of critique can be illustrated with reference to qualitative inquiry within the health sciences. The researcher who presents qualitative research findings to a health science discipline understands that the state of knowledge development is such that research results may well find their way into clinical applications regardless of the researcher's explicit assumptions about their origins. Thus the standards for health science research must be quite different than would be standards, for instance, in literary criticism. Health science disciplines exist because of a social mandate that entails a moral obligation toward benefiting individuals and the collective. This factor inherently alters a health sciences researcher's disciplinary responsibility in such a way that it extends beyond the reach of traditional evaluative criteria and into the domain of how findings might reasonably be interpreted or even used. Thus critique of qualitative research within the health sciences properly extends beyond mere consideration of adherence to the methodological rules and toward examination of the much more complex question of what meaning can be made of the research findings.

Evaluation Criteria

Although each qualitative methodological tradition includes distinct guidelines by which it may be judged as theoretically, epistemologically, and technically sound, various qualitative theorists have synthesized sets of general principles that are more or less accepted across the qualitative research spectrum. It is to these general principles that we turn when we consider the kinds of evaluative criteria that are typically applied to the products of qualitative research.

First, all qualitative research is expected to demonstrate *epistemological integrity* in the sense that there is a defensible line of reasoning from the assumptions made about the nature of knowledge through to the methodological rules by which decisions about the research process are explained. For the findings to be credible, the research process must reveal a research question that is consistent with the epistemological standpoint and an interpretation of data sources and interpretive strategies that follows logically from that question. We are necessarily suspicious of any research in which the findings reproduce the knowledge that the researcher wanted or expected to uncover. We therefore require that qualitative researchers demonstrate an appreciation of the nature of their epistemological positions and create decisional strategies that respect those positions (Koch, 1995; Simmons, 1995).

Second, qualitative studies ought to show *representative credibility* such that the theoretical claims they purport to make are consistent with the manner in which the phenomenon under study was sampled. For example, in a phenomenological single-case study of an illness experience, we would not expect claims about shared elements within experience. Similarly, where a grounded study of a phenomenon reflects the basic social processes of a dominant cultural group, we would not accept inferences that the processes are universal across cultures. We therefore recognize that classic conditions such as Glaser and Strauss's maximal variation (1966) are required before certain kinds of knowledge claims can be attempted on the basis of qualitative research. Findings based on prolonged engagement with the phenomenon are more likely to be afforded credibility than are those derived from more superficial involvement (Erlandson, Harris, Skipper, & Allen, 1993). To confirm our inherently constructed perception of an event or process, we generally value some form of triangulation of data sources. Similarly, to convey substantive completeness, we expect that qualitative researchers recognize knowledge beyond a single angle of vision, as depicted in the crystal images evoked by Breitmayer, Ayres, and Knafl (1993), Richardson (1994), and Sandelowski (1995).

Third, we expect reports of all qualitative studies to reflect an *analytic logic* that makes explicit the reasoning of the researcher from the inevitable forestructure (Miles & Huberman, 1994) through to the interpretations and knowledge claims made on the basis of what was learned in the research. It is never sufficient for a researcher to assure the reader that an inductive reasoning process occurred; rather, we require that evidence of that logic be apparent throughout the report to the degree that we can confirm or reject its credibility (Morse, 1994). Although it is well recognized that there is an inherently emergent nature to good qualitative research (Sandelowski, Davis, & Harris, 1989), the adequacy of the decision-making process must be accessible to the qualitative research consumer (Burns, 1989). A commonly applied principle is the generation of an audit trail, an explicit reasoning pathway along which another researcher could presumably follow (Erlandson et al., 1993; Leininger, 1994). Further, the traditional ethnographic principle of thick description (Erlandson et al., 1993) charges us with crafting reports that ground our interpretive claims in verbatim accounts from our data.

A fourth requirement is that qualitative studies reveal an *interpretive authority*. While we recognize that all knowledge is perspectival, we need assurance that a researcher's interpretations are trustworthy, that they fairly illustrate or reveal some truth external to his or her own bias or experience. For example, while we value a metaphor that makes our understanding of a complex phenomenon coherent, we demand sufficient information about the data in which the metaphor is grounded to be certain that it does not force-fit such structure (Janesick, 1994). In our evaluation of qualitative studies, we need to be confident as to which claims represent individual subjective truths and which might represent more common truths. Whatever our theoretical views on the question of generalizability, we must be able to grasp the researcher's intentions in revealing knowledge about the particular. Thus our reports must account for the reactivity that will occur within the research processes (Paterson, 1994). We build in systems to check our interpretations against those of our research subjects (Erlandson et al., 1993; Hutchinson & Wilson, 1992; Schwandt, 1994). We aim toward convincing our audience of our version of truth through what Altheide and Johnson (1994) refer to as "validity-as-reflexive-accounting."

The principles we generate to ensure rigor and credibility within our qualitative research processes all derive from an appreciation of the knowledge claims within which a method is grounded and an awareness of the social context into which our research reports will be directed. Taken together, these four principles form the basis of any articulation of evaluation standards in qualitative research.

Beyond Evaluation

Because we have access to an increasingly sophisticated set of evaluative standards against which research in the various qualitative traditions can be judged, one might be tempted to assume that merely following the guidelines will produce a product of high quality. However, as has been pointed out by several critics, rigid adherence to textbook approaches in qualitative research (fetishizing method, methodolatry, criteriology) can propagate weakness rather than strength in our research enterprises (Janesick, 1994; Sandelowski, 1993; Schwandt, 1996).

As I envision it, the domain of critique extends beyond evaluation and calls upon qualitative researchers to account for the ways in which their findings should or should not contribute to disciplinary knowledge (see Table 6.1). Within the health sciences, most qualitative research is applied in the sense that it aims toward knowledge that would eventually influence one or another health care practice (Simmons, 1995). For example, we seek to understand how people experience certain assaults of the body, mind, and spirit not in and of themselves but because we hope to be able to alleviate unnecessary suffering or harm and promote as much well-being as is possible under the circumstances. Because of this, a criterion against which all health science research ought to be judged is its *moral defensibility*. We need convincing claims about why we need the knowledge that we are extracting from people, what will be the purpose in having such knowledge

Table 6.1 Principles of Evaluation and Critique in Qualitative Research

Evaluation	Critique
• epistemological integrity	• moral defensibility
• representative credibility	• disciplinary relevance
• analytic logic	• pragmatic obligation
• interpretive authority	• contextual awareness
	• probable truth

once we obtain it. This principle extends beyond traditional ethical claims about the protection of our human subjects and into the realm of an appreciation for how knowledge is used in our society (Lipson, 1994). When we do research in sensitive areas (communicable diseases, ethnic diversities, vulnerable populations, for example), we must account for the possible uses of our findings even before we know what they will include (Sieber, 1993). Our rationale must link the findings to a potential benefit for the health care of those we serve before we will find it defensible to place any marginalized group at risk of social censure or antipathy because of the new knowledge we extract or because of the manner in which we make the knowledge accessible to those whose purposes may be distinct from a humanitarian health care agenda.

A related concern is that of *disciplinary relevance.* Beyond the question of whether or not society requires the knowledge we seek, critique properly includes the issue of whether the knowledge is appropriate to the development of the disciplinary science. A recent illustration occurred with publication in a prestigious nursing journal of research into career-oriented women with tattoos (Armstrong, 1991). Although such a study would not have raised an eyebrow in sociological circles, it generated considerable negative reaction within nursing, not only toward the author for the choice of topic but also toward the journal for using scarce publication pages for a seemingly irrelevant topic. The reaction suggested a deeply felt sense that researchers ought to be able to explain the relationship between their research and the disciplinary knowledge they seek to advance before the profession should accept otherwise competent research.

A third perspective from which critique is appropriate reflects the special problems inherent in the practical sciences, where matters of truth and opinion are often blurred around the edges. Apart from any knowledge claims within a health science discipline, whether they are expressed as limits to generalizability or a conviction about multiple coexisting realities, an agreement about what seems real and valid is prerequisite to action. This *pragmatic obligation* reflects the inherent tension within practice realities, in which respect for the uniqueness of individuals creates sympathy for an idealist epistemology at the same time that the moral mandate of a practice discipline requires usable general knowledge. Qualitative health researchers cannot therefore put forth their findings with the comfortable assurance that no one will apply them in practice before they become scientifically "proven." Rather, recognition of a practice mandate demands a position that no new idea should be understood as purely theoretical and therefore incapable of rendering harm. Thus researchers in this field are obliged to consider their findings "as if" they might indeed be applied in practice.

A fourth domain into which sound critique ought to venture is the *contextual awareness* revealed by a qualitative researcher. The epistemological claims upon which qualitative research methods are founded solidly locate knowledge within the societies that construct it. Even so, many qualitative researchers seem not to recognize that their own perspectives are inevitably bounded by their historical context as well as by their disciplinary perspective. Developments in the philosophy of science make it clear that we simply cannot see what we cannot yet see. Although those elements of our social historical context that are apparent to us can be accessed, bracketed, and explained, we must assume that we are as strongly influenced by other yet invisible assumptions. Because many of our tacit assumptions are social constructions, they are likely to be shared by others in the field and even by those we attempt to study. Therefore our research serves to re-create them "as if" they were factual (Herzlich & Pierret, 1985). It behooves qualitative researchers to articulate their findings as contextual in the recognition that many supposed accepted realities will not withstand a test of time.

Finally, critique of qualitative research demands a reverence for the ambiguous zone of validity and shared reality known in philosophical circles as *probable truth*. As has been pointed out in numerous thoughtful considerations of what validity might mean in qualitative research (Kvale, 1995; Lincoln, 1995), no set of standards against which we measure our procedures and products can fully account for the notion of truth, or representativeness within the real world, or ensure confidence that research findings are indeed entirely valid. In departing from a search for absolute truths, as all but the most postpositivist qualitative researchers must, we accept that there is value in recognition of some kinds of knowledge as "probable truth" (Johnson, 1996; Kikuchi & Simmons, 1996). Concurrently, we also must recognize that certain kinds of knowledge claims that appear to meet our very best truth criteria may in the end prove untrue (see Wolcott, 1994, for an exhaustive treatment of one such example). As Eisner (1981) points out, it can be useful to reconstruct our sense of why we do research as an effort not to seek truths but to create meaning, to construct images from which people's "fallible and tentative views of the world can be altered, rejected, or made more secure" (p. 9). Thus we arrive full circle in our search for truth standards at the portals of moral defensibility, disciplinary relevance, and pragmatic obligation. A sound critique of qualitative research beyond the surface level of adherence to a set of evaluative criteria therefore inevitably will reflect deep questioning as to why we select certain questions to ask, how we claim the knowledge gained will further certain kinds of meaning, and what might be the implications of acts based on what we have come to believe through the process of research.

Special Challenges to Critique
Within the Qualitative Enterprise

As it has been depicted here, critique of qualitative research demands solid grounding in the social and practical purposes of disciplinary knowledge as well as in the philosophy of science. Such a discussion moves us beyond questions of the validity of knowledge obtained through qualitative research methods and toward an examination of what we believe about knowledge and why. Two trends in the practice of current qualitative research raise additional complexities for the art of critique and therefore deserve consideration. They include the methodological shifts occasioned by the emancipatory movement within postmodern thinking and the interpretive shifts created when qualitative research is construed as extending scientific form into the realm of artistry.

The Emancipatory Thrust

The emergence of postmodern thinking among a new generation of qualitative health researchers has forced the location of knowledge claims into political, social, and historical context (Lincoln & Reason, 1996). As the cadre of qualitative researchers employing participatory, action, feminist, critical, and other emancipatory trends matures, truth notions in the empiricist/realist tradition are supplanted by acceptance of the notion of interpretive or constructed truths (Schwandt, 1994). An emancipatory application of qualitative research implies a normative world view, what ought to be instead of what is. It shifts the value of human inquiry away from straightforward knowledge acquisition and into the domain of generating useful or practical knowledge, interrupting patterns of power, participating in socially transformative processes toward such ideals as justice, equity, and freedom (Reason, 1996).

As Heron (1996) points out, this type of research illuminates a central "action paradox" within social reality; that is, our ability to understand our reality is heightened the more we try to change it. Action, then, is not only the outcome of research but also an inquiry tool. According to Harmon (1996), the very nature of our science is changing with these challenges to the traditions within our understanding of knowledge. In direct contrast to the requisite distance between knower and known, the researcher in an interpretivist, constructivist tradition must be prepared to be profoundly changed through the process of exploration. Such departures from the natural order within science force us to reconsider what it is that we take into account in a critique of emancipatory inquiry. As Lincoln (1995) points out,

> Just as the naturalistic/constructivist paradigm effectively brought about the irrelevance of the distinction between ontology and epistemology, so too does this paradigm and interpretive social science in general bring about the collapse of the distinctions between standards, rigor, and quality criteria and the formerly separate consideration of research ethics. (p. 286)

Such a view creates profound complications for the art of critique. First, it forces us to recognize that quality criteria are emerging rather than defined (Lincoln, 1995). Second, it places us in the disquieting position of challenging some of the very foundational standpoints upon which we operate as qualitative researchers. According to Schwandt (1994), without a critical purchase, qualitative researchers privilege the views of those identified as actors within a social reality. They co-construct interpretations of reality, thereby rendering themselves incapable of critically evaluating the social reality they seek to portray. Further, where participation and action are explicit research objectives, the community then becomes a primary arbiter of quality (Lincoln, 1995). However, even a rudimentary appreciation for the idea of knowledge as a social construction reveals that the community is not always the best source of truth, credibility, or even value.

The Poetic Imperative

A distinct trend, but one that may have equally penetrating implications for critiquing qualitative research, is the current tendency toward acknowledging and extending the artistry inherent in the production of research products. Arguing the improper fault line we have imposed between art and science, authors such as Eisner (1981, 1991) and Sandelowski (1994, 1996) have alerted us to their kinship in terms of shared origins and a mutual search for realities that represent a form of truth. As Sandelowski (1994) points out, "Artistic truths are often more true to life than scientific ones, providing us with visions of human nature more resonant with our own experiences than any psychological, sociological or other conventionally scientific rendering of it" (p. 52). Analysis of the rules of critique within art reveal that artists strive to be true to something beyond the mere facts and aim for essential and universal truths. When we represent our research findings in elegant language or artistic representational forms, we seek to create the conditions under which the truths within our newly acquired knowledge can resonate in an experiential manner with our intended audience.

Beyond calling on us to express the findings of our qualitative work in language and form that is less boring than our usual academic theory production (Tierney, 1995), that is accessible to those with whom we claim to share co-construction (Schwandt, 1994), this perspective challenges us to reconsider the roles of art and science within the truth-making enterprise. Sandelowski reminds us that "scientists no less than artists attempt to persuade their audiences of the value/validity of their findings by employing speaking and writing strategies to stake their claims" (p. 53). Understanding science in this way, we are forced to admit that presentation of data is in itself an art form, inseparable from the rules of writing it up, that strives for a persuasiveness we call "validity" or "credibility." Just as the artist chooses the medium, we choose which voices to privilege, which metaphors to make, and which representations to build. We do this in full consciousness that elegant and beautiful writing, the artistry in the presentation, will fire the imagination within our reader differently (and with more potency) than will the dry and deliberately scientific report.

The call to a poeticism within qualitative research writing strips away the surface layer of scientific reality from our epistemological positions. As Sandelowski (1991) points out, "A story once told as a tragedy can become a romance or comedy in another telling" (p. 164). It also permits us to turn to nonscientific sources such as art, literature, dance, and music for our inspiration and interpretation. However, it also creates a research climate in which it may become increasingly problematic to challenge questions of (even probable) truth when distinctions between science and story evaporate. As Clarke (1995) contends, creating story in the name of science, qualitative researchers often "wander from the kind of tight controls which ought to be the hallmark of scientific credibility" (p. 591). And Tierney (1995) points out that "in our postmodern rush to abandon complete understanding we retreat to the easy assumption that we can understand no one but ourselves" (p. 383). Taking the postmodern approach to the extreme, if all truths become a form of fiction, none are more or less valid. In a purely theoretical sense, such a position can be considered morally neutral. However, for researchers in applied fields such as health care, reflection upon social history forces us to recognize that both good and evil can be unleashed through the dissemination of persuasive distortions disguised as truths. Because of this, the social or health care scientist cannot ignore the social context in which truth claims are made.

In my opinion, as we aim for elegance and artistry within our qualitative research products, our obligation regarding their social impact becomes increasingly important. Unlike the poet attempting to capture the smell of a rose, or the painter trying to convey an essential emotion in visual form, qualitative social and health science researchers are engaged in the business of knowledge production for some purpose, and that purpose has very real social consequences. For example, if we define certain lifestyles as aberrant, certain ways of coping as inadequate, certain strategic choices as noncompliant, certain mind-sets as denial, and we make such knowledge claims as scientist/researchers, we may reinforce certain negative attitudes within health care providers and shape the consequent illness experiences of patients. Within the pragmatic obligation of a practice science, our capacity to render research findings using the persuasive traditions of both art and science makes those findings all the more potent in the social world. Although we might easily dismiss certain research findings on the basis of methodological weakness, our capacity to remain critical may not be as effective when those same findings are offered in a manner that fires our imagination or reinforces our most passionate convictions.

As the poetic imperative shifts our mode of knowledge transmission away from the rules of science and toward the rules of art, it will be important to maintain a grounding in the purpose of our research endeavors. When our research reports "have the look and feel of fine prose or poetry," they may "require modes of criticism aimed at disclosing and appraising literature" (Sandelowski, 1995, p. 206). However, critique drawn from the artistic domain does not take the place of the scientific, social, and disciplinary standards that ensure appreciation of the implications of our inquiries. In recognition of the potential social impact of knowledge, of the power of a good story, it would seem that the artfully crafted qualitative research report demands an even more rigorous standard of critique than does the dry scientific report.

Conclusion

On the basis of the arguments presented here, it seems evident that critique of qualitative research demands application of both art and science. An increasingly sophisticated set of evaluation standards provides us with mechanisms to establish rigor and credibility within our work. However, despite their obvious utility, such rules and guidelines will not ensure excellence within qualitative research. The critique we envision is analogous to connoisseurship, the art of apperception, the developed ability to experience the subtleties of form (Eisner, 1991). It describes, interprets, and appraises in such a manner that it reeducates the reader's perception (Schwandt, 1994).

In this chapter, an attempt is made to depict qualitative research excellence in the context of the purposes for which knowledge is sought, orientation toward actual and potential applications of the ideas produced, and reverence for the complexities of truth claims within the scientific enterprise. As postmodern emancipatory thinking challenges our comprehension of the role of knowledge within society, and deconstruction of distinctions between art and science blur our sense of how we know what we know, the foundations for critiquing qualitative research become increasingly translucent. At the same time, in acknowledging that there is both good and bad qualitative research, we must try to explain how we know that to be true.

References

Altheide, D. L., & Johnson, J. M. (1994). Criteria for assessing validity in qualitative research. In N. K. Denzin & Y. S. Lincoln (Eds.), *Handbook of qualitative research* (pp. 485-499). Thousand Oaks, CA: Sage.

Armstrong, M. L. (1991). Career-oriented women with tattoos. *IMAGE: Journal of Nursing Scholarship, 23,* 215-220.

Breitmayer, B. J., Ayres, L., & Knafl, K. A. (1993). Triangulation in qualitative research: Evaluation of completeness and confirmation purposes. *IMAGE: Journal of Nursing Scholarship, 25,* 237-243.

Burns, N. (1989). Standards for qualitative research. *Nursing Science Quarterly, 2*(1), 44-52.

Clarke, L. (1995). Nursing research: Science, visions and telling stories. *Journal of Advanced Nursing, 21,* 584-593.

Eisner, E. (1981). On the difference between scientific and artistic approaches to qualitative research. *Educational Researcher, 10*(3), 5-9.

Eisner, E. (1991). *The enlightened eye: Qualitative inquiry and the enhancement of educational practices.* New York: Macmillan.

Erlandson, D. A., Harris, E. L., Skipper, B. L., & Allen, S. D. (1993). *Doing naturalistic inquiry: A guide to methods.* Newbury Park, CA: Sage.

Glaser, B. G., & Strauss, A. L. (1966). The purpose and credibility of qualitative research. *Nursing Research, 15*(1), 56-61.

Harmon, W. W. (1996). The shortcomings of Western science. *Qualitative Health Inquiry, 2*, 30-38.

Heron, J. (1996). Quality as primacy of the practical. *Qualitative Inquiry, 2*, 41-56.

Herzlich, C., & Pierret, J. (1985). The social construction of the patient: Patients and illnesses in other ages. *Social Science & Medicine, 20*(2), 145-151.

Hutchinson, S., & Wilson, H. S. (1992). Validity threats in scheduled semistructured research interviews. *Nursing Research, 41*, 117-119

Janesick, V. J. (1994). The dance of qualitative research design: Metaphor, methodolatry, and meaning. In N. K. Denzin & Y. S. Lincoln (Eds.), *Handbook of qualitative research* (pp. 209-219). Thousand Oaks, CA: Sage.

Johnson, J. (1996). Nursing art and prescriptive truths. In J. F. Kikuchi, H. Simmons, & D. Romyn (Eds.), *Truth in nursing inquiry* (pp. 36-50). Thousand Oaks, CA: Sage.

Kikuchi, J. F., & Simmons, H. (1996). The whole truth and progress in nursing knowledge development. In J. F. Kikuchi, H. Simmons, & D. Romyn (Eds.), *Truth in nursing inquiry* (pp. 5-18). Thousand Oaks, CA: Sage.

Koch, T. (1995). Interpretive approaches in nursing research: The influence of Husserl and Heidegger. *Journal of Advanced Nursing, 21*, 827-836.

Kvale, S. (1995). The social construction of validity. *Qualitative Inquiry, 1*, 19-40.

Leininger, M. (1968). The research critique: Nature, function, and art. *Nursing Research, 13*, 444-449.

Leininger, M. (1994). Evaluation criteria and critique of qualitative research studies. In J. M. Morse (Ed.), *Critical issues in qualitative research methods* (pp. 95-115). Thousand Oaks, CA: Sage.

Lincoln, Y. S. (1995). Emerging criteria for quality in qualitative and interpretive research. *Qualitative Inquiry, 3*, 275-289.

Lincoln, Y. S., & Reason, P. (1996). Editors' introduction. *Qualitative Inquiry, 2*, 5-11.

Lipson, J. G. (1994). Ethical issues in ethnography. In J. M. Morse (Ed.), *Critical issues in qualitative research methods* (pp. 333-355). Thousand Oaks, CA: Sage.

Miles, M. B., & Huberman, A. M. (1994). *Qualitative data analysis* (2nd ed.). Thousand Oaks, CA: Sage.

Morse, J. M. (1994). "Emerging from the data": The cognitive processes of analysis in qualitative inquiry. In J. M. Morse (Ed.), *Critical issues in qualitative research methods* (pp. 23-43). Thousand Oaks, CA: Sage.

Parse, R. R., Coyne, A. B., & Smith, M. J. (1985). *Nursing research: Qualitative methods.* Bowie, MD: Brady Communications.

Paterson, B. L. (1994). A framework to identify reactivity in qualitative research. *Western Journal of Nursing Research, 16*, 301-316.

Reason, P. (1996). Reflections on the purposes of human inquiry. *Qualitative Inquiry, 2*, 15-28.

Richardson, L. (1994). Writing: A method of inquiry. In N. K. Denzin & Y. S. Lincoln (Eds.), *Handbook of qualitative research* (pp. 516-529). Thousand Oaks, CA: Sage.

Sandelowski, M. (1991). Telling stories: Narrative approaches in qualitative research. *IMAGE: Journal of Nursing Scholarship, 23*, 161-166.

Sandelowski, M. (1993). Rigor or rigor mortis: The problem of rigor in qualitative research revisited. *Advances in Nursing Science, 16*(2), 1-8.

Sandelowski, M. (1994). The proof is in the pottery: Toward a poetic for qualitative inquiry. In J. M. Morse (Ed.), *Critical issues in qualitative research methods* (pp. 46-63). Thousand Oaks, CA: Sage.

Sandelowski, M. (1995). On the aesthetics of qualitative research. *IMAGE: Journal of Nursing Scholarship, 3*, 205-209.

Sandelowski, M. (1996). Truth/storytelling in nursing inquiry. In J. F. Kikuchi, H. Simmons, & D. Romyn (Eds.), *Truth in nursing inquiry* (pp. 111-124). Thousand Oaks, CA: Sage.

Sandelowski, M., Davis, D. H., & Harris, B. G. (1989). Artful design: Writing the proposal for research in the naturalist paradigm. *Research in Nursing & Health, 12,* 77-84.

Schwandt, T. A. (1994). Constructivist, interpretivist approaches to human inquiry. In N. K. Denzin & Y. S. Lincoln (Eds.), *Handbook of qualitative research* (pp. 118-137). Thousand Oaks, CA: Sage.

Schwandt, T. A. (1996). Farewell to criteriology. *Qualitative Inquiry, 2,* 58-72.

Sieber, J. E. (1993). The ethics and politics of sensitive research. In C. M. Renzetti & R. M. Lee (Eds.), *Researching sensitive topics* (pp. 14-26). Newbury Park, CA: Sage.

Simmons, S. (1995). From paradigm to method in interpretive action research. *Journal of Advanced Nursing, 21,* 837-844.

Tierney, W. G. (1995). (Re)presentation and voice. *Qualitative Inquiry, 1,* 379-390.

Wolcott, H. F. (1994). *Transforming qualitative data: Description, analysis, interpretation.* Thousand Oaks, CA: Sage.

Advice: Publish or Perish

Boyle:　　One thing I am really wedded to is that I am utterly convinced that you must publish while you are a student. Whether you publish your dissertation, or parts of your dissertation—I guess it doesn't matter—but as long as you are working on a dissertation, it makes sense to publish that.

　　　　You can be absolutely certain, that if you have a good idea, someone else has it, too. And you need to publish it, and you need to get it out there, not only for your own reputation, but to help the progress of science and your colleagues.

　　　　I've had the very sad experience of seeing some very bright young faculty hired on at our institution in the last few years and not being able to get papers or articles published in the past few years, for all of the normal reasons—a couple of rejections, a heavy teaching load, a sick husband, a new baby—and when it comes time for tenure, they haven't made it. And it's been a very, very, sad thing. I mean, sometimes it destroys careers. I am more and more convinced that you need to come into a position, at least to a major university, with the publications already on your vita, and with *some sense* on how to go about getting an article published. And then you are not in a second-class position when the gate opens and you have to run down the tenure track—

7

Strategies for Overcoming
the Rage of Rejection

The Case of the Qualitative Researcher

Phyllis Noerager Stern

In the eyes of the writing public, when you become an editor you become
an instant expert on how to get published. Whether you're having great
success getting your own work in print seems to be beside the point;
you're asked to speak to various academic groups on getting published
anyway. Actually, it's not beside the point at all, because unless you have
a pretty good track record of published research, you're unlikely to
become an editor. And to my mind, any editor worth her or his salt
remains aware of the struggle, anxiety, and rage an author undergoes.

Stern (1995, p. v)

Just as our participants in research—our respondents—instruct us in
forming our analysis of qualitative data, so must we instruct our
editors, reviewers, readers, and dissertation advisees. At times we act
as mentors to students and authors. These categories are included

because I have had a number of experiences within recent history where I found myself in the multiple roles of aspiring author, peer reviewer, editor, and doctoral committee adviser. Why is it that nobody (including me) seems to be able to understand a first draft? In fact, it boggles the mind how something so simple as relating a qualitative research report can get so twisted in the perception of the other! On the one hand, when one has written it so clearly, why can't they see? And on the other, how can this writer have the gall to submit this piece of trash and call it grounded theory, or phenomenology, or ethnography?

In situations such as these, one must follow a series of social, psychological, physical, and vocal steps prior to editing, rewriting, or what have you. First, one rants and raves over the stupidity of the writer/editor. Next, one slaps the manuscript on the desk with all the force one can muster. Following the slapping activity, stomping out of the room and trapping the first hapless colleague one can find and roaring at the injustice of it all, until one or the other is spent, moves the process along. Next, and this is crucial, one avoids the manuscript for days or weeks. During the interim prior to taking up the task of revision or critique, one experiences the social psychological processes of disgust, despair, and lassitude, and contemplates tossing the whole project. In the end, one undergoes the basic social process in instructing audiences: *overcoming rage*. This is an interactive process involving writer, editor, peer reviewer, doctoral student, and adviser. Is this process peculiar to qualitative researchers? Probably not; no one likes to be rejected. The qualitative researcher, however, making no claims of being "objective," and becoming one with participants—the co-researchers—considers her or his work "subjective," personal. As the novelist Carolyn Chute (1995) has written, "So, yes, with this book, as with my other books, I have paid for it with my life." (p. 278)

Overcoming Rage: Tales From a Professional Winner and Loser

Story 1: Learning the Bitterness of Failure

Once, long ago, a methodological manuscript of mine on my research on stepfathers was accepted by phone for the next published issue of a respected research journal (Stern, 1980). This coming hard on not one but two rejections from a well-known nursing journal, I was ecstatic. The rejections came from a refereed periodical, which I shall call *Journal X*. The journal's reviewers wanted to know what stepfather families "have to do with nursing"? My private response to this query was, "What *hasn't* it got to do with nursing—have you read the remarriage statistics lately?" followed by, "If you're too stupid to see it, I can't explain it." I neglected to write this or any other response. Instead, I put the manuscript in a drawer, so no one could see my shame. In the case of *Journal X*, I was overcome by rage, rather than overcoming it. Had the reviews come in later in my career, I would have gone through the steps outlined above, and then carefully explained just what stepfamilies have to do with nursing, and kept explaining until they got it. Instead, I nourished my anger, went to other journals—with success—and never again submitted an article to *Journal X*. Now, who won? Not *Journal X*, because they didn't know what they were missing. Not me, because I closed off an avenue for my work as well as harboring bitterness for 20 years. That's not getting even, that's getting stupid.

Getting Smart

In 1995, I wrote an editorial, "Getting Published: View From the Editor's/Author's Desk," for my journal, *Health Care for Women International*, in which I explained, "If you're an academic and you lust not for your name in print, consider a career change" (p. v). And that's why being overcome by rage doesn't work—most promotion and tenure (P&T) committees demand some evidence of scholarly work. Even using Boyer's (1990) definition of scholarship, P&T committees want to see evidence of teaching research and service in some published form. The writer seeking tenure, then, has two options: to cave in to the reviewers or to make a substantiated argument.

Making rage work for you. To understand the anatomy of rage as it applies to writers and reviewers, we must accept that it is born of lust: the lust to get famous, the lust to read something worth your time. Lust rejected in authors/reviewers strikes at the heart of our beings. We suffer the dejection of the thwarted lover. It is the shield behind which we hide our suspicion of unworthiness. As such, rage is healthier than despair. It can provide the energy to swing us into action. To help students overcome the despair of rejection, I explain that the reviewers just didn't get it. I advise them to use the "listen stupid" technique; that is to say, "Listen stupid, I'm going to explain this so even you can understand." Sometimes writers find it necessary to go through the "ABCs" of what, to them, seems so basic that a reasonably bright high school senior could understand it. I console, "But if it was good enough to write in the first place, it's good enough to break down enough so they *do* get it."

The rejection that won't go away. There is a certain breed of peer reviewer who seems to find it insufficient to critique the work. This reviewer, rather than overcoming rage, vents it on the author. Whether it's overwork, oppressed-group behavior, early childhood rejection, or a sense of personal worthlessness, a disrespectful review is inexcusable. It is quite possible to say, "No," without adding, "because you're slime." As a result of a disrespectful review, some authors never write again. Some former students with whom I have cowritten never write for *that* journal again or that funding agency. The rejection that's particularly hard to shake is the one that comes from a reviewer who judges qualitative work from the point of view of quantitative research. In this case, it may be wiser to go to another journal or another agency; in other words, find the right home for the work, as whoever is handing out review assignments has failed to judge the talents of the referee. "What," you say, "this is still happening?" Sadly, I report that it is—more of this later.

Triumph over stupidity: Healing the unkindest cut of all. In recent years, more common than being judged by quantitative experts is getting back a review from a pseudoqualitative expert—"pseudo" not only because they don't agree with me but because they clearly are inexpert in the methodology. In 1993, when a new editor mounted the helm of a respected research journal, she wrote an editorial to the effect that the-finding's-the-thing; in other words, elaborate descriptions of the method are no longer necessary. Music to my ears (eyes). While we methodologists love splitting hairs over how a given method needs to be designed and exercised, these fine points are of little interest to the ordinary reader, who wants to know if findings make sense and if are they applicable to her or his world. Sometimes, in the academic world, we forget the salience of the findings, as well as the secondary import of the method in the final product.

For the editor above, I had just the piece in mind. Having spent the years from 1983 to 1991 in Canada, returning to the United States in August 1991, by 1993 I felt sufficiently settled in my job and reacculturated to tackle the time-consuming chore of writing up a major piece of research, the home fire victims study (Stern & Kerry, 1996) that had been put aside for purposes of earning a living, learning a new job, and relearning my country of origin. Frankly, I thought this article was pretty good, and I sought the wide audience the periodical of choice is famous for. But prior to submitting a manuscript, and with the agreement of my coauthor, I presented some of the concepts at research meetings, and I asked the official editor at my school, Phyllis Dexter, to give the paper a going over, which she did, pointing out several oversights—good. I also sent the work to the only other researchers I knew of who worked with fire victims (Jepson, Pickett, Keane, Tax, & McCorkle, in press; Keane, Pickett, Jepson, McCorkle, & Lowery, 1994). These authors returned helpful suggestions, one of which was to avoid the journal I had in mind, because the reviewers are particularly critical of qualitative work. But I like a challenge, so we submitted it. Time passed. When the reviews arrived in my office, and I read them, my secretary said, "Phyllis, that's the first time I've heard you really lose your temper—they can hear you down by the elevator!" Rage! I couldn't *believe* the reviews! One peer wanted irrelevant demographic data: the name, rank, and serial number of each participant—there were 105—rather than a conglomerate of the social scene under study. Another reviewer wondered why I hadn't "bracketed" anything. It also was clear that a synopsis of the method was unsatisfactory to these reviewers, in spite of the stated position of the editor.

We overcame our rage, and revised, explaining the ABCs of grounded theory. Instead of one lengthy paragraph, we covered three typewritten pages (so even *they* could understand). We explained that the term *bracket* is one phenomenologists use. We cited Stern (1980, 1985, 1991, 1994), Stern, Allen, and Moxley (1982), and Baker, Wuest, and Stern (1992). We also cited Glaser (1978, 1992, 1993, 1994), Glaser and Strauss (1967), and Strauss (1987) as substantiation for leaving out the name, rank, and serial number of the participants. This may seem like overkill, but part of overcoming rage is fighting back. Put another way, don't bring a knife to a gun fight.

Story 2: Perception, Persistence, and Peer Review

I suggested, in that 1995 editorial for *Health Care for Women International*, that "perception, persistence, and peer review" are the three most important ingredients "in seeing a manuscript through to printed work" (p. v). I have another article that has just been accepted for publication (Stern & Keffer, 1996) that illuminates these principles. In 1990, I evaluated a conference in New Zealand and used the findings for an endnote speech to those assembled (Stern, 1990). It was only a two-day conference, and my data were incomplete, but I stumbled on a basic social process that I thought had punch: I *perceived* that it was worth pursuing. I took on a coinvestigator and we engaged in theoretical sampling.

In 1993, I met an international visitor to Indianapolis, who told me that a new international scientific journal was being launched and invited me to submit an article. I thought the conference evaluation/cum grounded theory would be a good fit, and my coauthor and I were taken with the thought of going to press internationally. After suitable local *peer review*, we airmailed the article in March 1994. When we had no word that the manuscript had arrived by July, I faxed the editor. By September, we had no response, and the old rage started up. That is until I looked up the July fax, and realized I had used the wrong country code. I faxed again. I got an immediate response that they had never received the original article and asked that I fax the manuscript as they were nearing press time. Had I not *persisted*, our article would have remained in transworld-never-never land. But that's not the end of the story; I soon received a letter from the editor stating that they published only "scientific" articles (read "quantitative"), so the qualitative-quantitative mixup is still going on.

After a little editing, we sent the article to another journal in the spring of 1995. We got a letter acknowledging receipt, and then nothing for months. As an editor, I know manuscripts can get lost in stacks of paper, so in October 1995 I inquired about the progress of our manuscript. Just before Christmas, the reviews came back with a number of suggestions. It was March break 1996 before we could revise. In May 1996, we asked about the progress of the work. To our dismay, the article had been sent to a third reviewer, who made suggestions like this one: "If these are nurses, why is the term client used, why not patients?" This reviewer also made inappropriate comments about the methodology.

I was almost overcome by rage! It took three weeks before I could face the manuscript and explain the method so that even *this reviewer* could understand, and I took pains to point out that in most of the Western world, those whom nurses care for are referred to as "clients," reminding us that directly, or indirectly, our charges pay our salaries, and hence must be treated with respect. The reviewer did point out an error in our figure, thus *peer review* saved us from later embarrassment.

Story 3: The Dilemma of the Research Grant Proposal

As Cohen (1996) points out, one of the most vital components of qualitative research—its very essence—is emergence. Just as Sandelowski (this volume) notes that a program of qualitative research comes clear only after a series of studies are complete, the same is true of qualitative research itself. If we knew the population and variables going in, we would be testing rather than discovering—but try telling that to a funding agency that wants demographic particulars of the participants as a part of the proposal. The qualitative researcher is caught on the horns of a dilemma—either make up a number that seems plausible, or remain unfunded. If one chooses the former, one is stuck collecting data far beyond interpreting the problem, thus spending money, time, and *using* participants when it is no longer necessary. If one makes the latter choice of stressing emergence, one may do the study anyway, and get it published in a reputable journal, and yet one's curriculum vitae reflects little or none of the outside income universities love so well.

Following the triumphs of Morse and Sandelowski in successful qualitative funding, one would expect more of our peer grant reviewers to be expert in qualitative methods. The day may come when emergence will gain its rightful place in the funded grant proposal. However, at present, the field is still quantoid-dominated, and these quantoid-minded reviewers are generally present when proposals are reviewed. Three problems emerge: (a) As with manuscripts, proposals can be improperly assigned; (b) the reviewers may not have the experience and expertise that the researcher has, and their comments then are naive and out of sync; and (c) unfair criticism results in a higher score, which delays funding until the next cycle. Such procedures are inappropriate and unethical. Reviewers have a responsibility to be competent or they *must* decline the review.

Story 4: View From the Editor's Desk

Why do editors and reviewers become enraged at the transgressions of authors? For the same reasons authors rage at reviewers: The editor/reviewer's position in life is at stake. How can an author have the temerity to take up the time of a person of such stature? This is swine casting offal at pearls! I follow rage-reducing strategies before I tackle a response—my Girl Scout training won't allow me to write a *rejection that won't go away*.

Fortunately, most of the manuscripts submitted to my journal seem to be fairly high-quality work. But some authors clearly fail to do their homework. This is especially evident to me if the method is qualitative. A glance at the references may reveal only one methodological source, and that may be a single chapter in a book. Some manuscripts and proposals are just plain bad, in which case I let the author down as easily as possible, suggesting a consultant or another outlet for the author's work.

The problem I find with most qualitative pieces that don't come off is that they are underanalyzed. Perhaps the author has developed some categories but doesn't tell us how they fit together. Or the author strings a series of case studies together but fails to tell us how they contribute to our knowledge. A fatal flaw in a number of studies lies in the author's failure to link the findings with other theoretical works. She or he gives us no clue as to how this work goes beyond what other researchers have done. These are problems that can be solved, and I am often given to outlining how the paper can be fixed. This is a prereview reading of papers that wouldn't pass muster if I sent them to the review board, or if they did, I wouldn't want to publish them.

There are a few glaring errors that I won't abide. Unless the author is from overseas, I refuse to read a manuscript that follows another journal's publication style. This tells me the author hasn't even bothered to pick up the journal to find the contributor's guidelines. If the author doesn't even care that much, neither do I.

I received a manuscript to review for another journal recently that I almost sent back unread. The author began the manuscript with a story/case study that was printed in small-font italics. At the prospect of reading 4½ pages of this print, I almost gave up. I put it aside for a month. When I finally read it, the "story" part of the manuscript turned out to be quite touching. It was a sad incident that happened in the author's family. The problem was that the writing was amateurish. I wrote a four-page critique, because I knew the author had written from the heart. Part of that critique follows:

> It seems that within every scientific writer, there's an artist struggling to get out. The problem is that there's more to writing good artistic prose than struggle. . . . While the "story" . . . is poignant, and touching, the flow, syntax and phrasing need work. . . . Not hopeless, but very rough . . . this is particularly glaring on page 6 where the author uses the sentence, "so very, very quiet." . . . Is very × 2 more variable than × 1? . . . on page 7, we read a . . . lulu, ". . . lovely rural cemetery overlooking the mountain." Now does this mean the cemetery decided against the mountain, and so overlooked it in favor of a different spot, or does it mean the cemetery is up in the sky overlooking the mountain? . . . Story telling as a means of getting a message across can be effective if done well. If the author intends to use this medium, she or he needs to find an editor . . . and pay the price for a professional piece of work.

The rest of the review had to do with inaccuracies in the analysis of the case. Once the author overcomes her or his rage, she or he has every chance of writing a publishable article.

Transcending Variables: Uncovering
Virtue in a Blanket of Idiocy

When the rage clears, the reviews seem more rational. Sometimes my peers point out glaring errors. To quote my 1995 editorial again, when writing about the fire survivors article, one reviewer complained that "I would have assumed that NURSING [sic] should play a role in each article [of a nursing journal]. There is no mention of nursing" (p. vii). That was a pretty dumb oversight on our part. In that same article, the editor noticed an inconsistency in the analysis and in so doing saved us from committing an embarrassing gaffe. A competent review is, after all, free consultation, and as such should be shown respect.

Contained within the basic social process of *overcoming* rage lies the opportunity to learn something new. Once one concentrates on the reviews, the usual outcome is a better piece of work. The published work is worth the ego trampling one must undergo. *Getting smart* is a process and, as such, happens over time.

Conclusion

Painful though it may be, there is a price to pay in getting funded/published/graduated. If the reviewer is off base, the writer needs to substantiate her or his position. If the reviewer didn't get it, the writer simply has to try again—the best revenge is getting published. Sometimes, though, the reviewer, as an outside observer, can save the writer's reputation. Published work ends up in a federal repository, the Library of Congress, where one's errors can be held up to veneration or ridiculed by generations of latter-day scholars. A carefully executed review can make all the difference.

References

Baker, C., Wuest, J., & Stern, P. C. (1992). Method slurring: The grounded theory/phenomenology example. *Journal of Advanced Nursing, 17*, 1355-1360.

Boyer, E. (1990). *Scholarship reconsidered: Priorities for the professorate*. Princeton, NJ: Carnegie Foundation for the Advancement of Teaching.

Chute, C. (1995). *The Beans of Egypt, Maine: The finished version*. New York: Harcourt Brace.

Cohen, M. (1996, March). *Emergence: The sacrificial concept on the altar of mainstream acceptability*. Paper presented at the Midwest Nursing Research Society Conference, Detroit.

Glaser, B. G. (1978). *Theoretical sensitivity*. Mill Valley, CA: Sociology Press.

Glaser, B. G. (1992). *Basics of grounded theory analysis*. Mill Valley, CA: Sociology Press.

Glaser, B. G. (1993). *Examples of grounded theory: A reader*. Mill Valley, CA: Sociology Press.

Glaser, B. G. (1994). *More grounded theory methodology: A reader*. Mill Valley, CA: Sociology Press.

Glaser, B. G., & Strauss, A. (1967). *The discovery of grounded theory*. Chicago: Aldine.

Jepson, C., Pickett, M., Keane, A., Tax, A., & McCorkle, R. (in press). Experiences of African American and Caucasian women who survive residential fires. *Health Care for Women International.*

Keane, A., Pickett, M., Jepson, C., McCorkle, R., & Lowery, B. J. (1994). Psychological distress in survivors of residential fires. *Social Science and Medicine, 38*, 1055-1060.

Stern, P. N. (1980). Grounded theory methodology: Its uses and processes. *IMAGE: Journal of Nursing Scholarship, 12*, 20-23.

Stern, P. N. (1985). Using grounded theory in nursing research. In M. Leininger (Ed.), *Qualitative research methods in nursing* (pp. 149-160). New York: Grune & Stratton.

Stern, P. N. (1990, November). *Partnership in primary care: What do nurses think?* Paper presented at the First International Nursing Theory and Primary Care Conference, Massey University, Palmerston North, New Zealand.

Stern, P. N. (1991). Are counting and coding *a cappella* appropriate in qualitative research? In J. M. Morse (Ed.), *Qualitative nursing research: A contemporary dialogue* (pp.147-162). Newbury Park, CA: Sage.

Stern, P. N. (1994). Eroding grounded theory. In J. M. Morse (Ed.), *Critical issues in qualitative inquiry* (pp. 212-223). Newbury Park, CA: Sage.

Stern, P. N. (1995). Getting published: View from the editor's/author's desk. *Health Care for Women International, 16*(1), v-viii.

Stern, P. N., Allen, L. M., & Moxley, P. A. (1982). The nurse as grounded theorist: History, processes and uses. *Review Journal of Philosophy and Social Science, 7*, 200-215.

Stern, P. N., & Keffer, J. (1996). Strategies for solving client-nurse partnerships issues in primary care. *Scandinavian Journal of Caring Sciences, 10*, 219-244.

Stern, P. N., & Kerry, J. (1996). Restructuring life after home loss by fire. *IMAGE: Journal of Nursing Scholarship, 28*, 11-16.

Strauss, A. (1987). *Qualitative analysis for social scientists.* New York: Cambridge University Press.

Dialogue: The Downside of Blind Review

Thorne: I think it is very important *not* to keep your examples (of inappropriate reviewers' comments) to quantitative examples—you know, those ones in which they say the *n* is too small?

Hutchinson: It just happened to me where one reviewer said you cannot publish on the *Basic Social Problem*. You have to publish the whole theory. You could not pull a theory apart.

Boyle: Or the one who said to me, "You obviously don't know ethnography—this is grounded theory! And— [laughter]

Stern: And then they advised you to read Boyle!

Boyle: Yes! Yes! [laughter]

May: I would have hired a hit person! [laughter]

Boyle: They said, "Read Morse, '94." [laughter]

Morse: That shows you that the review process is blind!

Boyle: The message I get from editors is, "Cut it down, cut it down, cut it down!" They are not so entranced with methodology, they want findings. So you cut it down. And then this is what you get! They [the readers] don't know what you are doing.

Others: True, true.

Boyle: And read Boyle and expand!!

Responding to Criticism

Judith E. Hupcey

The public is the only critic whose opinion is worth anything at all.

Mark Twain (1870)

The art of criticism is held as a virtue in many professions such as art, music, and literature. Critics may interpret, describe, summarize, or evaluate the work with knowledge and propriety. They often discuss a work's historical context, thereby providing insight into an author's, artist's, or composer's purpose and meaning. Critics may not go into great detail about a particular work, but through the general discussion will provide information that will help a less knowledgeable person understand and interpret the work and define her or his own views about the work.

In science, criticism is a means of advancing knowledge by facilitating debate among scientists and scholars. Criticism serves to move science forward and ensures quality in our work. According to Aminoff (1994),

A major role of criticism is to determine whether the positive or negative conclusions of individual studies are justified, as well as to permit apparently conflicting studies to be reconciled by analyzing the differences between them. In this way public criticism is a secondary check on the quality of research—not only methodologically, but also correcting the values and ethics of research and its contribution and cost to society. (p. 1783)

Criticism is a skill that needs to be learned and practiced by a person knowledgeable about the particular subject. Although the term *criticism* many times brings with it negative connotations such as condemnation, dissatisfaction, and resentment, the purpose of criticism is to assist authors and researchers in molding and developing their work. However, many times criticism is not done in an appropriate manner. The criticizer may use careless or inflammatory language, which results in the recipient of the criticism being belittled and at times feeling devastated. This type of criticism erodes and destroys the development of one's work instead of advancing knowledge. In the words of Aminoff (1994),

Criticism must not . . . simply be destructive in nature for, in contrast to skepticism, it also has a constructive aspect . . . .[the] critic has a role of provocateur, generating new ideas or hypotheses, as well as an iconoclast serving to expose the weaknesses, flaws, and biases in established concepts. (p. 1783)

The scientific literature is replete with articles related to criticism; however, these works focus on the *need for and importance of criticism*, not a researcher's response to it. In addition, in journals from all the disciplines, there are numerous articles, editorials, and letters to the editor concerning forms of scientific misconduct, and the importance of detecting and responding to it. Included in this literature are plagiarism, ethics in research, falsification or misrepresentation of data, how and when an article should be retracted, and guidelines for authorship, with many editors expressing concern with poly- authorship. This body of literature appears biased toward the assumption that scientific misconduct has occurred, not how to respond when you are not guilty of scientific misconduct. In general, little has been written about the person being criticized. As a result, there are no guidelines to assist those researchers who are under scrutiny on when and how they should or should not respond to both constructive and destructive criticism.

The purpose of this chapter is to present strategies for responding to criticism, with the focus being responses to harsh and unjust attacks on a researcher's work. Next, responses to criticism of qualitative research will be discussed, again stressing unjust criticism. Finally, responding to both public and private criticism will be discussed. For public criticism, the following areas will be addressed: letters to the editor and commentaries in response to a published paper, questions at the end of a verbal presentation, discussions on the Internet, and misquotation and miscitations of oral presentations and written work. For private criticism, reviewers' comments on manuscripts and grant proposals will be briefly discussed (for more information, see Stern, this volume).

Strategies of Responding to Criticism

When a researcher's work is criticized, it is the responsibility of the researcher to respond. However, the style of response is contingent upon the nature of the criticism and the format and forum in which the criticism occurred, as well as the context available for the response. One broad principle is that the more heated and less rational the discussion, the more general the response should be.

Five types of criticism are discussed and the strategies for responding to each have been identified and are summarized in Table 8.1. Although these strategies have been developed from general patterns of responses, they are not necessarily independent of one another and can be used in combination. For instance, Strategy II, Justification of the Original Work, also may be combined with Strategy III, Diffusion of the Criticism, in the same response.

Strategy 1: Correction of the Original Work

There are times when a researcher's work, such as a submitted manuscript, is in need of further work or possibly major revisions prior to its being published. In this situation, the researcher needs to carefully read the criticism and use it in a constructive way to help further develop the work. At other times, an unintentional error or

Table 8.1 Strategies of Responding to Criticism

Strategy I: Correction of the Original Work
Used when the criticism is right/correct, or justified

Method
1. Clarify the issue.
2. Evaluate within own work/results.
3. If the point is correct, agree with and thank the questioner.

Strategy II: Justification of the Original Work
Used when there is a general attack on the research

Method
1. Read the commentary and identify the issues.
2. Place the issues within a higher conceptual level.
3. Respond to the greater issues in the context of the criticism.

Strategy III: Diffusion of the Criticism
Used when there is a global attack on the research topic, method,
results, and the author must respond (as with a commentary response)

Method
1. Select an issue or topical area that was mentioned.
2. Agree or disagree with the observation.
3. Thank the questioner for her or his important observation.
4. Discuss the issue, extending it beyond where the questioner has taken it.

Strategy IV: Counterattack
Used when the author needs to justify own approach/results
by selecting errors or poor examples from other research

Method
1. Identify the concerns.
2. Sort the literature into those who agree and disagree with your research.
3. Construct an argument to support your research by pointing out the errors, biases,
   or poor examples in the other research, including that conducted by the criticizer.

Strategy V: Choosing to Ignore the Criticism
Used when responding to criticism would result in a worthless
debate or a continued personal attack on the author

Method
1. Identify the issues and fully understand the concerns.
2. If you decide these issues have no scientific basis and that by responding the issue
   would escalate, the researcher may deliberately choose not to respond.

---

omission occurs in a researcher's work and the error is not detected until the work is presented. Sometimes when the error is pointed out, it becomes obvious; other times the error may not be clear and the nature of the concern must be clarified. Frequently the researcher must return to the data or check calculations before the error may be confirmed. When researchers become aware that a mistake has been made, it is their responsibility to make a public correction as soon as possible. The correction should be concise, without excuses, with acknowledgment and thanks to the researcher who raised the issue. The attitude of the researcher must be one of gratitude that the error was detected as soon as possible.

Strategy II: Justification of the Original Work

When the criticism is nonspecific but negative, such criticism may be generally damaging. The actual concerns of the criticizer may be difficult to identify, and it may be clear that the reviewer does not like or approve of the research.

In this situation, the first step is to read the criticism and identify all the issues and concerns of the criticizer. Often, because the review is so global, these will be difficult to identify. In other instances, the criticisms may be specific and numerous, or the review may contain both nonspecific and specific criticisms. Once identified, if these criticisms can be classified or grouped together under more abstract categories, the real concerns or misconceptions of the reviewer may be identified and the issues can be placed on a higher conceptual level. For example, if the reviewer does not understand the principles of qualitative sampling, he or she will present many criticisms concerning bias, adequacy, and the nature of the results. Responding to these concerns one by one will not assist the criticizer in understanding qualitative sampling. Rather, the researcher should present a short summary of the principles and assumptions that underlie qualitative sampling, criteria for adequacy, and appropriateness. This approach will help the criticizer understand that his or her many concerns extend from a lack of knowledge about a single issue.

Strategy III: Diffusion of the Criticism

Sadly, sometimes the criticism comes as a generalized attack on the research, involving the methods, the topic, and even the approach to the problem. In this case, the best strategy in the researcher's response is to diffuse the attack.

One strategy for diffusing the attack is to select an issue or a topic that is mentioned in the criticism. This may not be a major issue, and may even be one that is tangential to the issue being discussed. Begin the response by thanking the criticizers for their input, agree or disagree with the observation, then discuss the issue selected, even extending the discussion beyond the level introduced. In this way, an interesting response may be presented—albeit somewhat tangential to the original criticism.

Strategy IV: Counterattack

When the criticism is unjust and unwarranted, researchers may feel they have no recourse but to issue a "counterattack." Such an approach may be less painful to all concerned, if the attack is not a direct retaliation. Rather than defending one's research by attacking the criticizer's research, the debate can be made more general. First, identify the concerns of the criticizer. Next, identify research related to the concern and sort the research into teams—those in agreement and those not. Then, defend your research by citing poor examples or errors from the other team's research, pointing out that, without the error, their research would be stronger.

Strategy V: Choosing to Ignore the Criticism

Unfortunately, sometimes the criticism is so extraordinary that, clearly, no matter what response is given, it will fall on unreceptive ears. Rather than be rationally considered, any response will add "fuel to the fire" and escalate the situation. Although such attacks are unprofessional, they do occur, and anyone who publishes may be the target of such an attack. An example of a documented attack on someone's character, when the person being attacked did not openly respond to the allegations, is Glaser's (1992) written criticism of Julie Corbin after she coauthored *Basics of Qualitative Research* with Anselm Strauss (1990). Although Glaser admits that he had never read her work, he stated that she "tried to use grounded theory" (p. 125), "is not a scholar" (p. 126), and is immoral. A response by Corbin, no matter how benign, only would have fueled a fire that was already out of control.

When such attacks occur, they are best ignored—choosing not to respond is a deliberate choice, and silence holds power and dignity. Unfortunately, in a conference setting, should such an attack occur verbally, silence may also appear rude. When this occurs, the only course for the researcher may be to make a joke ("I'm sorry, we're only taking questions on farming") and then ask for a question from the next speaker.

Presenting Your Argument Versus Arguing Back

Presenting the argument may involve using Strategies II, III, or IV but usually involves a counterattack or a debate of the pertinent issues. The above strategies do not include "arguing back," which involves a more irrational response and/or a personal attack on the criticizer. Such a strategy is rarely constructive, and as new issues are constantly introduced into the discussion, such a format seldom leads to resolution. Thus it is recommended that the knee-jerk responsiveness of arguing back be avoided.

An example of a possibly unfitting personal attack, which occurred with both a "response" and a "rebuttal," was a result of Molly Dougherty's (1979a) review of the book *Transcultural Nursing: Concepts, Theories, and Practice.* The author, Madeleine Leininger (1979), not only responded to specific aspects of Dougherty's book review but based a good portion of her response on questioning the reviewer's ability to undertake such a review. Dougherty's rebuttal appeared to address and attack Leininger's model of transcultural nursing as much as it did the book being reviewed. This type of dialogue seemed more like personal attacks rather than an intellectual exchange.

Responses that are considered a personal attack on one's character rather than on the research itself have been shown to have the opposite effect of what was intended. For example, Leslie's (1990) long and passionate paper (which was later published), presented as an opening address at a Conference of the Social Sciences & Medicine, was in response to an article by Rushton and Bogaert (1989) titled "Population Differences in Susceptibility to AIDS: An Evolutionary Analysis," which used stereotypical racial depictions to describe the susceptibility to AIDS among various populations. Although many social scientists (for example, Lovejoy, 1990) were outraged by this article, many people were even more concerned with the manner in which Leslie handled his response to it. Leslie was criticized for presenting the paper as the opening address at a conference with a different focus and in which most of the audience had not read the article in question.

In addition, his remarks were felt to be excessively passionate, a personal attack on Rushton, and not just focused on Rushton's article (McEwan, 1990; Wilson, 1990). Leslie's concern with this article would have had greater impact if he had handled his criticism in a more befitting manner.

Criticism of Qualitative Work

In this section, common criticisms of qualitative research will be presented and the appropriate response strategy recommended. As with all research, the work of qualitative researchers needs to be constructively criticized so as to advance knowledge. There are times, however, when qualitative researchers are overly and unjustly criticized. This is of particular relevance when a reviewer does not understand the principles, assumptions, and methods inherent in qualitative inquiry. Reviewers have been known to wage fundamental attacks on the qualitative paradigm, stating that a study being presented is *not research* and *not science*, simply because they have little knowledge of or do not *believe in* qualitative research. Others criticize the rigor of qualitative inquiry, believing that qualitative research is not rigorous because it does not follow *quantitative* guidelines. A reviewer may criticize and reject the qualitative research itself. The research and the detailed descriptions of a topic can cut too close to home and make a reviewer uncomfortable, so the research is then rejected. The reviewer also may use an unacknowledged criterion for evaluating the research. Based on his or her own hypotheses or personal experiences, the reviewer does not believe the data presented, and therefore rejects the research results.

Responding to Criticism of Qualitative Work

When a criticizer has real questions about the qualitative work and/or research results, the suggested response would be to agree with the reviewer, if an actual problem is found—using Strategy I, Correction of the Original Work, or, if there is disagreement with the queries, Strategy IV, Counterattack (see Table 8.2).

The most general and negative comment a qualitative researcher may receive in response to his or her work is that it is "not science."

Table 8.2 Suggested Responses to Criticism of Qualitative Research

Criticism of Qualitative Research	Suggested Appropriate Response Strategy(s)
Real queries regarding the research and/or the results or discongruent results	Strategy I—if a true problem found Strategy IV—if you disagree with queries
Qualitative research in general is not considered "science"	Strategy V—ignore the criticizer or make a joke
Ignorant of qualitative approaches—considers qualitative methods "not research"	Strategy II or III—depending on what the forum will allow
Personal bias—a personal attack on the author, fear of competition by the questioner, or a disbelief of the result based on "personal experiences"	Strategy IV—counterattack Strategy V—if a personal attack and a response would add fuel to the fire

Such a comment dismisses the work instantly and in its entirety. No response will convince a reviewer who knows so little about qualitative methodology that your research has merit. It is recommended that the researcher simply not respond and use the silence recommended as Strategy V, Choosing to Ignore the Criticism. However, if the researcher needs to resubmit the manuscript to the same journal, it is recommended that a request be made to have a new and more appropriate reviewer assigned to the manuscript. If it is necessary to present it to a similar audience, it is recommended that the chair be alerted to expect particular problems and to control the question period accordingly.

Another comment of concern is that qualitative research is "not research." Criticizers who make such a comment also clearly are not familiar with the qualitative paradigm, and depending on the tone of the review, may be deserving of a response. If the researcher believes that the reviewers may be receptive to a response, the voice of reason, as described in Strategy II, Justification of the Original Work, or Strategy III, Diffusion of the Criticism, may be an appropriate way to reply. As Stern's chapter discusses, reviewers may need to be educated about qualitative methods.

If the comments suggest a personal bias on the part of the reviewer, Strategy IV, Counterattack, or Strategy V, Choosing to Ignore the Criticism, would be appropriate. If the criticism of the research appears to be based on the reviewer's past experiences ("I've worked in critical care for 20 years so I do not believe your results"), a counterattack may be appropriate. One may need to strongly support the results with other studies. However, if the criticism is based on a fear of competition, responding may not help because the response simply may fall on deaf ears. As discussed previously, criticism that is strictly an attack on one's character should be ignored unless one needs to defend oneself against slanderous statements.

Public and Private Criticism

Although criticism is, by and large, a public occurrence, with both the criticizer and his or her thoughts known both to the researcher and to the scientific community at large as it is spoken in meetings or printed in the literature, criticism also may be private. Reviewers' identities may not be known to the researcher or, in the case of reviews of journal articles, the reviewers and authors are concealed from each other. Both public and private criticism require that researchers decide whether they will respond and how they will respond. Responses to public criticism are of particular importance because the response or lack of response will also be under public scrutiny.

Responding to Public Criticism

Being criticized publicly allows the author/researcher an opportunity to respond to the criticizer. It, however, also allows the person being criticized to be exposed to public embarrassment. Learning to respond to these public attacks on one's work appears to be a difficult task. Passion and feelings of being personally offended are hard to set aside, but they must be held in check so that the response can be clear and logical, addressing the issues and not becoming a personal attack on the criticizer. Replying in a manner that expresses one's view, which is opposite or contradictory to that of the criticizer, requires that the responder respond with tact, and, as Emily Post suggests, a person should say something such as "I think it is this way or that way," not, "You're wrong and I'm right." Give your reasons for your point of view and listen carefully to the other person's side (Post, 1984, p. 223).

Letters to the editor, commentaries, and criticism of written work. Letters to the editor and commentaries (responses) are forums in which researchers can have a straightforward dialogue and/or debate over a research paper. These debates may relate to the design of a study, disputed errors, and interpretive uncertainty of published works (Horton, 1995). Concern has been expressed, however, as to the long-term benefit of these modes of exchange. According to Bhopal and Tonks (1994), studies have shown that even if letters are written that explain a study's flaws, the study still may be cited subsequently, while the comment letters are ignored. Many of these commentaries are not indexed and carry little weight. As a result, only those people who are hot on the topic actually write, and very few respond positively to an article. A final concern is that letters to the editor are not peer-reviewed. Although most letters are sound and encourage thoughtful dialogue, others may include only whimsical criticism, putting the author in an awkward position when responding to the commentary.

There are other ways that written work can be criticized. As described above, Leslie (1990) wrote an opening addressing criticizing the work of Rushton and Bogaert (1989). A book review can be written, as with Dougherty and Leininger. A response (or comment section) can be requested by the journal to be published following an article or, as in the case of Glaser (1992), a whole book can be written criticizing the work of others.

Most of the time, authors should respond to letters to the editor, a commentary (or response paper) that addresses a published paper, or other criticism of their work. There are instances, however, where a response/rebuttal would only cause more problems by encouraging a worthless debate or personal attack.

The goal of responding to criticism of your written work requires that the response be clear and concise, not bitter or sarcastic. An eloquent response that addresses the issues is most effective for getting a point across. It is important to pick out each salient point and address it. Ranting and raving or personal opinions can be ignored. If these are addressed, it will not prove to be an intellectual exchange. If the criticism has potential merit in terms of questioning the accuracy of the results and conclusions, researchers may need to make their data available for review and potentially allow the editors to work with the institution where the research is being undertaken to investigate the project (Horton, 1995). This may be the only way researchers can respond to major criticism of their work.

Questions at the end of a verbal presentation. Responding to questions at the end of an oral presentation involves the researcher deciding if the question will be directly addressed or if the issue should be skirted. First the presenter needs to decide why the person is asking the question. Does the person appear to have a genuine interest in the topic and want to bring up an interesting point or want some clarification of the research, or does the questioner have an "I'm smarter than you" attitude and want to stump the presenter?

If a question requires that part of the presentation be clarified or requires a simple explanation of part of the results, then it behooves the researcher to answer the question. If, however, the question or criticism of the study is based on opinion, personal experiences, or unpublished results, the presenter may respond nicely by telling a joke, or with one of the following: "That's an interesting point, next question," or "I look forward to reading about your results. When will they be published?" or "We'll look into that point in our next study." If the questioner is trying to stump the presenter, but the presenter has research to answer or defend his or her position, then a counter-attack may prove most beneficial. Again, it is better to answer the question, even if it is extremely critical, in a nonthreatening, nonsarcastic manner.

Discussions on the Internet. The Internet is a new means of having intellectual dialogue. These exchanges may occur among total strangers and, as a result, have the potential of developing into wonderful brainstorming sessions or deteriorating into harsh, unwarranted criticism of someone's work. What should one do if one is the recipient of criticism during one of these debates? The answer depends on the debate. A person should respond, if clarification of the work appears to be needed. However, harsh or sarcastic answers will only stifle the dialogue and not reflect well on the researcher.

Even though debates on the Internet are being carried out by anonymous individuals, Miss Manners says that there is still etiquette, or *netiquette*, that must be maintained. These exchanges should be treated as if you were responding to a person *in person*. "Flaming, or shouting on the Internet—defined by using capital letters—is an interesting problem now" (Goodman, 1996, p. 59) and should not be done.

Miscitations and misquotations. It is not an infrequent occurrence that an author is miscited and misquoted. Both errors can be very frustrating to an author, and both need direct responses. When one is cited incorrectly, others may not easily be able to find one's work. If a misquotation occurs, a direct response is required. The exact words and the context in which they were said or written should be pointed out and then clarified as to how they were misquoted. Responses to miscitation and misquotations could occur through a letter to the editor, in a written rebuttal, or in an oral forum.

Responding to Private Criticism

Because of the anonymous nature of private criticism, the author usually does not have the opportunity to respond directly to the criticizer. In the case of criticism of grant proposals, the only recourse is to revise the grant and respond to the criticizer in a special section of the proposal or to submit to another funding agency. Authors' responses to a reviewer's criticism of a submitted article are mediated by the journal's editor. As a result, the debate may or may not be allowed to continue through the editorial office.

Responding to reviewers' comments. The peer-review process for manuscripts and research proposals is an important one for ensuring that a work is clear, has scientific merit, is sound methodologically, and has or will obtain valid conclusions (Aminoff, 1994). In response to reviewers' comments related to a manuscript, an author should

alter the manuscript where you feel the criticism is fair and warranted; clarify; add or delete text where necessary; and ignore comments that appear nonsensical . . . resubmit with a cover letter briefly describing how you have responded to the reviewers' comments and listing the changes made. (Morse, 1996, p. 150)

If reviewers have widely disparate comments, it is up to the author to address each reviewer individually but only make changes to the manuscript that are deemed appropriate. Responding to criticism of a research proposal review may involve greater justification and a thorough description of the methods to be used (Cohen, Knafl, & Dzurec, 1993). Responding to unwarranted criticism of manuscripts and research proposals is a major problem. As discussed earlier, qualitative researchers are many times unjustly criticized simply because reviewers do not understand or buy into the qualitative paradigm. Authors may need to educate reviewers about the qualitative approach chosen by giving a meticulous description of the method. It is very frustrating to attempt to convince a true nonbeliever that qualitative methods are a scientifically sound and valid means of inquiry.

Summary

The art of responding to the criticism of one's work needs to be learned just as the art of criticizing needs to be learned. The process both of being criticized and of responding to it helps produce research that is stronger and of higher quality. Although being criticized may make us angry or humiliated or leave us feeling emotionally drained, it is necessary. The advice of Emily Post (1984) is apropos in this situation: It is "much better to withdraw unless you can argue without bitterness or bigotry. Argument between coolheaded, skillful opponents may be an amusing game, but it can be very, very dangerous for those who become hotheaded and ill-tempered" (p. 221).

References

Aminoff, M. J. (1994). Criticism in neurology and medicine. *Neurology, 44*, 1781-1783.
Bhopal, R. S., & Tonks, A. (1994). The role of letters in reviewing research. *BMJ, 308*, 1582-1583.
Cohen, M. Z., Knafl, K., & Dzurec, L. C. (1993). Grant writing for qualitative research. *IMAGE: Journal of Nursing Scholarship, 25*, 151-156.
Dougherty, M. C. (1979a, August). [Review of the book *Transcultural nursing: Concepts, theories, and practice*]. *Medical Anthropology Newsletter, 10*, 23.

Dougherty, M. C. (1979b, August). [Rebuttal to the author's response to the book review of *Transcultural nursing: Concepts, theories, and practice*]. *Medical Anthropology Newsletter, 10*, 24-25.

Glaser, B. G. (1992). *Emergence vs forcing: Basics of grounded theory analysis*. Mill Valley, CA: Sociology Press.

Goodman, S. (1996, March-April). Miss Manners, Judith Martin. *Modern Maturity, 39*, 56-63.

Horton, R. (1995). Revising the research record. *Lancet, 346*, 1610-1611.

Leininger, M. (1979, August). [Response to the review of the book *Transcultural nursing: Concepts, theories, and practice*]. *Medical Anthropology Newsletter, 10*, 23-24.

Leslie, C. (1990). Reflections on peer review, science and ideology. *Social Science & Medicine, 31*, 891-905.

Lovejoy, C. O. (1990). [Comments on the article, Scientific racism: Reflections on peer review, science and ideology]. *Social Science & Medicine, 31*, 909-910.

McEwan, P. J. M. (1990). [Comments on the article, Scientific racism: Reflections on peer review, science and ideology]. *Social Science & Medicine, 31*, 911-912.

Morse, J. M. (1996). "Revise and resubmit": Responding to reviewers' reports. *Qualitative Health Research , 6*, 149-151.

Post, E. L. (1984). *Emily Post's etiquette: A guide to modern manners* (14th ed.). New York: Harper & Row.

Rushton, J. P., & Bogaert, A. F. (1989). Population differences in susceptibility to AIDS: An evolutionary analysis. *Social Science & Medicine, 28*, 1211-1220.

Strauss, A., & Corbin, J. (1990). *Basics of qualitative research: Grounded theory procedures and techniques*. Newbury Park, CA: Sage.

Wilson, G. D. (1990). [Comments on the article, Scientific racism: Reflections on peer review, science and ideology]. *Social Science & Medicine, 31*, 910-911.

Dialogue: The Application of Theory

May: For instance, since my early work on expectant fatherhood,
         there have been maybe 10 people over the past decade who
         have developed instruments. And then they write to me and say,
         "I have developed this instrument—isn't this neat?" I have to say,
         "No, in fact, I am sorry—you have misinterpreted the uses to
         which the theory should be put." Because *instrumenting*, it
         means, "Now I am going to diagnose you, and then I am going
         to structure practice based on my diagnosis of your situation."
         When, in fact, the entire drift of the theory is to say, "Identify
         naturally occurring variations and bring to bear resources of
         support to assist the man to find his own path." And so, I have
         said, "Please don't do this, I would appreciate you not redirect-
         ing my work in this way." . . . But I handed in my final report (for
         my grant) at the time some clinical colleagues were building an
         antepartum nursing support service. And they just swung their
         intervention around to take into account some of what I had
         asserted was true in learning to live with preterm labor. So it
         just happened. But they did it in a way of *not* diagnosing people,
         not sticking people in boxes—but saying, "We are teaching
         nurses to watch for the naturally occurring variations here, and
         when they see this kind of pattern, then they may try to antici-
         pate and provide supports in this way. And when they see this
         other pattern, then they may try to—so this is the way that
         interventions get built.

Considering Theory Derived From Qualitative Research

Janice M. Morse

Theories . . . serve to satisfy a very human "need" to order the experienced world. The only instrument employed in the ordering process is the human mind and the "magic" of human perception and thought.

R. Dubin (1978, p. 7)

Despite the fact that the purpose of qualitative research is to develop theory, that is, "to order the empirical world," little attention has been paid to the nature, evaluation, and use of that theory. The sidestepping of these issues has had serious consequences for qualitative research as a whole. Qualitative researchers have been too glib in accepting the dictum that qualitatively derived theory

AUTHOR'S NOTE: I acknowledge Carl Mitcham, PhD, Elizabeth Lenz, PhD, FAAN, Sharon Wilson, RN, MEd, MN, Janice Penrod, RN, MN, and Gail Havens, RN, PhD, for their comments on earlier drafts of this manuscript. Research support was provided by NINR, 2R01 NR02130-08.

should be tested quantitatively prior to implementation,[1] too humble in the evaluation of the significance of their theoretical results, and too timid in making recommendations from this theory for practice. In short, the underestimation of the power of qualitatively derived theory has resulted in an impotence that has crippled and stigmatized the communication of qualitative research, the implementation of findings, and even the adoption of qualitative methods themselves. Results have been too easily dismissed with, "It's only a qualitative study," and qualitative researchers have not risen to the occasion and defended their work against such global attacks.

Theory is not theory, is not theory: Theory appears in many forms that vary in structure, sophistication, and modes of derivation. Suppe (1996) observes that middle-range theory is used in research in three different ways: (a) as an object to test, (b) as the scientific end product expressing knowledge, and (c) as theoretical frameworks for other research studies.[2] Quantitatively derived theory[3] *(QuanDT)* is developed prior to the planning of the research design and data collection and is perceived as "an object to test" (Suppe, 1996), with the goal of prediction (Dubin, 1978). Qualitatively derived theory *(QualDT)* is usually a product of the research process, with the purpose of providing understanding (Dubin, 1978). Practice derived theory *(PractDT)* is derived from clinical experience (or practice), from one's personal philosophy regarding nursing, and from the literature. As should be expected with different goals, the structure of qualitatively and practice derived theory does not resemble *QuanDT.* However, although *QualDT* and *PractDT* differ in important dimensions from theory used in quantitative inquiry, these differences have not been explicated.[4] All theory is measured by the criteria used to evaluate theory developed for quantitative research, despite the fact that qualitatively and practice derived theory are developed from different sources, in different ways, and serve different functions.

There has not been a discussion in the literature about the pragmatic implications of each type of theory. Without such a discussion, confusion remains about the value and purpose of the qualitative research process per se. In this chapter, first this issue will be explored and then the differences among qualitative, quantitative, and practice derived theory discussed. Second, the types of theory that emerge from qualitative inquiry will be examined, and a scheme for assessing *QualDT* as the end product of qualitative inquiry will be suggested.

What Is Theory?

> Science is not merely a collection of facts and formulas. It is preeminently
> a way of dealing with experience. The word may be appropriately used
> as a verb: One *sciences*.
>
> L. A. White (1938, p. 369)

Numerous definitions of theory exist in the literature. Some of these definitions are specific, stringently listing the components of theory. For example, theory is *"logically interconnected sets of propositions from which empirical uniformities can be derived"* (Merton, 1967, p. 39). Theories may be complex, providing a means for description, explanation, or prediction (Fawcett, 1993). Kaplan (1964) considers theory to be a fundamental explanation, and a model, a more explicit representation of reality. In a strict sense, he maintains, "all theories are not models" (p. 264). Maxwell (1996) defines theory as "a set of concepts and proposed relationships among these; a structure that is intended to represent or model something about the world" (pp. 29, 31). However, other authors suggest that a theory is "any general set of ideas that guide action" (Flinders & Mills, 1993, pp. xii), including "everyday explanations or a particular event or characteristic" (Maxwell, 1996, p. 31), and may even be "simply stated in one sentence" (Burton, 1974, p. 18).

While there are many conceptions of theory, these definitions are not associated with either the quantitative or the qualitative paradigms but are applied carte blanche to all theory. As stated, some authors have noted that theory is used for different purposes and the aforementioned criteria do not fit all types. In quantitative research, clearly prescribed methods for the presentation of the theory have been developed: Assumptions must be stated; propositions must be testable or assumed true; operational definitions must be measurable; the association of concepts must be clearly stated; and variables delineated. In this chapter, the less structured definition of theory is used. The former definition, requiring components and relationships to be present for a theory to be labeled as such, limits what may be included as *theory*. Although some authors have developed stringent and exclusive criteria for what constitutes a model and why a *model* is not a *theory*, such distinctions are unnecessary (Dubin, 1978); in this chapter, these terms will be used interchangeably. To enter a discussion that compares the disparate nature and uses of theory that develop from both quantitative and qualitative inquiry, and from practice, issues of structural components of theory must necessarily be put aside. Theory is notoriously inbred within disciplines. This restricted inbreeding has resulted in different views about what constitutes a theory, which conceptual components are included (Sandelowski, 1993), how it is tested and modified, and which criteria for application should be used. Adopting a definition of a theory that is as broad as possible will enable a discussion that encompasses as many dimensions of the problem as possible. Using a broad definition of a theory will enable the incorporation of the entire spectrum of theory and not, for instance, exclude studies that develop models or are primarily descriptive impressions that eventually have some influence on action.

Comparison of Characteristics of Quantitatively, Qualitatively, and Practice Derived Theories

It is not against a body of uninterpreted data, radically thinned description, that we must measure the cogency of our explications, but against the power of the scientific imagination to bring us in touch with the lives of strangers. It is not worth it, as Thoreau said, to go round the world to count the cats in Zanzibar.

C. Geertz (1973, p. 16)

When the characteristics of quantitatively, qualitatively, and practice derived theories are compared, interesting differences are evident. In this section, differences in the derivation, relationship to the empirical world, relationship to existing theory, relationship to inquiry, relationship to practice, and use/application of each type of theory will be compared. These are listed in Table 9.1.

The first characteristic differentiating qualitative, quantitative, and practice theories is related to their derivation. The *QuanDT* is "invented" or created by investigators through processes of reasoning and deduction using available knowledge, the wisdom of personal experience, and reasoning—a process, not surprisingly, known as "theorizing." Importantly, the theory is created apart from empirical data, but the results of previous empirical research may comprise some compo-

Table 9.1 Comparison of Characteristics of Theory Derived for Quantitative Research, for Qualitative Inquiry, and for Practice

Characteristic	Quantitatively Derived Theory (QuanDT)	Qualitatively Derived Theory (QualDT)	Practice Derived Theory (PractDT)
Derivation	Invented or created by extending previous research	Developed from empirical data	Created or developed from practice, from philosophy and personal beliefs
Relationship to empirical world	Conjectural and inferential • hypothetical • inferential • operational definitions may be vague • boundaries arbitrary	Represents empirical world • organizes reality • minimal inference • rich description • boundaries appropriate	Provides perspective, a framework for organizing practice
Relationship to existing theory	Foundation of existing theory • incremental modifications	May be innovative • linked to associated theory	Some reliance on existing theory
Relationship to inquiry	Primary guides investigation—conceptual framework for testing • deductive, purpose of investigation is to test • may be a poor fit (esoteric, hypotheses not verified) • intolerant of ambiguity	Primary product of investigation—verified representation of reality • purpose of investigation is to develop a reliable and valid theory • resembles reality (pragmatic, tolerates ambiguity)	Secondary guides inquiry—presents a perspective of reality • organizes studies within its framework
Relationship to practice	Secondary implemented after testing (often at least twice)	Secondary implemented after evaluation	Primary molds practice, implemented as practice
Utilization	Fit tested with empirical world • concepts not tested; rather, relationship between concepts explored • described distribution in population • development of measures	Represents empirical world • provides explicit insights into empirical world	Organizes the empirical world

nents of the theory. *PractDT* is developed from a process of synthesizing clinical praxis and developing innovative structures or models from this knowledge. On the other hand, *QualDT* is constructed from the empirical world during the process of inquiry. Although it is possible that after the stage of comprehension is reached (Morse, 1994), the theory suddenly may be comprehended or reached through instantaneous insight, more often it is conceived in small, incremental steps throughout the process of inquiry. The investigator makes conjectures and then confirms these conjectures with empirical data (i.e., observations or interview data) in small steps as inquiry proceeds. In this way, qualitative theory is systematically developed from both empirical data and the cognitive analytic practices of synthesizing, theorizing, and confirming.

The second area to consider is the relationship between the theory and the empirical world.[5] Because quantitative theory is "created" prior to commencing data collection, it consists of conjecture and inferences that are tested for correctness of fit with the world it reports to represent after the theory is articulated (see Figure 9.1). Thus, by its very nature, *QuanDT* is largely hypothetical and inferential. Researchers struggle with the twofold task of making operational definitions to meet the goals of *fit* (i.e., a good representation of the phenomenon/concept they try to represent) and *measurement* criteria. Because *QuanDTs* are created for the purpose of testing, the need to clearly outline the relationships between concepts is essential. Researchers create these relationships to be *testable*. Unfortunately, this often results in a theory that is intolerant of ambiguity, simplistic, and often with convenient, yet arbitrary boundaries. As Blumer (1970) notes, such theory is often divorced from reality.

Conversely, qualitative researchers develop theory that as accurately as possible *represents the empirical world* (Figure 9.1). Data analysis consists of organizing reality with inferences that are subsequently systematically confirmed in the process of inquiry. *QualDT* as a product is abstract but consists of minimal conjecture. These theories are rich in description, and the theoretical boundaries have been derived from the context and not from the researcher's arbitrary goals for delimiting the scope.

Finally, practice theory also is developed to represent the empirical world but is developed from the researcher's personal philosophy that

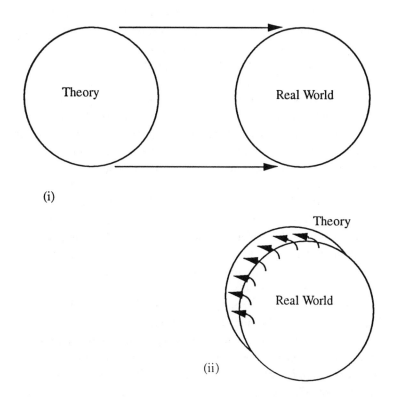

Figure 9.1: Relationship Between Theory and the Real World
(i) In quantitative inquiry, theory is tested for fit against the real world; (ii) in qualitative inquiry, theory is derived from the real world.

provides a perspective and a theoretical basis, from the researcher's personal knowledge of clinical praxis, and also from pertinent literature. It has not been tested, nor is it intended to be formally tested. Rather, is it considered a framework to organize and to guide clinical observations and practice, and is modified only when it does not meet this goal conveniently.

The third dimension is the relationship to inquiry. The purpose of *QuanDT* is to guide inquiry. Hypotheses are written at a manageable level—one that addresses a testable unit. If the theory is a poor fit or incomplete, hypotheses may not be verified. As quantitative theory is linked to existing knowledge, its relationship is therefore closely related to existing theory. When new theories are proposed, they are developed incrementally from previous research or extend existing theories. It is rare that an entirely new and innovative theory is proposed: Most researchers extend existing theory incrementally by one relatively minor dimension at a time.

On the other hand, because the qualitative investigator develops theory from empirical data, the theory produced is one that resembles reality. These theories are pragmatic and tolerant of ambiguity. As *QualDT* is developed systematically and invariably confirmed (tested) in the process of development, it is more likely to be creative, innovative, and less bound to existing knowledge. Thus the theory produced is more likely to be innovative. However, it usually is not devoid of linkages to other theories: Indeed, as newly developed concepts must fit with adjacent concepts (Bulmer, 1979), such linkages are a means for providing at least partial confirmation of the new model. Therefore, while in qualitative and quantitative research each method of inquiry is radically different, a confirmed theory—that is, the synchronization of a theory and data—is the final product.

PractDT may guide inquiry, in the sense that *PractDT* may be used as a framework that places the research in a practice context and serves as a framework to justify the proposed research as a nursing study (see Morse, 1996) (and is often kept relatively independent and separate from the research itself), rather than, as in *QuanDT*, serving as a framework that *is* actually tested.

Finally, we must consider differences in the ways that theory derived for each paradigm is used. In quantitative research, when testing the "fit" with the empirical world, the concepts per se are not "tested." Rather, it is the propositions, the proposed relationships between the concepts, that are examined. If the results indicate a poor fit, then the theory is modified and the process repeated. If the results indicate a good fit, then the model is extended, new relationships conceived and tested, and, in this way, in incremental steps, inquiry proceeds.

Critical to the use of *QuanDT* is the question of measurement. Because of the abstract measure of quantitatively derived theory in social sciences, the issue of measurement, and the issues of reliability and validity, testing and replication, are of primary importance. Instruments developed to measure the variables are the link to the usefulness of the theory. *QualDT* is a different story. Because the theory has been confirmed—*confirmed* in the process of development—the notion of testing is redundant. The theory by its very nature fits the empirical world. To retest this fit would be ridiculous and a waste of time— issues of how this testing should be conducted aside.

Given this degree of certainty for *QualDT*, does this theory still fit the definition of a theory? *Recall that theory is theory*, not fact, but as a theory is confirmed, it is moved into the realm of fact and is no longer theory (Morse, 1992). Because of the abstract nature of *QualDT* and because of the conceptual nature of the knowledge, *QualDT*, by and large, remains at the level of theory, not fact. Theory is not reality, but our *perception* or organization of reality, perhaps closely resembling reality, but *not* reality per se. It remains a representation of reality, malleable and modifiable. Qualitative researchers do not usually deal with concrete phenomena such as eye color, a knee-jerk reflex, cells, or bodily fluids—rather, we deal with concepts and constructs, which are, in themselves, theoretical entities.

Is it possible then that two researchers using qualitative methods could enter the same setting and return with divergent results? Of course! Recall that, with qualitatively derived theory, the first goal is to organize the empirical world and to make sense of human behaviors (actions and interactions). All research is guided by the question asked, by the disciplinary perspective and the agenda of the researcher, by methods used, and by the context. If two researchers with identical preparation, asking the same question and using the same methods, entered two similar settings, even though their data would not be identical, they would both develop a very similar theory.[6] However, as two researchers are rarely so similar, it is more likely that two researchers who enter the same setting will produce quite different theoretical schemes.[7] They may ask different research questions, focus observations and interviews on different phenomena, use divergent theoretical perspectives centering on different concepts, develop theories to different degrees of abstractness, and so forth. But, again, because of the abstraction of their work, the results still remain theoretical.

Does *QuanDT* ever move beyond the theoretical level? When relationships have been confirmed, is the theory transformed into fact? The answer is *perhaps*—depending on the level of abstractness of the concepts and the success in measuring the concepts. For instance, intelligence quotient (IQ) is a well-measured and replicated concept, but as a concept, it still remains at the theoretical level. Of even more serious concern, IQ is defined by its own measurement tool (see Blumer, 1970, p. 56). More concrete phenomena are directly measurable, less abstract, and more easily demonstrated. Therefore, they have greater opportunity to move into the domain of facts.

I have argued that theory is a tool (Morse, 1992), and the researcher must retain this methodological attitude using theory as a tool to guide research and as an instrument to assist with analysis, regardless of its derivation. Again, *QuanDT* is used deductively as a framework in which to sort data, and *QualDT* is formed as an emerging framework during the process of data collection and into which data are sorted as inquiry progresses. Treating theory as a *fact* is a pitfall for both qualitative and quantitative researchers because investigation ceases. When theory is treated as a fact, it becomes a "wall" that blinds the investigator, threatening validity and inhibiting inquiry.

Evaluating *QualDT*

> Good ideas are one test of theory. They last, people cannot resist using them. They cannot forget them. . . . Findings are soon forgotten, but not ideas.
>
> B. G. Glaser (1978, p. 8)

Although the quality of any theory developed is dependent in part on methodological rigor, adherence to such standards does little to inform us about the quality or value of the theoretical outcome of the research per se. Thus, in this section, I will argue that the assessment of qualitative research requires more than the inspection of an audit trail for such criteria as trustworthiness of the data and adherence to method.[8] I am suggesting that the process of review be expanded beyond method to include (a) assessment of the level of theory developed (according to such features as purpose, utility, scope) and (b) the theoretical elegance or structure of the theory (assessing coherence, clarity, and so on) (see, for example, Fawcett, 1993). Therefore, I am not suggesting that theoretical assessment replace standard methodological criteria for evaluating qualitative research but that it be used *in addition* to evaluation of the methods.

Assessment of the Level of Theoretical Development

Qualitative research as a *product* may be classified according to the level of theoretical abstraction. This ranges from the most descriptive research to the most abstract, generalizable research, and is outlined in Table 9.2.

Descriptive. This research consists of rich description of the phenomenon. Although description is used as the first step in all qualitative inquiry, it also may be an end in itself. Because descriptive research reports in detail about what is there, it serves an important function in documenting the *status quo*, confirming and legitimizing knowledge. However, the results remain close to the data, with minimal inferences and abstractions. Because descriptive research is primarily synthesis and has little abstraction, and because it is an essential preliminary to concept and theory development, it also may be a foundation for the development of more abstract theory.

The results of a descriptive study rarely present any new information to the readers who are familiar with the context. Descriptive research is the accurate portrayal of the phenomenon and the context (which cannot be recorded quantitatively); it forms the basis of evaluation research and also may be conducted using ethnographic methods. Observational methods, in particular those that do not incorporate interviews and therefore contain no interpretation (such as participant observation and qualitative ethology), also are the primary methods used for description.

What separates descriptive research from journalism? Remember that inquiry is theory focused. Although descriptive research does not produce a formal theory, this research still is conducted indirectly in a theoretical context. This means that although a theoretical framework does not guide data collection, concepts or theories do provide a backdrop that justifies conducting the research and also provide a context in which the results are reported.[9] For example, if we are interested in the way that patients interact with each other, we may conduct this study within the context of social support (What is the

Table 9.2 Characteristics of Qualitatively Derived Theory (QualDT)

Type	Purpose	Indicators	Use	Scope	Generalizability	Causality	Examples of Methods
Descriptive	Describes/confirms	"I know"	Documents	Primarily context bound	Local: limited to setting and tme	Limited	Ethnography Ethology Participant observation
Interpretive	Enlightens/informs	Instant recognition ("Oh!"; "Yes!")	Interprets	Limited to phenomenon	Local: limited to phenomenon	Limited	Phenomenology Ethnography Narrative inquiry
Disclosive	Reveals	Makes intricate complex processes obvious	Models	Process bound: stages and phases	Local: limited to phenomena over time	Yes (by disconfirming hypotheses and seeking negative cases)	Grounded theory Concept analysis
Explanatory	Explains comprehensive understanding	Provides	Predicts	Links macro and micro levels of knowledge	Broad	Yes	Triangulated methods

nature of support in patient-patient communication?) or patient education (What do patients teach each other about health and illness, or "learning the ropes of being a patient," and so forth?). It is this theoretical context that protects qualitative researchers from reviewers who may write, "So what?" It also provides a mechanism for making even descriptive research interesting to others and it provides limited generalizability. Miles and Huberman (1994) describe this as *local* generalizability. That is, it provides insight into the mechanisms, the temporal ordering of complex events. As the number of cases is increased, and the level of abstraction increased, so is the scope of the generalizability.

An example of such descriptive research is the research documenting the comforting role of the trauma nurse when the patient is conscious, in severe pain, and analgesics are delayed or ineffective (Proctor & Morse, 1996). This study, using videotaped data, linguistically described the talk of the trauma nurse as the patient attempted to maintain control. The speech pattern of these nurses was so distinct that it was described as the *comfort talk register*. This technique of comforting had not been described previously; this description will enable comfort talk to be taught and eventually formally integrated as a part of the roles and responsibility of nursing in trauma room situations.

Although descriptive research is often context-bound, the above study has implications for other settings. Usually descriptive work is not generalizable beyond the immediate setting, but if the phenomenon studied is a common behavior, the contextual features may permit generalizability. The role of the researcher in describing descriptive work should clearly delineate the scope and implications for practice. Note that descriptive research has only limited causal implications: In the above study, while further research must be conducted about the role and efficacy of the comfort talk register, description was an essential first step in establishing it as knowledge.

Often the descriptive portion of a study must be reported in a separate section prior to theoretical development. Such a strategy provides a means for the reader to appreciate the context and the data prior to the presentation of the theory. This is a common strategy used in case studies. For example, in a study by Morse and Carter (1995), the experiences of a burn patient were presented in verbatim segments in the first part of the article; the second part contained the identification of theory or model that enabled the case study to be generalized to others. It is important to note that this linkage is done conceptually—in this case, using the concepts of enduring and suffering—and it is this abstraction from the descriptive data that makes the study more powerful.

Qualitative researchers are theoretically timid. Some researchers may be more comfortable staying within the safety zone of their data; they may be unwilling to take the risk inherent in interpretation and move their analysis beyond the descriptive level. Theorizing is also work: Often researchers make the mistake of submitting their study for publication without making the effort to do the conceptual work necessary for the development of theory. Theoretically undeveloped submissions sometimes read as collections of quotations with minimal commentary from the researcher and virtually no interpretation of the meaning of the data apart from that expressed by the participants. This level of analysis, dubbed "transcription," barely meets the criteria for research, and these investigators should be encouraged to move their work forward theoretically to a more meaningful and useful level.

Interpretive. This research makes the implicit explicit. It allows the reader to experience instant recognition of the phenomenon ("Yes!!"), even when the reader is not a participant. Thus the research is not context-bound and it includes theoretical abstraction. However, this research often focuses on a single concept so that the theoretical linkages between concepts, which are necessary for modeling, are absent.

Interpretive theory may be evident in phenomenological research, ethnography, or narrative inquiry. Rich description is evident in descriptive research, but theoretical linkages are made to the literature, including the lay literature. Reflection and interpretation from the researcher are major components so that the reader appreciates the work on analysis beyond the collection of data. In this way, interpretive theory is generalizable: The reader is able to identify the descriptions in him- or herself or to recognize them in others. The scope is abstract and usually restricted to a single concept. Causality is limited and the purpose is to inform.

Examples of interpretive research include phenomenological study of the lived body during illness (Morse, Bottorff, & Hutchinson, 1994). By examining transcripts obtained from patients talking about their experiences of illness and reflecting upon these experiences in terms of the phenomenological literature, such categories as the *dis-eased body*, the *deceiving body*, the *disobedient body*, the *vulnerable body*, the *violated body*, and the *enduring body* were identified and described.

A more concept-focused example is the work of van Manen (1991) in which he delineates the concept of tact as it applied to teaching. The careful description and reflection of tact, linked carefully to data, provides an important and rich exposition of the concept that will facilitate its integration both into praxis and into educational theory.

Disclosive. Disclosive theory reveals the structure of knowledge and the intricate complexity linking concepts and delimiting stages and phases of a process. Primarily, methods such as grounded theory or concept development (Morse, Hupcey, Mitcham, & Lenz, 1996) are used, and these allow not only the identification of antecedents and consequences of the concepts but linkages to other concepts. The resulting theories are middle range and provide enormous potential for the development of applied knowledge (Lenz, 1996). The process of incremental confirmation of conjecture during the process of inquiry ensures that the resulting *QualDT* is as "solid" as possible. These theories are process-bound (that is, do not extend beyond the scope of the phenomenon, such as the particular illness described) and are generalizable to other contexts and to other participants experiencing similar phenomenon. The process in grounded theory of negative cases and discomfirming hypotheses, and Glaser's (1978) technique of comparing attributes of concepts on a 2 × 2 matrix provides some indicators of causality.

Glaser and Strauss (1967) and Glaser (1978, 1992) have differentiated between substantive (topic-focused) and formal (concept-focused) theory, arguing that formal theory is more abstract, more generalizable, and therefore more powerful than substantive theory. Note that in the typology presented in this chapter, disclosive theory encompasses both substantive and formal theory.

Examples of disclosive theory are numerous. Those investigators who have used grounded theory frequently model the stages and phases of the identified process, and because of the certainty of these models in development, if the study is methodologically sound, they may be ready for implementation into the clinical setting. Examples of such research are presented with descriptions of the data in *The Illness Experience: Dimensions of Suffering* (Morse & Johnson, 1991); in this volume, five authors address various issues such as in Johnson's "Adjustment After a Heart Attack," Chassé's "Experiences of Women Having a Heart Attack," and Norris's "Mothers' Involvement in Their Adolescent Daughters' Abortions."

Explanatory. In explanatory theory, concepts and linkages are identified and described. These theories are complex and important. However, few have been developed from qualitative research. Because of the limitations inherent in qualitative method in sample size and the context-bound nature of qualitative inquiry, theory that has been developed to this level has been developed using triangulated methods. Either these methods have been developed using two or more qualitative studies simultaneously (QUAL + Qual) or sequentially (QUAL → Qual) (see Morse, 1991). These theories are generalizable, and concepts may be operationalizable, so that the qualitative findings may be incorporated into larger studies and inform quantitative research. The scope of these studies is broad. Prediction of probability and causal relationships may have been established.

An example of such work is developing in the comfort project, with studies addressing such concepts as hope (Morse & Doberneck, 1995), suffering and enduring (Morse & Carter, 1996), nurse-patient relationships (Morse, Havens, & Wilson, in review), and patients' perspectives of comfort (Morse et al., 1994), integrated into a single theory. These studies are linked in smaller units, and the methods for integrating studies and linking concepts are still being developed (Morse & Penrod, in review). Thus explanatory theory may arise from a research program, or from the sequential conduct of interrelated projects developing interpretive or disclosive theory and through the effort of integrating this work. It is only by incrementally constructing theory from the other levels that theory in qualitative inquiry can reach the scope and attain the level of causality required for explanatory theory. However, despite the efforts to make each component of such work *certain*, this research remains at the level of theory.

Evaluating the Structure of *QualDT*

Given the differences between *QuanDT* and *QualDT* discussed thus far, it is clear that the criteria for evaluating *QualDT* must be different than or adapted for the evaluation of *QuanDT*. To date, three methods of evaluation have been suggested. First are the criteria for examining qualitative theory by Glaser and Strauss (1967) and Glaser (1978, 1992). These criteria state that *QualDT* must have fit, relevance, and be able to work; it must be modifiable; and it must be transcending. To transcend, it must be presented at a higher level of abstraction than the substantive area being studied. Although these components are important, they are criteria for theory as an *outcome*, a product. These reflect on the efficacy of the theory, but they reveal less about the theory itself.

The second method is to evaluate the quality of the research from which the theory was derived. Qualitative researchers have become distracted with criteria and standards for rigor, forgetting the contribution of insight and creativity to theory development and the significance of the quality of theory as a product. However, there is some relationship between methodological rigor and the quality of the theory developed. For instance, if the data are not trustworthy, there will be "holes" (i.e., inconsistencies, gaps, and lack of coherence) in the theoretical arguments. Therefore, the inadequacies in the theory will reflect the inadequacies of the data. Note that this is a circular argument: If the data are not trustworthy, then substandard theory will be produced; if the result is substandard or inadequate theory, one reason may be a lack of trustworthiness in the data. The value of the research necessarily consists of rigor plus the theoretical contribution: *Both must be evaluated.* However, neither of the above criteria provides a method for examining the theoretical structure or the theory itself, as does the criterion for *QuanDT*. In the next section, such a criterion will be discussed.

The third method is to examine the theory using techniques of critical reasoning to investigate such features as the congruence between the philosophical claims undergirding the theory and the theoretical content as well as criteria such as clarity, consistency, the logical connections between propositions, and so forth (Fawcett, 1993; Silva & Rothbart, 1983; Silva & Sorrell, 1992). Van der Steen (1993) notes that theory is always a compromise between achievement of the ideal (such as a lack of vagueness and ambiguity) and utility, that any assessment of a theory should be based on its context dependence and intended purpose.

Assessing QualDT

Once the level of development of the theory has been determined, the next step is to examine the theory for clarity, structure, coherence, scope, generalizability, and pragmatic application. This process is outlined in Table 9.3. Not all criteria described are appropriate for evaluating all levels of theory, and as each criterion is discussed, the type of theory for which it is appropriate will be noted.

Clarity. This criterion applies to all levels of theory, including the descriptive and interpretative. Clarity is achieved primarily through the use of thick description (Geertz, 1973). To achieve this level of description, the sample must be adequate and appropriate, and the data saturated. Ideally, there should be no hypothetical descriptions (e.g., if grounded theory is used, there should be no hypothetical cases in a 2×2 matrix).

The context must be described clearly to produce a picture, a mutual frame of reference for the reader, and to provide adequate detail on which to base our arguments. Note that these rationales are not analytic reasons in Glaser's sense. We describe the gender of participants not because gender is an important factor in the developing model[10] but to provide a complete representation of the scene.

The methods used must be clearly described, so that it is possible for the reader to understand what was done and why, and to be able to evaluate methodological rigor. Quotations that support the argument must be pertinent, succinct, and representative of both the topic and the data.

Finally, the researcher's commentary must be summative, synthesizing, and integrative. For descriptive theory, it is the richness and depth of the description, and the use of a theoretical context, that sep-

Table 9.3 Criteria for Evaluating the Structure of *QualDT*

Criteria	Assessment
1. Clarity	• Is the description detailed and complete? • Is the context clearly described? • Are the methods well explicated? • Are quotations used appropriately? • Is the commentary summative, synthesizing, and interpretive?
2. Structure	• Are the concepts clearly delineated? • Are the attributes identified? • Are the linkages well described? • Is the empirical content delineated from the theoretical? • Are the boundaries clearly marked?
3. Coherence	• Are macro-micro linkages plausible? • Is the theory consistent? Are the ambiguities explicit? • Is the theory clear? Are terms used consistently, defined and described? Is it parsimonious? • Is there a fit between categories and data?
4. Scope	• Is the theory stringent? • Is the theory appropriately linked to the phenomena?
5. Generalizabilty	• Is the theory an appropriate link between the concepts and the recommendations for practice? • Is the theory recontextualized for reapplication?
6. Pragmatic utility	• Does the theory work? • Is it relevant for research? Is it modifiable? • Are there realistic recommendations for practice?

arates research from journalism, that makes the study interesting and useful to others, and that moves descriptive research toward theory.

Structure. The theoretical structure is one of the most important features in determining the level of theory. While the structure increases in complexity with the increasing level of the theory, the structure also becomes more clearly defined. For example, in descriptive theory, concepts are usually not even identified; in interpretive theory, a concept may be identified and described as well as the focus of the phenomenological study, but the concept itself will not be developed. In disclosive theory, concepts will be identified and the antecedents and consequences also described—as linkages explaining the process, steps, or phases. Finally, in explanatory theory, the complexity of the theory is evident. Multiple concepts and constructs are linked to provide a comprehensive explanatory model of a complex phenomenon. Thus the attributes of the concept may be identified by interpretive theory, but conceptual linkages are not identified until disclosive theory. In explanatory theory, the number of concepts has increased, and the strength of the linkages are clearly elaborated.

Qualitative work is highly theoretical, and it is this aspect that enables the phenomena to be generalized.[11] However, the researcher must separate theory from data and the process of analysis, and also separate the process of inductive from deductive thought, and, as van der Steen (1993) advises, clearly separate empirical from theoretical statements.

Coherence. Qualitative theory must be coherent. Micro-macro linkages must be plausible, solid, and explicit. Inferences derived from the data must be described clearly and be obvious to the reader. Note that this notion differs from an "audit trail," which illustrates the development of analysis including discarded notions. Rather, interpretative linkages are presented as a final analysis and the theory as an end result.

Reality is complicated. Yet qualitative theory, like quantitative theory, should be consistent. As reality may consist of paradoxes and ambiguities, such factors must not be simplified in qualitative theory, but accepted and explained. This function of theory makes reality comprehensible and systematic. In the process, terms must be used consistently and be clearly defined and described. Glaser's (1978) criteria of fit—the fit of the data with the categories—must be evident.

Scope. In descriptive theory, scope simply cannot expand. Description remains pertinent only to the setting that it describes, and this setting must be delineated clearly. In descriptive studies, we need to know what kind of institution, which participants, and which questions were asked.

Interpretive studies are more abstract, but the scope is generally limited to a single phenomenon or concept. In disclosive theory, the scope increases to encompass a process—then, again, this is delineated. Although explanatory theory uses scope in its broadest capacity, the boundaries are still specified. The reader knows how the researcher specified inclusion-exclusion, what was ignored and what was emphasized, and how and why the theory was focused.

Generalizability. It is the level of abstraction reached, the quality of the interpretation, and the use of concepts and principles of abstraction that make the theory generalizable. In the process of abstraction, the analysis deconstructs data, isolating the essential and central features. Generalizability is obtained when the theory is recontextualized to another setting. With interpretive theory (for example, phenomenology), this is achieved by reflecting on the phenomenological literature and other sources describing similar experiences. In disclosive theory, the use of the theoretical scheme and Glaser's criterion of "Does it work?" as a framework both for research and for practice is important.

Pragmatic utility. As Glaser notes, "The theory must work." For researchers, the theory must extend inquiry and, as a result, be modifiable. For practitioners, it must "make sense" and be useful in practice. The use of abstract concepts in practice is difficult, and the theory must provide an adequate linkage to make such concepts relevant for use in the clinical setting. The researcher must bear some of the responsibility by making recommendations explicit for practice.

Discussion

Recall that *QualDT* is aimed at providing understanding, not prediction (Dubin, 1978). For this reason, the highest level of theory derived from qualitative research provides explanation. Future work on *QualDT* needs to address issues of prediction and to what extent, if any, the theory is able to predict. For example, does qualitative theory predict clinical outcomes? Geertz (1973), in part, answers this question. Regarding the example of clinical inference, he notes: "Cultural anthropology is not in the strictest meaning of the term, predictive. The diagnostician doesn't predict measles; he decides that someone has them, or at the very most *anticipates that* someone is rather likely to get them in the short term" (p. 26). He notes that this limitation does not mean that "interpretation is *post facto.*" However, it is not the primary use of *QualDT*. It does not mean that it "can only generate cogent interpretation of realities past," but it "also has to survive—intellectually survive—realities to come" (p. 26). Clearly, if we cannot label such "realities to come" as prediction, then there is a need for new language to describe these other characteristics of theory. Such precision may reduce some of the debate surrounding this issue.

At present, quantitative criteria (for example, those suggested by Whall, 1996) are being used to evaluate *QualDT*. The criteria for evaluating qualitative theory presented in this chapter are intended to replace quantitative criteria for evaluating qualitative work. However, at this time, they are not intended to be used as a gold standard by reviewers in the course of reviewing a journal article submitted for publication, although, over time, as the criteria become more accepted, this may become a more realistic aim. Rather, these criteria are intended to be used as a guide for qualitative researchers considering how to improve the structure of their own work, and are intended to draw the strength of qualitative inquiry to the attention of others.

It is important to note that *testability* is not a criterion for *QualDT*, and indeed it is this aspect that differs most from the quantitative criteria. The plain statement that it is not necessary to test *QualDT* may be controversial. However, this researcher could not find an instance where *QualDT* was tested, but there are many instances of implementation without testing. As late as 1992, Glaser noted that "if extant grounded theory needs to be verified, it would be done by researchers using rigorous methods of verification to test a few of its central hypotheses around which the core category is integrated" (p. 117). Two points are interesting about such a statement: (a) It is astonishing that Glaser himself has not questioned the long-standing assumption that grounded theory may need to be tested, and (b) he does not conceive it as possible that the model may be tested as a whole. Testing "a few central hypotheses" is not a very efficient or fair means to test a theory, for it reduces it from its comprehensive whole to small pieces. If qualitative work has preceded quantitative, the quantitative phase has generally not been for the purposes of testing but, instead, to extend investigation, using sequential triangulation. For instance, early qualitative work on adolescents' responses to menarche (Morse & Doan, 1987) was followed by a series of studies including the use of the qualitative data for Likert scale development and the establishment of normative attitudes toward menarche (for example, see Morse & Kieren, 1993; Morse, Kieren, & Bottorff, 1993).

Finally, it is necessary to reiterate that theory is not reality but a representation of reality. Its existence, as Geertz (1973) points out in his important example about anthropological knowledge not being in the real world, is in a book, representative of the world, in the archives of the discipline. It is the transformation of behavior, the interpretation, *the theory*, that is created. And if we did not have to *create* theory—if it already existed as an entity in the world—we would be unemployed. There would be no mystery, no interpretation, and no excitement to the puzzle of life.

Notes

1. For a discussion of the assumption that qualitative research is a preliminary step to quantitative inquiry, see Smith (1983, p. xiv).

2. However, I disagree with Suppe (1996) that a characteristic of qualitative middle-range theory is that it be objectively codable, so that the ultimate goal is measurement. Such a requirement then excludes all interpretive inquiry from middle-range theory, ignores the derivation, and denies the strength of qualitative inquiry.

3. Theory in quantitative research is derived by processes of creative formation, systematic testing, and subsequent modification.

4. Note that in this chapter we are only considering theory as it guides or is directly obtained from research. Sandelowski (1993) describes other uses of theory in research: as it is used as an interpretive framework or constitutes disciplinary assumptions and formulations that target inquiry. (See also the discussion by Steeves et al., 1996.)

5. For an excellent discussion of the debate between Glaser and Strauss and Merton on this topic, see Smith (1983).

6. Glaser (1992) responds to Strauss's comment on the replicability of grounded theory by noting that "no grounded theorist would waste his time trying [to replicate]" (p. 117).

7. Elsewhere (Morse, 1994), I have argued that it is this point, plus the additional knowledge that the investigator has about the data, that leads to interpretation and insight. Individual characteristics of the investigator lead to creative interpretation of data and provide justification for not using multiple coders and interrater reliability measures when analyzing unstructured data.

8. It is beyond the scope of this chapter to review criteria for the trustworthiness of qualitative research. A recent review of such criteria is presented by Lincoln (1995).

9. Schwandt (1993) notes that atheoretical research is impossible, and it's naive to think it can be achieved.

10. Glaser (1978) correctly notes that such factors must *earn* their way into the model.

11. Silverman (1989) provides an excellent example of the generalization of a case study using theory.

References

Agar, M. (1983). Inference and schema: An ethnographic view. *Human Studies, 6*, 53-66.

Blumer, H. (1970). What is wrong with social theory? In W. J. Filstead (Ed.), *Qualitative methodology: Firsthand involvement with the social world* (pp. 52-63). Chicago: Rand McNally College.

Bulmer, M. (1979). Concepts in the analysis of qualitative data. *Sociological Review, 27*, 651-677.

Burton, A. (Ed.). (1974). *Operational theories of personality.* New York: Brunner/Mazel.

Dubin, R. (1978). *Theory building* (2nd ed.). New York: Free Press.

Fawcett, J. (1993). *Analysis and evaluation of nursing theories.* Philadelphia: F. A. Davis.

Flinders, D. J., & Mills, G. E. (1993). *Theory and concepts in qualitative research.* New York: Teachers College Press.

Geertz, C. (1973). *The interpretation of cultures.* New York: Basic Books.

Glaser, B. G. (1978). *Advances in the methodology of grounded theory: Theoretical sensitivity.* Mill Valley, CA: Sociology Press.

Glaser, B. G. (1992). *Emergence vs forcing: Basics of grounded theory analysis.* Mill Valley, CA: Sociology Press.

Glaser, B. G., & Strauss, A. L. (1967). *The discovery of grounded theory.* New York: Aldine.

Kaplan, A. (1964). *The conduct of inquiry.* New York: Harper & Row.

Lenz, E. R. (1996, May). Role of middle range theory for research and practice. In *Proceedings of the Annual Rosemary Ellis Scholars Retreat* (pp. 78-116). Cleveland, OH: Case Western Reserve University.

Lincoln, Y. S. (1995). Emerging criteria for quality in qualitative and interpretative research. *Qualitative Inquiry, 1*(3), 275-289.

Maxwell, J. A. (1996). *Qualitative research design: An interpretive approach.* Thousand Oaks, CA: Sage.

Merton, R. K. (1967). *On theoretical sociology.* New York: Free Press.

Miles, M. B., & Huberman, A. M. (1994). *Qualitative data analysis.* Thousand Oaks, CA: Sage.

Morse, J. M. (1991). Approaches to qualitative-quantitative methodological triangulation. *Nursing Research, 40*(2), 120-123.

Morse, J. M. (1992). If you believe in theories . . . *Qualitative Health Research, 2*(3), 259-261.

Morse, J. M. (1994). "Emerging from the data": The cognitive processes of analysis in qualitative inquiry. In J. M. Morse (Ed.), *Critical issues in qualitative research methods* (pp. 23-43). Thousand Oaks, CA: Sage.

Morse, J. M. (1996). Nursing theory: Sense and sensibility. *Nursing Inquiry, 3*, 74-82.

Morse, J. M., Bottorff, J. L., & Hutchinson, S. (1994). The phenomenology of comfort. *Journal of Advanced Nursing, 20*, 189-195.

Morse, J. M., & Carter, B. J. (1995). Strategies of enduring and the suffering of loss: Modes of comfort used by a resilient survivor. *Holistic Nursing Practice, 9*(3), 33-58.

Morse, J. M., & Carter, B. (1996). The essence of enduring and the expression of suffering: The reformulation of self. *Scholarly Inquiry for Nursing Practice, 10*(1), 43-60.

Morse, J. M., & Doan, H. M. (1987). Growing up at school: Adolescents' response to menarche. *Journal of School Health, 57*(9), 385-389.

Morse, J. M., & Doberneck, B. M. (1995). Delineating the concept of hope. *IMAGE: Journal of Nursing Scholarship, 27*(4), 277-285.

Morse, J. M., Havens, G. D., & Wilson, S. (in review). The comforting interaction: Developing a model of nurse-patient interaction. *Advances in Nursing Science.*

Morse, J. M., Hupcey, J., Mitcham, C., & Lenz, E. (1996). Concept analysis in nursing research: A critical appraisal. *Scholarly Inquiry for Nursing Practice, 10,* 257-281.

Morse, J. M., & Johnson, J. L. (Eds.). (1991). *The illness experience: Dimensions of suffering.* Newbury Park, CA: Sage.

Morse, J. M., & Kieren, D. (1993). The Adolescent Menstrual Attitude Questionnaire, Part II: Normative scores. *Health Care for Women International, 14,* 63-76.

Morse, J. M., Kieren, D., & Bottorff, J. L. (1993). The Adolescent Menstrual Attitude Questionnaire, I: Scale construction. *Health Care for Women International, 14,* 39-62.

Morse, J. M., & Penrod, J. (in review). *Theoretical integration: Linking concepts of enduring, suffering, and hope.*

Proctor, A., & Morse, J. M. (1996). Sounds of comfort in the trauma center: How nurses talk to patients in pain. *Social Sciences & Medicine., 42*(12), 1669-1680.

Sandelowski, M. (1993). Theory unmasked: The uses and guises of theory in qualitative research. *Research in Nursing & Health, 16,* 213-218.

Schwandt, T. A. (1993). Theory for the moral sciences: Crisis in identity and purpose. In D. J. Flinders & G. E. Mills (Eds.), *Theory and concepts in qualitative research: Perspectives from the field* (pp. 5-23). New York: Teachers College Press.

Silva, M. C., & Rothbart, D. (1983). An analysis of changing trends in philosophies of science on nursing theory development and testing. *Advances in Nursing Science, 6,* 1-13.

Silva, M. C., & Sorrell, J. M. (1992). Testing nursing theory: Critique and philosophical method. *Advances in Nursing Science, 14,* 12-23.

Silverman, D. (1989). Telling convincing stories: A plea for cautious positivism in case-studies. In R. S. Cohen (Series Ed.), B. Glaser & J. D. Moreno (Vol. Eds.), *The qualitative-quantitative distinction in the social sciences* (Vol. 112, pp. 57-77). Dordrecht, the Netherlands: Kluwer Academic.

Smith, R. B. (1983). Cumulative social sciences: Paradigms, social research, and formal theorizing. In R. B. Smith (Ed.), *An introduction to social research: A handbook of social science methods* (Vol. 1, pp. 18-56). Cambridge, MA: Ballinger.

Steeves, R. H., Kahn, D. L., & Cohen, M. Z. (1996). Asking substantive theory questions of naturalistically derived data. *Western Journal of Nursing Research, 18*(2), 209-212.

Suppe, F. (1996, May). Middle-range theory and knowledge development. In *Proceedings of the Annual Rosemary Ellis Scholars Retreat.* Cleveland, OH: Case Western Reserve University.

van der Steen, W. J. (1993). *A practical philosophy for the life sciences*. Albany: State University of New York Press.

van Manen, M. (1991). *The tact of teaching: The meaning of pedagogical thoughtfulness*. Albany: State University of New York.

Whall, A. L. (1996). The structure of nursing knowledge: Analysis and evaluation of practice, middle-range, and grand theory. In J. J. Fitzpatrick & A. L. Whall (Eds.), *Conceptual models of nursing* (3rd ed., pp. 13-25). Stanford, CT: Appleton & Lange.

White, L. A. (1938). Science is sciencing. *Philosophy of Science, 5*(4), 369-389.

Dialogue: Generalizability

Boyle: You know, I was intrigued with the idea that we are even using the word "generalizability" because a few years ago it was a real "no-no!" in qualitative research, and we didn't use it. We talked about "confirmability" or "transferability."

Stern: Merton said you could! It's fascinating that we are using it again—

10

Generalizability in Qualitative Research

Excavating the Discourse

Joy L. Johnson

eneralizability typically has been held to refer to the extent to which research findings can be applied across, and are considered relevant to, different persons, settings, and times. The question of generalizability is a particularly problematic issue for qualitative researchers because discussions about generalizability are informed by epistemological standpoint, methodological preference, and discipline. It has been widely held that qualitative research is inherently ungeneralizable or that the term *generalizability* is not appropriately applied to qualitative methods. Accordingly, there are multiple lines of argument concerning the question of generalizability. Most recently, authors grounding their work in the postmodern perspective have raised serious questions about the very future of science (Kiziltan, Bain, & Canizares, 1990). An antifoundational era characterized by the loss of certainty and absolute frames of reference has emerged and with it new methods and new concerns regarding generalizability have been added to the discourse (Fine, 1986).

Tracing the lines of argument that have been put forward regarding generalizability in qualitative research is much like untangling a ball of yarn—with every knot untangled, another one appears. Despite the difficulty, this endeavor is worthwhile because from each line of argument we can gain valuable insights regarding the dimensions of generalizability, particularly as they apply to qualitative research. In this chapter, I examine the discourse that has emerged concerning generalizability in qualitative research. I proceed by considering six lines of argument that are prominent in the discourse with particular attention paid to the implications of these arguments.

The Qualitative-Quantitative Divide

Without a doubt, there is a fundamental opposition between the so-called *qualitative* and *quantitative* paradigms. From a semiotic standpoint, it is clear that the two terms are reciprocally defined: Each must refer, at least implicitly, to the other to establish its own meaning (Morrow, 1994). We see this contrast exemplified in discussions of generalizability in which claims regarding the generalizability of qualitative research are developed in reaction to those claims raised by quantitative researchers. This approach is not surprising given the dominance of quantitative approaches and the fact that the notion of generalizability was developed in relation to probability sampling techniques. The first line of argument to be considered focuses on how issues of generalizability in qualitative research have been contrasted with those claims made in relation to quantitative research. Qualitative researchers have tended to align themselves either with traditional approaches to generalizability or with new approaches that diverge from the aims and methods of traditional approaches. What unifies this line of argument is that positions have been developed in response to "traditional" quantitative approaches to generalizability.

It is interesting that qualitative researchers have tended to accord the procedures for establishing generalizability within the quantitative tradition more credence than they deserve, and more credence than many theorists consider appropriate. For example, in the following quotation, Guba (1981) implies that quantitative researchers assume they can achieve definitive results.

Within the rationalistic paradigm, applicability—external validity or generalizability—requires that the inquiry be conducted in ways that make chronological and situational variations irrelevant to the findings. If that condition can be met, the findings obviously will have relevance in any context. (Guba, 1981, p. 80)

Yet the notion that researchers of the rationalistic (read: quantitative) paradigm uncover findings that are relevant across all contexts is incongruent with the skepticism inherent in the approaches to scientific knowledge development described by Popper (1965) and other postpositivists. Popper recognized the theory-ladenness of facts and the limits of formal logic, and because of this, he grounded science in its general critical method—its fallibility. Consequently, scientific theorists were forced to back off claims about absolute eternal truths, because it was recognized that whatever we hold to be true today could be falsified tomorrow.

In light of the tendency to accord more credence than warranted to quantitative procedures for establishing generalizability, it is instructive to consider the origins of generalizability. The notion of generalizability that underlies quantitative research appears to rest on three assumptions embodied in conventional sampling theory: (a) Nature is uniform; (b) closed populations can be unambiguously defined; and (c) the defining characteristics of a population are shared by its members. Obviously these assumptions are easily violated and add to the complexity of making generalizations from quantitative work. It is important to note that making a generalization is an inferential process that involves making broad statements based on limited information. Such inference is a necessary part of the scientific process because all members of a defined population cannot be studied in all settings at all times. Hume's (1977/1748) truism that induction or generalization is never fully justified comes to mind and reminds us of the limits of generalizability. This truism was acknowledged by Campbell and Stanley (1963), recognized experts on generalizability in the social sciences, who conceded that the problems of generalizability are not solvable in any neat conclusive way. This is not to say that many quantitative researchers do not assume that generalizability is simply a matter of properly applying the rules of experimental design. But as Christensen (1994) pointed out, it is erroneous to draw conclusions about generalizability by simply summing up the threats to validity inherent in a design.

When contrasting qualitative and quantitative research, it is important that we not submit to the temptation to argue that quantitative researchers do not recognize the limits of their own science. It is all too easy to discount quantitative work on these grounds, thereby avoiding what might be fruitful discussions about the nature of generalizability. It is also essential that qualitative researchers not succumb to the temptation to mimic what some quantitative researchers have passed off as rules for developing generalizable findings. Such rules inevitably promise more than they can deliver.

There is evidence that at least some qualitative researchers do succumb to the temptation to use a set of rules or procedures to approach the question of generalizability. Sandelowski's (1986) work on rigor in qualitative research is probably the most widely cited work among nurses conducting qualitative research. Her work's appeal can be attributed partly to the fact that it has been interpreted by others as a set of procedures for obtaining rigorous and generalizable findings in qualitative research. It is easier to invoke a set of criteria than to seriously contemplate the strengths and limitations of one's findings. It is clear, however, that no such set of criteria exists. As Sandelowski (1986, 1993a, 1995) herself suggests, we must value the tension in qualitative research between the empirical and the aesthetic. To invoke a set of rules will only serve to destroy what is valuable in qualitative research.

Generalizability is not something that occurs when one follows a set of prescribed rules. Indeed, Ratcliffe (1983) correctly pointed out that unwavering adherence to a particular set of validity rules can bias the research process (regardless of the method employed) and can affect the outcome because one system of inquiry will not generate valid information across all classes of problems. Sandelowski (1993a) also cautions researchers that the rigid application of rules in general may inhibit or hinder researchers' sensitivity to a particular problem. The opposition that has developed between qualitative and quantitative approaches to generalizability is not necessarily warranted. It is clear that there is no easy solution to the problem of generalizability and that neither quantitative nor qualitative researchers should claim they have resolved the issue through a set of codified procedures.

The Relevance of Generalizability

The second line of argument to be considered concerns the relevance of generalizability. For some qualitative researchers, questions of generalizability are seen as irrelevant. "Naturalists eschew generalizations on the grounds that virtually all social/behavioral phenomena are context bound" (Guba, 1981, p. 86). Generalizability simply is ignored or dismissed as an oppressive, positivistic concept that hampers creative and emancipatory qualitative research. Generalizability, or external validity, is viewed as an evaluation criterion that is relevant only to quantitative work. Those who hold this position argue that generalizability as an evaluation criterion is nothing more than a socially constructed judgment and any attempt to discuss these judgments is futile. Ratcliffe (1983), for example, maintained that any rules purporting to guarantee generalizability ought not to be taken to represent reality. He claimed that such rules serve human purposes, are therefore normative, and simply prove we are "playing by the current rules" (p. 159). This seems to be a legitimate response to the codification of procedures for ensuring generalizability in quantitative research. Schofield (1990) maintains that one factor contributing to qualitative researchers' historical tendency to reject generalizability has been their close alignment with anthropology, with its focus on the study of unique cultures. "For researchers doing work of this sort, the goal is to describe a specific group in fine detail and to explain the patterns that exist, certainly not to discover general laws of human behavior" (p. 202).

Another related claim raised against generalizability as a legitimate concern for qualitative research concerns its dependence on abstraction and, consequently, its removal from context and individual experience. Lincoln and Guba (1985) argued that to generalize one must develop abstract theories, yet abstractions are not well grounded in what informants experience and think. Glaser and Strauss (1967) also recognized this dilemma and argued that it is for this reason that the researcher must, when collecting data, accumulate a diversity of experiences so that the emerging categories are sufficiently grounded in the everyday experiences of the informants. Schütz (1963) expressed this as a process of moving from the subjective contexts of everyday life to the objective contexts of social science. Similarly, Morse (this volume) maintains that broadly generalizable theory must be incrementally constructed from descriptive theories.

The potential discontinuity between the abstract and the particular was recognized by Douglas (1971), who maintained that the tension between situational and transsituational aspects of human existence is mirrored in the tension between the need to retain the integrity of the phenomenon and the need to produce useful knowledge about everyday life. The aim of the researcher is ultimately to make links, or to help the reader make links, between what he or she has observed in one situation and what is occurring in other situations. We engage in qualitative inquiry so that what we learn will be used or applied in other settings. In this light, questions of generalizability are highly relevant in that they bear directly on how research findings can be applied across individuals, settings, and time. The line of argument concerning the relevance of generalizability is instructive, however, in that it reminds us that what we gain in broad generalizability we often sacrifice in context and detail. In addition, the skepticism about generalizability claims is warranted, in that studies often have been judged solely on their ability to support sweeping generalizations. To reject the dogmatism that has been associated with generalizability claims is essential; to land on ground that supports total skepticism offers no alternative. Somehow we must move beyond this polarization and consider what is generalizable in qualitative research.

Reframing Generalizability

Rather than refuting the relevance of generalizability, some theorists have attempted to reframe or reconsider the question of generalizability by casting it in a new light. Guba (1981), for example, argued that traditional notions of generalizability rely on context-stripping techniques and are not applicable to qualitative methods. He recast the notion of generalizability by using the ordinary language term *trans-*

ferability. According to Guba, application or transfer of knowledge can occur across settings when one knows a great deal about both the transferring context and the receiving context. The transfer of knowledge is facilitated by what Geertz (1973) referred to as "thick description." If thick description demonstrates an essential similarity between two contexts, then, Guba argued, it is reasonable to hold that the findings of context A are likely to hold in context B. In a similar manner, LeCompte and Goetz (1982) adapted the concept of external validity to the case of ethnographic research. They argued that, in relation to generalizability, the challenge for ethnographers is to demonstrate either the typicality of a phenomenon or the extent to which it compares and contrasts with other relevant phenomena.

Lather (1993) radically reconsidered generalizability using a feminist, poststructural framework. She argued that validity is a notion that is becoming obsolete in the postmodern era, and addressed validity as an incitement to discourse, a fertile obsession, and used the postmodern problematic to reframe it. The frames of validity she discussed include ironic, paralogical, rhizomatic, and voluptuous. Rather than being focused on the traditional question of how findings apply across person, place, and time, she maintains that these frames help the reader to "think the unthought" or "see the unseeable." Parologic validity, for example, is aimed at refining our sensitivity to difference and reinforcing our ability to tolerate the incommensurable. Rather than seeking closure or claiming that the findings are saturated, this move is toward legitimizing heterogeneity and refusing closure. Rather than getting the story "right," paralogic validity is aimed at presenting "fruitful interruptions" that demonstrate a multiplicity of interpretations.

The problem with reinventing notions of generalizability is that it creates confusing terminology, and, as a result, discussions of generalizability are often obfuscated. Consider the following comment by Leininger (1994) in which she both rejects and affirms generalizability: "Because the goal of qualitative research is not to produce generalizations, but rather in depth understandings and knowledge of particular phenomena, the transferability criterion focuses on general similarities of findings under similar environmental conditions, contexts, or circumstances" (p. 107).

How do general similarities differ from generalizations? The difficulty qualitative researchers have in clearly specifying what is generalizable in their work is a threat to the credibility and advancement of qualitative research. If qualitative researchers cannot clearly specify the kinds of claims that can be based on their work, they will have difficulty convincing funding agencies, reviewers, and others of the merits of their approaches.

Sandelowski (in press) suggests that, rather than invent terms to describe the notions of generalizability inherent in qualitative work, we should reclaim the term *generalizability* for qualitative inquiry. She maintains that the retention and use of *generalizability* will help to keep at the forefront the problems that have caused many of us to consider abandoning the term. In addition, reclaiming the term will allow us to broaden our vision of generalizability.

The line of argument concerned with reframing generalizability raises serious questions about the nature and scope of generalizations, and reminds us that the goals of qualitative studies may differ from those of quantitative studies. It is not always clear, however, how the reframed discourse is distinct from traditional discourses on generalizability. In addition, as will be discussed in a subsequent section, the reframing of the generalizability question in qualitative terms tends to ignore distinctions among qualitative methods themselves.

Concepts of Truth and Generalizability

The issue of generalizability is often seen as a question of validity or representativeness. Three classical criteria of truth may be useful to consider here: correspondence, coherence, and pragmatic utility. The correspondence criterion of truth concerns whether a knowledge statement corresponds to the objective world. The coherence criterion refers to the consistency and internal logic of a statement. And the pragmatic criterion relates the truth of a knowledge claim to its practical consequences (Pollock, 1986). Although these three criteria are not necessarily mutually exclusive, different disciplines and philosophical traditions have tended to emphasize one over the other. The position one holds regarding the nature of "truth" has implications for how one conceptualizes generalizability. Those who subscribe to correspondence theories are concerned with whether qualitative researchers have adequately captured the nature of the phenomenon under study. Those who subscribe to coherence theories are concerned with how theories fit with existing social constructs and theories. Pragmatists' measure of generalizability is focused on whether findings offer solutions to problems or issues.

Although qualitative research most often is associated with a coherence or pragmatic view, the discourse on qualitative methods reveals that all three philosophical views of truth underlie qualitative researchers' thinking. Although many qualitative researchers fervently reject correspondence theory, we frequently note a concern about getting the story "right" and capturing the variation of a phenomenon. For example, Streubert and Carpenter (1995) maintain that "the new generation researcher assures that the representation is true by being immersed in the setting for a long period" (p. 265). Methodological procedures such as immersion in the setting seem to betray a concern about getting at the underlying nature of a phenomenon, a notion that is very much in line with correspondence theories of truth.

In contrast, implicit in concerns for description of context and for how findings of a qualitative study "fit the data" and fit with other theories, we note a conceptualization of truth as coherence. Findings that do not fit existing theories, or data that do not fit emerging theory, challenge us to continue to theorize. Similarly, "negative cases" challenge us to reconsider and extend emerging theories. It is the need for coherence that prompts qualitative researchers to continue to collect data and to theorize in the face of recalcitrant data. It is this sense of coherence that prompted Eisner (1991) to claim that the aim of qualitative work is consensual validation in which there is agreement among competent critiquers about the qualitative description and interpretation of a situation. Underlying this approach is the view that so-called objectivity is based on the premise that "we believe in what we believe in and others share our beliefs as well" (Eisner, 1979, p. 214).

Finally, underlying emancipatory forms of inquiry such as critical theory and participatory research, we find a philosophical vision of pragmatic truth. According to this vision, the truth is what is discovered to work in a given context. The effectiveness of our knowledge and understanding is demonstrated by the effectiveness of our actions.

Kvale (1995) points out that with pragmatic validation of a knowledge claim, justification is superseded by action. Accordingly, research becomes a means for solving problems and transforming cultures. It is clear that different conceptualizations of truth will lead to different criteria for making judgments about generalizability. Mishler (1990) pointed out that different communities of researchers use different criteria to warrant and evaluate scientific worthiness. Often within the debate, these three views of truth are pitted against one another. Yet, depending on the research question being considered and qualitative method employed, one might need to invoke a different criterion or use these criteria in a different combination. This is not to say that one's epistemology is informed by method but to point out that there are vital links between epistemology, method, and criteria for generalizability.

Horizontal Generalizability
Versus Vertical Generalizability

Stephens (1982) reminded us that those who tie claims of generalizability to quantitative sampling theory have narrowly defined the notion of generalizability. He makes a distinction between *horizontal generalization*, which is based on the claim that, if the same sampling procedures were performed on another sample from the same population, one would expect to have one's findings repeated, and *vertical generalization*, in which features of a situation are linked to more abstract and general considerations. Vertical generalizability is directed toward building interpretive theory, whereas horizontal generalizability is directed toward demonstrating that findings are applicable across settings.

Although it might be claimed that much of qualitative research does not possess horizontal generalizability, it is rich in its ability to illuminate existing theory. This notion of vertical generalization is similar to what Steeves, Kahn, and Cohen (1996) refer to as a second level of analysis in qualitative work in which one considers how the findings of a qualitative study contribute to the development of substantive theory. By "substantive theory," they mean theories that consist of formalized language describing the nature of ideas such as coping, uncertainty, hardiness, learned helplessness, and the like. Vertical generalization is accomplished by considering the texts generated by qualitative research and asking questions that will lead to insights regarding substantive theory. Morse (1992) similarly argued that the generalizability of a study is facilitated when links are made with the work of others. These links can emphasize either similarities or differences. Morse maintains that the generalizability of findings is enhanced when support for one's findings are located in existing theory. Likewise, Sandelowski (1993b) pointed out that a form of triangulation occurs when theory produced "in situ" is compared with established theories concerning a target population.

Schofield (1990) points out that in contrast to techniques that are aimed at improving the generalizability of a particular study, there are emerging techniques such as case study survey methods (Yin & Heald, 1975), qualitative comparative methods (Ragin, 1987), and meta-ethnography (Noblitt & Hare, 1988) that aggregate, compare, and contrast existing studies. The aim of these techniques is to enhance generalizability through the aggregation of the findings of independent studies.

The discussion about horizontal and vertical generalizability is instructive in that it underscores the multidimensionality of generalizability. In the following section, I expand on this notion of multidimensionality by considering whether there are other dimensions to generalizability.

Is the Choice of Qualitative Method Relevant to Generalizability Claims?

The distinction between qualitative and quantitative approaches has been based largely on distinctions between techniques for data collection and analysis, rather than the aim of the research. Rather than framing the argument on two different kinds of techniques (qualitative or quantitative), it is perhaps more appropriate to consider whether research is directed toward nomothetic explanations or idiographic interpretations. The idiographic approach assumes a unique case or limited set of cases as the unit of analysis, and is primarily concerned with interpretation and meaning. In contrast, a nomothetic focuses on more representative samples and the degree to which findings are representative of a particular sample, and is concerned with explanation (Morrow, 1994). Morse (this volume) makes a similar distinction between studies that are pretheoretical and whose purpose is to describe and enlighten, and those that are theoretical and whose purpose is to reveal or explain.

Underlying the distinction between the nomothetic and the idiographic are different ways we come to know and use knowledge. We generalize in a variety of ways: through formal inference, through attribute analysis, and through image matching (Eisner, 1991). Underlying nomothetic explanation is the use of formal inference, while idiographic interpretation relies on the ability of the reader to recognize attributes and match images. It follows that the claims one may make about generalizability, and the ways one might assess such claims, will differ if the research is directed at idiographic interpretation or nomothetic explanation. Contrary to this conclusion, the discourse related to generalizability within qualitative methods has tended to be generic in nature with various claims applied across qualitative approaches. There has been little acknowledgment that within the qualitative "paradigm," there are some approaches directed primarily toward idiographic interpretations (e.g., phenomenology) and others directed toward nomothetic explanations (e.g., grounded theory).

In that idiographic work is aimed at enriching understanding, enlarging insight, and capturing new possibilities, it seems wrongheaded to consider how findings might apply across persons and settings. Rather, what is of concern is how the research opens up new possibilities, or helps the reader to see things in new ways. In his discussion of phenomenology, van Manen (1990) recognizes this point when he acknowledges that phenomenological work is not directed toward general explanation but is directed toward the unique and the particular. He argues that through description of the particular, researchers provide readers with new insight, thereby enhancing thoughtful tactfulness. The phenomenological study does this by encouraging attentive awareness on the part of the reader.

It is through rich descriptions of the particular that some of the most profound insights might be gained. The idiographic explanation helps the reader move beyond *knowing* to *understanding* (Vendler,

1984). Seeking traditional broad forms of generalizability can lure the researcher to attend to facts capable of verification rather than stories that can convey meaning (Wolcott, 1994). It is for this reason that Wolcott considers himself an "anticomparativist," arguing that much can be learned from the single case. He recognized that the temptation to seek comparisons can rob a study of its unique insights. Eisner (1991) described the use of the particular to say something about the universal as "the concrete universal." Like Wolcott, Eisner recognized that through stories, pictures, and precepts, we can and do learn from the experiences of others. These "lessons" learned constitute a form of generalizability.

In contrast to idiographic approaches, some qualitative approaches are aimed at nomothetic explanation. In the case of grounded theory, the method is directed toward explaining the social and psychological processes that underlie a given experience. Grounded theorists are prompted to stretch and enrich the emerging theory through the consideration of negative cases and the use of theoretical sampling. The end product is a rich explanation of how individuals manage or cope with particular situations, problems, or transitions. The theory, if it has been developed in a rigorous manner, is applicable across numerous kinds of persons and contexts.

It is clear that different qualitative approaches are aimed at developing different kinds of knowledge. It is, therefore, inappropriate to assume that it is possible to develop a generic set of procedures for enhancing generalizability across all forms of qualitative research. If qualitative methods are to have a clear and convincing rationale, we must clarify the bases on which claims regarding the general relevance of findings are made, and we must develop practices that are congruent with those claims. In adopting an approach for use, researchers are buying into a set of choices with far-reaching implications. No one approach or strategy, and its accompanying choices, provides a perfect solution for the researcher; there is no ideal way to gain knowledge of the social world. All approaches and strategies involve assumptions, judgments, and compromises; all are claimed to have deficiencies. The challenge for researchers is to be aware of those deficiencies, to use techniques that limit them, and to refrain from making claims that extend beyond the purview of the research study.

Responsibility for Generalizability

A final line of argument to be considered concerns whether the responsibility for establishing generalizability lies with researchers or consumers of research. Some theorists maintain that generalizability rests with potential users of findings and not with researchers (Greene, 1990; Lincoln & Guba, 1985). Others maintain that researchers have a responsibility to consider how their findings may or may not be generalizable to other settings and groups. For example, Hammersley (1992) claims that the researcher must present evidence about the likely typicality of cases that are studied and must assess and present evidence about the validity of generalizations.

It seems misdirected to conclude that generalizability is up to either the user or the generator of research findings. It is all too easy to shift the responsibility for determining the relevance of findings to others. One major strength of qualitative research is its ability to expand the discourse concerning health issues among researchers, clinicians, consumers, and policymakers. All of these groups have a role to play in considering the relevance and utility of research findings. Benner (1994), for example, claims that interpretive phenomenology has a role to play in public policy by its power to make the concerns, voices, habits, and practices of people visible. It was perhaps recognition of the need to engage in a discourse about generalizability that prompted Geertz (1973) to claim that ethnographic research is aimed at increasing "the precision through which we vex each other" (p. 29). The researcher, practitioner, and consumer are all involved in mutual inquiry. The generalizability of much qualitative research is not located in *truth* per se but in its ability to refine perception and deepen conversation (Eisner, 1991).

No theory, no matter how it is derived, will be applicable to all situations in all contexts. For practitioners who are concerned with individuals, not aggregates, qualitative research is particularly useful because it can suggest possibilities and does not purport to dictate action (Donmoyer, 1990). Ultimately, questions of how qualitative findings are used to inform practice or policy rest with those who consider the findings. Glaser and Strauss (1967) remind us that theories must be tailored as they are used in practice:

The person who applies theory will, we believe, be able to bend, adjust or quickly reformulate a grounded theory when applying it, as he tries to keep up with and manage the situational realities that he wishes to improve. For example, nurses will be better able to cope with family and patients during sudden transitions from a closed context to one of pretense or open awareness if they try to apply elements of our awareness theory, continually adjusting the theory in application. (Glaser & Strauss, 1967, p. 242)

Both researchers and consumers of research play an essential role in the process of making generalizability claims in relation to qualitative research. It is for the researcher to be clear about the aim of the study, to defend the work, to consider its strengths and limitations, to relate the emerging findings to established theory, and, if appropriate, to speculate about how the findings may apply across settings, persons, and time. It is up to consumers of research to judge these claims, to weigh the findings' applicability in relation to their own practice or life situation, and, if new insights are obtained, to use these insights appropriately.

Conclusion

The question of generalizability is complex. From the lines of argument presented above, several suggestions for approaching the question of generalizability emerge. This chapter concludes by highlighting key suggestions.

1. Slavish application of rules of rigor will not necessarily lead to quality research. Ultimately, generalizability cannot be achieved by following a recipe.

2. If you are tempted to ignore the issue of generalizability, think again; perhaps you have defined generalizability too narrowly.

3. Sort out your epistemological position regarding knowledge development. Ultimately, decisions regarding generalizability must rest on these assumptions. Shifting assumptions may lead to indefensible work.

4. Thick description aids generalizability. Understanding the context in which a theory or insight arises helps the reader to make judgments about whether the findings fit similar contexts.

5. Enhance vertical generalizability by making links between findings and established substantive theory.

6. Be clear about the goal of the inquiry. Ask, is the study aimed at developing idiographic interpretation or nomothetic explanation? The way that issues of generalizability apply to a given study will depend on the nature and object of the inquiry.

7. Think of generalizability as a shared responsibility between researchers, consumers, and clinicians. Ultimately, the aim of researchers should be to foster a discourse concerning the generalizability of findings.

8. To foster the discourse regarding generalizability, be clear about how you are defining generalizability.

9. Ensure that the evidence you are using to support generalizability claims is congruent with your definition of generalizability.

The danger of offering such suggestions is that they will be interpreted as the final word on a subject that is bound to evolve and change. There is clear evidence that our notions about generalizability in qualitative research have changed over time. As we face new frontiers using qualitative methods, it is inevitable that new insights will be gained and our understanding of the subject enlarged. In other words, the discourse will continue.

References

Benner, P. (1994). The tradition and skill of interpretive phenomenology in studying health, illness, and caring practices. In P. Benner (Ed.), *Interpretive phenomenology* (pp. 99-127). Thousand Oaks, CA: Sage.
Campbell, D. T., & Stanley, J. C. (1963). *Experimental and quasi-experimental designs for research*. Boston: Houghton Mifflin.
Christensen, L. B. (1994). *Experimental methodology*. Boston: Allyn & Bacon.

Donmoyer, R. (1990). Generalizability and the single-case method. In E. W. Eisner & A. Peshkin (Eds.), *Qualitative inquiry in education: The continuing debate* (pp. 175-200). New York: Teacher's College Press.

Douglas, J. D. (1971). *Understanding everyday life*. London: Routledge & Kegan Paul.

Eisner, E. W. (1979). *The educational imagination*. New York: Macmillan.

Eisner, E. W. (1991). *The enlightened eye*. New York: Macmillan.

Fine, A. (1986). *The shaky game: Einstein, realism, and the quantum theory*. Chicago: University of Chicago Press.

Geertz, C. (1973). *The interpretation of culture*. New York: Basic Books.

Glaser, B. G., & Strauss, A. L. (1967). *The discovery of grounded theory: Strategies for qualitative research*. Chicago: Aldine.

Greene, J. C. (1990). Three views on nature and role of knowledge in social science. In E. Guba (Ed.), *The paradigm dialogue* (pp. 227-245). Newbury Park, CA: Sage.

Guba, E. (1981). Criteria for assessing the trustworthiness of naturalistic inquiries. *Education, Communication and Technology, 29*(2), 75-91.

Hammersley, M. (1992). *What's wrong with ethnography?* London: Routledge.

Hume, D. (1977). *An enquiry concerning human understanding*. Indianapolis: Hackett. (Original work published 1748)

Kiziltan, M., Bain, W., & Canizares, A. (1990). Postmodern conditions: Rethinking public education. *Educational Theory, 40*, 351-370.

Kvale, S. (1995). The social construction of validity. *Qualitative Inquiry, 1*, 19-40.

Lather, P. (1993). Fertile obsession: Validity after poststructuralism. *Sociological Quarterly, 34*, 673-693.

LeCompte, M. D. (1990). Emergent paradigms: How new? How necessary? In E. Guba (Ed.), *The paradigm dialogue* (pp. 246-255). Newbury Park, CA: Sage.

LeCompte, M. D., & Goetz, J. D. (1982). Problems of reliability and validity in ethnographic research. *Review of Educational Research, 52*, 31-60.

Leininger, M. (1994). Evaluation criteria and critique of qualitative research studies. In J. M. Morse (Ed.), *Critical issues in qualitative research methods* (pp. 95-115). Thousand Oaks, CA: Sage.

Lincoln, Y. S., & Guba, E. G. (1985). *Naturalistic inquiry*. Beverly Hills, CA: Sage.

Mishler, E. G. (1990). Validation in inquiry-guided research: The role of exemplars in narrative studies. *Harvard Educational Review, 60*, 415-442.

Morrow, R. (1994). *Critical theory and methodology*. Thousand Oaks, CA: Sage.

Morse, J. M. (1992). The power of induction. *Qualitative Health Research, 2*, 3-6.

Noblitt, G. W., & Hare, R. D. (1988). *Meta-ethnography: Synthesizing qualitative studies*. Newbury Park, CA: Sage.

Pollock, J. L. (1986). *Contemporary theories of knowledge*. Totowa, NJ: Rowan & Littlefield.

Popper, K. (1965). *The logic of scientific discovery*. New York: Harper Torchbooks.

Ragin, C. C. (1987). *The comparative methods: Moving beyond qualitative and quantitative strategies*. Berkeley: University of California Press.

Ratcliffe, J. W. (1983). Notions of validity in qualitative research methodology. *Knowledge, Creation, Diffusion, Utilization, 5*, 147-167.

Sandelowski M. (1986). The problem of rigor in qualitative research. *Advances in Nursing Science, 8*(3), 27-37.

Sandelowski, M. (1993a). Rigor or rigor mortis: The problem of rigor in qualitative research revisited. *Advances in Nursing Science, 16*(2), 1-8.

Sandelowski, M. (1993b). Theory unmasked: The uses and guises of theory in qualitative research. *Research in Nursing and Health, 16*, 213-218.

Sandelowski, M. (1995). On the aesthetics of qualitative research. *IMAGE: Journal of Nursing Scholarship, 27,* 205-209.

Sandelowski, M. (in press). One is the liveliest number: The case orientation of qualitative research. *Research in Nursing and Health.*

Schofield, J. W. (1990). Increasing the generalizability of qualitative research. In E. W. Eisner & A. Peshkin (Eds.), *Qualitative inquiry in education: The continuing debate* (pp. 202-232). New York: Teacher's College Press.

Schütz, A. (1963). Concept and theory formation in the social sciences. In M. A. Natanson (Ed.), *Philosophy of the social sciences* (pp. 231-249). New York: Random House.

Steeves, R. H., Kahn, D. L., & Cohen, M. Z. (1996). Asking substantive theory questions of naturalistically derived data. *Western Journal of Nursing Research, 18,* 209-211.

Stephens, M. (1982). A question of generalizability. *Theory and Research in Social Education, 9,* 75-86.

Streubert, H. J., & Carpenter, D. R. (1995). *Qualitative research in nursing: Advancing the humanistic imperative.* Philadelphia: J. B. Lippincott.

van Manen, M. (1990). *Researching lived experience: Human science for an action sensitive pedagogy.* London, Ontario, Canada: Althouse.

Vendler, Z. (1984). Understanding people. In R. A. Shweder & R. A. LeVine (Eds.), *Culture theory: Essays on mind, self, and emotion* (pp. 200-213). New York: Cambridge University Press.

Wolcott, H. F. (1994). *Transforming qualitative data: Description, analysis, and interpretation.* Thousand Oaks, CA: Sage.

Yin, R. K., & Heald, K. A. (1975). Using case survey methods to analyze policy studies. *Administrative Science Quarterly, 20,* 371-381.

Dialogue: On Labeling a Research Program

Lipson: I am like you—a dilettante! And I have refused to stick myself in one of those boxes. But when I look back over the 20 years of research, I guess there's a theme—

Stern: There's a theme! Sure there is!

Lipson: Yes—populations that are stigmatized, and somewhat vulnerable—but we are going from Afghans to disabled women—

Sandelowski: Are you planning some sort of synthesis of your work around marginalized people?

Lipson: I don't know if I would want to do that or not.

Sandelowski: I think we do have to take stock. I think once we have a label for it, I think the object is: "What is going to be your legacy?" And we will say, "This is what she had to say about marginalized people."

Boyle: You know, some programs are by their nature very broad and allow you to do several kinds of things. I think I am one of those dilettantes, too. Others are very, very narrow—I think of a colleague, who as long as I have known her, has focused on incontinence. And the best I can do is something related to culture and health. And I think there is a vast difference between a research program in incontinence and "culture and health."

May: The value of one's work is ultimately determined by the value of the contribution. And so those folks who stay with decubiti— it's highly focused, and it's easy to see. Before we know this, and now we know this, because of that person. And I think we do ourselves a disservice when we don't (and I'm talking to myself as much as anyone else) say, "This is what I have done. And for the *record*, this is what I have done." It's not to say *you* have to focus your own work—but I think we have to take stock and say this is what we have contributed here, for if we don't say it, the odds are others will miss that, especially if we are intellectually agile—which is a much better term than dilettante— [laughter]

Sandelowski: Let's talk about historians, nineteenth-century American women, for example. And they can articulate exactly what it is and how their work is tied together, how their work fits in with others. And I don't think we do this very well—a humanities model, or whatever it is—and I think we do have to do that. Instead of saying, "Oh I'm only 'culture and health' maybe," you need to talk exactly about what it spans, what's the framework, where are your studies, and ultimately, put something in your work or put something together.

Programmatic
Qualitative Research
Or, Appreciating the Importance
of Gas Station Pumps

Margarete J. Sandelowski

Programs of research, comprising planned, purposeful, and substantively and/or theoretically linked studies with demonstrable significance for the public welfare, have become the definition of scholarship and are determining factors favoring professional advancement in research universities. Researchers in the social science and practice disciplines now feel a special obligation not only to create such programs but also to defend them as likely to contribute to the advancement of practice or the development of policy to benefit the people asked to be research participants. Recent health care reform and other social policy initiatives have created a renewed urgency among various professional groups to show the benefits of their practices. There is also a new consciousness in these disciplines of how methodology, politics, and ethics converge in the research enterprise (e.g., Lincoln, 1995; Lincoln & Reason, 1996). Moreover, there is a new recognition of the self-serving nature of research as an activity that is necessary for professional advancement in the academy. That is, there is an awareness of the "violence of objectification required by turning another's life into information for academic trade" (Lather, 1995, p. 51).

In this chapter, I consider the increasing turn to programmatic research as it applies to qualitative inquiry. A curious state of affairs exists whereby qualitative methods have become increasingly popular yet are still viewed as somewhat dissociated from or only preliminary to "real" research, and as yielding largely insubstantial and unusable results for practice and policy. Moreover, engaging in qualitative research is still often perceived as hindering professional advancement, especially when both academic success and programmatic research are defined by the ability to secure money. Programmatic research tends to be conceived in linear, quantitative, and financial terms: that is, as research moving from so-called lower level description to highest level experiment supported with increasingly larger funds.

Given the prevailing emphasis on randomized controlled trials to document the effectiveness of various interventions, the increasing interest—in fields such as nursing—in biobehavioral research, and the limited funding available for research outside the conventional sciences, scholars with programs of qualitative research in science, history, philosophy, and other knowledge domains remain unlikely to secure large funds to support them. Yet, because of a coexisting (and frankly token) impetus to include qualitative components in largely quantitative research programs, a researcher could build a "program" of qualitative research solely on designing and executing adjunctive or ancillary studies in larger quantitative projects. Although these qualitative adjuncts are vital to ensuring the clinical significance of these quantitative studies (Sandelowski, 1996), their ancillary position in these studies serves to reinforce the secondary and even subservient position of qualitative research within the domain of inquiry.

The location of qualitative research on one side, and substance and success on the other, is all the more remarkable in light of the fact that knowledge in virtually all disciplines in the arts and humanities and in many of the social science disciplines is created with qualitative methods. Despite the rhetoric advocating other ways of knowing and more expansive and humanistic definitions of science, a narrowly scientific (and often scientistic) orientation to knowledge development still prevails. Accordingly, the time has come to consider the paradox and possibility carried in the very idea of programmatic qualitative research.

In this chapter, I consider the contradictions of programmatic qualitative research and the obligation that qualitative researchers, especially in the practice disciplines, have to develop and conduct programmatic research. Most important, I offer qualitative researchers a way of thinking about and communicating the coherence and significance of their work to others. That is, by expanding the notion of what it means to have a program of research, I provide qualitative researchers a way of recognizing and applauding the programmatic features of their work.

The Paradox of Programmatic Qualitative Research

To write about programmatic qualitative research may seem, at first blush, to be an (oxy)moronic and misdirected enterprise. After all, programs are, by definition, prearranged and fixed entities, while qualitative inquiry has been recurringly characterized as emergent and therefore not subject to advanced planning. Moreover, a program of research in a practice discipline ought, arguably, to emphasize the development of substantive knowledge involving the key questions or problems in the discipline, not its methods. That is, in the case of nursing, the emphasis should be on such matters as the clarification of human experiences of and responses to health problems and life transitions and the creation of effective means to favorably enhance these experiences and to resolve these problems. The preoccupation, in fields such as nursing, with debates about how to develop knowledge has often diverted scholars away from actually developing knowledge for practice. Both Meleis (1987) and Woods (1987) urged nurses to develop at least as much "passion" for the substance of nursing as they have shown for its methods.

In short, the idea of programmatic qualitative research appears antithetical to the open-ended and emergent nature of qualitative inquiry and it seems to perpetuate a preoccupation with process over product. This idea seems to place method ahead of substance and even to equate method with substance. This idea also seems to legitimate the twin desires to become a qualitative researcher as a worthy career goal and to do qualitative research as an end in itself. I have often heard both of these desires stated with no reference at all to what will be studied and what knowledge will be developed. Wanting to do qualitative research only for the sake of doing it seems as devoid of sense and significance as wanting to conduct factor analyses or experiments only for the sake of conducting them.

Yet, although the idea of programmatic qualitative research seems to be a contradiction in terms and an endorsement of a misplaced passion for method over substance, it also captures some distinctive truths about qualitative research that tend to be overlooked. First, scholars in disciplines wholly or largely employing qualitative methods, such as anthropology, history, philosophy, literature, and cultural studies, can be accurately described as engaged in programmatic qualitative research, although they would likely not describe themselves in this way or even have heard of the terms *qualitative* or *programmatic research.*

The reason that scholars in many of these fields would not find these labels useful lies in a second and postmodern truth that method is not so easily separated from substance in these or, indeed, in any other disciplines. As Horsfall (1995) observed, an unexamined truism is that the research problem should determine the method used. Although there is some truth to this ostensibly "simple rule," it overly simplifies the relationship between problem and method. As she argued, "such a simple rule has a technical orientation and denies the context within which the research activities take place" (p. 6). Wolfer (1993, p. 141) emphasized the ontological differences underlying different kinds of problems nurses investigate that require different methodologies. Accordingly, investigators drawn to problems largely of the "body," "mind," or "spirit" will, by necessity, be drawn to ways of knowing compatible with these different aspects of reality. Alternatively, investigators drawn to certain ways of knowing and even to certain kinds of data (such as numbers, stories, diaries, or artifacts) will, by necessity, be drawn to study certain kinds of problems.

(Scholars drawn to certain of these aspects of reality and ways of knowing them also will have developed an expertise in these methods. There is a prevailing but false assumption in the practice disciplines that investigators should and can have expertise in conducting all kinds of research. This assumption trivializes the notion of research expertise and the vast amount of knowledge, including technical skill and practical experience, and deep immersion any approach to inquiry requires for someone to claim expertise in it. Although investigators in practice disciplines ought to have an acquaintance with, appreciation of, and even some minimal level of competence in prevailing modes of inquiry in their specific disciplines, they simply cannot have expertise across such a wide and diverse range of approaches. To continue to trivialize research expertise is to consign ourselves to producing trivial work. Investigators trained primarily in quantitative approaches and engaged in quantitatively driven [Morse, 1991] research programs with qualitative components should include colleagues specifically trained and experienced in qualitative methods.)

Researchers also may be drawn to certain forms of knowledge and acquire expertise in certain kinds of "forming." All human inquiry results in the creation of form; theories, paintings, and pots are kinds of form by means of which scientists, artists, and crafts(wo)men create worlds that are coherent, understandable, and meaningful (Eisner, 1985). Scholars in the social science and practice disciplines newly concerned with the writing and (re)presentation of research findings have emphasized the artificiality of separating not only substance from method but also method from the presentation of findings; that is, the informational content of a (re)presentation cannot be separated from its form. Whether scientific or artistic, "the form of the work (in)forms us" (Eisner, 1985, p. 25). Indeed, like artists, qualitative researchers often consciously "exploit the power of form to inform" (Eisner, 1991, p. 7) and it is this possibility alone that may attract them to qualitative inquiry and the kinds of questions and concerns most amenable to qualitative inquiry.

Moreover, qualitative research is itself trans- and interdisciplinary and, accordingly, picks up substance by virtue of its location across and between disciplines and their rich and varied philosophical, theoretical, social, and political commitments. Researchers ask certain questions about the world that reflect these disciplinary commitments, and these questions may be about aspects of reality more amenable to qualitative research. Researchers also may have orientations to knowledge development that influence their methods. For example, Krathwohl (1985, pp. 156-190) proposed that synthesizers, theorizers, multiperspectivists, humanists, and particularists prefer qualitative and case-oriented methods, while pragmatists and analyzers prefer quantitative methods. Methodology, or the sum total of methods of inquiry and the personal and disciplinary orientations that surround and shape them, can thus drive substance.

Adding to the seeming paradox of programmatic qualitative research is the fact that such programs may comprise studies linked not by substantive or theoretical content per se but by social goals. For example, there are researchers who choose certain kinds of participatory and action research informed by critical theories because of their commitment to raising the consciousness of the participants in their studies. These investigators see their programs of research as programs of intervention in the service of pluralist and emancipatory goals (Parsons, 1995; Reason, 1994).

Knowledge Accumulation in Qualitative Research

Further confounding the problem of programmatic qualitative research are concerns regarding whether and how qualitative research contributes to the synthesis and accumulation of knowledge for practice. Knowledge for practice typically has been conceived as the result of an aggregation of findings accumulated from programs of research in specified areas.

Yet there continues to be some confusion concerning what knowledge accumulation means in any domain of inquiry. According to Eisner (1991, pp. 209-211), dollars accumulate because they are in a common system of currency and because there are rules for calculating equivalencies. Yet there is no such common ground nor are there such established rules in research, given the wide variation in theories, concepts, and methods used within and across disciplines that are embedded in, or inextricable from, the knowledge they produce.

Alternatively, garbage accumulates merely because its volume increases, but few scholars would want to compare knowledge accumulation in the disciplines to a growing garbage pile. Accordingly, as Eisner proposed, if knowledge can be said to accumulate at all, its growth is more horizontal than vertical. That is, there is no way to add the knowledge of human development produced from an Eriksonian perspective to the knowledge produced from a Skinnerian perspective. Instead, what accumulates are the perspectives available to scholars to choose to guide their inquiries about the world. Knowledge accumulation is, thus, less about knowing more than it is about having more perspectives from which to know. Accordingly, qualitative research contributes to the advancement of thoughtful practice and policy by creating more resources with which to think about and act in the world. Laudan (1977) observed that progress in knowledge is achieved not by addition but by the reformulation of "facts" and aspects of reality that lead to the satisfactory resolution of problems central to a discipline. In demonstrating the "fecundity of the individual case," Jardine (1992) argued that the goal of interpretive inquiry was not the "simple accumulation of new objective information [but] rather the transformation of self-understanding" (p. 60).

Challenges to prevailing notions of knowledge accumulation call into question common conceptions concerning the synthesis and generalizability of qualitative findings. These misconceptions have often been used to diminish the relevance and utility of qualitative research. Eisner's conception of knowledge accumulation as horizontal implies that all generalizations, including the greatly prized formal or nomothetic generalizations in quantitative research typically conceived as applicable to populations, are ultimately naturalistic or idiographic, as they are drawn from and within particular perspectives.

Eisner does not deny the need for or the possibility of making larger connections between perspectival worlds, but the making of these connections is as much the responsibility of the reader as of the creator of research findings. Creators of research findings are obliged to provide sufficiently contextualized presentations of them so that readers can evaluate their relevance in other contexts. Readers of qualitative research findings are obliged to become sufficiently schooled in qualitative research to make appropriate judgments about such matters as the generalizability and overall utility of a work. Qualitative researchers must also develop their skills in the use of analogy, metaphor, verbal and conceptual translation, and other techniques to create meta-syntheses, or larger combinations or integrations, of qualitative findings. Ideally, such syntheses will remain faithful to the complexity of individual findings and yet yield new perspectival worlds for future inquiry and practice (Estabrooks, Field, & Morse, 1994; Noblit & Hare, 1988). As Noblit and Hare (1988, p. 11) proposed, we have an overly technical and falsely additive view of knowledge development. This view is replaced in the qualitative domain with an interpretive and even culinary vision. As Eisner concluded (1991):

> [The horizontal] model of knowledge accumulation is less like making deposits to a bank account than preparing a fine meal. Indeed, a fine meal is much more apt an image than either the tidy rationality of a bank account or the redolence of a garbage dump. In the meal, each course connects with and complements the other. Such an image is not a bad model for knowledge accumulation in qualitative research. (p. 211)

In addition to the obligations of readers of qualitative texts to read well and the creators of those texts to create well, all qualitative researchers bear the individual burden of locating their work within and against other inquiry in a field. Qualitative researchers too often conduct study after study with data sets inadequate for the stated aims and/or with little or no substantive, theoretical, or other connection to each other or even demonstrable knowledge of other quantitative and qualitative studies in the field. They legitimate their naïveté as being in the service of "bracketing" or a cleansing of their minds from the so-called contaminating influences of existing knowledge. Yet researchers who fail to locate their individual studies within a larger field of scholarship often do nothing more than reinvent the wheel. Mind*less* researchers can only produce mindless research.

Models of Programmatic Research

The idea of programmatic research typically conjures up a scientific, linear, and hierarchical model of inquiry moving from so-called lower level descriptive studies that may involve qualitative methods to so-called higher level explanatory and prescriptive studies involving exclusively quantitative methods. If qualitative methods play any role at all in this model, it is typically an adjunctive rather than central role. Qualitative methods are used largely to collect in situ descriptions of experiences and events at the beginning of a program of research. They are seen here as contributing "only" to description (a concept that tends to be trivialized in quantitative discourse) and as contributing nothing to the explanation of events or the testing of ideas. Two empirical variants of this familiar and conventionally scientific model include programs of research aimed at intervention testing and instrument development. This model typically requires the collaborative efforts of a research team and large sums of money to support the numbers of investigators and research subjects required to conduct such programs, as validity and significance are "mathematized," or "intimately linked (with) quantities and enumerable surface repetitions" (Jardine, 1992, p. 54).

Alternative Models of Programmatic Research

For qualitative research to move from its position as merely adjunctive in largely quantitative programs of research, we need a more expansive and interpretive notion of programmatic research. For example, programs of research may be centrally organized around (a) "real-world" problems requiring understanding or resolution, such as facilitating recovery after certain illnesses or injuries, or preventing the occurrence of certain disorders or impairments; (b) conceptual problems, such as elucidating and theorizing about "suffering" or "comfort"; (c) substantive domains, such as examining various aspects of patient-caregiver communication; and (d) methodological domains, where the substantive area is itself the development of research methodology.

We also need to give more than lip service to the varieties of ways of knowing other than the conventionally scientific and to recognize and reward programs of research that draw their substance and form from both human science and the traditional humanistic disciplines. Individuals, as opposed to teams of researchers, often conduct humanistically oriented studies. In contrast to the conventional science model, where the scholarly products of a research program are a sufficient quantity of articles published in refereed journals, the product desired may be a university press monograph or book, visual object, or scholarly performance.

The end points of research programs in these disciplines may be a "tested" intervention or specified practice, in addition to larger and deeper historical, philosophical, cultural, critical, or other meta-understandings of events, including narrative and theoretical descriptions and explanations. As linguistic concepts and practices, neither *testing* nor *explaining* belong exclusively to the quantitative domain, as these words have meanings beyond the mathematized definitions they hold in that domain. Researchers may indeed move directly from the development of a grounded theory of an event to the application and qualitative and/or quantitative evaluation of an intervention derived from that theory, without moving through the intervening steps of quantitative theory testing or instrument development. The process of creating grounded theory itself entails establishing its theoretical validity and generalizability (Maxwell, 1992). Grounded theory is, by definition and purpose, theory tested against human experience.

Programs of qualitative research may be directed toward developing and evaluating formal theory describing human responses to chronic illness, narrative explanations of how individuals manage illness, ethnographic explanations of how culture informs health behavior, or historical explanations of why nurses have adopted certain nursing therapies. Such meta-understandings are foundational; that is, they are themselves the "interventions" on which all others are based, which permit human beings interpretive control of their worlds, and without which no other interventions are possible. Benner and Wrubel (1989, p. 11) suggested that we often fail to *understand* understanding *as* therapy or healing in our cultural drive toward "instrumental interventions." The essential aim of all human inquiry is the making of meaning and of sense (Eisner, 1985), whether sense-making is in the form of the formal generalizations of quantitatively produced science, the idiographic generalizations of qualitatively produced science, the meta-understandings of history and philosophy, or the singular understandings of the arts. There is as great a need in nursing for critical ethnographies of intervention programs, studies in the ethics and politics of intervention, intellectual and social histories of nursing intervention, and philosophical studies of the compatibility between current technical notions of intervention and nursing as there is for experimental studies of interventions themselves.

Our notion of programs of research ought also to include efforts to make the most of data already collected, such as the deliberate pursuit of multiple analytic paths within a data set that are later synthesized as well as secondary analysis and meta-synthesis projects combining data sets or findings from different studies. In my own study of the transition to parenthood of infertile couples, the more than 450 interviews conducted yielded information contributing to different substantive fields of knowledge: for example, knowledge about the personal experience of infertility; the interaction between technology, gender, and culture; and parent-fetal/infant relations. There is so much more information to mine in the rich vein of data typically collected in qualitative projects of any significant size, but too much "methodological forbidding" (Sharrock & Anderson, 1979, p. 82) that may prohibit the use of these data. Investigators should work toward and be tangibly supported for developing methods that make as much worthwhile use of materials as possible, regardless of their kind or quantity. Conventional methods often "constrict (the) imagination" (p. 82) when imagination is the most critical factor in research design and in the treatment of data. We need to strive toward, value, and support programs of research directed toward innovative treatments and narrative and theoretical syntheses of data already collected and of findings from completed analyses. Such programmatic work will enhance the conceptual and instrumental use of these data and findings and, in the process, enlarge our understanding of knowledge use itself (Larsen, 1981). Moreover, it will relieve persons already vulnerable by virtue of their health conditions or life stage from the burdens of participation in yet more studies yielding data that already exist.

My Program of Research

I came up in academic nursing at a time when there was generally little attention given to building research programs. Only recently did I name (with the assistance of a very wise colleague, Janice Morse) the thematic thread running through all my intellectual efforts. I had a program, but I did not know it. I had a program, but it was not a conventionally scientific one.

Although discovered in hindsight, my studies reveal a consistent attraction to and enduring interest in the intersection among gender, technology, and culture, in feminist criticism, and in modes of inquiry falling between disciplines and definitely outside of what is commonly understood as science. These interests were evident well before I entered a doctoral program in American Studies, in the very first book I wrote on women and health (Sandelowski, 1981), and in the doctoral dissertation that was later published as part of a series in medical history (Sandelowski, 1984). My subsequent studies of cesarean birth, infertility (the book-length treatment of which was recognized as a contribution in ethnography; Sandelowski, 1993), and conceptive and prenatal diagnosis technology, as well as my current efforts in the history and philosophy of technology in nursing, have continued to reflect these interests and have involved a variety of qualitative methodologies.

American Studies is itself an interdisciplinary field that emphasizes the use of all kinds of sources (e.g., written texts, oral histories, archival documents, and material artifacts) and domains of knowledge (e.g., history, literature, art, popular culture, and science) to study "American culture." I remember how impressed I was with a presentation in which an "Americanist" interpreted changing designs in gas station pumps. I marveled at everything such a familiar and taken-for-granted artifact could reveal and that it could be the basis for enhancing our understanding of ourselves. By virtue of its substantive emphasis on concerns in the humanities, my program in American Studies also emphasized *qualitative* methods, although I had no consciousness of this term as signifying certain modes of inquiry until they were discovered in nursing as qualitative research. In American Studies, as in most humanities fields, method is not separable from substance; as a student of American Studies, I learned method by reading the classic works in the field.

In short, American Studies provided me with an intellectually satisfying and aesthetically appealing orientation to inquiry. Combined with my background in nursing, it gave me a panoramic view of culture and a correspondingly panoramic approach to inquiry and how to conceptualize foci for inquiry. I learned that knowledge could not be confined to disciplinary or methodological boxes, and that it was not acquired or accumulated in a straight line. I learned that the creation of knowledge cannot be separated from the way it is produced or from the way it is (re)presented. Most important, I learned that knowledge can be "found" even in gas station pumps.

Conclusion

The idea of programmatic qualitative research makes sense if we understand and value the different ways that scientists, humanists, and artists organize and contribute to knowledge. The practice disciplines, in particular, must have all these knowledge creators for these disciplines to advance and remain relevant. The idea makes sense if we pay more than lip service to the idea that researchers in practice disciplines, such as nursing, both draw from and contribute to knowledge in the sciences, humanities, and arts. These researchers are not simply borrowers of other scholars' ideas and methods but are transformers of these ideas and methods and, more important, creators of new ones. The idea of programmatic research makes no sense so long as we adhere to rigid notions of programmatic research and equate scholarship with numbers (that is, with measurement and dollars), and so long as qualitative researchers fail to articulate how their work addresses certain disciplinary or empirical problems and how it connects to (or draws from, enlarges upon, or diverges from) other work.

Inquiry addresses an inherent human need for aesthetic satisfaction (Eisner, 1985). Yet, in the practice disciplines, investigators have a special obligation to contribute to knowledge that ultimately will (in)form practice, whether that (inform)ation contributes to a difference in the way events are configured (that is, the conceptual use of knowledge) or to a measurable difference in practice (that is, the instrumental use of knowledge) (Larsen, 1981). The most valuable program of research is the one that satisfactorily combines the aesthetic inclinations of the investigator with a concern to improve the quality of life. The public welfare is well served by programmatic qualitative research because it enlightens; it results in knowledge individuals can use to solve problems—but even more important, use to make sense of their lives and worlds.

References

Benner, P., & Wrubel, J. (1989). *The primacy of caring: Stress and coping in health and illness.* Menlo Park, CA: Addison-Wesley.

Eisner, E. (1985). Aesthetic modes of knowing. In E. Eisner (Ed.), *Learning and teaching the ways of knowing: Eighty-fourth Yearbook of the National Society for the Study of Education* (Pt. II, pp. 23-36). Chicago: National Society for the Study of Education.

Eisner, E. W. (1991). *The enlightened eye: Qualitative inquiry and the enhancement of educational practice.* New York: Macmillan.

Estabrooks, C. A., Field, P. A., & Morse, J. M. (1994). Aggregating qualitative findings: An approach to theory development. *Qualitative Health Research, 4,* 503-511.

Horsfall, J. M. (1995). Madness in our methods: Nursing research, scientific epistemology. *Nursing Inquiry, 2,* 2-9.

Jardine, D. W. (1992). The fecundity of the individual case: Considerations of the pedagogic heart of interpretive work. *Journal of Philosophy of Education, 26,* 51-61.

Krathwohl, D. R. (1985). *Social and behavioral science research.* San Francisco: Jossey-Bass.

Larsen, J. K. (1981). Knowledge utilization: Current issues. In R. F. Rich (Ed.), *The knowledge cycle* (pp. 149-167). Beverly Hills, CA: Sage.

Lather, P. A. (1995). The validity of angels: Interpretive and textual strategies in researching the lives of women with HIV/AIDS. *Qualitative Inquiry, 1,* 41-68.

Laudan, L. (1977). *Progress and its problems: Towards a theory of scientific growth.* Berkeley: University of California Press.

Lincoln, Y. S. (1995). Emerging criteria for quality in qualitative and interpretive research. *Qualitative Inquiry, 1,* 275-289.

Lincoln, Y. S., & Reason, P. (Eds.). (1996). Quality in human inquiry [Special issue]. *Qualitative Inquiry, 2*(1).

Maxwell, J. A. (1992). Understanding and validity in qualitative research. *Harvard Educational Review, 62,* 279-300.

Meleis, A. I. (1987). ReVisions in knowledge development: A passion for substance. *Scholarly Inquiry for Nursing Practice, 1,* 5-19.

Morse, J. M. (1991). Approaches to qualitative-quantitative methodological triangulation. *Nursing Research, 40,* 120-122.

Noblit, G. W., & Hare, R. D. (1988). *Meta-ethnography: Synthesizing qualitative studies.* Newbury Park, CA: Sage.

Parsons, C. (1995). The impact of postmodernism on research methodology: Implications for nursing. *Nursing Inquiry, 2,* 22-28.

Reason, P. (1994). Three approaches to participative inquiry. In N. K. Denzin & Y. S. Lincoln (Eds.), *Handbook of qualitative research* (pp. 324-339). Thousand Oaks, CA: Sage.

Sandelowski, M. (1981). *Women, health, and choice.* Englewood Cliffs, NJ: Prentice Hall.

Sandelowski, M. (1984). *Pain, pleasure, and American childbirth: From the Twilight Sleep to the Read Method, 1914-1960.* Westport, CT: Greenwood.

Sandelowski, M. (1993). *With child in mind: Studies of the personal encounter with infertility.* Philadelphia: University of Pennsylvania Press.

Sandelowski, M. (1996). Using qualitative methods in intervention studies. *Research in Nursing & Health, 19,* 359-364.

Sharrock, W. W., & Anderson, D. C. (1979). Directional hospital signs as sociological data. *Information Design Journal, 1,* 81-94.

Wolfer, J. (1993). Aspects of "reality" and ways of knowing in nursing: In search of an integrating paradigm. *IMAGE: Journal of Nursing Scholarship, 25,* 141-146.

Woods, N. F. (1987). Response: Early morning musings on the passion for substance. *Scholarly Inquiry for Nursing Practice, 1,* 25-28.

Dialogue: Research Programs

Sandelowski: One of the things the discussion raises is that a program of research shouldn't be an adjective like qualitative or quantitative. Although, by virtue of the fact that you can be an expert in methods, you are often very necessary for a program to advance. But I think there is a danger of always placing qualitative research in that secondary role—and that's another way to do it—and I think we do need to say when students come up and say, "I want to be a qualitative researcher," that's like saying, "I want to be a factor analyst"—it doesn't make any sense. What you should be saying is, "I want to do research on quality of life with AIDS patients," or something like that. *Then* look at what you have to do to get there. You don't make a career of a method, per se. But you can make an argument that is your substantive area. But that's a whole other ball of wax.

Morse: There are certain kinds of styles of research programs, and one would be by *methods;* another would be by *substantive area,* that's your quality of life in AIDS patients; another would be by *concept*—quality of life.

Sandelowski: I see that as substantive, too.

Linking Qualitative and Quantitative Research

New Avenues for Programmatic Research

Joan L. Bottorff

Qualitative research methods encompass various methods for vali-dating results such that when a "sufficient level of plausibility" is reached, qualitative investigations are often an end point within a substantive area (Glaser & Strauss, 1966). The findings can be applied and adjusted to many situations to guide understanding, forestalling the need for further research. When additional related analyses follow initial qualitative investigations, the main purpose often is to "discover more" rather than to test or correct. The need to follow qualitative research with a quantitative study, therefore, is seen as inappropriate, unnecessary, and often impossible by many researchers. However, even among qualitative researchers, there has not been unanimous agreement on this issue.

Glaser and Strauss (1966, p. 60) were perhaps among the first to suggest that we might profit from other ways of validating qualitative analyses "to raise the level of plausibility of some hypotheses," pointing to situations where specific action plans were being developed or when researchers were working in well-developed substantive areas. Others have offered strong support for this suggestion. Hammersley (1992, p. 182) argues that to maximize the confidence we legitimately can have in a theory, we need to "open the theory up to [the] maximal threat" of systematic testing without retreating into research paradigms. To emphasize the importance of this testing, he draws on Eckstein's (1975) remarks regarding practitioners of macropolitics, suggesting that they apply equally to social researchers:

> One may consider it reprehensible that so many comparativists are willing to stop where only that much (i.e., plausibility), or little more, has been accomplished, and then go on to new, still merely plausible, ideas on new subject matter. We certainly have no right to bewail the fact that others do not take up our ideas if we ourselves drop them far short of the point to which they could be taken. (p. 110)

Although it makes sense that methods used for any further empirical validation of qualitative analyses should be compatible with the research situation, Glaser and Strauss (1966) recommend that further research could be accomplished by a variety of methods, including through more rigorous or extensive fieldwork or through experiments and surveys.

Although others have agreed that the sequential use of qualitative and quantitative methods could be useful in advancing our knowledge, they are critical of those who advocate this approach for demonstrating the validity or scientific worthiness of qualitative analyses. The problem with suggestions that qualitative analyses are in need of quantitative verification is that by inference epistemological assumptions about ways of knowing prioritize one type of research over another rather than acknowledging paradigmatic differences. The important question is how we can combine findings from paradigmatically distinct studies of the same phenomena in ways that preserve the integrity of both method and findings (Morse, 1991a; Sandelowski, 1995). It has been suggested that the value of subsequent quantitative investigations lies in their ability to extend the results of a qualitative study in a complementary or corroborative but distinct way (e.g., to determine the distribution of X qualitative concept in a particular population) rather than to "test" or "verify" qualitative results per se (Morse, 1991a; see also Morse, this volume). Qualitative researchers have pointed out that quantitative studies fall short in their ability to evaluate the full complexity of many qualitative theories (e.g., when operational definitions of concepts and concisely expressed hypotheses appear to be weak representations of the qualitatively derived theory on which they are based) and as such provide inconclusive and inadequate evaluations of these theories. Nevertheless, it is possible that supporting evidence from quantitative research, if adequately grounded in aspects of a qualitative analysis, could potentially provide some level of confirmation about what the qualitative researcher knew all along or, alternatively, new directions for further inductive work. Whether this constitutes a "test" of the qualitatively generated theory or whether it is even necessary remains a topic of debate.

For the purposes of this chapter, a position will be taken that well-designed quantitative studies, that have as a foundation inductively derived concepts or theories, provide one kind of opportunity for evaluating, extending, and revising theory. In doing so, this particular type of quantitative research provides an important avenue for extending our knowledge. In this chapter, available sources of insight related to the use of this approach will be used as a foundation for exploring its strengths. Selected examples from the literature will be used to identify specific ways quantitative methods have been linked to qualitative studies and to build a set of beginning guidelines for the use of this approach.

Methodological Triangulation

The widespread use of triangulation has resulted in a confusing variety of interpretations and applications, the impetus for which Sandelowski (1995) attributes to the need to minimize differences among modes of inquiry. Nevertheless, although efforts have focused on clarifying the types of triangulation (Jick, 1983; Kimchi, Polivka, & Stevenson, 1991; Patton, 1990) and the purposes that triangulation can serve (Knafl & Breitmayer, 1991; Sandelowski, 1995), it is methods triangulation and the appropriateness of combining qualitative and quantitative research methods that have stimulated the most debate and discussion (see, for example, Blaikie, 1991; Flick, 1992; Goodwin & Goodwin, 1984; Myers & Haase, 1989; Powers, 1987). Morse (1991a) argues that it is the findings obtained through the use of qualitative and quantitative methods that are triangulated (not the methods themselves). To ensure that the findings obtained through each method are sound, it is important that both qualitative and quantitative methods be used without violating their respective assumptions. To accomplish this, Morse proposes a reconceptualization of methods triangulation to differentiate two types of combinations of methodological approaches to clarify how qualitative and quantitative research should be linked, namely, simultaneous and sequential triangulation.

Simultaneous methodological triangulation involves the implementation of qualitative and quantitative methods at the same time (Morse, 1991a). The findings related to each method are used to complement one another at the end of the study to enhance theoretical or substantive completeness. Suggestions for study design and data analysis to support this type of triangulation have been made (Breitmayer, Ayres, & Knafl, 1993) and issues related to its use have been brought forward (Sandelowski, 1995).

In contrast, with sequential triangulation, research methods are used independently and in sequence (Morse, 1991a). For example, the qualitative component of the study is completed before the quantitative methods are used, or vice versa, depending on the nature of the problem under study. The results of one method provide a critical foundation for the next stage of the study involving the other method. For the purposes of this chapter, our interest lies in the research sequence that begins with a qualitative study, a necessary starting point when there is a lack of theory or previous research related to the concept under study or there are indications that existing theory may be incomplete, inaccurate, or biased. In this case, the results of the first study (qualitative) generate theories and ideas that then may be used as a foundation for conducting a quantitative investigation. The results of the second study (quantitative) can be used to support, extend, or revise the theory. In sequential triangulation, qualitative and quantitative studies are completed independently of one another.

Yet they are inextricably linked. Without the results of the qualitative study, it would not be possible to conduct the quantitative investigation. Each makes an important and unique contribution to theory building.

In this discussion of sequential triangulation, it may appear I am suggesting that qualitative methods are only used for discovery and theory building, while quantitative designs are only used for verification or theory testing. Clearly this is not always the case, because quantitative methods also have been used in theory building and qualitative methods often involve theory testing. Furthermore, I am not suggesting that the use of quantitative methods is any less error-prone than other approaches to evaluating theory, that it avoids any of the issues related to what constitutes truth, or that any number of such studies providing support for a theory can ever guarantee its validity (Silva & Sorrell, 1992). Rather, it is but one approach often used to evaluate and advance theories.

A qualitative research study is complete in itself and should not be seen *only* as a pilot study or as preliminary to quantitative research (Morse, 1991b). It must be clear that this approach to sequential triangulation is not meant to suggest that qualitative methods are in any way of inferior quality or importance. Rather, in sequential triangulation (qual → quant), excellent qualitative work is critical to equally excellent quantitative work. There is some consensus in the literature that in some instances it makes good sense to use quantitative methods to support or extend the results of qualitative research, whether theoretical frameworks, newly identified concepts, hypotheses, or theory (Carey, 1993; Ford-Gilboe, Campbell, & Berman, 1995; Glaser & Strauss, 1966; Hammersley & Atkinson, 1993; Kristjanson, 1992; Morse, 1991a, 1991b; Sells, Smith, & Sprenkle, 1995; Smith, 1985; Strickland, 1993; Tripp-Reimer, 1985). In this sense, qualitative research provides the groundbreaking work for beginning a program of research. There is no doubt about the importance of the qualitative work in this sequence. This initial work has a direct impact on defining the theoretical foundation and conceptual parameters of the discipline and as such provides the necessary direction for evaluating, refining, and extending a growing body of knowledge (Morse, 1994) that holds both theoretical interest and practical relevance (Carey, 1993).

There are a few examples of this sequential approach to research in the literature. It is unlikely that these examples represent the extent to which sequential triangulation (qualitative → quantitative) has been used. Reports of such investigations would not be encouraged by journals specializing in one type of methodology or the other. In addition, if sequential triangulation is used, publications may be separated by several years in disparate journals, making it difficult to determine the links between studies or, alternatively, highlighting only the quantitative findings. One example clearly demonstrates some of the difficulties encountered in locating examples of sequential triangulation. Morse and Doan published their qualitative study of adolescents' experiences of menarche in 1987 in the *Journal of School Health*. Six years later, this was followed by a publication in *Health Care for Women International* describing the development and initial psychometric evaluation of a new instrument designed to measure adolescents' attitudes toward menstruation (Morse, Kieren, & Bottorff, 1993). The instrument was theoretically grounded in the results of the previous qualitative study. Not only are the two studies published in different journals, some years apart and by different groups of investigators (with the exception of Morse), it is impossible to recognize the sequential link between these studies using typical computerized literature search strategies. In spite of these difficulties, some examples of sequential triangulation found in the literature are provided here to help describe the use of sequential triangulation as a model of research, to increase awareness of the merits of this approach, and to serve as a basis for developing some specific guidelines for its use. These examples are unlikely to represent the diversity of approaches to sequential triangulation but provide an important beginning to explicating this kind of research.

Sequential Triangulation (Qualitative → Quantitative): Examples From the Field

The results of qualitative research often have been used to supplement theoretical literature and empirical studies to provide a theoretical basis for instrument development (e.g., Dempster, 1990; Hilton,

1994) or to enhance later stages of the research process. As an example of the latter, qualitative methods have been used to improve subsequent quantitative data collection (e.g., by ensuring that appropriate language is used in formulating questionnaire items or by taking advantage of close relationships developed with informants to enhance response rates). However, for the purposes of this chapter, the quantitative investigations of primary interest are those that are solidly based on some aspect of inductively derived theories, theoretical frameworks, or concepts identified through qualitative studies. Accordingly, the types of sequential triangulation (qualitative → quantitative) can be divided into three categories based on how qualitative results are used by quantitative researchers, namely, those sequences that are based on qualitatively derived measures, interventions, or relationships.

Deriving Measures From Inductively Generated Concepts

Theory not only serves as a basis for explanation, it also determines what can be counted as an observation. Furthermore, Hayduk (1996) reminds us that we "only know what we are measuring when our concepts and hence measurements, behave in relation to one another as they theoretically should" (p. 71). Thus, given that our measures are theory laden, it is not surprising that researchers have looked to qualitative research as an important theoretical source.

The term *concept synthesis* has been used to describe the process of developing or clarifying a concept using qualitative methods (Mishel, 1989; Walker & Avant, 1988). A variety of qualitative analytic techniques used in phenomenology, ethnography, ethnoscience, and grounded theory have been identified as particularly useful in facilitating the description of concepts (Morse, Hupcey, Mitcham, & Lenz, 1996). Qualitative analyses that make explicit new conceptualizations or challenge the status quo by revising existing conceptualizations are then used to guide the development of new measures. This is a significant departure from the usual practice of relying on existing theoretical literature to clarify a concept (referred to as concept analysis) or redefining concepts borrowed from other fields (concept derivation) to provide the necessary foundation for instrument development (Mishel, 1989).

Table 12.1 Illustrations of Sequential Triangulation
(Qualitative → Quantitative)

Author	Qualitative Method	Quantitative Method	Theoretical or Conceptual Framework Evaluated
Deriving measures from inductively generated concepts			
Olson (1990) Olson & Morse (1996)	ethnoscience	instrument development, psychometric evaluation	BSE Frequency Model and its ability to discriminate between those who do and do not do BSE
Morse & Doan (1987) Morse et al. (1993)	content analysis of qualitative data	instrument development, psychometric evaluation	multidimensional construct of menstrual attitudes
Tilden, Nelson, & May (1990a, 1990b) Tilden, Hirsh, & Nelson (1994)	content analysis of qualitative data	instrument development, psychometric evaluation	multidimensional construct of interpersonal relationship networks
Bottorff & Morse (1994) Bottorff (1994)	qualitative ethology	quantitative ethology	patterns of behavior reflecting patterns of nurse attending
Imle (1983) Imle & Atwood (1988)	grounded theory	instrument development, psychometric evaluation	Transition to First-Time Parent Construct
Hall (1987, 1991, 1993)	grounded theory	instrument development, psychometric evaluation	construct of role enactment as it applies to combining work parenting
Garro (1990)	ethnographic	structured survey, consensual analysis	cultural model of blood pressure beliefs
Deriving interventions from qualitative research			
DeJoseph, Norbeck, Smith, & Miller (1996) Norbeck, DeJoseph, & Smith (1996)	feminist qualitative	clinical trial	the efficacy of a social support intervention developed through a qualitative study

Table 12.1 Continued

Author	Qualitative Method	Quantitative Method	Theoretical or Conceptual Framework Evaluated
de Vries, Weijts, Dijkstra, & Kok (1992)	a variety of qualitative methods	survey and program evaluation	the efficacy of a smoking prevention program developed on the basis of qualitative study of students' beliefs and needs assessment
May (1994) Jenssen (1996)	grounded theory	program evaluation	the usefulness of a risk appraisal guide developed on the basis of a grounded theory of experiences during preterm labor
Deriving relationships from inductively generated theory			
Duffy (1984, 1994)	grounded theory	longitudinal descriptive correlational design	associations among variables as predicted in the Theory of Transcending Options

In this approach to sequential triangulation, concepts identified and explicated through qualitative methods are operationalized into observable indicators. Care is taken to capture the language and expressions used by informants during qualitative interviews while simultaneously reflecting essential features and dimensions of the concept. Although on the surface this appears to be a straightforward procedure, in most cases it is not. Maintaining the qualitative meaning while transforming qualitative data into decontextualized measurable items that can be subject to psychometric testing has been particularly challenging. Furthermore, the complexity and interrelatedness of qualitative data sometimes make it difficult to adequately address all dimensions within the constraints of a structured questionnaire (Coreil, Augustin, Holt, & Halsey, 1989) and to create subscales that are conceptually distinct from one another (Hall, in review). These difficulties continue to stimulate researchers to explore more effective ways of representing the complexities of human experience. Thus far only a few procedures have been reported to preserve the meaning of inductively generated data while reflecting the characteristics of the concept (Fluery, 1993; Hall, in review; Imle & Atwood, 1988; Tilden et al., 1990b). For example, Fluery (1993) recommends that several interrelated steps (i.e., understanding the concept within a theoretical context that reflects the complexity of experience, specifying the essential dimensions of the concept, and generating items to correspond with inductively generated data from each dimension) be combined with continual immersion in the qualitative data, along with participant feedback on the instrument, to ensure that researchers and informants view the data in a consistent way.

Psychometric evaluation of newly developed instruments typically involves an evaluation of both reliability and validity using quantitative approaches. The results of these evaluations are used to support or refine the inductively derived conceptualization. Sequentially linking and using the unique contributions of qualitative and quantitative methods of inquiry to evaluate inductively generated concepts through the development and evaluation of quantitative measures has several advantages, including the potential for producing a measure with a high degree of relevancy and salience to the target group as well as a high level of formal reliability and validity (Carey, 1993; Mahoney, Thombs, & Howe, 1995; Morse et al., 1993).

Since Glaser and Strauss (1966) suggested that qualitatively generated material was a viable means of meeting the need for new measures, researchers have begun to operationalize qualitatively generated concepts into instruments that are amenable to psychometric testing. Concepts that have provided this important foundation for instrument development have been products of grounded theory (Fluery, 1993, 1994; Hall, 1993; Imle, 1983), ethnoscience (Olson, 1990), ethnographic interviews (Garro, 1990), qualitative ethology (Bottorff, 1994), and content analysis (Morse et al., 1993; Tilden et al., 1990a). Of this broad array of methods, it is only ethology that has a long tradition of encouraging the sequential use of qualitative and quantitative methods, with qualitative ethological methods facilitating the identification of significant behaviors that should be observed in subsequent quantitative studies of the phenomena of interest (Morse & Bottorff, 1990). On the basis of the remaining examples from the literature, researchers appeared to take advantage of new or revised conceptualizations—some of which rendered previous forms of measurement inappropriate or inadequate—to develop new instruments. In evaluating the reliability and validity of these instruments, researchers have addressed the dimensionality of concepts and the predictive validity of their measures as determined by the inductively generated theories in which these concepts were embedded.

The use of sequential triangulation in this context is not without problems. Researchers interested in developing measures can misinterpret or misuse qualitative findings. For example, in May's (1980) grounded theory, she describes a typology of behavioral styles reflecting expectant fathers' experiences, along with the kind of resources that fathers may need to find the best way to manage this experience. Overly ambitious researchers, keen to "diagnose" expectant fathers' behavior patterns, have attempted to use this grounded theory as a basis for developing instruments to evaluate whether interventions have been successful in changing fathers' behaviors. What these researchers have overlooked is that the theory proposes it is the expectant father that needs to determine the best course of action and not the nurse, which makes a diagnostic tool for nurses inappropriate. This example illustrates that researchers using qualitative results as a basis for instrument development need to have an adequate understanding of the qualitatively generated theory and/or concepts and that the proposed instrument needs to make sense or "fit" within the context of the theory.

For the most part, a factor analytic perspective continues to underlie the evaluation of qualitatively derived measures. However, a full evaluation of measurement structures requires that researchers also consider the precursors to, or the consequences of, the relevant concepts. The clearest meaning of concepts arises when they are viewed within a particular context and are embedded in a theory. Although the results of qualitative research typically embed identified concepts into a theoretical context that reflects the complexity of individual experience and patterns of living, full advantage of this understanding often is not taken in subsequent psychometric testing. Concepts are granted meaning not only through links with their indicators but also with their links to other concepts (Blalock, 1982; Hayduk, 1987). Continued evaluation of these newly developed instruments is needed using a variety of approaches. One particular approach that should be considered is structural equation modeling. It provides the opportunity, within a single test, to evaluate the theory-implied nature of our grounded measures not only through links to their respective concepts but also by links among concepts, representing a significant advance over factor analytic approaches. Furthermore, the meaning of concepts can be adjusted using the measurement structure of indicators (Hayduk, 1987; Ratner, Bottorff, Johnson, & Hayduk, 1996), a potentially useful strategy when even our best indicators fall short of capturing the full meaning of the inductively generated concepts we are trying to measure. This can be achieved by fixing measurement reliabilities to reflect information about the adequacy of our measures in capturing complex conceptualizations.

Deriving Interventions From Qualitative Findings

Some researchers interested in designing new interventions that acknowledge the complex lives and experiences of potential recipients and are shaped by them, have looked to qualitative research findings as a starting point when insufficient data have been available to guide the development of specific interventions. They have recognized that themes generated from the qualitative data potentially could be used to identify the most appropriate foci, timing, and processes for a successful intervention. The efficacy of such a theoretically grounded intervention could then be determined through a quantitative study (e.g., a [quasi]experimental trial or use of quantitative program evaluation methods). Although some might argue that such studies simply evaluate the intervention, the findings will also shed some light on the theory or interpretive work on which the intervention was based.

In searching for studies that reflected this type of sequential triangulation, several examples were eliminated because of inadequate links between the qualitative and quantitative studies. In some applications of this type of sequential triangulation, qualitative findings are used simply to guide the selection of already existing intervention strategies rather than the development of a new intervention. For example, ethnographic methods were used to explore breast cancer-related knowledge, attitudes, and behaviors among Latinas, Anglo women, and physicians (Hubbell et al., 1995). Patterns of dissimilar beliefs among Latinas and Anglo women, subsequently confirmed through a telephone survey, were then used to guide the design and pretesting of a breast cancer control strategy. What is interesting about this example is that the differences in beliefs about breast cancer identified through the initial qualitative study helped researchers to determine which preexisting theories (in this case, Bandura's self-efficacy theory and Freire's empowerment pedagogy) to use as a basis for their intervention strategies. Thus qualitative methods only indirectly influenced the design of the intervention, thereby missing one of the key features of this approach to sequential triangulation.

Examples of this approach to sequential triangulation that reflect strong links between qualitative and quantitative research can be divided into two groups based on how the intervention was derived from the qualitative results. In the first group of studies, researchers appear to begin their qualitative work with the objective of developing a specific type of intervention. This objective shapes the qualitative data collection and analysis process. For example, to obtain an adequate foundation for developing a social support intervention for lower income, socially isolated, pregnant, African American women, researchers used focus groups and open-ended interviews to learn about the difficulties involved in being African American and pregnant, the stresses women experienced, and the personal resources they used to manage those stresses, including the characteristics of their supportive relationships (DeJoseph et al., 1996). On the basis of this qualitative study, researchers recognized that, while they would not be able to intervene in some of the basic stressors in these women's lives (e.g., poverty), there were two needs that were within their purview: the need for skill building to develop self-esteem and the need for access to support and acknowledgment of their lives and experiences. An intervention consisting of a series of interactive sessions subsequently was designed to focus on skill building and to foster a relationship through which a pregnant woman's stories could be acknowledged and valued. African American women were active collaborators, fully participating in all phases of the research, to ensure that the concerns that were studied were important to women and that the intervention was tailored to their situation. This project was followed by a clinical trial to determine whether this intervention could make a difference in low birth weight among lower income African American women (Norbeck, DeJoseph, & Smith, 1996).

Similar approaches have been used to develop interventions to meet the needs of specific groups including a smoking prevention program for adolescents (de Vries et al., 1992) and culturally appropriate educational strategies to enhance cervical screening among First Nations women (Clarke et al., in review; Deschamps et al., 1992). The involvement of potential recipients of an intervention in the research process appears to be a critical element in all of these examples.

Unlike the previous approach, some researchers interested in developing and evaluating interventions have simply taken advantage of a preexisting qualitative analysis(es) as a springboard for this work. One way this has been done is through the development of assessment guides, the foci of which are derived from qualitative findings. These assessment guides become the basis of a clinical intervention. For example, taking advantage of a grounded theory to explain experiences related to preterm labor (May, 1994), May collaborated with clinicians to develop a risk appraisal tool to increase nurses' awareness of levels of emotional distress and family disruption to guide the selection of nursing interventions. Although the risk appraisal was originally developed as an intervention tool, researchers have also used it to evaluate the results of specialized nursing care during preterm labor (Jenssen, 1996). Changes in emotional distress and family disruption were not only in the expected direction but also were supported by scores obtained using standardized instruments. These findings provide some support for the potential usefulness of the risk appraisal in practice and, in turn, provide support for the grounded theory on which this intervention was based. While a similar approach to developing interventions from qualitative results has been taken by Beck (1995) in the development of a guide to assess depression in women and by Morse and her colleagues (Morse & Doberneck, 1995; Morse & Penrod, in press) in the development of a guide to assess hope, the efficacy of these interventions remains to be demonstrated. What is important to note is that these assessment guides are not finely tuned measures that should be subjected to psychometric testing. Rather, they are flexible, often brief, easy-to-use clinical tools that sensitize nurses to particular nuances of human experience, the foci of which are determined by the nature of the experience as it is captured and represented by qualitative researchers.

Others have taken advantage of models based on an accumulated body of qualitative research to develop intervention protocols. For example, one group of researchers operationalized the major abstract concepts comprising the Corbin and Strauss Trajectory Model (1991) by designing phase-specific protocols that could be used as a basis for evaluating nursing care (Robinson et al., 1993). The strategies for facilitating the development of the protocols included using anecdotal data to examine the applicability of concepts to actual clinical situations, using case studies to help differentiate phases, drawing extensively on the diverse professional experiences of the research team, and clarifying aspects of the model with one of the investigators. Although further research is needed to determine if the phase-specific protocols accurately describe the care that is needed to achieve the goals at each phase, they represent an important beginning.

Regardless of the approach taken, these examples illustrate the potential that qualitative analyses hold for developing innovative, highly relevant interventions. What we need are detailed descriptions of the strategies that researchers use in transforming qualitative findings into interventions that can be used consistently enough to evaluate their efficacy in different contexts. Which approaches to the development of interventions are most appropriate for particular types of qualitative results remains unclear. In addition, issues related to designing studies to demonstrate the efficacy of interventions derived from qualitative research, while still acknowledging the complexities of human experience from which they are derived, have not been addressed.

Deriving Relationships From Inductively Derived Theory

Qualitative researchers have provided many in-depth theories about human experience that order concepts and describe relationships. In this approach to sequential triangulation, researchers take advantage of relationships embedded in qualitatively generated theories to formulate research hypotheses. Results obtained from testing these hypotheses in quantitative studies can provide support for our theories, extend our knowledge (e.g., by determining the strength of such relationships), or provide direction for theory revision. One example is presented here to illustrate this approach. In a grounded theory study of the health behaviors of female single parents, Duffy (1984) identified important variables associated with health behavior practices in the context of the Theory of Transcending Options. On the basis of this theory, she predicted that certain variables were associated with the number of health behaviors practiced by divorced women with children, and then tested this hypothesis (Duffy, 1994). Standardized instruments were selected to represent the relevant concepts. For example, the Norbeck Social Support Questionnaire (Norbeck, Lindsey, & Carrieri, 1981, 1983) was used to measure social support. Duffy (1994) acknowledges that this instrument provided only a gross measure of the value of social support to women in this study and did not adequately capture the characteristics of "sustaining" and "motivating" as represented in her grounded theory. This points to problems associated with selecting instruments that arise from theoretical frameworks that may not be compatible with or do not adequately address the complexities captured by the grounded theory from which hypotheses have been derived. One of the most important challenges in using this approach to sequential triangulation appears to be finding appropriate ways to operationalize concepts that are consistent with qualitative findings. In this regard, there are still more questions than there are answers.

Another important consideration in designing studies to evaluate relationships derived from qualitative research is the dynamic nature of qualitative results. For example, testing hypotheses related to the emergence of "transcending options" as reflected in Duffy's (1984) grounded theory would require not only particular types of research designs (e.g., cross-sectional or longitudinal) but also particular analytic techniques to evaluate hypothesized changes in health behaviors as reflected in the dynamic process underlying this theory. Wood (1994) has suggested that the identification of trajectories may provide a useful basis for testing theories in a dynamic way. Multivariate techniques, such as LISREL, also hold potential for testing changes over time (e.g., see Bottorff, Johnson, Ratner, & Hayduk, 1996). It is also important to keep in mind that changes in experiences and behaviors captured by qualitative methods are often substantive (rather than simply changes in the frequency of an experience or behavior), suggesting the need for different indicators or measures of a behavior or concept at each phase to conduct an adequate evaluation of the theory. Finally, it may not be feasible to test hypotheses that capture complex qualitatively derived theories in their entirety. Evaluations of any part of the theory still provide valuable information in that the selected components must operate as theorized for the overall model to succeed. If adequate tests of selected components of the theory fail, one can only conclude that the theory should be reconsidered.

Guidelines for Using Sequential Triangulation (Qualitative → Quantitative)

Although the overall merit of sequential triangulation in supporting, extending, and refining qualitative research results remains to be determined, selected examples from the literature indicate the potential value of this approach in particular situations. Qualitative findings generated from methods such as grounded theory, ethnoscience, ethnography, and qualitative ethology can provide an important and useful foundation for quantitative studies. Notably absent from the literature is the use of sequential triangulation in conjunction with phenomenological methods. There is good reason for this. Phenomenological description does not offer effective explanatory or predictive theory that quantitative researchers can take advantage of. Rather, these interpretive descriptions of lived experiences provide the possibility of understanding the nature of these experiences in a deeper way, stimulate further reflection on their meaning, and provide the possibility of "plausible insight" that brings us in direct contact with the world being investigated (van Manen, 1990).

There are several guidelines that can be gleaned from the work of investigators using sequential triangulation (qualitative → quantitative):

1. The quantitative research project in sequential triangulation must be clearly focused theoretically or conceptually on qualitative results. Without this, judgments about how well the results of a quantitative study support, refute, or extend relevant aspects of the theory or interpretation cannot be made and the potential contribu-

tions of sequential triangulation to knowledge development will not be realized. The potential benefits of sequential triangulation depend less on the type of qualitative and quantitative methods used in this sequence than on the quality of the qualitative study on which this sequence is built and the strength of the theoretical links between the investigations. Consequently, only the best qualitative studies should be used as a foundation for this type of triangulation. Furthermore, it behooves quantitative researchers to have an adequate understanding of the qualitative results they use and for qualitative researchers to provide the necessary guidance and advice to ensure this happens.

2. The qualitative-quantitative sequence provides an important avenue for evaluating, extending, and revising theory. However, it is unlikely that only one quantitative study will be sufficient in this sequence. This has been recognized by researchers involved in instrument development, although it may be too early to expect most of these investigators to have completed additional evaluations when initial tests have provided supportive evidence. In addition, consideration should be given to evaluating new theories generated from qualitative research against existing competing theories (e.g., see Olson, 1990) as well as to the need for further qualitative work when aspects of the theory are not well supported (e.g., see Duffy, 1994) or when new questions are raised by quantitative investigations (Kim Lutzen, personal communication, July 29, 1996).

3. The transformation of qualitative results into forms that can be studied with quantitative methods requires special attention. Although some procedures have been suggested to facilitate this process, researchers will likely need to continue to experiment with new strategies to accommodate the wide variety of qualitative data. Sharing both successful and unsuccessful experiences will be important.

4. In all situations, the usefulness of sequential triangulation will need to be evaluated in light of the particular phenomena of interest. There is often a span of several years between the completion of a qualitative project and the beginning of a quantitative study, particularly if additional funding is required. As such, the value of moving to a phase of quantitative research can depend in part on the degree to

which phenomena that have been the focus of qualitative research take on new dimensions before quantitative investigations can be accomplished (Glaser & Strauss, 1966).

5. As in all research designs that involve the use of qualitative and quantitative methods, investigators need to pay special attention to ensuring the integrity and quality of each (Sandelowski, 1996). If either the qualitative study or the subsequent quantitative study are ill-conceived, the potential benefits of using sequential triangulation will not be realized.

6. Developing a program of research from inductive theory building to deductive theory testing up to now has been carried out primarily by the same investigator or investigative team. This approach implies that researchers who use this approach to sequential triangulation need to be experts in all methods. Clearly, this is not the case and may in part explain the lack of examples of sequential triangulation that we see in the literature. Quantitative researchers could be encouraged to take advantage of the growing body of qualitative research as a basis for their investigations. In addition, ways to provide quantitative researchers more access to qualitative data also may be necessary. Alternatively, investigative teams comprising both qualitative and quantitative researchers should be formed to undertake this kind of research.

Conclusion

Although it is not suited to all research purposes, the linking of qualitative and quantitative research through sequential triangulation harnesses the strength of both research methods to enhance productive programmatic research. It is without question that theories we propose as qualitative researchers can provide new avenues for quantitative research. The number of examples in the literature using sequential triangulation (qualitative → quantitative) suggest that it is both possible and useful to use this approach to evaluate, extend, and refine inductively generated theory.

References

Beck, C. T. (1995). Screening methods for postpartum depression. *Journal of Obstetric, Gynecologic, & Neonatal Nursing, 24,* 308-312.

Blaikie, N. W. (1991). A critique of the use of triangulation in social research. *Quality & Quantity, 25,* 115-136.

Blalock, H. M., Jr. (1982). *Conceptualization and measurement in the social sciences.* Beverly Hills, CA: Sage.

Bottorff, J. L. (1994). Development of an observational instrument to study nurse-patient touch. *Journal of Nursing Measurement, 2,* 7-24.

Bottorff, J. L., Johnson, J. L., Ratner, P. A., & Hayduk, L. A. (1996). The effects of cognitive-perceptual factors on health promotion behavior maintenance. *Nursing Research, 45,* 30-36.

Bottorff, J. L., & Morse, J. M. (1994). Identifying types of attending: Patterns of nurses' work. *IMAGE: Journal of Nursing Scholarship, 26,* 53-60.

Breitmayer, B. J., Ayres, L., & Knafl, K. A. (1993). Triangulation in qualitative research: Evaluation of completeness and confirmation purposes. *IMAGE: Journal of Nursing Scholarship, 25,* 237-243.

Carey, J. W. (1993). Linking qualitative and quantitative methods: Integrating cultural factors into public health. *Qualitative Health Research, 3,* 298-318.

Clarke, H. F., Joseph, R., Deschamps, M., Hislop, T. G., Band, P. R., & Alteo, R. (in review). *Listening to First Nations women: Acting on their perspectives.* Unpublished manuscript.

Corbin, J. M., & Strauss, A. (1991). A nursing model for chronic illness management based upon the trajectory framework. *Scholarly Inquiry for Nursing Practice: An International Journal, 5,* 155-174.

Coreil, J., Augustin, A., Holt, E., & Halsey, N. A. (1989). Use of ethnographic research for instrument development in a case-control study of immunization use in Haiti. *International Journal of Epidemiology, 18*(4, Suppl. 2), 33-37.

DeJoseph, J. F., Norbeck, J. S., Smith, R. T., & Miller, S. (1996). The development of a social support intervention among African American women. *Qualitative Health Research, 6,* 283-297.

Dempster, J. S. (1990). *Autonomy in practice: Conceptualization, construction, and psychometric evaluation of an empirical instrument.* Unpublished doctoral dissertation, University of San Diego, CA.

Deschamps, M., Band, P. R., Hislop, T. G., Clarke, H. F., Smith, J. M., Ng, V. T. Y., & Math, M. (1992). Barriers to cervical cytology screening in Native women in British Columbia. *Cancer Detection and Prevention, 16,* 337-340.

de Vries, H., Weijts, W., Dijkstra, M., & Kok, G. (1992). The utilization of qualitative and quantitative data for health education program planning, implementation, and evaluation: A spiral approach. *Health Education Quarterly, 19,* 101-115.

Duffy, M. E. (1984). Transcending options: Creating a milieu for practicing high level wellness. *Health Care for Women International, 5*(1-3), 145-161.

Duffy, M. E. (1994). Testing the theory of transcending options: Health behaviors of single parents. *Scholarly Inquiry for Nursing Practice: An International Journal, 8,* 191-202.

Eckstein, H. (1975). Case study and theory in political science. In F. Greenstein & N. Polsby (Eds.), *Strategies of inquiry: Handbook of political science* (Vol. 7, pp. 79-137). Menlo Park, CA: Addison-Wesley.

Flick, U. (1992). Triangulation revisited: Strategy of validation or alternative? *Journal for the Theory of Social Behavior, 22*, 175-197.

Fluery, J. (1993). Preserving qualitative meaning in instrument development. *Journal of Nursing Measurement, 1*, 135-144.

Fluery, J. (1994). The Index of Readiness: Development and psychometric analysis. *Journal of Nursing Measurement, 2*, 143-154.

Ford-Gilboe, M., Campbell, J., & Berman, H. (1995). Stories and numbers: Coexistence without compromise. *Advances in Nursing Science, 18*, 14-26.

Garro, L. C. (1990). Explaining high blood pressure: Variation in knowledge about illness. *American Ethnologist, 15*, 98-119.

Glaser, B. G., & Strauss, A. L. (1966). The purpose and credibility of qualitative research. *Nursing Research, 15*, 56-61.

Goodwin, L. D., & Goodwin, W. L. (1984). Qualitative versus quantitative research or qualitative and quantitative research? *Nursing Research, 33*, 378-380.

Hall, W. A. (1987). The experience of women returning to work following the birth of their first child. *Midwifery, 3*, 187-195.

Hall, W. A. (1991). The experience of fathers in dual-earner families following the births of their first infants. *Journal of Advanced Nursing, 16*, 423-430.

Hall, W. A. (1993). Development and early testing of the role enactment questionnaire. *Canadian Journal of Nursing Research, 25* (4), 57-65.

Hall, W. A. (in review). *Transforming qualitative data to quantitative items: An illustration of the process.*

Hammersley, M. (1992). *What's wrong with ethnography?* London: Routledge.

Hammersley, M., & Atkinson, P. (1993). *Ethnography.* London: Routledge.

Hayduk, L. A. (1987). *Structural equation modeling with LISREL: Essentials and advances.* Baltimore, MD: John Hopkins University Press.

Hayduk, L. A. (1996). *LISREL: Issues, debates and strategies.* Baltimore, MD: Johns Hopkins University Press.

Hilton, B. A. (1994). The Uncertainty Stress Scale: Its development and psychometric properties. *Canadian Journal of Nursing Research, 26*(3), 15-30.

Hubbell, F. A., Chavez, L. R., Mishra, S. I., Magna, J. R., & Burciaga Valdez, R. (1995). From ethnography to intervention: Developing a breast cancer control program for Latinas. *Monographs—National Cancer Institute, 18*, 109-115.

Imle, M. A. (1983). *Indices to measure concerns of expectant parents in transition to parenthood.* Unpublished doctoral dissertation, University of Arizona, Tucson.

Imle, M. A., & Atwood, J. R. (1988). Retaining qualitative validity while gaining quantitative reliability and validity: Development of the Transition to Parenthood Concerns Scale. *Advances in Nursing Science, 11*, 61-75.

Jenssen, P. (1996). *Antepartum home care pilot program: Interim evaluation.* (Available from British Columbia Women's Hospital and Health Centre Society, 4500 Oak Street, Vancouver, BC, Canada V6H 3N1)

Jick, T. D. (1983). Mixing qualitative and quantitative methods: Triangulation in action. In J. V. Maanen (Ed.), *Qualitative methodology* (pp. 135-148). Beverly Hills, CA: Sage.

Kimchi, J., Polivka, B., & Stevenson, J. S. (1991). Triangulation: Operational definitions. *Nursing Research, 40*, 363-366.

Knafl, K. A., & Breitmayer, B. J. (1991). Triangulation in qualitative research: Issues of conceptual clarity and purpose. In J. M. Morse (Ed.), *Qualitative nursing research: A contemporary dialogue* (pp. 226-239). Newbury Park, CA: Sage.

Kristjanson, L. J. (1992). Conceptual issues related to measurement in family research. *Canadian Journal of Nursing Research, 24*(3), 37-52.

Mahoney, C. A., Thombs, D. L., & Howe, C. Z. (1995). The art and science of scale development in health education research. *Health Education Research: Theory and Practice, 10*(1), 1-10.

May, K. A. (1980). A typology of detachment and involvement styles adopted during pregnancy by first-time expectant fathers. *Western Journal of Nursing Research, 2*, 445-561.

May, K. A. (1994). *Final report: Impact of preterm labor on families* (Grant R01 NR 02377, 1990-1993). Bethesda, MD: National Institutes of Health, National Institute of Nursing Research.

Mishel, M. H. (1989). Methodological studies: Instrument development. In P. J. Brink & M. J. Wood (Eds.), *Advanced design in nursing research* (pp. 138-284). Newbury Park, CA: Sage.

Morse, J. M. (1991a). Methods of qualitative-quantitative methodological triangulation. *Nursing Research, 40*, 120-123.

Morse, J. M. (1991b). Qualitative nursing research: A free-for-all? In J. M. Morse (Ed.), *Qualitative nursing research: A contemporary dialogue* (pp. 14-22). Newbury Park, CA: Sage.

Morse, J. M. (1994). Qualitative research: Fact or fantasy? In J. M. Morse (Ed.), *Critical issues in qualitative research methods* (pp. 1-7). Thousand Oaks, CA: Sage.

Morse, J. M., & Bottorff, J. L. (1990). The use of ethology in clinical nursing research. *Advances in Nursing Science, 12*, 53-64.

Morse, J. M., & Doan, H. M. (1987). Growing up at school: Adolescent's response to menarche. *Journal of School Health, 57*, 385-389.

Morse, J. M., & Doberneck, B. (1995). Delineating the concept of hope. *IMAGE: Journal of Nursing Scholarship, 27*, 277-285.

Morse, J. M., Hupcey, J., Mitcham, C., & Lenz, E. (1996). Concept analysis in nursing research: A critical appraisal. *Scholarly Inquiry for Nursing Practice: An International Journal, 10*, 257-281.

Morse, J. M., Kieren, D., & Bottorff, J. (1993). The Adolescent Menstrual Attitude Questionnaire, Part 1: Scale development. *Health Care for Women International, 14*, 39-62.

Morse, J. M., & Penrod, J. (in review). *Strategies for assessing and fostering hope: The Hope Assessment Guide.*

Myers, S. T., & Haase, J. E. (1989). Guidelines for integration of quantitative and qualitative approaches. *Nursing Research, 38*, 299-301.

Norbeck, J. S., DeJoseph, J. F., & Smith, R. T. (1996). A randomized trial of an empirically-derived social support intervention to prevent low birth weight among African American women. *Social Science and Medicine, 43*, 947-954.

Norbeck, J. S., Lindsey, A. M., & Carrieri, V. L. (1981). The development of an instrument to measure social support. *Nursing Research, 30*, 264-269.

Norbeck, J. S., Lindsey, A. M., & Carrieri, V. L. (1983). Further development of the Norbeck Social Support Questionnaire: Normative data and validity testing. *Nursing Research, 32*, 4-9.

Olson, K. (1990). *Factors associated with the practice of breast self examination.* Unpublished doctoral dissertation, University of Alberta, Edmonton.

Olson, K., & Morse, J. (1996). Explaining breast self-examination. *Health Care for Women International, 17*(6), 587-603.

Patton, M. Q. (1990). *Qualitative evaluation and research methods*. Newbury Park, CA: Sage.

Powers, B. A. (1987). Taking sides: A response to Goodwin and Goodwin. *Nursing Research, 36*, 122-126.

Ratner, P. A., Bottorff, J. L., Johnson, J. L., & Hayduk, L. A. (1996). Using multiple indicators to test the dimensionality of concepts in the Health Promotion Model. *Research in Nursing & Health, 19*, 237-247.

Robinson, L. A., Bevil, C., Arcangelo, V., Reifsnyder, J., Rothman, N., & Smeltzer, S. (1993). Operationalizing the Corbin & Strauss Trajectory model for elderly clients with chronic illness. *Scholarly Inquiry for Nursing Practice: An International Journal, 7*, 253-264.

Sandelowski, M. (1995). Triangles and crystals: On the geometry of qualitative research. *Research in Nursing and Health, 18*, 569-574.

Sandelowski, M. (1996). Using qualitative methods in intervention studies. *Research in Nursing and Health, 19*, 359-364.

Sells, S. P., Smith, T. E., & Sprenkle, D. H. (1995). Integrating qualitative and quantitative research methods: A research model. *Family Process, 34*, 199-218.

Silva, M. C., & Sorrell, J. M. (1992). Testing of nursing theory: Critique and philosophical expansion. *Advances in Nursing Science, 14*(4), 12-23.

Smith, R. B. (1985). Introduction: Linking quality and quantity. In R. B. Smith (Ed.), *Quantitative methods: Focused survey research and causal modeling* (pp. 1-51). New York: Praeger.

Strickland, O. L. (1993). Qualitative or quantitative: So what is your religion? [Editorial]. *Journal of Nursing Measurement, 1*, 103-105.

Tilden, V. P., Hirsch, A. M., & Nelson, C. (1994). The Interpersonal Relationship Inventory: Continued psychometric evaluation. *Journal of Nursing Measurement, 2*, 63-78.

Tilden, V. P., Nelson, C. A., & May, B. A. (1990a). The IPR Inventory: Development and psychometric characteristics. *Nursing Research, 39*, 337-343.

Tilden, V. P., Nelson, C. A., & May, B. A. (1990b). Use of qualitative methods to enhance content validity. *Nursing Research, 39*, 172-175.

Tripp-Reimer, T. (1985). Combining qualitative and quantitative methods. In M. M. Leininger (Ed.), *Qualitative research methods in nursing* (pp. 179-194). Orlando, FL: Grune & Stratton.

van Manen, M. (1990). *Researching the lived experience: Human science for an action sensitive pedagogy*. London, Ontario, Canada: Althouse.

Walker, L. O., & Avant, K. C. (1988). *Strategies for theory construction in nursing*. Norwalk, CT: Appleton Lange.

Wood, N. F. (1994). Response to "Testing the Theory of Transcending Options: Health behaviors of single parents." *Scholarly Inquiry for Nursing Practice: An International Journal, 8*, 203-205.

May: What *is* practice? What is *intervention?* I think we could make the argument that an expanded repertoire in the random access memory of a nurse *is* [intervention]. It has got to improve practice. It has got to improve the experience of humans receiving nursing care. Now if we can get dinosaurs to figure out that does not translate to clinical trials—but it must be measured differently—then I think we can talk about it.

Morse: But does it have to be measured?

May: I mean "measure" in the broadest sense. What good is it if you understand me, and I am your patient, and I do not experience better, more sensitive care, what do I care that you understand? Do you see what I'm saying? The understanding has got to pay off somewhere.

Stern: I think the next step is to action research. I mean, I don't think qualitative research lends itself to testing and measurement. You may want to do an intervention and action research—fine.

Thorne: That may be true to a limited sense. Action research only applies to certain types of questions and problems. I think it is a generalization problem at this point.

May: Can we bring this out into an example for a minute? When I finished the preterm labor study, I *understood* the experiences of those women who were struggling with activity restriction in a profoundly different way. And when I tell others I understood the experience, I can expand their repertoire of everything that they could potentially do. And it's not testable except in the very largest sense of improvements in practice. They develop risk-free interventions based on their expanded understanding. But you can't test it at the level of "identify, plan, implement, and evaluate." It's got to be evaluated almost at the level of the person's experience of that care.

Carey: The next step to test is to ask is what dollars are spent as a direct result or an indirect result of nursing understanding more—of better care provided—and then are the patients, community, clients somehow better according to some standards? That's what I think NINR [National Institute for Nursing Research] is pushing for.

May: But that is not "testing the theory." That is evaluating practice.

Carey: Practice should be based on theory, and theory can help you inform practice, and practice results can help you modify theory.

May: Well, it's just the last part I didn't like. To say that this theory is no value unless it is tested, and my argument is that the best test is to use it. But you cannot test the theory—you can evaluate the practice!

Lipson: You can figure out if it works!

Morse: Is there a step then that is the preparation of whatever models you've got for practice, a part of the research process that should be paid for by NIH? Who does that piece? Who takes all of these comfort studies and puts them together in a whole for the practitioner, or do they just stay around like a lot of stones in the literature?

Carey: If you are not able to apply them, should you be doing the research? Should you be paid to do the research, if it doesn't have some effect on the overall? And then how on earth can you document that?

Schreiber: What you are looking at is teaching nurses as an intervention study?

Sandelowski: We are arguing about two things: We are arguing about how you get funded by NINR, and how you test. Now I think a word like *test*, is used very narrowly. It can apply to qualitative work. We have a "Test and Measures" definition of test. That whole thing about words having liabilities and we let other people own the words, when, in fact, the words are in the English language and anybody can use them. And they have gotten a very small mathematized definition, and we end up buying into it.

Wuest: Well, it seems to be that even if you follow things back epistemologically, it makes no sense to test qualitatively derived models.

Others: That's right.

Clinical Utilization/ Application of Qualitative Research

Janice M. Swanson

Roberta F. Durham

Judith Albright

"Application" is a hard word for many to accept. It suggests some extraneous tool ready-made and complete which is then put to uses that are external to its nature. But . . . application of 'science' means application *in*, not application *to*. Application *in* something signifies a more extensive interaction of natural events with one another, an elimination of distance and obstacles; provision of opportunities for interactions that reveal potentialities previously hidden and that bring into existence new histories with new initiations and endings. Engineering, medicine, social arts realize relationships that were unrealized in actual existence. Surely in their new context the latter are understood or known as they are not in isolation.

J. Dewey (1925, pp. 161-162).

The Application/Use of Research Results in Practice

The problem of how to provide information about the results of research to practitioners is a challenge faced by every practice discipline (Cronenwett, 1995a; Manderson, Almedom, Gittelsohn, Helitzer-Allen, & Pelto, 1996; Patton, 1986; Selker, 1994). Time lags to knowledge use have been well documented in many disciplines, ranging from the lag in adoption of citrus juice to prevent scurvy on British ships (264 years), to the use of hybrid corn (25 years) and the oral contraceptive (9 years) (Burns & Grove, 1993; Glaser, Abelson, & Garrison, 1983). That little research has been used in practice has been well documented in the literature (Brett, 1987; Coyle & Sokop, 1990; Patton, 1986, 1990; Rossi & Freeman, 1993). Yet research as a basis for practice is currently presented as critical for professionals in varying roles, from those at elementary levels (Carter, 1995; Cronenwett, 1995b) to those at more advanced levels (Phillips, 1995; Selker, 1994).

There are many constraints to the use of research by practitioners in the field (Carter, 1995; Cronenwett, 1995a, 1995b; Durward & Baer, 1995; Funk, Tornquist, & Champagne, 1995; Glasser, 1994; Llorens, 1990; Rossi & Freeman, 1993). These authors suggest that barriers to research utilization by persons in practice are myriad and may be due, for example, to characteristics of the practitioner, such as limited education in research methods; characteristics of the setting, including administrative constraints such as lack of exposure to ongoing research programs or other research development opportunities; the way research is carried out, usually by academicians rather than by practitioners or in collaboration with practitioners, or the way research findings are presented, in academic settings or scholarly conferences that are not readily accessible to practitioners.

The use of qualitative research findings in practice has been addressed in the literature; however, the literature is sparse, appears unevenly throughout a number of practice disciplines, and is contradictory.[1] Lacking in this body of literature are review articles addressing this topic as well as a model for application of qualitative research findings in the world of practice. For example, the field of education has used qualitative research methods in teacher education, to advance research on instruction, and in program evaluation. Collaborative teams of teachers and researchers have used stories, collaborative autobiographies, and narrative inquiry in group settings in initial teacher education to capture the experience of the teachers as members of families, peer groups, and classrooms as well as in carrying out initial course work and field experiences (Carter, 1995). Researchers then assisted in identifying major patterns, themes, and issues from the collective stories and developed the concepts and categories to formulate an interpretive explanation, which was then validated both by the neophyte teachers and by the researchers, who observed in classrooms themselves. The early practice of teaching was then built upon a process of negotiating meaning in teaching, grounded in evolving images. Rosenshine (1995) has described the use of qualitative research in improving instruction in the classroom. Researchers observed and recorded classroom instruction styles and strategies used by teachers and then evaluated these instructional procedures by testing student achievement outcomes. Those instructional behaviors associated with gains in student achievement were then taught to a group of teachers, and student outcomes were compared with those of a group of teachers who continued teaching as usual. Education has also led the way in the use of qualitative research methods in program evaluation (Patton, 1990).

Anthropology, particularly medical anthropology, has developed a body of qualitative research findings that have been applied in practice. For example, Lipson and Omidian (1993), in their fieldwork study of the health of Afghans living in the United States, noted unexpected individual changes in health practices reported by participants who were interviewed and who attended community meetings that discussed health practices as a part of data collection activities. Another example is the journal of the Society for Applied Anthropology, *Practicing Anthropology*, which is devoted to communicating scholarly but practical experience in the application of anthropological research. Using this venue, reports have included the practical application of qualitative research in fields as widespread as engineering (Baba & Falkenburg, 1994), archaeology (Garrow, 1993), and social welfare (Churchill, 1994). An entire issue of *Practicing Anthropology*, "AIDS Outreach, Education, and Prevention: Anthropological Contributions" (O'Connor & Leap, 1993), has been devoted to reports of how anthropologists have contributed successfully to the development of HIV prevention programs. However, the 1995 annual meeting of the Society for Medical Anthropology featured a session, "Theory to Practice: Anthropologic Approaches to HIV/AIDS Prevention," in which it was acknowledged that while qualitative investigators, including anthropologists, have made marked contributions to AIDS research, "[their] own theory has had a minimal impact on AIDS research and prevention agendas" (Lindenbaum & McQueen, 1996, p. 67). The application of theory in this discipline to HIV/AIDS prevention was identified as a needed area of research endeavor.

Allied health disciplines such as nursing, physical therapy, and occupational therapy are generally limited in their literature as it addresses the need for the use of research, in general, for practice (Cronenwett, 1995a, 1995b; Durward & Baer, 1995; Llorens, 1990; Selker, 1994; Wuest, 1995). Nursing, specifically, has developed models of research utilization for the purpose of assisting the practitioner in application of quantitative research findings in practice (Cronenwett, 1995a, 1995b; Stetler, 1994; Titler & Goode, 1995).

Practice should provide a testing ground for research findings (Goode, 1995). Qualitative research, like quantitative research, should be of value and used in practice settings. Qualitative researchers investigate naturally occurring phenomena and describe, analyze, and theorize on the phenomena and their context and relationships. This kind of work is conducted in the "real world," not in a controlled situation, and yields important findings for practice. Practitioners may not be aware of qualitative research findings, or, if they are, they may not have available avenues to application of the findings. Reports of qualitative research should be more readily understood by persons in practice as they are conveyed in language that is more understandable to the practitioner than is most quantitative research. Story lines from qualitative research are often a more compelling and culturally resonant way to communicate research findings, particularly to staff, affected groups, and policymakers (Sandelowski, 1996). Despite the fact that qualitative research is conducted in the "real world" and is more understandable to many practitioners, as with quantitative research utilization, a gap exists between the world of qualitative research and the world of practice. A creative bridge between these worlds is needed.

Approaches to the Application/Use of Research

The field of evaluation research involves research that has systematically applied social research procedures to assess the design, implementation, and use of social programs and outcomes in the fields of education and public health since before World War I (Rossi & Freeman, 1993). Early efforts were focused on educational programs to increase literacy and occupational training as well as public health programs to decrease mortality and morbidity due to infectious diseases. Applied social research received a boost during World War II and afterward with the widespread use of large-scale evaluation programs in areas such as family planning, nutrition, public housing, and community development both in the United States and abroad. The social programs in the 1960s generated evaluation research and policy analysis at the federal level that continue today, as seen in the use of program evaluation to combat emerging new problems such as acquired immunodeficiency syndrome (AIDS) and homelessness (Spicer, Willenbring, Miller, & Raymond, 1994).

MODELS OF RESEARCH UTILIZATION

In the field of evaluation research, the utility of evaluations may be viewed as (a) direct or instrumental, (b) conceptual, or (c) persuasive (Rossi & Freeman, 1993). The direct use of evaluations includes documented use of findings by persons such as decision makers or other stakeholders. Conceptual use occurs when the findings do not lead to changes in programs or policies but influence thinking about issues more generally. The persuasive use of findings refers to the use of evaluation results to support or attack political positions such as in setting policy.

Cronenwett (1995b), asserting that the purpose of research is to improve practice, reviews two models of research utilization found in the literature: (a) decision driven and (b) knowledge driven (Caplan, 1979; Cronenwett, 1995a, 1995b; Weiss, 1980). Decision-driven models are typical of research utilization in which a clinical problem is identified, the literature is reviewed, and a *decision* or course of action is taken that leads to a specific outcome, such as a change in policy, procedure, or program. The knowledge-driven model of research utilization is conceptual and involves the influence the research findings have on *thinking* rather than on a decision or some course of action. In this model, the practitioner may read research journals or attend research conferences, which expose her or him to new knowledge. A specific practice question is not in mind, but the findings of various research reports will cause the practitioner to question assumptions about basic practice or to pose possibilities about a new theory in other areas of clinical practice. This type of research utilization has been called "knowledge creep" by Weiss (1980) and "cognitive application" by Stetler (1985). Decision-driven or instrumental models and knowledge-driven or conceptual models of research utilization, as currently defined, are models for the application/use of quantitative research in practice and are useful as they trigger new awareness and new direction from quantitative study. Summaries of selected examples of these models and their use are presented below.

Decision-Driven Models

Zimiles (1993) presented a case study of the use of quantitative or "hard data" versus qualitative or more subjectively derived data in an evaluation of the effects of infant day care as opposed to maternal care on the young child. The evaluation based on "hard data" precipitated a pattern of social change of major proportions that has been viewed by many child development specialists as a "matter of fact," and that has become a common, everyday practice. The three adverse effects from the "adoration of hard data" (p. 384) as presented in the case study are as follows: (a) The research process is limited in its ability to generate valid findings; (b) collaboration between clinician/practitioners is interrupted, hence preventing a mode of working that could produce needed knowledge; and (c) the clinician/practitioner is alienated by the findings that present an image of reality not in keeping with the complexity reflected in clinical practice.

Although classic projects to promote the use of research to improve nursing practice began in the 1970s with the Western Interstate Commission for Higher Education in Nursing (WICHEN), the Conduct and Utilization of Research in Nursing (CURN), and the Nursing/Child Assessment Satellite Training (NCAST) projects (Burns & Grove, 1993), a review of these models reveals a perspective that lies primarily in the quantitative paradigm. The research dissemination models reviewed discuss research utilization exclusively in terms of evaluation of quantitative research (Horsley, Crane, Crabtree, & Wood, 1983; Krueger, 1978; Stetler & Marram, 1976). Examples in these models that describe their use discuss evaluating quantitative and intervention-based research.

Although nurses have been writing about bridging the gap between research and practice for almost three decades (Burns & Grove, 1993), published papers of models of research utilization in practice remain exclusively in the quantitative research tradition (Butcher, 1995; Cronenwett, 1995a). In fact, a recent volume of *Nursing Clinics of North America* on research utilization deals exclusively with quantitative research (Titler & Goode, 1995). To exemplify existing use models, one of the models of research utilization first published in 1976 (Stetler & Marram), and further developed by Stetler in 1983, in 1985, and in 1994, will be discussed.

Stetler/Marram Model of Research Utilization

The Stetler/Marram (Stetler, 1994) model of research utilization proposes a six-phase process to facilitate critical thinking about the application of research findings, to bring about the use of research in daily practice, and to prescribe a decision-making model for the use of research in clinical practice (see Table 13.1). The initial phase assists in identifying the purpose of the research review. The next two phases consist of validation, the critique of the research, and a comparative evaluation. The comparative evaluation phase pertains to feasibility, clinical fit, basis for practice, and substantive evidence to support the use of the findings (White, Leske, & Pearcy, 1995); this results in accepting or rejecting the research. Phase IV, decision making, involves deciding whether to use the findings: to consider

Table 13.1 Stetler Model of Research Use

Phase I	Phase II	Phase III	Phase IV	Phase V	Phase VI
Preparation	Validation	Comparative Evaluation	Decision Making	Translation/Application	Evaluation
• study selection	• research critique	• fit of setting • feasibility • current practice • substantiating evidence	• use • consider use • delay use • reject	• concept integration and/or • practice detail	• outcome clarification

SOURCE: Adapted from Stetler (1994).

using them, to delay use, or to reject them. Phase V, translation/ application, involves an analysis of the generalizability of the research findings and is discussed in terms of measured variables. The final component, the evaluation phase, encompasses exploration of outcomes.

This model, appropriate for evaluating quantitative research, does not fit as a model to evaluate qualitative research. The difficulty begins with the second of the six phases. In examples of the use of these research methods, terms are used that fit a quantitative paradigm. For example, *validity* is discussed. Although there are guidelines for evaluating credibility (Glaser & Strauss, 1967), density (Strauss & Corbin, 1990), and confirmability (Leininger, 1994) in qualitative research, validity previously has been a criterion used to critique quantitative research. Similarly, when evaluating a qualitative study, answering the question "Was the sample size appropriate?" involves more than a power analysis. Appropriate sample size in qualitative research is one that permits deep, case-oriented analysis that results in a new and richly textured understanding of a phenomenon (Sandelowski, 1995). Comparative evaluation includes the fit between the research context and the proposed practice context. This may be facilitated with qualitative research because the context of the research environment and participants may be more richly described and considered in qualitative work, which makes this evaluation easier. Difficulties in application of the model in the evaluation phase would be encountered as well, because these processes are narrowly defined only in terms of measured variables as outcomes.

Knowledge-Driven Model

The knowledge-driven model of research utilization (Cronenwett, 1995a, 1995b), which is more conceptual than the decision-driven model, and thus leads to changes in thinking about practice issues in the clinical setting, is a model that is more in keeping with the use of qualitative findings in practice. In Cronenwett's (1995a, 1995b) interpretations of this model, she focuses on how exposure to research abstracts, conferences, and even tables of contents of research journals will increase thinking about changes and may prompt the practitioner to try changes in practice at a later date. Cronenwett (1995b) reminds us that "healthy nurses may have no idea what it feels like to experience a particular illness or surgery or to care for someone who has that experience" (p. 69). She recommends that nurses in practice read qualitative research reports to sensitize them to human responses to the experience of illness as well as how patients and families adapt. She states that nurses will use what they read:

> You see the actual words of patients and families, and these words lead you to do a better job of eliciting your own patients' experiences and perceptions. As a result, you will understand your patients and families better than you have in the past, and you will plan your nursing care differently—and thus change your practice. (Cronenwett, 1995b, p. 69)

Cronenwett's contributions are important in that they point in a needed direction, a direction that will focus more on concepts generated from the research on the "whole,"that is, on the theory generated.

Models such as these have been useful in assisting the practitioner in application of quantitative research findings in practice. They serve as important stepping stones to new directions in the development of models for the use of qualitative findings in the practice world.

Use/Application of Qualitative Research

Theory functions in the service of action—it has no other purpose—but effective (and moral) action is possible only through theory that apprehends the true nature of reality.

A. L. Strauss (1978, p. 23)

The key to the application or use of qualitative research in practice is reflected in the quotation above. That is, an effective and moral action is an action that may come about through theory that discerns or captures the "true nature of reality" (p. 23) rather than preformed images. Realities, or meanings, come about as people go about their daily lives interpreting things or events that happen to them (Blumer, 1969). Through interacting with others, meanings or realities are modified to enable a person to cope with his or her world. As persons constantly interact with others, meanings are continuously modified and shared, and individual behavior is aligned with that of others as well as groups. Thus people in interaction are forming and transforming their lines of action in terms of those of others. The "sphere of life under study" is thus "a moving process" as persons constantly define and interpret the acts of others and fit together their lines of action (Blumer, 1969, p. 53). If one is to have firsthand knowledge of the ongoing group life in the area under study, then one must "lift the veils" that obscure what is going on (Blumer, 1969, p. 39). Meanings are conveyed through behavior—both verbal and nonverbal. Preformed images will not "lift the veils," but firsthand knowledge that comes about through entering the world of the group under study through observation of interactions will. This is done through activities such as direct observation, interviewing, listening, reading diaries, arranging for group discussions, or consulting existing records, as indicated by the circumstances. Studying interaction in natural settings, entering the participants' worlds, is necessary. It is also necessary to examine the rules and ideologies that depict shared meanings under changing conditions and that affect behavior. Through analysis of interactions, symbolic meanings of events are posed.

The authors of this chapter have found the following questions helpful in assisting practitioners to consider qualitative research for use in practice. Answers to the questions will help determine if the researcher has "lifted the veils" that obscure what is going on in the world of the persons under study. In posing the questions, what we do *not* want to convey to practitioners about the nature of qualitative research findings is a focus on the usual quantitative aspects of the study, such as the sample size, what proportion of the sample elect that predetermined option, or an unusual fact. On the other hand, what we *do* want to convey to practitioners about the nature of the findings is that a great range of options exist—to chart new territory, to open up one's thinking about possibilities about the range and variation that exist related to the nature of the problem as well as the processes that attempt to resolve the problem faced by the participants. For example, in the classic study by May (1980) of styles adopted during pregnancy by first-time expectant fathers, she described an "observer style," that is, a man who was emotionally distant from the pregnancy, a bystander, as opposed to other styles that described men who were more involved with the pregnancy, either emotionally or as a caretaker or manager. May's study opened up a line of inquiry regarding men's roles in the childbearing process and provided new and useful information about the range of types of involvement of expectant fathers for practitioners who were seeking to "involve" men in the childbearing process.

The following set of questions is not exhaustive but is presented to serve as a guideline for practitioners in developing areas of inquiry in evaluating a theory, or findings, from a qualitative research study for use in practice.

1. What is this study about?

   Is there a "story line" (or theory)? What is the story line/theory about? What is happening here? What are these informants doing? Why? How? With what consequences?

2. Does the "story line"/theory fit with my experience in my practice, or do I feel I have to force a fit?

A story line (meaning a theory about why something occurs) must *fit*, very closely, the substantive area chosen for its use (Glaser & Strauss, 1965). The problem of fit between a theory and the substantive area to which it will be applied is of utmost importance to the use of qualitative research in practice. Sociology, among other disciplines, has been accused of "borrowing" concepts and theories from other disciplines. As noted by Glaser and Strauss (1967), "Blumer remarked in his classes that sociologists perennially import theories from other disciplines that do not fit the data of sociology and inappropriately apply sociological theories developed from the study of data different from that under consideration" (p. 238).

So, too, have other health professionals been accused of "borrowing" concepts and theories from other, more established disciplines (Chenitz & Swanson, 1986). Attempts have been made by nursing, for example, to reformulate concepts for nursing from sociological literature, such as "deviance" and "labeling theory" (Trexler, 1996). Glaser and Strauss (1967) caution, however, that to make practical applications from a formal theory, one must make a major assumption that the theory's concepts and hypotheses fit. Because this assumption is made when the theory's concepts and hypotheses in fact do not fit, one is left to force or distort the data into preexisting sociological (or other discipline) categories. Furthermore, relevant data that do not readily fit the existing theory must be ignored. Another important point noted by the authors is that many theories are static; few theories account for change over time. This may require a forcing and distortion of data when the theory is applied to an everyday reality that is constantly changing. In contrast, a theory that is *induced* from data reflecting multiple daily realities over time will be more applicable in the practice setting.

3. Can I understand what the investigator(s) is trying to say?
   Is there jargon, or is it understandable to me or a layperson?

A theory must be easily *understandable* to laypersons working in this area (Glaser & Strauss, 1965). As above, a theory that reflects the realities of a phenomenon will be sensible and understandable to the persons who work in the substantive area. It is necessary for the theory to have concepts that bridge the gap between the theoretical thinking of the scientist and the practical thinking and clinical considerations of the people who are concerned with the substantive area. Thus the concepts must be sufficiently abstract as to designate properties of concrete entities without designating the entities themselves, yet be sensitive enough to be meaningful for the person working in the area. For example, the concepts "nothing more to do" and "lingering" from *Awareness of Dying* (Glaser & Strauss, 1965) are properties of dying patients that are both abstract or analytical to the scientist, yet meaningful to persons who work in a hospital. They give the scientist "a feeling for" the daily realities faced by persons in the substantive area, yet enable the persons who work in the area to grasp and even manage the theory (Glaser & Strauss, 1967, p. 241). The authors then state that a reading of their chapters on how families react in both "closed" and "open" awareness contexts could serve staff in their efforts to deal with families and their reactions to the dying patient.

Hospital personnel who are aware of the theory could better understand the kinds of problems faced by varying types of hospital services and the solutions tried by the staff.

4. Is the theory general enough to apply to situations I encounter in practice on a daily basis?
5. Does the story line account for the wide range of behavior seen in my practice over time?
6. What are the concepts presented in the findings? Are they just named or are they supported by their characteristics (properties) and the range and variation of those characteristics (dimensions)? Are the concepts supported by anecdotal data? Are any of the concepts linked to one another? Do any of the concepts give me an "ah-hah" reaction? Have I seen this or experienced it?

A theory must not be limited in its applicability to only a specific type of situation; instead, it must be sufficiently *general* to be applicable to a wide range of situations found on a daily basis in the substantive area (Glaser & Strauss, 1965). According to Glaser and Strauss (1967), the realities of practice require "the continual adjustment and reformulation of theory" (p. 243). Thus the categories conceptualized in the theory not only must balance abstraction with sensitizing ability but must be abstract enough to serve as a "guide to multi-conditional, ever-changing daily situations" (p. 242). The theory must be flexible enough to account for a wide range of changing situations, yet be flexible enough to be reformulated when applied to practice, even "on the spot" if need be (p. 242). Because the qualitatively derived theory gathers multiple realities or "facts" in multiple situations from multiple persons over time, it generates a theory with concepts and identifies relationships among them that are sufficiently general to account for a wide range of behavior. When conditions that are specified in the theory change, the theory allows for and accounts for change. When the practitioner attempts to apply the theory in a new setting, the relationships among the categories are qualified and changed in direction and magnitude by new conditions. Thus the practitioner who applies the theory in practice is expanding the theory inasmuch as the theory is viewed as *process*, that is, as ever developing.

In contrast, the quantitative approach to theory development is bound by gathering "facts" that change quickly, even using large surveys, and are too few in number and insufficiently complex to account for the myriad changes in a substantive area. Therefore, the variables or concepts derived quantitatively account for only a partial picture of what is going on in the substantive area. The theory is viewed as "correct" and, as such, fails to allow for the adjustment and reformulation needed by those facing the realities of practice. The theory should be in a continual process of development as it is reformulated by those in practice.

7. Are there conditions that show how the theory varies? Are these sufficiently broad to encompass my practice experience?

8. Can I expand on the theory by thinking of other conditions under which the theory would be applicable?

9. Do the investigators state how the theory can be applied in practice? Can I refute their claim(s) or add to their list of applications?

A theory must allow the user partial *control* over both the structure and the process of daily situations as they vary over time (Glaser & Strauss, 1965). The substantive theory should have sufficient general concepts, and possible interrelations among them, to provide practitioners in the substantive area not only with understanding but with situational controls and access to various situations so that practitioners are able to exert the controls. Thus, when physicians must make decisions about whether to disclose to patients and their families that patients are dying, and the physicians base their decisions on the substantive theory *awareness of dying*, they will be guided by a great range of concepts, as well as their possible interrelations, drawn from the theory, and this will equip these physicians to consider the many possible situations that they may have to deal with in addition to the patients. Glaser and Strauss (1967) state that the person must be able to produce and control change through what are termed "controllable" variables and "access" variables. Controllable variables must have maximum explanatory power; that is, they must make a difference. One such controllable variable is *awareness context*, which explains much of what happens with dying patients as a result of the prevailing context of awareness. Also, such a theory can give persons in a substantive area, such as nurses who control information about a dying patient, a broader guide to what they are already doing, and may enable them to increase their effectiveness. Objects and physical spaces such as screens, doors, and the way a room is arranged are also important variables that facilitate the control of situations and the behavior of people in the setting. Access variables are the social structural variables that give persons in the setting access either to the controllable variables or to the persons who control them. These include professional rules that, for example, give the physician the primary role in disclosing the terminal status of the patient. Professional rules and the organizational structure of the hospital, in this example, are other access variables. Controllable and access variables should be included in a grounded theory if they do not readily emerge because they will increase the application of the theory in practice.

10. Does the theory (e.g., findings) increase awareness of sociological, psychological, moral, ethical, or organizational aspects of practice?

11. Does the theory suggest accountability for sociological, psychological, moral, ethical, or organizational aspects of practice rather than for technical aspects of practice only?

12. Does the theory suggest application/use including pre- and postinstitutionalization?

13. Does the theory suggest concepts that will serve to guide the practitioner regarding aspects of application/use such as "trajectory" or "biography"?

14. Are issues presented from the research that can be raised among the general public?

Glaser and Strauss (1968) made recommendations for improving the nursing and medical care of dying patients based on extensive study of the temporal aspects of dying. Their recommendations are for correcting and improving care by changing the "deficient social and psychological aspects of contemporary terminal care" (p. 252). The recommendations are guided by their theory of dying trajectories and are made as a "package" of recommendations not to be implemented piecemeal. They ask that (a) extensive training in schools of nursing and medicine for giving terminal care be deepened to include the social, psychological, and organizational aspects of care, rather than just the technical aspects; (b) the social, psychological, and organizational aspects of care of the terminally ill be planned, carried out, and reported on just as technical aspects of work are (i.e., staff should be held accountable for such work based on knowledge of the dying trajectories on their wards rather than having the decision to perform this important work left up to the individual staff); (c) planning should be explicit for the different phases of the dying trajectory including those that are pre- and posthospitalization; and (d) discussion of issues in terminal care that transcend professional responsibilities should be encouraged among the general public by nursing and medical personnel (e.g., such as the unnecessary prolonging of life and the withholding of "addicting drugs" when a patient is dying).

15. Does the research address empowerment issues for consumers, families, and/or communities?

16. Does the research address the role of the social system (such as the health care system or the educational system) in addressing the social problem?

Strauss and Glaser (1975) made major recommendations based on qualitative research on living with chronic illness for consumers, families, and the health care system personnel:

1. Sick people, when at the health facilities, would have a generally greater participation in the decisions made both about their care and its implementation.

2. The health care "system" would be extended in systematic ways so that health personnel could play more of a role in aiding sick people, and their families, to cope with problems attendant on chronicity. (p. 134)

The authors' recommendations are again based on the importance of staff knowing the patients and their multiple biographies (e.g., experiences with their disease, experiences with medical personnel and health care, and social encounters with family, friends, colleagues, and others) rather than "doing" medical or procedural tasks. Interviewing by staff should occur as "action interviews," or "conversations," to obtain general biographical information regarding types of patients seen by staff that can be shared and that can lead to making specific efforts to respond to these patterns by promoting accountability and organizational responsibility. In essence, the plea is made, based on a body of qualitative research in chronic illness, that persons with chronic illness, who are managers of *their* lives at home, be helped by staff *who learn about patients' lives*, rather than by staff without this knowledge who usurp responsibility for the lives of patients at times when they seek medical or health care.

Practice, then, must be based on a broad view of reality or meaning. Asking the above questions related to fit, understanding, generality, and control of a theory will assist the practitioner in assessing the utility of qualitative research for practice.

Few explicit applications of qualitative research have been found in the literature. Examples of two such applications are presented below.

An explicit application of grounded theory to clinical practice by Kus (1986) presents six case studies that show how the prior theory (Kus, 1980) was applied to clients who were having a difficult experience in the process of "coming out" to themselves. The chapter focuses on how the difficulty in coming out to oneself and embracing a gay identity as a gay person can affect one's physical and mental health, as well as how nurses and other health professionals can assist gay people to move through the process in a timely manner, as defined by the client, so as to view a gay identity as a positive state of being.

Most applications of qualitative research in practice are straightforward, as found in the above monographs and texts (e.g., Glaser & Strauss, 1965; Kus, 1980, 1986). Journal articles that present qualitative research findings also often contain implications for practice. Little in the literature, however, has been found that presents a model for application of qualitative research findings in practice. One exception follows.

Stern and Harris (1985) present the use of a meta-analysis of qualitative research findings as a model for application of qualitative research in practice. The model suggested that the self-care nursing processes may be "enhanced" or "interrupted" as a result of the symbolic meaning and values brought by the patient and the nurse to the interaction and how these were interpreted. The meta-analysis was of seven qualitative nursing research studies in which the authors were involved and examined the variables, contexts, and paradigms related to perspectives of self-care between nurse and client. A description of a model of four paradigms (two congruent—teamwork and forced dependency—and two noncongruent—troublemaker and noncompliance) provided "a guide to self-care readiness that the nurse may use in practice" (p. 152). The authors explain how an understanding of the four paradigms can assist the nurse in assessing the self-care readiness of both the client and the nurse. In a case study, Harris and Stern (1985) illustrate the theory of the self-care paradox and develop a predictive model of self-care readiness.

Evaluation research also has an extensive literature on patterns of implementation for practical problem solving by those in the field. A brief overview of some of the patterns of implementation are described below.

Patterns of Implementation From Evaluation Research

Much has been written about the use of qualitative methods for "practical" problem solving, mostly in the evaluation literature (Patton, 1986, 1990). Utilization-focused evaluation plans for use of the findings from an evaluation prior to the conduct of the evaluation. Thus the intended users of the information work with the evaluator at the onset of the study to focus the relevant questions from which flow the appropriate methods and analysis. Patton (1986) describes this approach as having been developed using qualitative methods to determine the variations in the actual use of evaluations. Examples of the appropriate use of qualitative methods in evaluation include those reviewed by Patton (1990) as "capturing differences among people and programs" (p. 104): (a) doing process evaluations in which the focus is on studying how something occurs rather than on the outcomes; (b) evaluating individualized outcomes, or matching services in a program to the individual needs of clients; (c) developing unique case studies to explain the puzzling case (the case who excels, or fails, or drops out of the program); and (d) documenting and describing local community needs or diversity within state or national programs.

Qualitative methods can also be used to evaluate program implementation by giving insight into how the program was carried out. Utilization-focused evaluation (Patton, 1986) calls for finding out what is happening in the "black box" of treatment that is normally limited to pre-post outcomes evaluation only; this can involve describing the process of participating in the intervention (Swanson & Chapman, 1994). Another use is to clarify or determine discrepancies within a program by describing the "espoused theories," or what people say they do in a program, versus the "theory-in-use," or what their real priories are (Patton, 1990). Important outcomes such as quality of change or quality of care can be enhanced through the use of highly descriptive clinical case files. Prevention evaluation is yet another use of qualitative methods in program evaluation; important insights into why attitudes and behavior changes occurred, or why prevention programs worked, can be enhanced through use of qualitative methods (Janz et al., 1996). Qualitative methods are also amenable to involving participants in studying themselves in collaborative research efforts, called participatory research or participatory evaluation; the purpose of such shared inquiry is to improve practice (Patton, 1990).

The use of qualitative methods in intervention studies also has the potential to improve knowledge related to the process of carrying out the study and the outcomes themselves. For example, in AIDS prevention research, elicitation research has been viewed as critical to designing effective programs (Fisher & Fisher, 1992). Elicitation research is research activity used to gain feedback from the target population regarding the sensitiveness of the format and delivery of the intervention and the appropriateness of research tools to be used for evaluation, prior to the conduct of the actual study. Data collection methods in elicitation research are usually qualitative, such as interviewing or conducting focus groups. Sandelowski (1996) has outlined a number of creative ways that qualitative methods can be used to enhance clinical trials, including clarification of interventions and description of individual variation.

Although the use of evaluation research has focused largely on the "practical purposes and useful application of qualitative methods" (Patton, 1990, p. 139), the emphasis has tended to focus more on the use of the methods, at times piecemeal, rather than on the use of the overall findings, the generated theory, or the "Gestalt" of the study. One exception is the report of the many problems encountered by an attempt to implement Guba and Lincoln's "Fourth Generation" evaluation (1989) theory using a constructivist approach via hermeneutic circles among senior science teachers in black townships and rural schools in South Africa (O'Neill, 1995). Guba and Lincoln's theory involves a naturalistic evaluation approach that promises empowerment of stakeholders, valuing the constructions of all stakeholders equally, consensual constructions among stakeholders, and use of the process and product of the evaluation. O'Neill (1995) reports his experience in carrying out naturalistic evaluation that varies from the original theory at each phase of the process. Variances from the theory found by O'Neill were many, and the author presents evidence for and argues that these variances should "be taken as a natural and legitimate phenomenon" (p. 14) rather than being seen as "variances." The author further questions Guba and Lincoln's statement that evaluation reports based on their theory produce "action," and calls for a more realistic view, "to aim instead for a *process* that can be of gradual conceptual use" (p. 16).

The following section addresses how the overall findings of qualitative studies may be used in practice, focusing on examples from grounded theory studies.

Creating Ways to Apply/Use Qualitative Research in Practice

Investigators who conduct qualitative research in naturalistic settings are in a prime position to participate in bridging the gap between research and practice. This can be accomplished in a number of ways. For example, investigators may disseminate research by taking their findings back to the settings where the data were collected, or distribute their findings in the form of a report to staff, management, or administrators in the field. They may collaborate with nurse researchers in clinical settings in presenting innovative in-service education for staff concerning findings of qualitative research. They may also teach persons in the practice setting how to critique such research using current guidelines as developed by Thorne (this volume). In viewing research as an interactive process with persons in the clinical or field setting, investigators are also in a key position to generate relevant research questions from current clinical problems, thus contributing meaningful studies to practice.

Dissemination of Research Findings to Practice

The dissemination of research findings in the practice world is imperative. Dissemination includes a set of activities that will make research findings available to relevant audiences. Cronenwett (1995a) cautions, however, that dissemination must be carefully planned due to the fact that practitioners cannot be expected to be research experts; in addition, they are extremely busy carrying out their practice, and they are working under serious time constraints and have difficulty keeping up with new knowledge. Patton (1986) cautions that "not all information is useful," and that "not all people are information users" (pp. 298-299). Getting information to the right person in the right format is crucial. Rossi and Freeman (1993) distinguish between primary and secondary dissemination. *Primary dissemination* refers to the communication of research findings via a technical report, as in the publication of findings in a journal or book. *Secondary dissemination*, however, should involve a number of creative ways to communicate research findings to "stakeholders," or persons in practice. In today's fast-paced workplace, secondary dissemination should not be overlooked as a medium of dissemination for both busy administrators and persons in practice.

Research findings must be disseminated to persons at many levels throughout an institution. As important as information may be for the person in practice, practitioners' characteristics, values, skills, and awareness along with other factors may create barriers to research utilization (Funk, Champagne, Wiese, & Tornquist, 1991). Management, or those with a research role such as a clinical nurse or reading specialist, may be better suited to implement change whether on decision-making or knowledge-driven levels, than persons in practice. For example, a common use of research in practice is the routine updating of the policy and procedure manuals for practitioners in health care institutions. The use of the decision-driven model of research utilization of quantitative research findings may be appropriate to keep abreast of policies regarding teaching breast-feeding or how to flush a heparin lock; these policies and procedures are usually implemented by administration following the updating of the policy or procedure by delegated senior staff, who may or may not have a research role.

Staff interpretation of other policies and procedures could, however, benefit from the use of the knowledge-driven or conceptual model of research utilization as well as by use of the decision-driven model, particularly in addressing issues in practice that are difficult or unresolved, such as pain management. For example, one medical center in the West cites standards of care for the nursing diagnosis of pain (Patient Care Services, 1995; see Table 13.2). Both outcome and process standards are presented. Some are quantitative standards, such as assessing the pain experience of a patient using a scale of 0 to 10; other standards, however, address dimensions of the pain experience that call for qualitative judgments, such as assessing the pain experience of a patient for aggravating factors as well as coping mechanisms, and teaching patients and significant others nonpharmacological measures to relieve pain and potential patient responses. Use of qualitative research findings could contribute to knowledge of pain management under varying conditions and in many social contexts. For example, through quantitative research, pain has been studied by developing and using measures for assessing, for example, pain in children (Wong & Baker, 1988) and pain in children and adolescents (Beyer, Villarruel, & Denyes, 1995; Savedra, Holzemer, Tesler, & Wilkie, 1993; Savedra, Tesler, Holzemer, Wilkie, & Ward, 1989; Tesler et al., 1991). On the other hand, through qualitative research, a theory of pain management has been generated by studying persons' responses to pain, including premises about pain and the meaning of pain to patients as well as the multiple persons working with people experiencing pain, within a social context and in an organizational environment (Fagerhaugh & Strauss, 1977).

The usual prescription for dissemination of research findings is to publish research findings in clinical journals as well as in research journals (Burns & Grove, 1993). Other means of dissemination may be necessary for the practice world. To present findings that will have meaning for persons in the practice world: (a) Write using a style and language appropriate for the target audience, and (b) use other creative avenues of informing persons in practice (Rossi & Freeman, 1993).

Table 13.2 Standards of Care

Nursing Diagnosis: Pain

Definition	A state in which an individual experiences, demonstrates, or reports the presence of severe discomfort or an uncomfortable sensation
Major defining characteristics	Verbal reports of pain, splinting, guarding, shallow breathing, altered time perceptions, decreased ability to concentrate, restlessness, irritability, insomnia, loss of appetite, withdrawal, diaphoresis, BP and pulse changes
	Decreased mobility of painful part; fear; facial appearance of pain: wincing, grimacing, flat affect, lackluster, pupil changes, crying, moaning, sighing
Related nursing diagnosis	Impaired nutrition, impaired mobility, potential for injury, impaired gas exchange
Outcome standard	1.0 The patient will report or be observed to be in a pain-free state or that the status of pain is minimal enough to carry out ADL.
	1.1 Decreased complaints of pain
	1.2 Decreased behavioral manifestations of pain
	1.3 Descriptions of reduced intensity and durations of painful episodes
	1.4 Vital signs and respiratory pattern appropriate for age and condition
Process standard	1.0 The nurse will monitor the patient for the presence/absence/changes in the quality and nature of pain throughout hospitalization.

1.1 Assess pain experience for the following:
* aggravating and relieving factors
* effects of pain on activities of daily living (appetite, activity, sleep)
* intensity using a numerical scale of 0–10
* location
* onset, duration
* support systems, coping mechanisms
* quality
* effectiveness of pharmacological and nonpharmacological pain relief measures

1.2 Document administration of pain medication on a scheduled basis rather than PRN when pain predictably occurs as well as effect.

1.3 Teach patient to request pain medication as soon as pain begins and use nonpharmacological strategies to decrease pain (relaxation/distraction).

1.4 Document effectiveness of interventions.

1.5 Teach patient and significant others various forms of pain relief measures (pharmacological and nonpharmacological) and their potential side effects/patient responses.

1.6 Pain medication is withheld for respirations less than 10 unless physician order is obtained.

1.7 Respiratory rate is evaluated before and after administration of narcotics.

An appropriate style and language are critical to research dissemination (Rossi & Freeman, 1993). Even chief executive officers may not have or take the time to read entire research reports, nor may they have the esoteric research jargon at their disposal. Abbreviated versions of studies such as abstracts, "executive summaries," special reports, or even memos may be more likely to be read by the busy executive; the same may be true for staff. Still more creative approaches include videotapes, audiotapes, slide presentations, drama, or even movies (see the chapter by Norris in this volume). Investing in expert help in staging a qualitative presentation may be called for, as presenting anecdotal data in the traditional poster session or oral presentation alone may not serve to adequately capture and present the findings for this intended audience (see the chapter by Wilson and Hutchinson, this volume). Offering to give an in-service or continuing education session, or to start a journal club or other activity, highlighting application/use of qualitative research findings for management or staff can be important, even if the research was carried out by others elsewhere.

It is important to teach management and staff how to apply/use qualitative research in practice. For example, existing studies pertinent to practice issues could be reviewed with staff using the guidelines above, such as studies involving the experience of volunteers in an inner-city housing project (Freidenberg, 1993) or of husbands during their wives' chemotherapy (Wilson, 1991), privacy in a nursing home (Applegate & Morse, 1994), or stories and local understandings in teacher learning (Carter, 1995). Collaborative forums for communicating qualitative research findings across disciplines within the community need to be devised. For example, a review of qualitative studies on childhood violence might be of benefit when presented in a forum that includes nurses who practice in urgent care or emergency rooms, ethnographers who are conducting research in a women's shelter, and elementary school educators.

Conclusion

In the current era of cost containment, practitioners must know what is going on in the worlds of their clients because practitioners are limited to interacting with clients within an ever smaller window of time and space. Qualitative research can assist in bringing practitioners an awareness of that larger world and its implications for their scope of practice. Utilization of research can no longer be left for the elite to implement via policies and procedures related to state-of-the-art, technical tasks that have been drawn only from bodies of quantitative literature. This decision-driven model of research utilization must be integrated with a knowledge-driven model in which research findings influence conceptual thinking and cause practitioners to question assumptions and possibilities about a theory in related areas of practice (Cronenwett, 1995b).

Note

1. Methods included electronic and manual searching of the following databases: MEDLINE, CINAHL, ERIC, PSYCH INFO Abstracts, SOC Abstracts, ANTH Abstracts, SOCIAL WORK Abstracts, Women's Studies, and DISSERTATION Abstracts as well as retrieval of selected cited works from SOCIAL SCIENCE CITATIONS, SCIENCE CITATIONS, and NURSING CITATIONS INDEX. Findings rely heavily on work based on qualitative research methods originally developed by Glaser and Strauss (1967).

References

Applegate, M., & Morse, J. M. (1994). Personal privacy and interactional patterns in a nursing home. *Journal of Aging Studies, 8*(4), 413-434.

Baba, M. L., & Falkenburg, D. R. (1994). Anthropologists and engineers: Partners in the field. *Practicing Anthropology, 16*(1), 19-22.

Beyer, J. E., Villarruel, A. M., & Denyes, M. J. (1995). *The Oucher user's manual and technical report.* Bethesda, MD: Association for the Care of Children's Health.

Blumer, H. (1969). *Symbolic interactionism: Perspective and method.* Englewood Cliffs, NJ: Prentice Hall.

Brett, J. L. (1987). Use of nursing practice research findings. *Nursing Research, 36*(6), 344-349.

Burns, N., & Grove, S. (1993). *The practice of nursing research: Conduct, critique, and utilization.* Philadelphia: W. B. Saunders.

Butcher, L. (1995). Research utilization in a small, rural, community hospital. *Nursing Clinics of North America, 30*(3), 439-446.

Caplan, N. (1979). The two-communities theory and knowledge utilization. *American Behavioral Scientist, 22*, 259-470.

Carter, K. (1995). Teaching stories and local understandings. *Journal of Educational Research, 88*(6), 326-330.

Chenitz, C., & Swanson, J. (1986). *From practice to grounded theory: Qualitative research in nursing.* Menlo Park, CA: Addison-Wesley.

Churchill, N. (1994). Welfare-to-work: Planners, practitioners, and participants. *Practicing Anthropology, 16*(4), 8-11.

Coyle, L. A., & Sokop, A. G. (1990). Innovation adoption behavior among nurses. *Nursing Research, 39*(3), 176-180.

Cronenwett, L. (1995a). Effective methods for disseminating research findings to nurses in practice. *Nursing Clinics of North America, 30*(3), 429-438.

Cronenwett, L. (1995b). Evaluating research findings for practice. In S. Funk, E. Tornquist, M. Champagne, & R. Wiese (Eds.), *Key aspects of caring for the acutely ill: Technological aspects, patient education, and quality of life* (pp. 66-76). New York: Springer.

Dewey, J. (1925). *Experience and nature.* Chicago: Open Court.

Durward, B., & Baer, G. (1995). Physiotherapy and neurology: Towards research-based practice. *Physiotherapy, 81*(8), 436-439.

Fagerhaugh, S., & Strauss, A. (1977). *The politics of pain management: Staff-patient interaction.* Menlo Park, CA: Addison-Wesley.

Fisher, J., & Fisher, W. (1992). Changing AIDS-risk behavior. *Psychological Bulletin, 111*(3), 455-474.

Freidenberg, J. (1993). Ethnicity and volunteerism in an inner-city housing project. *Practicing Anthropology, 15*(3), 3-5.

Funk, S. G., Champagne, M. T., Wiese, R. A., & Tornquist, E. M. (1991). BARRIERS: The barriers research utilization scale. *Applied Nursing Research, 4*(1), 39-45.

Funk, S. G., Tornquist, E. M., & Champagne, M. T. (1995). Barriers and facilitators of research utilization: An integrative review. *Nursing Clinics of North America, 30*(3), 395-407.

Garrow, P. H. (1993). Ethics and contract archaeology. *Practicing Anthropology, 15*(3), 10-13.

Glaser, B., & Strauss, A. (1965). *Awareness of dying.* Chicago: Aldine.

Glaser, B., & Strauss, A. (1967). *The discovery of grounded theory: Strategies for qualitative research.* Chicago: Aldine.

Glaser, B., & Strauss, A. (1968). *Time for dying.* Chicago: Aldine.

Glaser, E. M., Abelson, H. H., & Garrison, K. N. (1983). *Putting knowledge to use.* San Francisco: Jossey-Bass.

Glasser, I. (1994). Anthropological contributions to welfare policy and practice. *Practicing Anthropology, 16*(4), 3-4.

Goode, C. (1995). Evaluation of research-based nursing practice. *Nursing Clinics of North America, 30*(3), 421-428.

Guba, E. G., & Lincoln, Y. S. (1989). *Fourth Generation evaluation.* Newbury Park, CA: Sage.

Harris, C. C., & Stern, P. N. (1985). Women's health and the self-care paradox: Case study and analysis. *Health Care for Women International, 6*, 165-174.

Horsley, J., Crane, J., Crabtree, M., & Wood, D. (1983). *Using research to improve nursing practice: A guide, CURN project.* New York: Grune & Stratton.

Janz, N. K., Zimmerman, M. A., Wren, P. A., Israel, B. A., Freudenberg, N., & Carter, R. J. (1996). Evaluation of 37 AIDS prevention projects: Successful approaches and barriers to program effectiveness. *Health Education Quarterly, 23*(1), 80-97.

Krueger, J. (1978). Utilization of nursing research. *Journal of Nursing Administration, 8*(1), 6-9.

Kus, R. J. (1980). *Gay freedom: An ethnography of coming out.* Unpublished doctoral dissertation. University of Montana, Missoula.

Kus, R. J. (1986). From grounded theory to clinical practice: Cases from gay studies research. In W. C. Chenitz & J. M. Swanson (Eds.), *From practice to grounded theory: Qualitative research in nursing* (pp. 227-240). Menlo Park, CA: Addison-Wesley.

Leininger, M. (1994). Evaluation criteria and critique of qualitative research studies. In J. Morse (Ed.), *Critical issues in qualitative research methods* (pp. 95-115). Thousand Oaks, CA: Sage.

Lindenbaum, S., & McQueen, K. (1996, April). Session review: Anthropological approaches to HIV/AIDS prevention. *Anthropology Newsletter*, p. 1.

Lipson, J., & Omidian, P. A. (1993). Health among San Francisco Bay Area Afghans: A community assessment. *Afghanistan Studies Journal, 4*, 71-86.

Llorens, L. A. (1990). Research utilization: A personal/professional responsibility. *Occupational Therapy Journal of Research, 10*(1), 3-6.

Manderson, L., Almedom, A. M., Gittelsohn, J., Helitzer-Allen, D., & Pelto, P. (1996). Transferring anthropological techniques in applied research. *Practicing Anthropology, 18*(3), 3-6.

May, K. A. (1980). A typology of detachment/involvement styles adopted during pregnancy by first-time expectant fathers. *Western Journal of Nursing Research, 2*, 445-453.

O'Connor, K. A., & Leap, W. L. (Eds.). (1993). AIDS outreach, education, and prevention: Anthropological contributions. *Practicing Anthropology, 15*, (4), 1-72.

O'Neill, T. (1995). Implementation frailties of Guba and Lincoln's *Fourth Generation* evaluation theory. *Studies in Educational Evaluation, 21*, 5-21.

Patient Care Services. (1995). *Standards of care: Nursing diagnosis: Pain.* Oakland, CA: Summit Medical Center.

Patton, M. Q. (1986). *Utilization-focused evaluation.* Beverly Hills, CA: Sage.

Patton, M. Q. (1990). *Qualitative evaluation and research methods.* Newbury Park, CA: Sage.

Phillips, J. R. (1995). Nursing theory-based research for advanced nursing practice. *Nursing Science Quarterly, 8*(1), 4-5.

Rosenshine, B. (1995). Advances in research on instruction. *Journal of Educational Research, 88*(5), 262-268.

Rossi, P. H., & Freeman, H. E. (1993). *Evaluation: A systematic approach.* Newbury Park, CA: Sage.

Sandelowski, M. (1995). Sample size in qualitative research. *Research in Nursing and Health, 18*, 179-183.

Sandelowski, M. (1996). Using qualitative methods in intervention studies. *Research in Nursing and Health, 19*, 359-364.

Savedra, M. C., Holzemer, W. L., Tesler, M. D., & Wilkie, D. J. (1993). Assessment of postoperative pain in children and adolescents using the Adolescent Pediatric Pain Tool. *Nursing Research, 42*(1), 5-9.

Savedra, M. C., Tesler, M. D., Holzemer, W. L., Wilkie, D. J., & Ward, J. A. (1989). Pain location: Validity and reliability of body outline markings by hospitalized children and adolescents. *Research in Nursing and Health, 12*, 307-314.

Selker, L. G. (1994). Clinical research in allied health. *Journal of Allied Health, 23*(4), 201-228.

Spicer, P., Willenbring, M. L., Miller, F., & Raymond, E. (1994). Ethnographic evaluation of case management for homeless alcoholics. *Practicing Anthropology, 16*(4), 23-26.

Stern, P. N., & Harris, C. C. (1985). Women's health and the self-care paradox: A model to guide self-care readiness. *Health Care for Women International, 6*, 151-163.

Stetler, C. (1983). Nurses and research: Responsibility and involvement. *Journal of National Intravenous Therapy Association, 6*(3), 207-212.

Stetler, C. (1985). Research utilization: Defining the concept. *IMAGE: The Journal of Nursing Scholarship, 17*(2), 40-44.

Stetler, C. (1994). Refinement of the Stetler/Marram model for application of research findings to practice. *Nursing Outlook, 42*, 15-25.

Stetler, C., & Marram, G. (1976). Evaluating research findings for applicability in practice. *Nursing Outlook, 24*(9), 151-155.

Strauss, A. L. (1978). *Negotiations: Varieties, contexts, processes, and social order.* San Francisco: Jossey-Bass.

Strauss, A. L., & Corbin, J. (1990). *Basics of qualitative research.* Newbury Park, CA: Sage.

Strauss, A. L., & Glaser, B. (1975). *Chronic illness and the quality of life.* St. Louis: C. V. Mosby.

Swanson, J. M., & Chapman, L. (1994). Inside the black box: Theoretical and methodological issues in conducting evaluation research using a qualitative approach. In J. M. Morse (Ed.), *Critical issues in qualitative research methods* (pp. 66-93). Thousand Oaks, CA: Sage.

Tesler, M. D., Savedra, M. C., Holzemer, W. L., Wilkie, D. J., Ward, J. A., & Paul, S. M. (1991). The Word-Graphic Rating Scale as a measure of children's and adolescents' pain intensity. *Research in Nursing and Health, 14*, 361-371.

Titler, M., & Goode, C. (1995). Research utilization. *Nursing Clinics of North America, 30*(3), xv.

Trexler, J. (1996). Reformulation of deviance and labeling theory for nursing. *IMAGE: Journal of Nursing Scholarship, 28*(2), 131-135.

Weiss, C. H. (1980). Knowledge creep and decision accretion. *Knowledge: Creation, Diffusion, Utilization, 1*, 381-404.

White, J. M., Leske, J. S., & Pearcy, J. M. (1995). Models and processes of research utilization. *Nursing Clinics of North America, 30*(3), 409-420.

Wilson, S. (1991). The unrelenting nightmare: Husbands' experiences during their wives' chemotherapy. In J. M. Morse & J. L. Johnson (Eds.), *The illness experience: Dimensions of suffering* (pp. 237-314). Newbury Park, CA: Sage.

Wong, D. L., & Baker, C. M. (1988). Pain in children: Comparison of assessment scales. *Pediatrics Nursing, 14*(1), 9-17.

Wuest, J. (1995). Breaking the barriers to nursing research. *Canadian Nurse, 91*(4), 29-33.

Zimiles, H. (1993). The adoration of "hard data": A case study of data fetishism in the evaluation of infant day care. *Early Childhood Research Quarterly, 8*, 369-385.

Dialogue: On PAR

Boyle: Why would you bother to do Participatory Action Research? Why is it important?

Wuest: What makes it worthwhile to the community, is whether it is somehow personally worthwhile to those people. The difficult thing about this is keeping all these various people, who have dogs and kids and wives and other interests; "Why bother? Why would I want to go out and do these focus groups on WHAT? You know, I would really rather be a teacher." And it's only that it informs some personal meaning in their personal or work lives that keeps them in there. It's sort of like the personal and the political. It's the reverse. The personal is political, and the political is also personal. If the participants can't see it at a personal level, then they just, "hey ——." But somehow—

Boyle: The *how* to balance that research to make it worthwhile not only for you, but for your participants?

Wuest: I mean, if we have gone into a group and said, "We want a social action focus group, they would have said, 'Good, go do it!' " There would not have been a whole lot of interest. But when we were able to relate it to what they were doing, then—

Participatory Action Research

Practical Dilemmas and Emancipatory Possibilities

Judith Wuest

Marilyn Merritt-Gray

Action-oriented research with its underpinnings of *empowerment, partnership*, and *participation* is gaining favor as a relevant model for health and social research within systems influenced by primary health care and community development frameworks. Despite the principle of social justice inherent in the participatory action model, there are methodological and practical concerns that threaten the credibility of its foundational assumptions and jeopardize its usefulness. Frequently, participatory action ventures are put forward as ideal

AUTHORS' NOTE: This chapter originates in the work of the HEAR (Helpers Exploring Abuse and Responding) Research Team, Muriel McQueen Fergusson Centre for Family Violence Research, University of New Brunswick, Fredericton, NB, Canada. This research was supported by the Muriel McQueen Fergusson Foundation, Imperial Oil Research Grant.

but little direction is available from the literature to deal with the stumbling blocks inevitably encountered when the theory is translated into practice. We initiated a participatory action project when women in our feminist, grounded theory study of the process of leaving abusive conjugal relationships (Merritt-Gray & Wuest, 1995) were dissatisfied by the passive nature of their involvement in the research. Our experience has revealed that while action research has many benefits, serious challenges arise when implementing the approach.

Our goals in writing this chapter are to review the place of action-oriented research in the research spectrum, to clarify the range of action research, and to highlight the salient dilemmas and problems of such research while suggesting some strategies for minimizing their deleterious effects on the research endeavor. Exemplars will be taken from our experiences with participatory action research.

The Place of Action-Oriented Research in the Research Spectrum

Dissatisfaction with the limitations of the quantitative designs of traditional positivist research has led many health researchers to qualitative methods within the naturalistic or constructivist paradigm (Guba & Lincoln, 1994). Rather than seeking prediction and control by uncovering universal truths, these investigators seek understanding of multiple realities. Although qualitative interpretive research is a means of gaining contextual understanding from the perspective of social actors, issues of hierarchy and power in the research relationship and usefulness of the research process to those who participate remain unaddressed. Research within the critical paradigm moves beyond this goal of understanding to one of emancipation and change (Ford-Gilboe, Campbell, & Berman, 1995; Labonte, 1993). In contrast to interpretive research, which results in theory that explains what is, critical research results in generative theory with a focus on what could be (Kvale, 1995).

The Critical Paradigm

The hallmarks of research within the critical paradigm are critical reflection geared toward uncovering the power imbalances in social and political structures and processes, and taking action for change. Critical theory emphasizes group reflection facilitated by the expert investigator with a goal of critiquing the system, revealing oppression, and eventually effecting political change. Freire (1970), from his work with impoverished populations in South America, labeled these steps *problematization, conscientization,* and *praxis*. Part of the transformation is the process of participants becoming aware of power imbalances previously hidden from their consciousness. Action research differs from critical theory in the degree of participant awareness of issues. In the action-oriented approach, no longer does the outside expert control the investigative process. Typically, a collective knowing that problems exist within the larger system brings together people with diverse expertise and experience of the issue. Together, they investigate, expanding their understanding of the dimensions of the problem, and develop relevant strategies for change. Changes occur both during the research process as participants gain new perspectives and as a consequence of the research findings.

Action-Oriented Research

Action research originated with the work of Kurt Lewin as a means of discovering ways to deal with social problems while simultaneously generating knowledge about the social system, but it soon became used largely to address intraorganizational and work life problems (Elden & Chisholm, 1993). Action-oriented research is not a singular entity (Chisholm & Eldon, 1993; Elden & Chisholm, 1993; Fals-Borda, 1996; Small, 1995). The variation in action-oriented research is related to the emphasis placed on raising the consciousness of participants and effecting social change through empowerment of the oppressed. Small (1995) described four types of action-oriented research, each with slightly different agendas: action research, participatory research, empowerment research, and feminist research. *Action research* focuses on finding solutions to practical concerns as well as developing scientific knowledge. *Participatory research* is "a self-conscious way of empowering people to take effective action toward improving conditions in their lives" (Park, 1993). Both the research process and its outcome effect change. *Empowerment research* is concerned with change that occurs as a result of participants discovering and using their own strengths and abilities (Small, 1995). *Femi-*

nist research attempts to seek solutions to the social and political problems of women by uncovering androcentric, race, and class bias (Maguire, 1987). Although action research varies, particularly in its application in industrialized and developing nations, there are core similarities (Fals-Borda, 1996). Couto (1987) suggested that all variations of action-oriented research have the following commonalities: (a) The problem originates in the community; (b) the goal of the research is political or social change; (c) community investigators control problem definition, information gathering, and resulting actions; and (d) community researchers and professional investigators are partners in the research process. A final critical characteristic is that the process is "based on continuous interaction between research, action, reflection, and evaluation" (Hart, 1996, p. 454). Research with these attributes often is called participatory action research (Rains & Ray, 1995). The appeal of such research is that research and practice are brought closer together (Hart, 1996). Action and change occur *during* the research process, not just as a final outcome.

Salient Dilemmas and Strategies for Their Solution

The research process in participatory action research is neither singular nor linear. Participatory research has an emerging design. When the study begins with dialogue among participants, the direction and even the goals of the research may be unknown. Only once the dialogue is under way is the design determined. The possibilities for the participatory action design are informed by the diverse perspectives of the investigators. Greenwood, Whyte, and Harkavy (1993) observed that the eclectic design "mobilizes theories, methods, and information from whatever sources the participants jointly believe to be relevant" (p. 178). The use of a wide knowledge of interpretive methods and frameworks adds rigor, depth, and breadth to the research approach and outcome (Denzin & Lincoln, 1994) but it creates challenges in the process. Additional complexity arises from the desire in participatory action research to move beyond understanding from a subjective viewpoint to understanding from a systemic viewpoint (Reason, 1993).

The research design that does emerge may include both quantitative and qualitative methods, depending on the goals of the work. Qualitative methods produce data that more fully reflect the voices and stories of the community, and thus are consistent with the epistemology of participatory action research. However, qualitative approaches are not concrete and the complexity and difficulty of the research process are increased.

Mangham (1993, p. 1247) complained about the "aridity" of papers discussing participatory projects.

> There is little or no sense of engagement, or researchers and co-researchers *researching*. There is little or no sense of issues emerging, of issues being defined and redefined, of false starts and disappointments, of flesh and blood involvement. What action researchers need to do is to invent a *way* of talking about the *what*. A *way* that captures the essence of the activity—explorations around and constructions of a new social reality.

The complexity of this iterative process of participatory research is difficult to capture in text. We intend that our focus on the problems in action-oriented research will reveal some of the practical considerations, illuminate the pitfalls in the method, and clarify some essential elements of an effective research process.

The Abuse Project

The discussion of problematic dimensions of participatory action research will be illustrated by references to a project in a rural county of Atlantic Canada. The research team who designed the project included community researchers (13 lay and professional helpers and 3 survivors of woman abuse) and external researchers (2 nursing faculty members who were not community members). The team was interested in assisting survivors and preventing woman abuse in the community. Through group discussion, team members identified that despite professional and community efforts to educate about woman abuse and provide services to abused women, women continued to be abused. Women, particularly those living in more geographically isolated areas, rarely sought help and viewed public services as inaccessible and designed for others. Team members wanted to be more effective helpers. Based on their experiences, team members believed that rural culture has a unique influence on both violence and the social response to abuse. They conducted 20 repeat focus groups with naturally occurring groups (Women's Institute, hockey team, Chamber of Commerce) to explore the meanings of and responses to abuse in their town, rural, and island communities for the purpose of designing more meaningful prevention and helping strategies.

What Is Research?

Most investigators turn to participatory research relationships because they are uneasy with the traditional research process. Although participant perspectives and contexts are recognized in naturalistic investigations, the benefits to informants may be neither immediate nor meaningful in pragmatic ways. An underlying assumption that informs participatory research is that the research process itself, not just the outcomes, will effect change or transformation that will be part of the solution. As outside researchers, we were uncomfortable with a research process that failed to give primacy to the community of survivors and helpers who were dealing with woman abuse on a daily basis. We believed that their meaningful involvement in the research process was essential for enduring change. In addition to solving practical problems and developing knowledge, the goal of participatory research is to make change "a self-generating and self-maintaining process" that continues after the research is over (Elden & Chisholm, 1993, p. 125).

Within the abuse project, these assumptions were not articulated initially. Community researchers were interested in addressing the problem of women abuse in their locale; they were action focused, and tasks such as developing the research question, designing the project, learning how to conduct focus groups, and preparing protocols for ethical review took priority. Only after the first round of focus groups had been conducted, and the data analyzed, did it emerge that the dominant perception of research held by community researchers was traditional. For many, the focus was the research outcome, not the process. Some thought they were participating in research that would provide the answers that they would be taking back to the focus groups. They were disappointed that some of the findings only confirmed what was already known. "So this is news?" said one team member after examining a summary of initial findings. Some were unsure about seeking clarification and further discussion of new emerging themes when they returned to the focus groups, believing that group participants also wanted answers. As external investigators, we were dismayed and felt that somehow we had failed the group.

This discovery suggests that an essential element of any participatory research project is discussion of each team member's view of research and their desired outcome, initially and periodically throughout the project, as a part of the ongoing team building. Such discussions will not be lengthy initially because team members may not see the worth of such discussion, and the momentum of their work cannot be disrupted. Dialogue among team members as the project proceeds is important for illuminating the ways that the research process itself is addressing the problematic issues identified by the group and for ensuring that there is some level of common understanding of the research process and outcomes. Through discussion of their experiences with the focus groups in the abuse project, team members pondered the influence of simply discussing woman abuse with 200 people across the county. They noted their own increased understanding of how services were viewed by the broader public, and observed their increased understanding of each other's roles in dealing with abuse. This did not take place in a large team meeting but in smaller groups, and incidental to other agenda. The primary consequence of participatory research is the development of practical skills and competencies, which in turn inform knowledge (Heron, 1996).

No doubt, community team members are attracted to participatory projects out of a desire to find useful solutions to issues that affect their lives. However, there is power associated with taking on this new role of *researcher* in the community that is the antithesis of the assumptions of the transformative research process. There is potential for the development of hierarchical relationships between participants and the rest of the community. This raises the following questions: "Who is the community?" and "Does the participatory process eliminate hierarchy in the research process?"

Communities and Hierarchy

Most literature on participatory action research refers to partnership with the community without identifying who and what constitutes the community or specifying the nature of the research relationship other than as a partnership.

Who Is the Community?

When an investigator seeks to move into participatory research, a central challenge is finding a community-based aggregate with which to work. In the Freire model, the community is often a geographic entity; the researcher engages whole villages in reflection on their current reality and identification of ways that things can change (Freire, 1970). The researcher initiates the work to help the community identify that they have a problem and to take action. In action initiatives, the community can be defined geographically or as an aggregate that has come together with a common interest. Our experience suggests that the defining characteristic of the action-oriented initiative is a critical mass of people who are interested and committed to change. Ideally, the research problem is identified by this aggregate and the project moves forward on their initiative. But more often in participatory action work, an outside person with research skills connects with an existing community group to help them develop a research project that addresses the issue they have previously identified. Chisholm and Elden (1993) indicated that the outside investigator is the catalyst for this "community" to address its common desire for change, but this assertion may overemphasize the importance of the outside researcher. In the abuse project, the commitment for action was preexisting; our involvement only augmented the change process with a different investigative style.

In participatory projects, the outside investigator, frequently an academic, remains somewhat peripheral to the community and is often seen as the research expert, despite attempts at partnership. Community researchers are willing to engage in this alliance because they see benefits for themselves as individuals and for the larger community, especially if there is funding available for the project. Although community team members may all have a common interest, it cannot be assumed that they have a homogeneous view of the problem or of the ways it should be addressed. Cornwall and Jewkes (1995) noted:

> The very act of the "community" engaging with outsiders necessitates a simplification of their shared experiences into a form and generality

which is intelligible to an outsider. This simplification may imply notions of sameness that border on fiction and often would not pass within the community. (p.1673)

As the work of the project proceeds, community diversity emerges and individual agendas become apparent. A central challenge then is maintaining balance between the team agenda and the individual agendas such that the work continues and individuals feel the work is worthwhile.

In the abuse project, the community came from a group of lay and professional helpers and survivors who already had formed a Family Violence Committee. They had previously endorsed our research exploring the process of leaving abusive relationships and many members were interested in becoming involved in a participatory action project that addressed family violence in their community. When we became aware of funding available for projects that focused on woman abuse in rural areas, we initiated an exploratory session with interested members of the Family Violence Committee. Despite our commitment to participatory research, upon reflection we were forced to acknowledge that we had exerted considerable control on the project. We had defined the community by choosing to approach only the Family Violence Committee, and had defined the research focus broadly by indicating the availability of funding. Of interest, at no point in the initial development of the research team was there any suggestion by Family Violence Committee members that other local people should be invited to participate in the endeavor, which indicated that they saw themselves as the local experts on woman abuse.

A risk inherent in the external researchers maintaining control of key aspects of the research process is that community researchers' knowledge of their system and culture will be outweighed by the outsider's view of reality (Chisholm & Elden, 1993). Theoretically, this should have been problematic in our work. However, community researchers in the project were less concerned. They viewed women abuse as a worthy focus and our initiative as an opportunity to bring funding into the community.

Lack of homogeneity of perspective among team members did emerge over time. Focus group transcripts revealed that although all team member facilitators asked the same questions, the time spent on particular issues varied according to individual agendas. For example, transition house workers probed more about people's understanding of the availability and use of transition houses, teachers were interested in how safe teens felt in approaching school-based helpers, and investigators from the justice system pursued issues of police and court response. Although, in traditional scientific research, this might be seen as a threat to validity, in this situation such diversity simply increased the breadth of the information gleaned. Elden and Chisholm (1993) noted the necessity of community members generating "valid knowledge as partners in a systematic empirical inquiry based on their own categories and frameworks for understanding and explaining their world" (p. 128). The categories and frameworks used by each investigator for making sense of the inquiry will be slightly different regardless of how much the group discusses its work. These differences lead to the development of theoretical perspectives that account for variation and contribute to diverse social actions throughout and following the research.

Hierarchy in the Research Process

There are three possible sites for the development of differential power structures in participatory action research: the relationship between the community researchers and the external researchers, the relationship between the community researchers and the community at large, and the relationships among community researchers.

Community researchers versus external researchers. According to the variation of action research used, the research process varies along a continuum of domination by the external researcher to collaborative management by all parties of all steps (Chisholm & Elden, 1993). When the research process is one of domination, the community members may have input but the control of the research design, data collection, and analysis remains with the expert researchers. The collaborative ideal suggests that community and external researchers participate equally in all steps of the process. We found that although we endorsed the collaborative ideal, it was impossible to fully achieve. For example, deadlines for proposal submission necessitated that we write the proposal quickly, albeit with considerable input from the team. Nevertheless, because the proposal guided the whole project, our action further contributed to our control of the direction of the research. When the community investigators took on the entire data collection process, organizing and conducting focus groups, we accepted the responsibility for data analysis of the first round of focus groups. Only when we took the findings back did we realize that isolating the team members from the data analysis left us with divergent perspectives on what we had learned. We had the opportunity to read and work with all of the data; each community researcher only had the experience of one to four focus groups. In discussion, we all concluded that, while community members really did not wish to have the work or responsibility of analysis, there were ways that they might have been more effectively included. For example, each team member could have reflected on the transcript of their particular focus group and identified themes. Sharing these themes within the larger forum would have allowed more inclusive ownership of the analysis and might have produced a richer view of emerging patterns.

Community researchers versus the community at large. Unless the project focuses on an issue that affects only the community investigators, the team goals necessitate data collection from the community at large. The literature offers no insights into the relationship between community researchers and the larger community. In our case, researchers from the local Family Violence Committee included survivors of woman abuse, community members, shelter workers, clergy, and professionals from the health, social services, education, and justice systems. They used their wide-ranging community contacts to set up and conduct focus groups with community members. As the work progressed, queries arose from the public's perspective about who the community investigators represented. In one focus group, a participant commented about people who become community spokespersons such as those on the research team, "Those people are the ones that make the big bucks: they don't represent us!" This feedback demonstrated that participatory action research can imitate the more traditional hierarchical research model and called into question the legitimacy of asserting that this was a community partnership.

Partnerships cannot be formed with all community members, and unquestionably community investigators have greater local credibility and are more knowledgeable of the ways to tap into their communities than outsiders. But it is necessary to acknowledge that participatory research has the potential to differ little or not at all from conventional naturalistic or scientific research in the actual data collection. The people from whom the data are collected are not always partners, and the same risks for marginalization or oppression exist as in conventional research. This perhaps explains why those who are partners may see themselves as having the power of the traditional researcher. In the abuse project, community investigators found it challenging to facilitate focus groups when the perspectives aired therein were the antithesis of their own views. Faced with participants whose behavior and attitudes seemed to be part of the problem, not the solution, it was difficult for community researchers to hear these views and to imagine that this could be the milieu for initiatives to prevent woman abuse. Even arranging focus groups was problematic when key contacts denied the existence of woman abuse in their communities. Because team members had little time both to meet as a group and to do the work of conducting focus groups, members' time for sharing strategies and concerns was informal and often incidental. Over time, however, community investigators found that focus group experiences constructively challenged their assumptions, caused them to reflect upon their own helping practice, and reinforced their commitment for further community action.

Power issues emerge in the actual process of data collection. Because community researchers may have helping relationships with those from whom data will be collected, issues of coercion and power must be addressed in the recruitment of community participants and in the actual data collection process, especially if the method used allows only for confidentiality and not anonymity. Community researchers' strength is their understanding of the nuances and issues in the application of ethical principles to their practice in their communities. The dilemma in participatory action research is how to harness that expertise in the service of the ethical requirements imposed by outside ethical review boards. Finding these solutions requires dialogue over time, willingness to relinquish habitual interpretations, and negotiation toward new ways of addressing ethical dilemmas.

In the abuse project, community researchers had envisioned conducting focus groups in the community groups with which they had the best links. When group discussion uncovered the potential violation of privacy and coercion inherent in such situations as clergy conducting focus groups with members of their congregation, new strategies had to be developed. In several situations, this resulted in the loss of particular focus groups because the potential participants were willing to meet with the person who knew them well, but less willing to meet with strangers.

Community investigator versus community investigator. Community researchers may not have equal legitimacy in each other's eyes. Professional members may view themselves as having more to offer than community volunteers or, in this case, survivors (Derkson & Nelson, 1995) and some professionals may see themselves as less legitimate than others (Fiorelli, 1988). Because community investigators have shared histories and expected roles within their day-to-day work, it may be difficult for them all to be equal partners in this community venture. Professionals who have been accustomed to exerting control in their work lives may have difficulty relinquishing control to collective decision making. Equally problematic is the way those who see themselves as less powerful may speak less in discussion but readily take on tasks such as making coffee. Although the disparities of resources such as funds, technical support, writing skills, and training in research between community and academic researchers are addressed in the literature (Drevdahl, 1995), rarely are the disparities among the community members considered. Yet our experiences suggest that unless efforts are made from the outset to identify and support the unique and potential contribution of each community member, the project can become the work of the most powerful.

In this project, during the process of learning how to do focus groups, outside consultants demonstrated the approach to conducting focus groups by conducting a focus group with the team members and asking questions about experiences with abuse in the workplace. We all spoke of things within the group that revealed personal dimensions previously unrevealed. Ultimately, this knowledge helped us to appreciate each other's strengths. Another useful strategy is having powerful members try new roles within the group, revealing that they too are learners. When two articulate, respected group members volunteered to role-play a focus group and demonstrated their need for support from other group members, it became possible for less secure participants to reveal their uncertainties about this new role. Rains and Ray (1995) recommend that outside researchers act as a coach for team building, which ultimately allows each member to contribute her or his unique expertise to the work of the team and be valued for that contribution. This leads us to the question: What constitutes participation?

What Is Participation?

How much and what form of participation is appropriate for the endeavor to be considered participatory? Greenwood et al. (1993) suggested that participation is a process: "It begins with participatory intent and continues by building participatory processes into the activity within the limits set by the participants and the conditions" (p. 176). Although the level of participation will vary over time and among researchers, the key consideration is whether investigators continue to feel they are able to make a contribution that is significant both personally and to the research group, while continuing to attend to their other individual commitments. Central issues that may emerge include the unpredictability of the research course, the availability of time for the work of the group, the varied nature of tasks, and the team's response to the fluctuation of involvement over time.

Unpredictability

The research process in participatory research is unpredictable, which makes it difficult to keep all team members involved at all times. Time constraints of individual team members influence the progress of the project, and time lines are subject to continuous modification. This variation makes it difficult for team members to remain committed. Additionally, the longer the project continues, the more likely it is for life events such as pregnancy, job change, or moving to contribute to attrition in the team. In the abuse project, the first round of focus groups took six months longer than expected to complete and analyze. Hence, for some group members, almost a year passed between the first and second focus groups.

Time

Another issue of participation is the availability of time to commit to the research endeavor. Although some community investigators may have research time built into their workday, most operate on their personal time. In contrast, for most outside investigators, research constitutes a significant portion of their work, and encroachment on personal time is resisted. These differences have implications for team building, communication among researchers, and project work. What facilitates concession making by all parties is their personal commitment to the project. In the abuse project, the investigators had decided to conduct focus groups to uncover the unique ways abuse was socially or culturally defined and the ways abused women were treated in their communities. The processes of learning how to facilitate focus groups and developing the focus group guide actively engaged almost all group members. Some tasks, such as drafting a list of groups to approach for participation in focus groups, were taken on by subgroups. The endless process of revision of these documents was wearing. It was eight months from the first meeting of the research team until the investigators were prepared to do the first focus group. The time that action-oriented projects take can be a barrier for community members who seek practical changes. In this situation, some members withdrew until it was time to begin the focus groups.

A question that emerges from this process is whether the work would have been better facilitated and the interest of investigators better maintained if the outside researchers had taken on specific tasks such as preparing consent forms and ethical review documents. In addressing that question, researchers need to consider the balance between what is gained and what is lost because, clearly, community-based investigators have important contributions to make in all aspects of the work. Often, projects that are called participatory are actually completely controlled by scientists or academics with community participants only collecting the data (Cornwall & Jewkes, 1995). We think that an essential way the group has ownership in the project is by participating in the foundational work. After four months of the abuse team meeting monthly for two-hour periods, we all realized that we needed more concentrated periods of time together and scheduled three full-day sessions that allowed for team building, acquisition of the necessary research skills, and heightened sensitivity to the community milieu. Community investigators took days away from employment to engage in this work and billeted us overnight. This concentrated time together created an opportunity for more meaningful and purposeful participation in the research process.

Varied Nature of the Tasks

The varied nature of the tasks in the research endeavor present challenges for team participation. Researchers may want to engage only in portions of the project that are well matched to their interests or skills. The complexity of most people's lives inevitably results in periodic absences from meeting sessions. If participants do not attend all planning sessions, they may not have input into critical decisions. This may result in investigators carrying out future parts of the project in ways that are not consistent with the intent of the group or the goals of the research. Our experiences suggest that such inconsistencies are inescapable in participatory action research. Rather than expending energy insisting that all members participate in all phases of the project, investigators need to collectively determine the places where such variation would seriously jeopardize the team's functioning or the research credibility. In the abuse project, participation in the development of the information sheet/consent form and the generation of the focus group questions was seen as important.

Fluctuating Involvement

The fluctuating involvement of researchers and the reaction of the team to people's varied participation raises further questions. Typically, expectations and enthusiasm of the team are high initially when identifying the research question and developing broad strategies for conducting the research. However, those who are new to the formalized research process may become discouraged by the time commitment and the tedious process of developing a proposal, hammering out administrative details, rigorously preparing for data collection, and the ongoing work of collecting data. Because there is no external measure for how much participation is enough in a participatory action project, the norm for participation is socially determined early in the life of the team. Investigators observe each other's behavior and measure their own involvement against that of the others whom they most respect. Therefore, the issue is not the actual time or effort expended but the comparative perceptions of each other's efforts. When members see themselves as not measuring up or doing too much, energy is diverted from the investigative tasks. Traditional group process would dictate the need for confrontation of these issues in a full team meeting. Our experience suggests that serendipitous, small, informal discussions are more effective in addressing issues of difference. This forum provides a safer environment for testing perceptions, receiving feedback, solving problems informally, and, most important, saving face.

Issues Related to Qualitative Methods

The use of qualitative methods within a participatory action investigation produces unique challenges. Specific issues include investigator confidence in qualitative methods, identification of an acceptable level of consistency, reaching a system perspective, and stamina and tolerance.

Confidence in Qualitative Methods

The broad public perception of research is statistically based science; qualitative approaches are not so familiar. Most people have some familiarity with questionnaires and basic statistical analyses. At first glance, qualitative data collection and analyses appear elementary and amorphous. Helpers, accustomed to hearing and processing people's stories, may question how the process of qualitative interviewing differs from their normal practice: How is this research? Additionally, they often believe that, to create systemic change, statistics are needed to convince those in power. Although qualitative information may be seen as enlightening and engaging, community investigators question how useful it will be in facilitating change. This reaction necessitates intensive work as a group directed at increasing investigator trust in the credibility of the qualitative approach collectively chosen. Engaging the research team in developing a structure for the investigation helps to make the approach more concrete. Frequently, doubts about the qualitative method recur throughout the research process as investigators move from data collection to analyses and, finally, action.

In the abuse project, investigators turned to a qualitative approach because traditional scientific approaches had not furnished them with either enhanced understanding or direction for change. Nevertheless, they still had reservations about the credibility of the qualitative approach. The focus group method selected by the research team demanded dialogue around tangible activities such as creating the focus group guide, learning how to facilitate the focus group, recording of focus group interaction, and recruitment of participants. This work helped the investigators to see the method as rigorous and manageable, and thereby enhanced their confidence. Investigators' confidence in qualitative methods was further challenged by the question of consistency in the approach.

Consistency

Consistency is important in traditional scientific research as a factor in ensuring internal validity, or isomorphism between research findings and a singular external reality. In qualitative research, the question is more whether the reconstruction in the research find- ings represents the constructed realities of the participants (Guba & Lincoln, 1989). When the multiple players in a participatory action effort choose to use a qualitative method, their understanding of how truth value is established in research stems from experience in the positivist mode. It was not unusual in the abuse project to have community investigators raise questions about random sampling and interrater reliability. A central role for the external investigators may be to help team members broaden their understanding of ways that credibility can be established through evidence of recurrent patterning of themes in the data, confirmation and clarification in repeat engagement with participants, and ongoing dialogue about findings among investigators to reach consensus. In addition, the investigators may need support to endorse the somewhat intuitive notion of pragmatic validity, where the credibility of the findings is evaluated by their usefulness in action (Kvale, 1995).

Consistency, however, remains an issue. In a qualitative study, the investigator is the instrument for data collection and the vehicle for data analysis. When many investigators are simultaneously reaching out into a community to collect data, all members must be conveying the project in a similar light, respecting participant rights, and gathering information in agreed upon ways. The abuse team reached consensus on the information sheets and consent forms, the strategies for convening focus groups, and a focus group guide. We role-played the focus group process from greeting people at the door through to debriefing. We chose to have a facilitator and recorder for each group, and worked through processes for tape recording, taking notes, and dealing with disruption caused by latecomers or participants who found the topic upsetting. Role-playing brought to light problematic issues in facilitation such as how far to probe and how the facilitator might react when he or she strongly disagrees with a participant. This preparation process increased team confidence but, most important, enabled the development of an acceptable level of consistency among investigators.

Although this general consistency seems critical to ensure that the qualitative method is implemented in a way that allows the research goals to be reached, within this framework there is room for variability among investigators. Each investigator's way of carrying out the research work will be influenced by his or her unique knowledge, skills, and understanding. Such variation can be tolerated because of the foundational assumption in qualitative research that there are multiple realities that are socially constructed. In fact, the diversity contributes to the richness of the data. However, what is essential is that the variation be drawn upon during the data analysis process to clarify salient themes and patterns across the data.

In the abuse project, the analysis of data collected from the initial round of focus groups was analyzed by a hired research assistant who worked with the external investigators in isolation from the community researchers. This was a major error in design. Although the community researchers were comparing their experiences and information gleaned from the focus groups informally, they did not have an opportunity to examine the transcripts of their focus groups or to participate in formal discussion of the themes that were emerging until quite late in the analysis process.

A Systems Perspective

A critical challenge when doing qualitative analysis within a participatory action process is to ensure that understanding of the problem studied moves to a system level. This requires shifting away from a subjective experience by teasing out and interpreting patterns of behavior, their mutual interaction, and the influence of social, economic, and political structures. If many players are collecting data, the dilemma is to reach some level of agreement on the emerging patterns and their meaning in terms of understanding both what is happening in the larger community and what actions are necessary. This process is one of negotiation and synergism; new perspectives do not negate existing patterns but stretch or augment them. This process of developing knowledge is well suited to group work; it may be difficult, however, for those who value and work well in teams but are accustomed to doing their best thinking alone. Although common themes in the data may be readily identified, the stretch to seeing patterns and interpreting them in terms of the larger system may be more demanding. In the abuse project, investigators had no difficulty relating to the common themes. They did have difficulty seeing the patterns, largely because they had worked only with their own data, not across data. For example, in all the focus groups, there was a consistent theme that in a rural community it is difficult to keep secrets; everyone knows everyone else's business. Yet in almost every focus group, a participant would reveal a past abuse experience to which other group members would respond in amazement, "I never knew that!" This apparent paradox only became evident across data.

Another barrier to achieving a systems perspective is the tendency for society to examine problems from an intra- or interpersonal perspective. We are schooled to question what is wrong with the individual when a problem arises. Helpers have broadened their perspective from the intrapersonal to the interpersonal but rarely have opportunities in their work to pursue a systemic resolution to problems. Therefore, it is more difficult for the investigative team to be sensitive to patterns in the data that reveal dimensions of the problem that emanate from the larger social structure.

Stamina and Patience

Investigators who work in qualitative participatory action projects require stamina and patience to deal with the competing demands for immediate action versus meaningful participation. As the qualitative research process evolves, demands on personal time and energy may be unpredictable and may exceed those originally anticipated. The emerging design inherent in action-oriented research demands that the research process be reflexive. Such reflexivity requires commitment and energy that may be difficult to sustain over the life of the project, particularly in the face of competing personal and professional responsibilities. Without reflexivity, the promise for participation and empowerment disappears into a cloud of expediency. Patience with self and others is necessary as assumptions are challenged, new skills and personal knowledge developed, and ways of working together reframed. "When we engage in action research we are engaging in a human process of building communities of inquiry" (Reason, 1993, p. 1269).

Why Bother?

The foregoing discussion highlights the complexities of the participatory research process and suggests strategies for avoiding or managing difficulties. It may leave the reader wondering why researchers, knowing the problematic nature of such investigations, would choose a participatory action route. The benefits of participatory research for both community and external investigators are many. From a theoretical stance, the value of participatory research relates to social justice, partnership, and empowerment. Participatory research facilitates progressive and sustainable social change. The research process addresses the research problem in practical and meaningful ways with people at a grassroots level gaining new perspectives on their situations. There is a development of personal knowing that is transformative and empowering. Knowledge discovered in this way has a pragmatic validity. This rationale appeals to academic researchers, particularly those in practice disciplines, who are concerned with existing social inequities and are committed to socially just outcomes. It also is appealing to community members who are weary of outsiders who invade their communities, ignore their expertise, and fail to give anything meaningful in return.

For some, these rewards are outweighed by the practical implications for the investigator. Academic researchers who approach review for tenure and promotion face considerable risk in choosing participatory research. Although publications and papers are legitimate in such research (Heron, 1996), their production is so time consuming, especially in qualitative participatory projects, that it may exceed the academic time frame or leave the investigator with little time to participate in other necessary scholarly endeavors. Community-based investigators may find that the fit between the research process, increasing work demands, and other community responsibilities is unmanageable for the duration of the endeavor.

There are practical rewards in participatory research that go beyond action at the grassroots level. Participatory proposals may have economic benefits for the community, a characteristic that is attractive to community researchers. Research budgets must then include funding for training, travel, and remuneration of team members who do not have research identified as a responsibility of their work life roles. Time lines must allow for the lengthy processes of building a community-based research team, developing new qualitative research skills, and responding to the emerging design. For academic researchers, the pragmatic appeal may lie in funding opportunities that would be unavailable without community linkages. Currently, funding agencies require authentic interdisciplinary, community partnerships and expect pragmatic outcomes. Participatory research proposals satisfy these conditions.

Most rewarding for all investigators are the myriad tangible spinoffs that occur during the research process. The goals of empowerment, social justice, and emancipation seem to require large systemic change. In our experiences, such systemic change stems from smaller gains at personal, interpersonal, or small community levels, and it is those smaller benefits that keep people engaged in the lengthy process. One basic benefit from working in a participatory project is developing new networks with lay and professional helpers and academics, networks that have spinoffs both for the project and for other work. Another is the acquisition of new personal skills and understandings that increase individual competencies and confidence to take on new roles both within the project and in the community. In the abuse project, interdisciplinary relationships became strengthened as team members planned the project and learned the skills for conducting the research using qualitative methods. When networking produced an opportunity to be paid coordinators of parenting groups for abused women as part of another research project, several team members felt competent to volunteer.

A compelling reward is visible evidence within the project community that indicates that the research process is making a difference. In the abuse project, such evidence emerged when investigators began the second round of focus groups. In many groups, participants spoke of their increased awareness of the issue of woman abuse and how they were talking about it more in their communities. Many groups suggested strategies for educational efforts and community support, but others had specific plans for what they could do. A group of plant workers found the first focus group so helpful that they brought their friends to the second focus group and made plans to continue meeting on a regular basis. This tangible evidence that the participatory project is making a difference in the local community sustains investigator commitment.

Conclusion

The hallmark of action-oriented research is the commitment to social responsibility. Qualitative methods used within such research invite the full expression of community voice. However, honoring the action-oriented process while dealing with the complexity inherent in the qualitative approach is problematic. Our experience suggests that there are no singular or simple solutions or ways to manage the challenges of the research process. Ongoing surveillance, openness to dialogue, and commitment to be responsive to the competing demands for participation and action are essential to the participatory process. Attending to these challenges is critical in the realization of social justice through authentic involvement and pragmatic problem solving within the participatory action process.

References

Chisholm, R., & Elden, M. (1993). Features of emerging action research. *Human Relations, 40,* 275-297.

Cornwall, A., & Jewkes, R. (1995). What is participatory research? *Social Science and Medicine, 41,* 1667-1676.

Couto, R. (1987). Participatory research: Methodology and critique. *Clinical Sociology Review, 5,* 83-90.

Denzin, N., & Lincoln, Y. (1994). Introduction: Entering the field of qualitative research. In N. Denzin & Y. Lincoln (Eds.), *Handbook of qualitative research* (pp. 1-17). Thousand Oaks, CA: Sage.

Derkson, B., & Nelson, G. (1995). Partnerships between community residents and professionals: Issues of power and social class across the lifespan of neighbourhood organizations. *Canadian Journal of Community Mental Health, 14,* 61-77.

Drevdahl, D. (1995). Coming to voice: The power of emancipatory community interventions. *Advances in Nursing Science, 18,* 13-24.

Elden, M., & Chisholm, R. (1993). Emerging varieties of action research: Introduction to the special issue. *Human Relations, 46,* 121-141.

Fals-Borda, O. (1996). The north-south convergence on the quest for meaning. *Qualitative Inquiry, 2,* 76-87.

Fiorelli, J. (1988). Power in work groups: Team members' perspectives. *Human Relations, 41,* 1-12.

Ford-Gilboe, M., Campbell, J., & Berman, H. (1995). Stories and numbers: Coexistence without compromise. *Advances in Nursing Science, 18,* 14-26.

Freire, P. (1970). *Pedagogy of the oppressed.* New York: Seabury.

Greenwood, D., Whyte, W., & Harkavy, I. (1993). Participatory action research as a process and as a goal. *Human Relations, 46,* 175-191.

Guba, E., & Lincoln, Y. (1989). *Fourth Generation evaluation.* Newbury Park, CA: Sage.

Guba, E., & Lincoln, Y. (1994). Competing paradigms in qualitative research. In N. Denzin & Y. Lincoln (Eds.), *Handbook of qualitative research* (pp. 105-117). Thousand Oaks, CA: Sage.

Hart, E. (1996). Action research as a professionalizing strategy: Issues and dilemmas. *Journal of Advanced Nursing, 23,* 454-461.

Heron, J. (1996). Quality as primacy of the practical. *Qualitative Inquiry, 2,* 41-56.

Kvale, S. (1995). The social construction of validity. *Qualitative Inquiry, 1,* 19-40.

Labonte, R. (1993). *Health promotion and empowerment: Practice frameworks.* Toronto, Canada: Centre for Health Promotion and ParticipACTION.

Maguire, P. (1987). *Doing participatory research: A feminist approach.* Amherst, MA: Center for International Education.

Mangham, I. (1993). Conspiracies of silence? Some critical comments of the action research special issue, February, 1993. *Human Relations, 46,* 1243-1251.

Merritt-Gray, M., & Wuest, J. (1995). Counteracting abuse and breaking free: The process of leaving revealed through women's voices. *Health Care for Women International, 16,* 399-412.

Park, P. (1993). What is participatory research? A theoretical and methodological perspective. In P. Park, M. Brydon-Miller, B. Hall, & T. Jackson (Eds.), *Voices of change: Participatory research in the United States and Canada* (pp. 1-20). Toronto: OISE Press.

Rains, J., & Ray, D. W. (1995). Participatory action research for community health promotion. *Public Health Nursing, 12,* 256-261.

Reason, P. (1993). Sitting between appreciation and disappointment: A critique on the special edition of *Human Relations* on action research. *Human Relations, 46,* 1253-1269.

Small, S. (1995). Action-oriented research: Models and methods. *Journal of Marriage and the Family, 57,* 941-955.

Brainstorming: Sorting Out Meta-Analysis

Morse: There is something that we haven't talked about: Qualitative researchers don't replicate. So if there are two studies in the literature on the same topic, it's coincidental.

Stern: Yes.

Morse: So therefore you don't have a bank of replicated studies—

Sandelowski: But you have similar—complementary—

Morse: But studies overlap in different ways. They overlap because they are about the same phenomenon or the same concept, or they overlap because they are about the same disease entity, or they overlap because they are about something else. And you have to make your decision about what it is you are collecting studies on. And people go around collecting studies about *illness*. Now when Joy [Johnson] and I put together all of those studies on illness, we were criticized because people said that Norris's study was about abortion, and "abortion wasn't illness." This is ridiculous. And when I told Judy [Norris], she said, "My study wasn't about abortion; it wasn't about illness—it was about soul ache."

So what our theory is about is human responses to a threat to the self, or whatever. And if you look at it that way, then Judy's study fits perfectly. If we create these artificial boundaries and don't let these studies, as Glaser says, "earn their way into the data," then you get into a whole lot of trouble, and you have a tremendous threat to validity—if you want to use that bad *V* word.

So that's why I think you have to start with the most abstract concept and work down.

May: That's a nice bit of intellectual footwork! But 99% of folks who attempt to do that, can't do that. Even in my field if you took all the qualitative work on at-risk childbearing—there are not very many, but you could pile them up on the table. But then to push through and find out what the study *really* was about. And to think: this one is about "technological management of conditions." And this one is about "suffering and anticipatory grief."

Do you see it's a level problem? You've got apples and Tuesdays. And the source data don't necessarily tell you [what it's about]. Jan [Morse] had to get inside those studies and then say, "But what did they really do?"

Morse: But it is false for us to go and collect studies on heart attacks and strokes.

Sandelowski: But it's the way you start. In order to get to the point where you are—that's something that's invented by the analysis. And in order to get there, you have to go through this process. A naturally occurring way to start is, "Gee, I am interested in people's responses to heart attack," and then to say the essence of this thing is not the heart attack, per se. The main part of the analytic work is *getting there*—you don't get there first.

Morse: You are totally right. But I don't know if you have to do the coding, or if you have to be theory-smart—the problem is, if you start off with the data, you get bogged down. You get into not seeing the forest for the trees thing—you can't get there. To do a meta-analysis, you have to be so broadly read, and as Joy [Johnson] said, you have to decide on your goal before you start. So you are doing this analytic stuff and working almost deductively, organizing your theory.

Sandelowski: It's like any qualitative person who goes in with an orientation, but not a fixed question. You think you are interested in one thing and that's very interesting to me, and that's what gets me in there. But I don't know if that's how I'm going to leave. And that's what's different about qualitative work. You have some idea about where you want to go, but that may not be where you end up. And I think the same principle holds true here, but what you have to do is show that process, and that's one of the differences in doing this work. There is no way to look up in the computer the sort of thing we end up with. But you do have to start somewhere like looking up research on heart disease.

Morse: What I was trying to do was to lift these grounded theory studies up into a higher level of abstraction of "suffering and enduring" and kinds of suffering and enduring, which encompasses all kinds of illness responses. And maybe there will be something above that. And *that's* what's useful to nursing—not the medical taxonomy of diseases.

Johnson: I think the other thing though is that we have to let go of the idea of statistical meta-analysis—of getting *every* study.

Carey: How on earth do you theoretically sample?

Boyle: It's like theoretical sensitivity. Somehow, by knowing something about the literature, you know where to go; as you read more, you get more insight.

Sandelowski: And even more than that—you have some idea about where you want to go.

Question: How is this different from "formal theory"?

Others: It *is* formal theory!

Qualitative Meta-Analysis

Rita Schreiber
Dauna Crooks
Phyllis Noerager Stern

Meta-analysis in quantitative research has long been accepted as a legitimate method for pooling research findings. In quantitative meta-analysis, the primary purpose is to combine a number of studies exploring the same research question, so that with the increase of sample size, the effectiveness of interventions may be more readily assessed. Methods for quantitative meta-analysis techniques are well developed and described. However, in qualitative research the purpose of meta-analysis is not to evaluate treatment effects or causal relationships but to develop theory at the grand or midrange level or to develop theoretical description. At this time, the methods are relatively poorly developed. The purpose of this chapter is to explore

AUTHORS' NOTE: The authors wish to thank the other authors in this volume for their helpful feedback in the preparation of the manuscript. In addition, they would like particularly to thank Judith Wuest, Eleanor Covan, Patricia Munhall, and Barney Glaser for their invaluable contributions.

311

the various uses of the synthesis of qualitative studies and to explore methods by which this is achieved. Finally, we present a number of philosophical and methodological considerations inherent in the synthesis of interpretive findings.

Qualitative meta-analysis is a way of knowing-what-we-know and further extending findings. Qualitative meta-analysis presents a number of challenges, and the researcher undertaking the task must be aware of, and prepared to sort through, a variety of philosophical and methodological considerations. Techniques used at this time are poorly understood, underdeveloped, and lack clear description. Although this leaves some room for creativity and ingenuity, the meta-analyst must take care to ensure that the procedures undertaken are congruent with the naturalistic paradigm (Noblit & Hare, 1988). Further, because techniques are still evolving, for future examination, documenting the process used will assist in methodological development through reflective practice.

Challenges for the Qualitative Meta-Analyst

As research findings proliferate, investigators are urged to wrestle with the problem of developing ways to synthesize what is known in their fields of study. But the challenge remains: How do we, as qualitative researchers, determine what we know about a particular phenomenon? How do we identify what we do not know? How do we uncover what has remained hidden so that it might be studied? How do we compare studies that are bound to different contexts? And, if meta-analysis is accomplished, will the synthesis of research ultimately make a difference in the lives of people or develop knowledge in a substantive way?

Clarification of Terms and Interrelationships

The term *qualitative meta-analysis* was first used by Stern and Harris in 1985 to refer to the synthesis of a group of qualitative research *findings* into one explanatory interpretative end product. Because meta-analysis is a process of synthesizing findings from a group of naturalistic studies, the findings themselves are considered to be data for analysis. This contrasts with *secondary analysis*, in which the researcher has access to the original data from a study or group of studies and uses this to reanalyze and/or synthesize results, usually to answer a different question or to view the data with a different analytic focus or even using a different qualitative method (see Thorne, 1994).[1] Our limited use of the term *secondary analysis* differs from other uses (Estabrooks, Field, & Morse, 1994; Jensen & Allen, 1996, 1994) in that we confine secondary analysis to reanalysis of original raw data. Further, meta-analysis differs from methodological triangulation (see Denzin, 1970) in important ways: Meta-analysis is usually conducted by researchers other than the investigators of the original studies who have no access to the original data, with certain important exceptions (Glaser & Strauss, 1971; Stern & Harris, 1985), as explained in a later section.

Currently, the variety of conceptualizations of meta-analysis is seen in the variation in related terms used to describe the synthesis of qualitative findings. Noblit and Hare (1988) have synthesized ethnographic findings in what they term *meta-ethnography*. Stressing the interpretive nature of meta-analysis and of naturalistic research in general, these authors found that translating studies into one another's metaphorical languages could be used to synthesize ethnographic findings. Estabrooks et al. (1994) used the term *aggregating findings* and consider it a means of increasing the level of abstraction and thus developing midrange theory. However, they view this as a type of secondary analysis that increases the generalizability of findings through theoretical development.

Finally, the term *meta-study* is used to signify an analysis that includes more than examination and synthesis of findings (Paterson, personal communication, 1996), to place and interpret the results of a most comprehensive meta-analysis within a temporal or historical context. Thus a meta-study may consist of a series of meta-analytical studies, comparing and contrasting the results in delimited segments of time, to discover changing theoretical orientation of the research. Paterson and her colleagues (1996) have found that their examination of theoretically and methodologically diverse studies has moved the investigation in different directions. Because of this, Paterson coined the terms *meta-method* and *meta-theory* to describe the process.

What is the difference between meta-analysis and a review of the literature? A classical literature review consists of a summary of research questions, findings, variables, methods, conclusions, limitations, and suggestions for future investigation, and reflects the current state of knowledge about a certain topic. Note that the topic may be broad, encompassing an area, rather than as in meta-analysis, being driven by a research question. Although the literature review is an excellent means of identifying and summarizing findings to date, contrasting with meta-analysis, a literature review contains no mechanism for meaningful, interpretive synthesis so that the reader can make sense of the aggregated results. Even an integrative literature review, in which the researcher uses the report of findings as a means in itself rather than a proposal for future research, fails to do this. Qualitative researchers can use the literature review to identify sensitizing concepts as well as for writing research proposals; however, they can do no more than that. As Noblit and Hare (1988) state: "Literature reviews in practice are more rituals than substantive accomplishments" (p. 15).

So, what is meta-analysis? Mish (1989) defines *meta* as "a prefix meaning 'among,' 'along with,' 'after,' 'behind,' and often denoting change, found chiefly in scientific words" (p. 745). The same source defines *analysis* as "separation of a whole, whether a material substance or any matter of thought, into its constituent elements as a method of studying the nature of a thing or of determining its essential features" (p. 82). Using this definition, meta-analysis becomes the bringing together and breaking down of findings, examining them, discovering the essential features, and, in some way, combining phenomena into a transformed whole. We propose that qualitative meta-analysis is *the aggregating of a group of studies for the purposes of discovering the essential elements and translating the results into an end product that transforms the original results into a new conceptualization.* This is similar, in many ways, to Noblit and Hare's (1988) translating the results into one another's language.

Uses of Meta-Analysis

To date, we have identified meta-analytic techniques used in three distinct ways: theory building, theory explication, and theoretical description. The methodological techniques used for each purpose may differ, and for each approach the questions posed above will be answered somewhat differently. However, the emergence of three somewhat distinct purposes of qualitative meta-analysis should be considered before methodological techniques are described.

(1) Theory building. Meta-analytic techniques are ideal for theory construction. They enable the analyst to begin with description and systematically bring the research to higher levels of abstraction. For example, Glaser and Strauss (1965, 1967, 1968, 1971) in their studies of dying patients and their families, on further examination, discovered the concept of status passage, or passage through meaningful benchmarks of life, and its impact on the lives of individuals. After searching the work of other authors, they further developed the theory of status passage (1971) as life changes through salient experiences. Thus, what began as research on dying, became a theory of salient life events.

In this way, meta-analytic techniques enable researchers to use data from diverse sources and to push the level of theory beyond the level possible using data from only one sample. In this way, the end product is developed to the level of formal theory.

(2) Theory explication. The second approach shows the researcher doing theory explication (Morse, this volume), which would begin with the most abstract concept, for example, *self*, and move outward to study and "flesh out" all that emerged that was hermeneutically a part of the original concept. Note that the lateral and deductive analytic processes result in the reconceptualization of the studies included in the meta-analysis.

(3) Theoretical development. The third approach to meta-analysis involves the synthesis of findings into a final product that is thickly descriptive, and comprehensive—somewhat like a meta-phenomenology or ethnography. In this way, the final product is more complete and comprehensive than any of the original studies. This type of meta-analysis would not necessarily result in theory development, although it could do so. More likely, it lays an excellent foundation for concept and theory development, depending on the analytic methods used by the researchers as well as the desired end product.

These three purposes of meta-analysis may not be exhaustive, or mutually exclusive. Rather, they may be complementary and overlapping. In each of the three meta-analyses, the researcher would use different approaches to sampling, data, analysis, and so forth. These are summarized in Table 15.1.

Philosophical/Methodological Issues

When conducting qualitative meta-analysis, a number of significant philosophical issues arise that directly affect the methodological choices to be made. For instance, the researcher must determine the purpose and expected outcome of the analysis, given the three purposes discussed above. Researchers must decide what will be considered to be data, how the literature will be sampled, as well as what is to be included or excluded. The researcher must consider the context of the final analysis and level of abstraction to be achieved in the analytic process.

Therefore, much of this discussion will highlight the complexity of the decision making in the meta-analysis process. At this stage, considering the level of evolution of qualitative meta-analytic techniques, documentation of the decision trail is essential. This process enables the reader to retrace the analytic process, to evaluate the decisions and the findings, and to report accurately on the conceptual processes used during analysis.

Data. The earliest decision for the meta-analyst is to determine: "What are my data?" The researcher must decide what will be included and why. This decision involves both the scope of the study and the importance of maintaining congruence with the naturalistic paradigm used in the study. It also involves issues of standards of qualitative research.

For instance, in a theory-building meta-analysis on the relationship between enduring, suffering, and hope, the concept of *uncertainty* emerged (Morse & Penrod, in review). Although the significance of this concept could not be appreciated at the commencement of the study, a theoretical decision had to be made on whether to allow uncertainty to force its way into the analysis, or whether to remain focused on the three original concepts. Such a decision obviously affects the validity and the comprehensiveness of the completed theory, but it also broadens the scope of the study, which, in turn, could also reduce the density of the theoretical product.

Table 15.1 Proposed Models of Qualitative Meta-Analysis

	Models		
Issues	Theory Building	Theory Explication	Description
What is the purpose of this meta-analysis? (or: What is my research question?)	• to build midrange or formal theory from a group of studies of related concepts	• to develop mid-range or formal theory from a group of studies related by a single concept	• to examine a group of studies to discover the essential naturalistic interpretation/ understanding of a phenomenon
What are the assumptions underlying the question?	• Everything is data.	• Findings must be deconstructed.	• The final analysis is in the text.
What is the usefulness of the potential end product?	• creating theory • generating research questions • identifying gaps in knowledge	• development of theory • generating research questions • identifying gaps in knowledge	• informing practice • informing policy • identifying gaps in knowledge • discovering substantive theory
What are the boundaries of the study?	• Boundaries are emergent and follow the unfolding of the study results.	• Boundaries are predefined.	• Boundaries could be either prede-fined or emergent.
What are the assumptions underlying the methodology of the meta-analysis?	• inductive/emergent approach to theory building	• deductive approach to theory building	• theory not neces-sarily a desired outcome • findings grounded in, and close to, the data
What constitutes my data?	• studies of related concepts or phenomena	• studies of the same concept	• could use any qualitative study
How will I analyze my data?	• by constant comparison	• by deconstruction, reconstruction, and constant comparison	• could use phenome-nology, hermeneu-tics, or ethnography
What sampling procedure do I use? How do I know what to include?	• can start anywhere and follow it through to higher levels of abstraction • studies related by concepts	• must start with the most abstract concept and follow with related, less abstract concepts • studies related by a single concept	• could start with a diagnostic category (people with breast cancer, for example)
How do I ensure the scientific rigor of the meta-analysis?	• Constant compar-ison will allow the core variable to emerge.	• The methodology must have careful illumination.	• The findings should be immediately rec-ognizable to those who have experi-ence with the phe-nomenon of study.

Must the sample only include articles that use one methodology? It has been suggested that it would make sense to include for analysis findings that are at roughly the same conceptual context. In other words, from this perspective, phenomenological findings that yield rich description could not be combined with findings from grounded theory in the same meta-analytic study. Not only do phenomenology and grounded theory have different philosophical underpinnings, but temporally, the process focus of grounded theory does not fit well with the more limited, but in-depth focus of phenomenology. At best, a phenomenological study would only illuminate one stage of the grounded theory process. However, those who hold the "do not mix" perspective may combine studies from grounded theory and ethnography because the results are philosophically more structurally alike.

Other researchers might be less concerned about the issue of incompatibility of ontological/epistemological parameters. For example, a grounded theorist may appropriately combine findings obtained from studies that use different methods, using grounded theory-based techniques to synthesize the results at a more abstract level. In this way, findings from any qualitative study become "grist for the synthesis mill." As Strauss (personal communication, 1974) noted, "Everything is data." These researchers appear to be less concerned about specific methods, and focus more on the same substantive area when synthesizing studies (Covan, personal communication, 1996; Glaser, personal communication, 1996; Miles & Huberman, 1994).

Thus the decision on whether or not to include articles using different qualitative research methods in the meta-analysis is a philosophical one that depends on the worldview of the researcher. Although bringing together data collected by different techniques to confirm and elaborate the findings may be considered triangulation, in this view the fact that the findings were from varied methodologies has limited impact on the end result. Ultimately, when deciding what should be included in the meta-analysis, the researcher must consider the purpose of the study, its intended audience, and what the end product will be.

Sampling. A second major question for the researcher and one that is closely related to the previous section is this: "How will I sample?" Qualitative researchers accept the notion of some type of purposive or theoretical sampling as a necessary principle that guides the sampling process. Can one theoretically sample in a qualitative meta-analysis? If so, how is it done? If not, what can be done instead that will be sufficiently congruent with the naturalistic paradigm to be both plausible and acceptable? Again, the principles guiding the theoretical sampling technique depend on the research questions, the desired end product, and the ontological/epistemological parameters discussed above.

Another sampling issue is that of rigor. Must the researcher limit the sample on the basis of some criteria for rigor? Does the rigor of the original studies have an effect on the meta-analysis, and, if so, how is the issue of standards and quality to be handled? Jensen and Allen (1996) suggest that imposing restrictions on inclusion based on scientific merit is likely to result in eliminating "data germane to the purpose of the investigation" (p. 557).

Finally, there is scope: How does the researcher decide what is pertinent to the meta-analysis and what is not? According to Glaser, it is a matter of the theoretical needs of the study. A researcher using constant comparison continues using examples of what is and what is not a part of a concept, until the researcher reaches the desired level of abstraction. In his words: "As far as comparing apples and oranges, they're both fruit, they both have skin, they are both sweet, so what's the difference?" (Glaser, personal communication, 1996) Thus, for Glaser, the process of sampling is analogous to multivariate analysis: The cells need to be filled with data, and saturation must be achieved.

Can a researcher sample *from* a study, or must it be accepted in its entirety? Depending on the research question, in some studies the factors of interest in the meta-analysis may not be the central issue. For example, the researcher may want to include only those portions of study results that relate directly to the researcher's meta-analysis. Maxwell (1979) did just that when she used grounded theory techniques to synthesize one portion of multiple ethnographies pertaining to mentoring relationships between older mentors and younger protégés. In doing so, she reviewed numerous studies in their entirety of material and sampled (or theoretically selected) only those parts that addressed the research question. Thus Maxwell's sample included only those portions of the extant ethnographic literature that pertained to elder-protégé interactions as the unit of analysis.

Outcomes. Preoccupied with the research questions and with issues of defining data, theoretical sampling, and the process of doing the meta-analysis, the researcher may lose sight of the end goal. Researchers must ask: "Why am I doing this meta-analysis? What outcome is expected?" Some direction is necessary. It is necessary to guide the direction of the "unfolding" process. Keeping the purpose of the study in mind provides guidance for the sampling and data collection processes. Consideration of outcomes necessarily overlaps with consideration of the relationship of the meta-analysis to theory. For example, if the purpose of the study were to develop a comprehensive, descriptive understanding of a phenomenon of study, such as developing an applied theory of the experience of depression for women, sampling and data collection would be more clearly delineated. The researcher would seek out studies based in the naturalistic paradigm that are concerned with women and depression, with little consideration of the levels of theoretical development within the studies. The group of studies might well include different methods and quite different study populations, from different contexts, but all that have relevance for clinical application. The end product might be a descriptive analysis that was sufficiently dense and comprehensive that it could be used to inform practice and policy. In this case, the researcher would not seek out studies of related topics, such as development of self that arose in the individual studies. The focus would remain on the initially defined conceptual area, and the sampling and data would be confined to women and depression.

The researcher may, however, have a more emergent view of the phenomenon of study, so that she or he may follow a more inductive path to data collection. For example, the researcher may begin with a study of persons with renal failure and discover Sloan's (1986) concept of "broken promises." The discovery of this concept might prompt the researcher to sample studies of disappointment and move into transformation. In other words, by remaining open to the theoretical possibilities within the data, the researcher might wind up taking a very different path from that which was initially imagined. This process uses a very different data set than the first study and results in a more theoretical understanding of a different set of phenomena.

By contrast, if the researcher begins with a particular theory and deductively selects studies that fit a particular paradigm, the outcome of the meta-analysis is an explicated or formalized theory. Consideration of the possible purposes and outcomes of a qualitative meta-analysis makes the decision trail significant, although it may be complex and convoluted. The decision trail also will enable the researcher to define what is needed for the particular study under consideration because data requirements shift the sampling frame.

Contexts. In addition to the issues of data, sampling, and outcomes, the researcher must clarify a number of important, but less obvious issues related to context. How does one handle studies conducted in markedly different contexts that result in markedly different central metaphors? An example of this is the contrast of Wilson's (1989) and Wuest, Ericson, and Stern's (1994) studies of Alzheimer's disease. In the Wilson study, the central metaphor was "surviving on the brink," reflecting, in part, the participants' context within the U.S. health care system. Caregiver participants in this study shared as a factor a concern over how to manage the financial burden of providing care for a demented loved one. The Wuest study, by contrast, was conducted in Canada, a country with comprehensive health care for its citizens. In this study, the central concept was "becoming strangers": an interactive process in which both the caregiver and the demented relative discover that the person they once knew and loved is gone and has been replaced with a strange, new person.

These two grounded theory studies of the same phenomenon from different perspectives and in different contexts resulted in strikingly different findings and central metaphors. The main contrast between the studies is that while both looked at caregivers, the Wuest et al. (1994) study examined the interaction between the caregivers and their relatives suffering from Alzheimer's disease. It might be, upon further examination, that the two could not be combined in meta-analysis because there was no apparent congruity. It might, however, be postulated that there is some sort of hierarchy of contexts, so that once the financial issues of health care costs were addressed, then the interpersonal issues come to the foreground. A secondary analysis of the two studies might yield some interesting results.

In addition to the context issues presented by the individual studies, there are several other contextual matters that affect the process and outcome of a meta-analysis concerned with the contexts of researchers involved. For example, what difference would it make to examine findings from a variety of disciplinary traditions? Would data be enriched by such a sample or would the process become too muddled (Baker, Wuest, & Stern, 1992)? How much does the variation in philosophical viewpoints and hidden assumptions of the individual studies influence the process of analysis? Can one meaningfully combine a Parseist (nursing) phenomenological study (Parse, 1990) with one using van Manen's (1990) method that arose within education? And, if so, would it be useful?

In addition, the historical context of the studies involved influences the findings (Paterson, personal communication, 1996). If the meta-analyst collapsed the data from different periods without consideration of the historical context, the emerging results would be different and less specific than if a tem- poral analysis were conducted. On the other hand, a well-constructed grand theory tends to be timeless. For example, Durkheim's (1889/ 1966) tracing of the process of suicide and the progression of anomie to hopelessness is as relevant today as it was 100 years ago. Depending on the skills and interests of the meta-analyst as well as the envisioned end product and uses of the result, one approach may be more suitable than the other.

Finally, a word of warning: Do not unwittingly sacrifice context for synthesis. Noblit and Hare (1988) have suggested that even the best intentioned researchers can inadvertently lose valuable contextual information in attending to areas of commonality.

Analysis of data. How do meta-analysts analyze data? One approach is Morse and Penrod's (in review) suggestion that the study findings must be "unraveled," so that the researcher attends to the information and rich material that is synthesized in the original studies as themes, categories, and processes, rather than working with the concepts per se. By considering the minor concepts and attributes that are presented "under" the theoretical formulations, the researcher is then able to begin to compare and interpret data of various studies. In this way, the researcher can also "get beyond" the apparent obstacle of comparing findings that use divergent central metaphors. For example, if study A found "soul ache," and study B found "grief," the researcher could ask questions about the data and compare the studies. It is this comparison that leads to the synthesizing of studies through what Noblit and Hare (1988) refer to as "translation": recognition that meta-analysis, like all naturalistic research, is interpretive in nature.

By contrast, Glaser (personal communication, 1996) suggests that with examination of sufficient findings using constant comparison, the central category reaches a higher level of abstraction. Haddan and Lester (1994) have proposed grounded theory techniques as the means for synthesizing ethnographic findings. The researcher uses grounded theory methods of conceptualizing to arrive at a taxonomy from the less abstract ethnographic findings. Adaptation of grounded theory techniques in such circumstances is legitimate as long as the researcher clearly documents exactly what she or he is doing and does not call the product "grounded theory."

Researcher. The question remains: Who should undertake meta-analysis? Should it be a single investigator or a team? If it is a team, who should be involved? We would suggest that there is a need to have variation in expertise, so that both experienced methodologists and content experts participate in the analysis. This would provide more lenses through which to view and question the data, and lead to richer results and perhaps improved scientific merit.

Conclusion

Currently the literature addressing qualitative meta-analysis is sparse, methodologically barren, and marked by a striking lack of consensus. Despite the fact that there are strong, informed voices supporting various positions on issues discussed in this chapter, the area of qualitative meta-analysis is still developing, and it is a time when creativity can flourish and new approaches can be developed. At the same time, these meta-analytic developments must arise with care: Researchers would do well to think through carefully how they will manage the methodological and philosophical issues that we have listed. The complexity of the issues that arise when considering the synthesis of findings from within the naturalistic paradigm is vast. This should not be a cause of despair; rather, the meta-analyst can take comfort knowing that the challenges and problems are shared by all who would attempt the process. In time, and with practical application of the techniques, the issues should begin to be clarified.

General principles: A summary. To help in the process of conducting a meta-analysis, the following general principles should be followed. These principles will develop over time, and as methods develop, so will our understanding of the complexity of the issues.

1. The researcher must identify the purpose and envisioned outcome of the meta-analysis clearly and early in the process. At the same time, however, this decision should not be binding, but changes in directions must be made thoughtfully and consciously and be carefully documented.

2. The researcher must adhere to the philosophical tenets of the naturalistic paradigm and make decisions congruent with it. Do not sacrifice context for commonality.

3. The researcher must create a decision trail, in diary format, so that the research process used may be easily described. All decisions related to sampling, scope, and strengths and limitations should be documented for later justification and reporting.

4. While conducting the analysis, the researcher should maintain a perspective regarding the purpose of the study and the intended relationship of the analysis to theory development.

5. For each study sampled, the issues related to context should be clarified.

In closing, we see meta-analysis of qualitative findings as a necessary and important dimension in the development of qualitative research. It is a way of bringing together the qualities of interpretive studies in a richer, more meaningful way. It is a means to develop more solid, higher level theory and more solid descriptive work—entirely new knowledge for clinical application. The adaptation of existing methodologies for use in qualitative meta-analysis will require careful documentation to avoid "muddling" of methods (Stern, 1994).

But with your generosity, it is done . . . we break the rules together.

Carolyn Chute (1995), *The Beans of Egypt, Maine*

Note

1. In practice, secondary analysis has often been done by the authors of the original studies, as Glaser and Strauss (1965, 1967), Strauss and Glaser, (1970) and Jezewski (1995) have done.

References

Baker, C., Wuest, J., & Stern, P. N. (1992). Method slurring: The grounded theory/phe-nomenology example. *Journal of Advanced Nursing, 17*, 1355-1360.
Chute, C. (1995). *The Beans of Egypt, Maine: The finished version.* New York: Harcourt Brace.
Denzin, N. (1970). *The research act.* Chicago: Aldine.
Durkheim, É. (1966). *Suicide: A study in sociology* (J. A. Spaulding & G. Simpson, Trans.). New York: Free Press. (Original work published 1889)
Estabrooks, C. A., Field, P. A., & Morse, J. M. (1994). Aggregating qualitative findings: An approach to theory development. *Qualitative Health Research, 4*(4), 503-511.
Glaser, B. G., & Strauss, A. (1965). *Awareness of dying.* Chicago: Aldine.
Glaser, B. G., & Strauss, A. (1967). *Anguish: Case study of a dying patient.* Chicago: Aldine.
Glaser, B. G., & Strauss, A. (1968). *Time for dying.* Chicago: Aldine.
Glaser, B. G., & Strauss, A. (1971). *Status passage.* Chicago: Aldine.
Haddan, S. E., & Lester, M. (1994). Grounded theory methodology as a resource for doing ethno-methodology. In B. G. Glaser (Ed.), *More grounded theory methodol-ogy: A reader.* Mill Valley, CA: Sociology Press.
Jensen, L. A., & Allen, M. N. (1994). A synthesis of qualitative research on wellness-illness. *Qualitative Health Research, 4*(4), 349-369.
Jensen, L. A., & Allen, M. N. (1996). Meta-synthesis of qualitative findings. *Qualitative Health Research, 6*(4), 555-562.
Jezewski, M. A. (1995). Evolution of a grounded theory: Conflict resolution through culture brokering. *Advances in Nursing Science, 17*(3), 14-30.
Maxwell, E. K. (1979). Modeling life: Elder modelers and their protégés (Doctoral dissertation, University of California, 1979). *Dissertation Abstracts International, 39*, 7531A.
Miles, M. B., & Huberman, A. M. (1994). *An expanded sourcebook: Qualitative data analysis* (2nd ed.). Thousand Oaks, CA: Sage.
Mish, G. C. (Ed.). (1989). *Webster's ninth new collegiate dictionary.* Springfield, MA: Merriam-Webster.
Morse, J. M., & Penrod, J. (in review). *Theoretical interpretation: The relationship between suffering, enduring and hope.*
Noblit, G. W., & Hare, R. D. (1988). *Meta-ethnography: Synthesizing qualitative studies.* Newbury Park, CA: Sage.

Parse, R. R. (1990). Parse's research methodology with an illustration of the lived experience of hope. *Nursing Science Quarterly, 3*(1), 9-17.

Sloan, R. S. (1986). *A hermeneutical study of the medical treatment decision for end stage renal disease patients and their families.* Unpublished doctoral dissertation, University of Kentucky.

Stern, P. N. (1994). Eroding grounded theory. In J. M. Morse (Ed.), *Critical issues in qualitative research methods* (pp. 212-223). Thousand Oaks, CA: Sage.

Stern, P. N., & Harris, C. C. (1985). Women's health and the self-care paradox: A model to guide self-care readiness. *Health Care for Women International, 6,* 151-163.

Strauss, A., & Glaser, B. (1970). *Anguish: The case history of a dying trajectory.* San Francisco: Aldine.

Thorne, S. (1994). Secondary analysis in qualitative research: Issues and implications. In J. M. Morse (Ed.), *Critical issues in qualitative research methods* (pp. 263-279). Thousand Oaks, CA: Sage.

van Manen, M. (1990). *Researching the lived experience.* London, Ontario, Canada: Althouse.

Wilson, H. S. (1989). Family caregiving for a person with Alzheimer's disease: Coping with negative choices. *Nursing Research, 38,* 94-98.

Wuest, J., Ericson, P. K., & Stern, P. N. (1994). Becoming strangers: The changing family caregiving relationship in Alzheimer's disease. *Journal of Advanced Nursing, 20,* 437-443.

The Dead Dog Section: Explaining Methods

May: What do you do when they ask you to explain how you did your work? Because that's extraordinarily difficult. It's real easy to say, "Well, we sent out the survey to 250 people, and this is what we found. But to try to explain grounded theory methodology to a reporter who's on a deadline—forget it! It won't work.

Boyle: Try phenomenology—Here, this Heideggerian thing!
        [laughter]

Stern: Well, one trick, too, is to talk about the number of hours of interview data, rather than the number of people.

May: Well, they said, "Tell us how you did this project." And like the good interviewee, I took a deep breath and explained "theory making."

Sandelowski: It's rather like when a child asks you, "Where do I come from," and they want to know they're from New York!
        [laughter]

May: Yeah! Exactly right! Well, I walked right into it! And five minutes later, their eyes had glazed over. They were no longer writing. But, you know, I thought I had done a really good job in explaining grounded theory method, and how your goal was to build theory, 'cause blah, blah, blah. So I learned real quick not to do that anymore. So, in subsequent reports in the media, they don't even talk about how the information was analyzed. They only talk about what can be gleaned from the project, which, in some ways, has no scientific integrity.

Wilson: Well, in 1974, when I first started to study with Glaser and Strauss, methodology sections of dissertations consisted of: "I hung out and I got insight." [laughter] So, maybe we could return to that as our methodological statement.

        But seriously, what I have seen people do that works reasonably well, that seems to work, is to use some analogy, so that rather than go into open coding and all that stuff, say something like, "It's something like the work of _____," and name some well-known field researcher whom most people are familiar with, and with whom you wouldn't mind being associated. Or you say, "This is like the work that anthropologists have done, where you spend time with people"—

Stern: Or like a detective story. But you can't learn a method in a sound bite!

CHAPTER

The Politicking of
Research Results

*Presenting Qualitative Findings
in the Public Arena*

Katharyn A. May

M ost researchers have recently come to grips with the fact that
dissemination of research results beyond scientific meetings and
journals is now part of "doing science." Many do not enjoy the public
limelight of media exposure, and some actively avoid it; nevertheless,
the work of science is a matter of public discussion, and scientists are
expected to be able to speak and write about their work in ways that
make the results accessible to those outside academic circles.

AUTHOR'S NOTE: I wish to acknowledge the contributions of pithy and perfect
quotations to this chapter, gleaned in conversations with Mr. D. Ruth and Drs. M.
Sandelowski, P. Stern, and H. S. Wilson, among others.

In his book titled *The Third Culture: Beyond the Scientific Revolution*, Brockman (1995) notes that early in this century, scientists were not expected to be effective in communicating their work directly to the general public. Rather, "men of letters" or so-called literary intellectuals read original scientific works and wrote about them. In so doing, they synthesized and shaped scientific knowledge in the public realm. However, by the 1950s, science and technology had begun to take center stage in Western culture. A cadre of scientists emerged who communicated quite effectively through the mass media and who, in a sense, popularized science and the image of the scientist. By the 1990s, evidence of the rise in "scientific literacy" could be seen everywhere, ranging from the best-selling books written by scientists for public consumption to the growing numbers of full-time health and science reporters in print and broadcasting who regularly work the university and research meeting circuits.

Increasingly, governmental and private agencies see dissemination of findings from research beyond scientific circles as part of the researcher's responsibility, especially if tax or charitable dollars underwrote the cost of the research. In a world where scientific breakthroughs have become almost commonplace, universities and research institutes often rely on investigators who can portray their own research (and thus the institution for sponsoring it) in a favorable light.

From a societal perspective, science reporting has literally become big business. In the United States, the number of newspapers regularly devoting a special section to science and health coverage nationwide tripled between 1980 and 1985, and broadcast coverage pertaining to research and technology is routine, even in very small media markets (Friedman, Dunwoody, & Rogers, 1986). In many universities and research institutes, the field of "media relations" has all but replaced the practice of "public relations."

Thus the process of "politicking" research findings has become an important activity of researchers—not in the sense that researchers enact a political process for professional gain but in the sense that they must argue the practical wisdom of communicating research findings. The desired result of this politicking is quite simple: that research findings are reported in the public realm where they may be heard both by those who might benefit from this new knowledge and by those with power (influence, money) to act on it for the public good.

The challenge of meeting and handling the media is one faced by all scientists who care about informing the public about their work. However, those who do qualitative research (as one journalist once said to me, those who are "working without numbers"—he said it as if it were akin to "working without a net") have some particular challenges in getting their stories out into the public realm. This chapter focuses on those challenges and is based to a very large extent on my own experience in presenting qualitative research to print and broadcast media. Because of its specific focus on dissemination of qualitative research, a full discussion of techniques for engaging with the media is beyond the scope of this chapter, although some material in that vein is presented here. I have relied on few references and would refer readers with a general interest in the topic of science and the media to Friedman et al. (1986) as well as to materials usually available from scientific and professional associations and media relations departments in most academic institutions.

The first section of this chapter focuses on the notion of "communicating with the communicators," that is, with journalists. The second section focuses on strategies to describe qualitative methods and findings to nonscientists, including journalists and laypeople with a topical interest in the work. Throughout, I will include accounts of my own successful and less than successful contacts with the media, all of which taught me some valuable lessons.

Communicating With the Communicators (To Whom Are You Talking and Why Should They Listen?)

Although it seems obvious that, to communicate effectively, one must understand one's audience, I am surprised at how often highly intelligent and well-educated researchers forget this when discussing their research outside the relatively safe world of academe. Presenting research findings to a journalist or to laypeople with an interest in the topic is a qualitatively different process than presenting findings to a scientific audience; unfortunately, researchers often fail to make the distinction and thus fail to capture effective media exposure.

The Communicators: Who They Are and How They Work

Journalists in the print and broadcast media tend to share a common set of views about themselves and their work, and understanding some of these views can help the researcher in managing media contact. Journalists are professional communicators. Increasingly, they have professional training in journalism, and have very well-developed verbal and writing skills; quite logically, they assume they are better communicators than the average researcher and, in most cases, they are correct. Their skills are honed in a high-pressure industry where performance is judged solely on how much "good film" or "good copy" they produce and how quickly they produce it.

Most journalists are not particularly well paid and do the work because they love it, not because they will become famous, influential, or wealthy by doing it. Journalists usually see themselves as public servants providing an essential role in society by conveying information about matters of importance to their audience (readers, listeners, viewers). What topics are regarded as important and worthy of attention by journalists will depend on a number of factors: the "agenda" or "voice" of their employer (newspaper, magazine, station); timeliness and scope of the story (How many people affected? How much? How long?); the presence of conflict or change in the story; the reputations involved (people or organizations); and its entertainment or interest value. Usually stories of most interest to those in the print and broadcast media involve human interest and action (conflict, change) that can be extrapolated into the future and that affect a group and can be linked to the community.

Journalists who do "news" usually work under very tight deadlines (minutes or hours) while those who write "features" or have particular "beats" can often take more time (a day or two) to complete a story. Whether an informant can meet their need for information by a deadline is often a major determinant of whether a reporter pursues a story and with whom. Other factors taken into account in deciding whether to pursue a story include whether the topic can be explained at a ninth-grade reading level for print, can be made visual for film, or can be talked about for broadcast. Although journalists themselves usually determine which stories they pursue, they rarely decide what stories actually run; editors or producers ultimately decide what goes to print or is broadcast.

Getting the Communicator's Attention (or Avoiding It)

The first decision that researchers must make is whether to seek media exposure for a research project, and, if so, when. Usually journalists are interested in stories that can be tied to some event in time (publication in a major journal, presentation at a scientific meeting, public policy decisions based on the research), and that often means waiting until the project has been completed. However, some projects have sufficient "human interest" that preliminary findings can be pitched for media coverage.

Topics that are (or can be made to be) controversial should be given very careful consideration before contacts with the media are made, and the advice of media relations officers can be especially valuable in this regard. If a sensationalistic interpretation of findings is possible, that is probably the angle that will appeal immediately to a journalist, even if that angle is of little interest to the researchers themselves. Thus researchers should think through all of the possible angles before pitching a story to a journalist and decide if they are prepared to have any one of those "sidebar issues" become "the main story" (see the section below). If the researcher is not confident that the negative or sensationalistic interpretation can be avoided, it may be best not to invite media attention without considerable support from a media relations consultant. Even when such support is available, researchers must consider carefully whether the benefits of pitching a story that may become controversial will be offset by the personal costs in time and emotional energy.

In some cases, it may be possible to prevent "a negative spin" on research findings in the media by executing what might be called a "preemptive strike" (D. Ruth, personal communication, August 1996). In this case, a balanced first story can be put out in which the researcher has some control over its direction (i.e., in a community or university newspaper or on a local public interest broadcast), where it may attract the attention of regional or national media. This can have the effect of directing journalistic interest in a desired direction and preempting more negative coverage.

Working with media relations staff. Once a decision is made to "go public" with a story, rarely are researchers required to handle all aspects of media contact alone. Most institutions that employ working scientists also employ media relations specialists who can provide valuable assistance. These individuals will develop and circulate a press release based on information provided by the researcher, advise whether a press conference is likely to generate interest and, if so, will organize and manage the press conference, and can "pitch" the story to journalists who regularly cover health and science beats. They often handle routine communication with journalists, will assist in preparing for interviews, will give advice on answering questions, and are especially helpful in anticipating problems that may arise. However, they often cannot assist during the actual interview (unless this is a major media event), so researchers must usually be prepared to handle the interview by themselves.

Clarifying Expectations

Prior to the interview, it is important that researchers clarify with the journalist what reasonably can be expected in regard to conduct of the interview and any coverage that may result. The following questions should be asked and answered:

- What is the time line in which the journalist is working?
- Will questions be submitted in advance? Will the researcher have an opportunity to read the story (view the film, hear the taped interview) prior to release? If not, how will the journalist reassure the researcher that the material, especially matters of fact and direct quotations, is correct?
- What is the specific topic to be discussed? Where and when will any resulting coverage appear? Will the researcher be provided with a copy?

If answers to these questions are not satisfactory, researchers should consider declining an interview, or at least enlisting the assistance of a media relations officer. It may be possible to negotiate on a number of the points above, depending on how earnestly the journalist wants the story and how much time is available to get it. However, compromise may not be forthcoming if the researcher is more interested in getting media coverage than the journalist is in modifying routine practices.

Table 16.1 Tips for a Positive Media Interview

- Know what you will be expected to discuss, and decide what is most important to convey. If you don't have that "main message" clearly in mind at the beginning, it is unlikely that the reporter will at the end. Remember, you are the expert.

- Focus on *why* this story should be told (Who is affected? How much?). Talk about the public's interest.

- Do your homework. Anticipate tough questions. Practice your answers. Brush up on facts and figures.

- Make your statements clear and to the point, but avoid "yes" or "no" answers. When necessary, respond, "I don't know, but I'll find out for you by . . ." Set and keep a reasonable deadline.

- Have some quotable material ready, mentally and on paper. If that material contradicts or supports other information on the subject, say so.

- Do not allow a reporter to put words in your mouth. If you don't like the way something is phrased, don't repeat his or her words in your answer. If you don't want to see a statement of yours published, don't make it.

- Tell the reporter how to reach you after the interview. At the end, smile, shake hands, and say you hope you have been able to answer at least some of the reporter's questions.

SOURCE: Adapted from a presentation outline by P. Bradley, Kellogg National Leadership Fellows Media Workshop (August 1990).

Handling the Interview

A full discussion of techniques for handling a media interview is far beyond the scope of this chapter. One bit of encouragement should be taken from the fact that researchers who do interviews themselves in the course of their work are probably in a much better position to manage media interviews successfully than are those for whom the interview experience is rather foreign. Table 16.1 provides specific advice for ensuring a positive interview experience.

Allowing a sidebar to become the story. There are times when permitting a journalist to focus on a tangential issue rather than on more substantive aspects of the story can be an acceptable, although slightly anxiety-producing strategy. This might be the case where the risk is not that coverage will be negative but simply that there will be some undeserved media attention to a quirky and relatively unimportant aspect of the research, or to a topic within the researcher's expertise but unrelated to the specific research findings. Agreeing to be interviewed in this situation may be a way for a researcher to get some media experience, and can have the benefit of achieving some exposure for the researcher, if not the research itself.

For example, in the early 1980s, I completed my dissertation work—a grounded theory study on the social psychological experience of first-time expectant fatherhood—and because I had just been appointed to a faculty position there, my university's media relations office generated a well-balanced press release that went out to local print and broadcast media. The first interest shown in my work was from a writer working on an article focusing on couvade syndrome (male pregnancy symptoms) for *Glamour Magazine*. I agreed to a telephone interview and, in anticipation, provided the writer with copies of my research publications.

The actual interview focused exclusively on couvade syndrome, and the writer was not interested at all in the more substantive aspects of my work. Despite the fact that couvade syndrome was not a major element in my findings and I didn't even consider it a particularly interesting topic, nevertheless I was a bit dazzled by the attention, and so told the writer everything I knew about the topic. Because I had just completed my graduate work, I knew most of the literature, and willingly volunteered one or two pertinent anecdotes from my own study.

When the story appeared, the magazine itself sent out a press release that was picked up by the wire services. My comments in the interview were featured rather prominently in the magazine article and mentioned briefly in the press release. A journalist who worked on pieces "off the wire" for newspaper and television news bureaus wrote a story on couvade syndrome (citing the magazine article and my comments in the interview) and sent it to NBC News, who subsequently sent it to an assistant producer of *The Today Show*. I was contacted by the program and screened for a possible appearance on the show in a segment on male pregnancy symptoms. Two weeks later, I was appearing on live television nationwide talking about what was essentially a "sidebar" story from my research program.

Subsequent to the *Today Show* segment, I was contacted by a number of radio stations to do live and taped interviews, and several talk shows were devoted to the topic of men and pregnancy. In these situations, I was able to exert more topic control, by redirecting my comments (and focusing my answers to questions) toward the more important information I had to share about men and pregnancy, rather than focusing on the quirky topic of couvade syndrome. Through their questions, listeners on talk shows also provided me opportunities to give a fuller presentation of my research findings than had been possible in the much tighter television format. These advantages far outweighed the disadvantages of doing live radio interviews over the telephone, with no direct contact with radio reporters and talk show hosts and little sense of connection or rapport with them.

Looking back on this experience of allowing a sidebar issue to become the main story, I doubt I could have redirected the initial media interest toward the more substantive aspects of my research; that simply was not what had caught the journalists' interest. However, because I was well versed in the topic that did interest them and was enjoying the excitement, I went along for the ride. Now, with more experience and less time to devote to such diversions, I might decline the invitation and refer the journalist to a colleague working on the topic of interest, or try to redirect some interest to the broader and more substantive issues related to it.

Handling the Consequences of Media Coverage

Even before a story runs, researchers should give some consideration to how the consequences of media coverage will be handled. For instance, decisions should be made on matters such as who will respond to telephone inquiries, how requests from other journalists for follow-up interviews will be handled, and who will monitor the developing coverage when wire services or networks pick up the original story.

If coverage was positive or neutral, dealing with its aftermath (the flurry of excitement and a brief moment of "fame") is usually rather enjoyable. However, if the coverage was negative or disappointing, there is little that can be done but grit one's teeth and resolve to learn from the experience. Media relations personnel should be advised if there is the possibility that the story could represent a public relations problem for the sponsoring institution or organizations associated with the research project.

It is usually pointless to demand a retraction, unless the error is a point of fact (rather than perspective) or the researcher can "prove" the journalist misquoted her or him, a defense usually possible only if the researcher kept an audiotape of the interview. Even if a retraction is issued, it usually fails to effectively correct any misimpressions created by the original story. However, researchers should express their concerns directly to the journalist involved, stressing the importance of providing the public with accurate information, rather than complaining about damage to the researcher's reputation (an argument that will be seen as self-serving).

Strategies for Describing Qualitative Methods and Findings

Presenting qualitative research findings to the media poses some unique challenges and opportunities for investigators. The challenges arise from the fact that qualitative methods are sometimes difficult for researchers to explain simply and succinctly, and journalists are accustomed to "facts and figures" rather than *theory* or *thick description;* in fact, use of the latter terms is almost guaranteed to put a journalist off. The opportunities that arise in presenting qualitative research findings in the media stem from the similarities between qualitative research and journalism: reliance on first-person accounts of events, an orientation toward describing the human condition in human terms, and every journalist's appreciation for the power of a well-told story.

Describing Qualitative Research Methods: The Preamble, Not the Story

When discussing findings of qualitative research with a journalist, the researcher should take care not to make the method become the story. As scientists, we work hard to describe our methods completely and clearly to colleagues in the time-honored tradition of science, and it may be that those who do qualitative research feel the need to work harder at this description than others. Thus it is not uncommon for researchers to place a much greater emphasis on method than is strictly necessary when discussing their research findings in the public arena.

Rarely is there any advantage in providing that much detail on the actual conduct of the study, and usually it discourages journalistic interest. Providing even the pared-down version of methodology appropriate for a 15-minute research presentation is quite likely to backfire in a media interview. Such explanations tend to convince the journalist that the researcher is just another scientist who can't communicate and also may convince him or her that the findings of the study aren't worth the effort required to find them among the jargon.

Probably my most embarrassing experience with a reporter was the result of a well-intended effort to explain grounded theory methodology. The newspaper reporter asked how I gathered my information—Did I give a questionnaire or something?—and somehow, my novice's insecurity about qualitative method pushed me into an explanation of "theory building." I thought I was doing a good job of keeping it simple, but I was wrong. In hindsight, what probably would have sufficed in this situation was a description of method common in the early days at UCSF when students were learning grounded theory method—an explanation that went something like "I hung around and got insight" (H. Wilson, personal communication, August 1996).

In my case, I had seriously overcompensated in the other direction. My mistake was assuming that the reporter wanted information about the method, when, in fact, he wanted something much more specific—whom I talked to, and what I had found. The situation was comparable to when a child asks, "Where did I come from?" and receives a lecture on sex when the appropriate answer would have been "Philadelphia" (M. Sandelowski, personal communication, August 1996).

By the time I came to my senses, the reporter's eyes had glazed over and note taking had ceased. What I should have done in that situation was to explain how my process of interviewing and analysis rather similar to that of reporters: Find people with a story to tell, listen to the stories, and write them up so that you capture something of the shared as well as the unique experiences. I should have told him how many informants I interviewed and something about who they were, how many hours of audiotape I had analyzed, and how long the study had been under way. I could have compared what I did with the methods used by other researchers who write in the public arena or with methods used by journalists in investigative reporting.

This is not to say that a fuller, more scientific explanation of method might not be appropriate or even required in some media situations. Reporters who regularly write on science and health may be much more familiar with conventional scientific methods, and may raise questions about qualitative method. In this situation, it is probably best not to launch into a discussion of epistemology but to give a bit more detail about the method, cite other important studies using this method, and draw parallels between the work under discussion and the widely accepted fieldwork traditions in anthropology, psychology, and sociology. Researchers also may choose to be more detailed in describing methodology to a science journalist as part of the story itself. For example, if part of the desired message is to highlight the appropriateness of qualitative methods in certain kinds of research questions, or the validity of qualitative research findings for certain kinds of applications in practice, then the researcher must prepare to spend more time in an explanation of method for the reporter to grasp the overarching message.

However, even when talking with a scientifically sophisticated journalist, it is important to keep one's language clear and concise and to avoid explanations that have been developed and rehearsed through repetition but for very different audiences and purposes. Often qualitative methodologists use jargonistic, complicated, even incomprehensible language to describe methods, not so much as an attempt to be scholarly or impressive but more probably out of habit. Lee Smolin, a theoretical physicist and author of a book for the general public titled *The Life of the Cosmos: A New View of Cosmology, Particle Physics and the Meaning of Quantum Physics*, commented on the challenge of being comprehensible:

> It is difficult, but I need to be able to communicate a theory of quantum gravity outside the physics community. . . . When I listen to people in the humanities, I realize that they have similar problems with regard to communicating difficult ideas. I can't read them line by line, because their language is based on Hegel and Heidegger, or whomever, and it doesn't make any sense to me. They have some romantic idea about being difficult is good, and this is wrong. Why they do it, and why it's become popular is something I don't understand. . . . One of the differences between the traditions of science and the humanities is that the humanities have become traditions of reading and writing. People in these fields don't talk to each other. . . . Scientists speak to each other, first and

foremost. Go to a talk given by somebody in philosophy or literary theory. Notice that they invariably will read something that they've written, word for word. Very few scientists will ever do that. (in Brockman, 1995, pp. 30-31)

Although one may argue with Smolin's characterization of the humanities, I suggest that some of his analysis fits patterns of behavior seen "in qualitative circles." Overreliance on language that has become rote and comfortable in the academic world ultimately compromises our ability to communicate outside of it. There are few situations where this is more unfortunate than in interaction with the media, because their interest, first and foremost, is the story.

The Story: Discussing the Findings

Returning to my disastrous interview situation, I had failed to recognize that I had, literally, "gone off the deep end." In my own defense, this reporter was uncharacteristically passive and did not interrupt. In a valiant effort to recover the interview situation described above, I stopped talking about method and tried to salvage the situation by "cutting to the theory itself." This was my second and lethal mistake, because it simply compounded the problem. This reporter didn't want to hear about theory, he wanted to hear about the experiences of men during unexpected cesarean births of their babies.

I should have given him some facts and figures about cesarean birth: how frequently it occurred, how often men were present or wanted to be present at those deliveries, and what local hospital policies were. I should have told a few specific stories about individual men's experiences, and then linked them together, showing the similarities and differences among them. Literally, I should have described what happened to men in the context of an unanticipated cesarean birth, and what it meant in their lives as new fathers. I might have read him direct quotes from my data set, or perhaps volunteered to connect him with an informant who could describe the experience in his own words. Then I could have wrapped up with some points about what health professionals should know, what expectant parents should know, and, finally, what I hoped would happen in the future as a result of this study.

Unfortunately, by the time I realized my second mistake, this patient reporter had clearly concluded I was a flake or, worse, just another academic who couldn't communicate. I could not reestablish any real rapport with him, and that newspaper article was never written. If I had only thought through the message I wanted that reporter to take away, I would have recognized that, as a colleague so aptly put it, "You can't present theory in a sound bite" (P. Stern, personal communication, August 1996).

Conclusion

In the final analysis, the politicking of qualitative research results requires the researcher to have certain basic skills in dealing with journalists and their mass media orientation to the world, as well as some advanced skills in describing complex concepts and processes in simple and clear terms. These skills can be learned well only through practice, thus it is more or less a requirement that researchers, especially novices, suffer through some mildly embarrassing encounters to gain proficiency. Rarely is any permanent damage done in the learning process, except to an investigator's slightly inflated view of self and the importance of her or his work.

If researchers communicate insecurity about their methods, their results, and their place in the scientific pecking order, savvy journalists will pick up that undercurrent and, in their search for the truth, will usually resort to probing for the weakness they sense is there. If researchers are secure with the methods used and the results obtained in their scientific work, and are willing to spend time working on commonsense ways of explaining both, then journalists will accept their expertise as a given and focus on the story.

In the final analysis, qualitative research is remarkably easy to profile in the public realm. Findings often have a "ring of truth" and often present views of the human condition and real-world implications that command attention. Usually the researcher feels a strong personal connection to the subject at hand, and this is a definite advantage in piquing a reporter's interest. If researchers will capitalize on these advantages and discipline themselves to use clear, concise language to describe qualitative research findings, journalists will respond. The result will be the presentation of those findings in a form accessible to wider audiences than scientists can ever hope to reach on their own, where those findings, in the end, may contribute substantially to the public good.

References

Brockman, J. (1995). *The third culture: Beyond the scientific revolution.* New York: Simon & Schuster.

Friedman, S., Dunwoody, S., & Rogers, C. (1986). *Scientists and journalists: Reporting science as news.* New York: Free Press.

Dialogue: As Hired Guns

May: There is the notion of being typecast as a methodologist. I think there is a pattern in the development of qualitative work in our discipline because there were so few of us who knew what we were doing, some of us did, in fact, become hired guns. We got attached to whoever needed help, regardless or not if we knew anything about the substantive field. I hope we have gotten past that.

Stern: I don't think so.

May: You are right. People come to me and say, "You are the expert in grounded theory . . ." And to prevent sloppy work, I will really bend my brain against someone else's project, 'cause what they are doing is really inadequate. So I clean it up, and say, "Now, here's where you might consider doing it this way." So I feel I am contributing to a greater good by doing that. But I have increasingly become sensitive to this— 'cause I make fun of the number crunchers who are methodologists. I say, "Gosh, what a shame. What a tragedy, a waste of a good brain!"

Qualitative Research in Policy Development

Martha Ann Carey

Health policy formulation and the allocation of resources to programs have far-reaching impacts on society. The development of programs and policies, ideally, uses the best available information. Often, policy issues are complex, the time frame for decisions short, and the audiences very diverse in terms of goals and experiences. Some policy questions may have practical constraints that limit the applicability of quantitative methods and can only be answered through qualitative approaches. For example, in some settings, political and/or ethical considerations prohibit research designs with random assignment of participants.

To optimize the role and usefulness of qualitative methods for policy and program development, one must understand the information needs of policymakers, how qualitative methods can contribute, and how best to design research and report results.

Information Needs and Policy Development

A rational model of policy development includes assumptions of (a) purposive development (b) based on accurate information and (c) a reasonable understanding of causal relations (d) in an iterative sequence of preparation, development, implementation, evaluation, and refinement (Bots & Hulshof, 1995). However, in actual practice, policy making and program planning occur within highly political systems with pressures that render this rational model prescriptive rather than descriptive. For example, policies on approval of medications for use with AIDS patients have been greatly affected by the pressures from concerned patients and communities.

In the United States, there are two general levels of policy making and program development: national and state/local. At the national level, Congress has responsibility for addressing broad issues while the federal agencies (e.g., the Department of Health and Human Services) implement and monitor programs (e.g., Medicare). State and local agencies have responsibility for more direct service programs. Although the functions differ, agencies' information needs are roughly similar in terms of targeted and timely information that is credible, generalizable, and accurate. The time frame for the usefulness of information may be brief, as when information is needed before a vote on legislation. The format must be quite concise because often the executive summary with bullet items is the only section read by most policymakers and staff. The remainder of the document unofficially functions as an appendix.

As described within the prevailing quantitative paradigm, the broad types of needed information are *anecdotal*, to portray the humanness of the data; *distributional* and comparative, such as a survey to assess the magnitude of an issue across groups; and *outcome*, to examine the impact or effectiveness of services (Scallet, 1996). From this narrow perspective, qualitative research can have virtually no usefulness. However, some funded research does use qualitative approaches to study new and novel problems. Later in this chapter, I describe useful approaches to enhance the contributions of qualitative research.

External influences shape the availability and impact of information. Special interest groups often provide persuasive data as well as apply political pressure. The media function in a role of gatekeeper in the selection and presentation of information. Maney and Plutzer (1996) discuss the role of the press as "interpreters of scientific information." The general public also plays a role in policy development. Henry (1996) describes an example of the weight of public sentiment in determining public programs, in conflict with guidance from scientific findings.

A postpositivist approach to policy development questions the criteria upon which decisions are made. Addressing the sentiment that the public does not trust technocrats and does not accept the artificial division between experts and ordinary citizens, Fischer (1995) recommends an integration of the four methodological orientations in the social sciences: empirical outcome analysis, phenomenological science, systems analysis, and political philosophy. He describes a multiple level approach to the concern that political problems are not given facts but are socially constructed. Although not a common approach, this paradigm invites a process of participatory democracy that could be used more broadly.

Responsibilities and Contributions of Qualitative Research

It is increasingly considered a responsibility of the researcher to plan to get results used. There is a sentiment that "knowledge is productive only if it makes a difference" (Drucker, 1993, p. 193), which includes an obligation to clearly communicate the research findings to promote their use (Sandelowski, 1996). Although not divided into two separate categories, research use may be a contribution (1) to basic knowledge or (2) to the development of information upon which to base practice or policies. In any one study, a researcher generally would have to choose between a policy-relevant research question and a question that addresses basic knowledge. A program of research or research synthesis may be able to address both purposes.

A large body of literature documents the advantages of qualitative research, particularly in studying complex and new problems. Among the strengths are the capability to examine context and provide an in-depth look at elements and systems, and to communicate results in a compelling manner. Increasing awareness of multiculturalism requires a knowledge base that is developed from a wide range of methods, including qualitative approaches (Basic Behavioral Science Task Force of the National Advisory Mental Health Council, 1996). Referring to the merits of case studies, Sechrest, Stewart, Stickle, and Sidani (1996) suggest that when the information is important, dependable, and relevant, and the proposed action is feasible and effective, then the persuasiveness of a study will be optimal.

Contributions of social science research to policy and program development involve more than a direct and immediate impact of research results. Weiss (1977) emphasized the importance of long-term and diffuse effects in reducing uncertainty and clarifying issues. Incremental effects may only be noted in long-term effects.

Results from research that uses only qualitative methods have an additional burden because these methods are not as well known and are not as formulaic; that is, the process is not as well understood or highly structured as a quantitative analysis technique such as factor analysis. The burden of conveying the usefulness of the results to policymakers lies with the researcher. Fetterman (1993) provides several suggestions on how best to communicate and collaborate.

At the U.S. federal level, most funding support for qualitative studies comes from the National Institute of Nursing Research and the National Institute of Drug Abuse, both at the National Institutes of Health. Although direct impact on policy and programs from these studies has been minimal, there has been some application, such as NIH-funded studies of HIV prevention needle-exchange projects, which are based, in part, on studies of drug dens. More recently, health services research programs have included a qualitative component to help understand the experiences of patients and the role of service interventions.

Useful Qualitative Approaches

Combination of Qualitative and Quantitative Methods

Previously, there was some degree of an adversarial relationship between qualitative and quantitative approaches; this seems generally to have dissipated (Dennis, Fetterman, & Sechrest, 1994; Reichardt & Rallis, 1994). In contrast to the paradigmatic incompatibility stated earlier by Guba and Lincoln (1989), more scientists currently see common ground in the acceptance of value- or theory-laden facts (Cook & Campbell, 1979) in contrast to the generally discredited paradigm of logical positivism. In general, the combination of methods has been recommended for purpose of comparison and synthesis, not for the development of theory (Morse & Field, 1995). Planning in the research design phase should balance the strengths and weaknesses of each approach. Morse (1991) has described a framework for selection of multimethod designs.

Qualitative approaches have been used in combination with quantitative approaches in sequence or concurrently to reinforce, explain, or expand. Reinforcement is the purpose when concurrent results from two methods are used to reinforce confidence in results, a process called *triangulation* of methods. To help explain quantitative results, focus groups were used to understand the unanticipated results of quantitative studies when the psychosocial instruments were for a new population (Carey & Smith, 1992).

An example of sequential use to expand and explain study possibilities is the use of epidemiologic data and a grounded theory approach in a study of the young adults living with a diagnosis of herpes. In a grounded theory study, Swanson, Remy, Chenitz, Chastain, and Trocki (1993) found very high drug use. In the subsequent statistical analyses (log-linear models) that compared their study population findings with a national database, they found significantly higher use in herpes clients and recommended that clinics serving populations with sexually transmitted diseases should routinely screen for drug use. The program of research then used a qualitative approach to examine why this population had such a high use of drugs and found that the need to self-medicate to control stress was the main factor.

Qualitative Inquiry

Is It Qualitative? Is It Research? Does the Label Matter?

The label does matter because it denotes an understanding of a study's purpose and process, and therefore guides the appropriate interpretation and use of research results. Morse (this volume) describes the purposes for different levels of theoretical abstraction in qualitative research, ranging from description to formal theory that is generalizable.

Method possibilities include not only an either-or approach and the combination of methods, but also an approximation/adaptation of the usual approaches. The approach recommended by Miles and Huberman (1994) includes the data display, organization, and synthesis processes that lead to useful information, and in some instances to causal statements. This approach of systemic inquiry is not intended to build formal theory or produce the insights associated with phenomenology but *to provide cognitive leverage on rich data.* A systematic, descriptive analysis with the presentation of qualitative data is often the optimum way of handling the information required by policymakers.

When a clear purpose is defined, adequate description of analyses is provided, and appropriate interpretation of analyses is given, it can be a useful approach to inquiry and contribute to understanding. Most U.S. policy and program information needs do not require the development of theory but, instead, require knowledge to address immediate, practical needs.

A recent example of this approach is the study being done for the Office of Safe and Drug Free Communities of the U.S. Department of Education (White, personal communication, July 1996). The program targets adolescents who have been expelled from school due to weapons violations and assists them to make a successful reentry into their communities. Projects vary widely in approach from boot camp-type projects to back-to-basics programs with vocational services. There has been no evaluation and only a little description of this program. Through examining the nine projects that are considered to have good outcomes, this study will build matrices to explore what these projects have in common, such as small size, communication processes, and atmosphere, and will distill what leads to success in these "promising practices." This information is needed for the development of other projects, and the usual research time line of a few years won't meet policy development needs. The systematic, documented, and rigorous approach is expected to provide credible and therefore useful information that can readily be translated to program planning.

Enhancing the Use of Results

In any communication, it is important to understand the needs and expectations of the information receiver. Scallet (1996) describes what the ideal form for presenting information to policymakers should include:

- answers a precise question specified by the policymaker,
- specifies assumptions and biases,
- is concise and easy to use, and
- is instantaneously accessible. (p. 13)

The message should be brief and clear, focusing on key findings. Especially for qualitative results, which are not familiar to most policymakers, precise language is important and clear definitions are essential.

High standards of rigor with a documented audit trail in the analysis also will be needed. Triangulation of data sources and collection methods will strengthen confidence in results as will a large body of results from a program of research or a meta-analysis.

Timely information will be hard to plan for, and therefore Scallet (1996) recommends that researchers keep up with current concerns that may benefit from timely studies, and also keep an up-to-date file of synopses of results handy to mail quickly to the appropriate policymaker. First, one must learn who the policymakers are and get to know them if possible. If appropriate, send them brief (one-page) summaries of relevant results. Often the key person is not the agency head or elected lawmaker but a senior staffer on an appropriations committee.

Validity/Credibility

Some results just seem to ring true—the message is persuasive and heart tugging. We see this when a suffering patient appears before a committee hearing as a vivid example of some preventable tragedy. This can, and does, affect policy decisions and program resource allocations. However, it makes researchers shudder. Rather than being a good use of credible information, it is instead excellent theater. Although a vivid example to illustrate solid research can be an excellent format in which to communicate results, decisions should be based on information, not emotional responses.

Validity is the key to credibility and usefulness. Messick (1995) defines *validity* as "an overall valuative judgment of the degree to which empirical evidence and theoretical rationales support the adequacy and appropriateness of interpretations and actions on the bases of test scores or other modes of assessment" (p. 741). The concern with validity is relevant to any systematic inquiry.

It is the perception of validity that is important for federal work. How is validity perceived by the stakeholders? The federal environment is predominantly quantitative, but one in which the realization is dawning that the qualitative or quasi-qualitative approach may be the wave of the future. Distilling the knowledge that can seem hidden in the folk wisdom of project staffs or clients presents a challenge for which some quantitatively trained staff welcome, although warily, the cognitive leverage of qualitative approaches. The trustworthiness of the data, analysis, and interpretation will be enhanced by (a) the well-documented adequacy and appropriateness of the purposive sampling selected for the concept or theory driven by analysis; (b) systematic analysis process with clear rationale, that is, no method slurring; and (c) interpretation well supported by analysis.

Design and Report

Considerations in designing a study include who will use the information and how it will be used. Potential implications of probable results for policy and programs should be considered. Legislators are interested in *concrete information:*

- What does the program do? How much does it cost?
- What does the program produce? For whom?
- Does the program resolve the problem? Can you measure it? (Scallet, 1996, p. 8)

After the selection of a clearly stated, important, and relevant question, planning should include incorporating input from as many stakeholders as possible and at as many stages of the research process as is practical. The sampling design should permit the appropriateness and adequacy of the data to be easily recognized. Because the use of inductive process will produce sounder and probably more innovative information, it likely will lead to more use because this approach reflects the social context of the participants more authentically.

The importance of documenting the audit trail has been well described by Morse and Field (1995), Miles and Huberman (1994), and several others. It would be particularly important for the potential user who is not well versed in qualitative methods (including most federal staff) to be able to easily follow the decisions in analysis.

The usefulness of the research project is directly affected by the quality of the research report. Wolcott's (1990) monograph has some excellent, practical suggestions for the critical stage of writing up the research results. He suggests that the writer conceptualize the report in three components: statement of purpose, outline of project, and basic story. Miles and Huberman (1994) provide a review of related references. With the understanding that knowledge is not "self-implementing" (p. 305), and support is generally required for actually using research results, they recommend that researchers identify the basic message they wish to convey, the audiences to reach, the targeted level of use, and the groups and organizations to work with. Planning for the report should begin at least at midpoint in the project.

Summary

There is a continuing need for information from qualitative approaches in policy development. As the benefits of qualitative approaches are better understood by policymakers, federal staff, and the general public, and as qualitative researchers improve their understanding of the needs of policymakers, it is likely that these methods will be increasingly used.

References

Basic Behavioral Science Task Force of the National Advisory Mental Health Council. (1996). Basic behavioral science research for mental health. *American Psychologist, 7*, 722-731.

Bots, P., & Hulshof, J. (1995, June). *Applying multi-criteria group decision support to health policy formulation.* Presentation at the ISDSS conference, Hong Kong.

Carey, M. A., & Smith, M. W. (1992). Enhancement of validity through qualitative approaches: Incorporating the patient's perspective. *Evaluation and the Health Professions, 15*, 107-114.

Cook, T. D., & Campbell, D. T. (1979). *Quasi-experimentation: Design and analysis issues for field settings.* Chicago: Rand McNally College Publishing.

Dennis, M. L., Fetterman, D. M., & Sechrest, L. (1994). Integrating qualitative and quantitative evaluation research methods in substance abuse research. *Evaluation and Program Planning, 17*, 419-427.

Drucker, P. (1993). *Post-capitalist society.* New York: Harper Business.

Fetterman, D. (1993). *Speaking the language of power: Communication, collaboration and advocacy.* Washington, DC: Falmer.

Fischer, F. (1995). *Evaluating public policy.* Chicago: Nelson-Hall.

Guba, E., & Lincoln, Y. (1989). *Fourth Generation evaluation.* Newbury Park, CA: Sage.

Henry, G. (1996). Does the public have a role in evaluation? Surveys and democratic discourse. *New Directions for Evaluation, 70*, 3-15.

Maney, A., & Plutzer, E. (1996). Scientific information, elite attitudes, and public debate over food safety. *Policy Studies Journal, 24*, 42-56.

Messick, S. (1995). Validity of psychological assessment. *American Psychologist, 50*, 741-749.

Miles, M. B., & Huberman, A. M. (1994). *Qualitative data analysis* (2nd ed.). Thousand Oaks, CA: Sage.

Morse, J. M. (1991). Approaches to qualitative-quantitative methodological triangulation. *Nursing Research, 40*, 120-123.

Morse, J. M., & Field, P. A. (1995). *Qualitative research methods for health professionals* (2nd ed.). Thousand Oaks, CA: Sage.

Reichardt, C. S., & Rallis, S. (1994). Qualitative and quantitative inquires are not incompatible: A call for a new partnership. *New Directions for Program Evaluation, 61*, 85-91.

Sandelowski, M. (1996). Focus on qualitative methods: Using qualitative methods in intervention studies. *Research in Nursing and Health, 19*, 359-364.

Scallet, L. (1996). *What policy makers want: A guide for evaluators.* Unpublished manuscript prepared for and available from the Human Services Research Institute, 2336 Massachusetts Ave., Cambridge, MA 02140.

Sechrest, L., Stewart, M., Stickle, T., & Sidani, S. (1996). *Effective and persuasive case studies.* Prepared for and available from the Human Services Research Institute, 2336 Massachusetts Ave., Cambridge, MA 02140.

Swanson, J., Remy, L., Chenitz, C., Chastain, R., & Trocki, K. (1993). Eliciting drug abuse among young adults with genital herpes. *Public Health Nursing, 10*, 197-203.

Weiss, C. (1977). *Using social research in public policy making.* Lexington, MA: D. C. Heath.

Wolcott, H. F. (1990). *Writing up qualitative research.* Newbury Park, CA: Sage.

The Dead Dog Section:
What to Do When Stumped by the Media

Stern: Well, I had an interesting experience in beautiful downtown Edmonton—well, it was at the Mall. They put me on the local station, right? And they had my CV. They had the paper I was going to present. And I talked to these two people, for at least 45 minutes. And we talked about a number of things that I am expert at. But when I got on the air, they said, "What about the nurses' strike?" [laughter] And then they brought up some stuff about euthanasia going on—I don't know—

Well, as I looked at the tape—they were good enough to give me a tape—I didn't do too badly. But what I should have done was to say, "I was not prepared to talk about this subject!" I mean, that's what politicians do. They say, "I'm not going to release that information."

I hadn't experienced that kind of sandbagging before. It was sort of like a doctoral defense! [laughter]

Policy as Forethought in Qualitative Research

A Paradigm From Developing Country Social Scientists

Marjorie A. Muecke

The Variety of Health Researcher Perspectives on Context

What challenges for health researchers do the following contexts have
in common?

- Crowded underserved urban centers of under- and unemployment
- Rural and hill areas isolated from telecommunication and urban services
  and markets

AUTHOR'S NOTE: The section on Egypt was written in collaboration with Jocelyn
DeJong, PhD, Program Officer, Reproductive Health and Population, The Ford Foundation, Cairo, Egypt.

- Squatter communities settled along the banks of rivers that are intoxicated with chemical and biologic wastes
- Agriculture-dependent communities working eroded effete soil

Whether at home or abroad, health researchers working in such areas are compelled to confront the consequences of and contributors to poverty—high morbidity and mortality compounded by inadequate or inappropriate health care resources. However, quantitative and qualitative researchers tend to interpret and respond to these challenges differently.

Worldwide, biomedical scientists, epidemiologists, and scientists of related positivistic perspectives have chronicled health information in terms of aggregate statistics of disease and death rates, and in terms of the objectified individual "case" history. These researchers have given us decades of important comparative national data on morbidity, mortality, health care providers, and use of health care resources that have informed policy and program planning at all levels of government. However, these data, by definition, obscure within-group variations and extremes, and ignore socioenvironmental context as determinants of the health outcome measures. Qualitative researchers, on the other hand, act on the knowledge that socioenvironmental history and context shape patterns of sickness and death, and that they do so with increasing severity as poverty worsens. Qualitative researchers working in areas whose people are slackened by poverty tend to see the excess sickness and death as fallout from the biases of wealth and privilege in social policy. Qualitative researchers, particularly those working in areas of poverty, tend to prioritize thinking about how their research work might inform social policy so as to reduce economic discrimination and its selective denigrating effects upon the health of the poor.

When faced with the competition for paltry resources of diverse urgent needs for basic education, nutrition, clean water, sanitary waste disposal systems, and health care, all of which are clearly but profoundly interrelated, one of the most common and daunting first questions raised by North American researchers is this: "Where to begin?" or "How best to prioritize research topics or projects?" We would most likely want to whittle down the scope of our agendas to manageable discipline-specific pieces in which we (individually or as an organization) could "make a difference" in the foreseeable future, that is, in a future that we could see. Our proclivity as researchers would often be to find a niche for our area of expertise and to conduct exploratory or intervention research in it. As foreign researchers working abroad with some self-consciousness about our status as guests or aliens in a host nation, we would be even more unlikely than when at home to link our research questions and designs to policy-making processes. In choosing our research topic, we would likely prioritize generating knowledge for its own sake over policy-relevant research, thereby assuring, however inadvertently, that our ultimate findings would serve academic rather than political purposes.

In contrast, indigenous researchers—that is, researchers who have grown up intimate with the comprehensive nature of harms that perch on the various edges of poverty and oppression—may be more likely than those raised in privileged countries to be applied and activist in their research purposes. Although few in number and scattered geographically into small discrete programs where they are faced with the immediacy of many interrelated and urgent needs, health social scientists in developing countries[1] tend to prioritize research questions and designs that can inform public policy. This orientation is sometimes facilitated by the happenstance that some developing country researchers have held government positions or can realistically expect to hold one during their professional careers. Being part of an elite that was educated with public funds, then they may feel a special obligation to their country. Having a foot in both worlds, research and government, makes it more reasonable and feasible for them to think of research as a political undertaking, and to realize that there would be little change unless it was mandated through government policy.

Although not all developing country social science researchers treat policy as a forethought in selecting their research issues, and admitting that there are developed country researchers who do frame their research activities in terms of their relevance to policy,[2] in this chapter I will tout selected developing country qualitative researchers and research organizations for demonstrating through their work that research can be linked to policy as a forethought during its conceptualization—as well as during its implementation and dissemination.

The Challenges to Qualitative Researchers

In much of the developing world, the dominance in research of the scientific method and of epidemiological and demographic survey techniques continues to hold the legitimacy of qualitative, participatory, and applied approaches in question. Rigid structures within both academic and medical institutions contribute to the hegemonic hold of the biomedical paradigm on health by preventing an easy exchange of ideas among health scientists[3] and social scientists and among researchers, communities, and policymakers. This is particularly evident in relatively new areas such as reproductive health, where few training opportunities exist for social scientists.[4] Health social scientists, and social scientists conducting research in health and reproductive health,[5] consequently face major challenges in their efforts to establish a paradigm for applied qualitative research. As Chowdhury, Egerö, Myntti, and Rees (1996) have said,

> The new agenda in sexual and reproductive health will lead us to ask new questions and requires us to use new methods or combinations of methods in our research. Institutions strong in traditional approaches to family planning, demographic or biomedical research may not have persons with the requisite vision or skills to lead the way in research in sexual and reproductive health. This . . . will require new commitments . . . for research capacity-building. (p. 19)

The tenacity of the biomedical paradigm is apparent in the fact that 50 years after the World Health Organization defined health as the total well-being of a person and not just the absence of disease and infirmity, many medical research and education institutions and policymakers still tend to regard health from only a medical perspective, neglecting its broad social and structural determinants and dimensions. Although interdisciplinary subspecialties such as health economics, health psychology, medical anthropology, medical geography, and medical sociology have developed over the past 20 years, the social sciences continue to be marginalized in medical, epidemiologic, and population training and research centers.

The marginalization of the social sciences and particularly of qualitative research has been accentuated in developing countries since World War II by governmental oppression of the social sciences (such as by recent military regimes in Argentina, Brazil, and Chile) and, more pervasively, by major international funders pursuing development models for developing countries that prioritize continuous capitalist expansion over social welfare programs (e.g., the World Bank's structural adjustment programs) ("Editorial," 1996; Lurie, Hintzen, & Lowe, 1995). These models for development linked scientific technology with economic growth and assessed development in terms of purely economic indicators. Unfortunately, these efforts promoted neither the autonomy of the recipient countries nor equity in the distribution of the benefits and burdens of development. However, because social and political difficulties persist in countries with high as well as with low gross national products, we know that economic growth has not solved the problems of development. Women in particular have been sidelined by the economic development policies, in part because economic indicators eschew the informal sector, that is, the parallel economy where women predominate (Kabeer, 1994), and partly because men control the national and international economic institutions that privilege policies that favor men.

The 1990s Tilt Toward Recognition of Social Context as Shaping Health

Today there is evidence that a paradigm shift is beginning toward a more holistic human-centered perspective that aims to put a human face on development. In 1993, for example, the World Bank, a major financier and authoritative source of health policy ideas, and longtime proponent of a purely economic definition of development and of using death (mortality) as the chief indicator of health, shifted course (Buse, 1994; World Bank, 1993). To assess the effectiveness of health care, it introduced a way to include morbidity into a measure of health, the disability-adjusted life year (DALY). The DALY is an index that shows the number of healthy years of life lost due to various (mostly medical) causes.[6] It was initially heralded for providing a functional basis that takes account of quality of life for making decisions about health policy ("Editorial," 1993). This is progress toward a more human-centered approach to the measurement of health status than offered by the biomedical model. However, critics point out numerous limitations of the DALY from the perspectives of the social sciences.

One criticism made by qualitative researchers is that the DALY measures only functional limitations of disease, not individual or psychosocial limitations. AbouZahr (1996), for example, points out that "in some countries a menstruating woman cannot cook, have sex with her husband or pray. These are real burdens in the sense that they impede daily life and activities. Yet there is no way of taking account of them using the DALY methodology." For another trenchant example, she points out that infertility is not physically disabling and therefore does not weigh heavily in the measure despite the suffering it causes, particularly for women in societies where a woman's worth is assessed by her capacity to reproduce (AbouZahr, 1996). Another critique refutes "health" measures like the DALY for their rootedness in disease rather than in persons, so they do not capture what people want or what contributes to individual well-being. For example, the success or failure of a family planning program would be more ethically determined by linking a woman's intention to conceive or to avoid pregnancy to her subsequent (non)pregnancy than by ascertaining whether or not she was a contraceptive acceptor (Jain & Bruce, 1994). Meanwhile, the World Health Organization's Human Reproduction program and Division of Family Health are working to define more appropriate, person-centered indicators for assessing and monitoring reproductive health (Shah & Mundigo, 1996).

There are numerous other signs of a shift toward a broader and more health-oriented interpretation of development that takes account of local context and the macro-level political economic influences on it. Progressive voices, often those of activist qualitative researchers, now call for reducing the social and economic costs of industrialization's wastes and pollution, and of undoing economic policies like structural adjustment that prioritize exports over health and human services (Harcourt, 1994). Nongovernmental organizations (NGOs) have emerged as an important voice in United Nations development efforts and conferences in the 1990s, inspiring *socio-economic* paths to development. In effect, we are riding on a wave of interest in the social and cultural contributions and barriers to health and quality of life that calls for more qualitative research and heightened visibility of its analyses.

Researcher Responses to the Challenges

The social sciences are part of this transformation (Gulbenkian Commission, in press; Gupta, Trakroo, & Bamezai, 1994). Just as the women's movement's worldwide spread challenged previous development models for being hegemonic and androcentric, brought the local to global attention, and raised the value of voice, diversity, alliance, and agency, the social sciences are also undergoing a transformation, becoming self-conscious and critical, and beginning to cross disciplinary boundaries for new partnerships in the search for understanding.

In the context of massive threats to quality of life, developing country scholars express an urgency that social science research be an integral part of and contribute to the direction of social change. Their methods for becoming part of social change include situating research in the everyday realities of people's lives, bringing a gender perspective to research questions and designs, and using research findings to inform health policy decision making (Alan Guttmacher Institute, 1995; Harcourt, 1994). The role sought for social sciences in general and qualitative research in particular is to challenge the vision of any singular truth, that is, to undo the notion that one knowledge is privileged with universality over another (e.g., to challenge hegemonic interpretations of biomedicine). Social scientists often have to think against the mainstream of tradition or authoritarian systems and therefore need exposure to thinking that is beyond the terms of the society in which they live.

Developing country social scientists recognize there is a vital role that qualitative research can play in development efforts: It is to put people and culture back into health and development theory and practice. They often have to find ways to work across deep-seated traditional divisions between research and practice, and among academic disciplines. Theirs is potentially a revolutionary agenda because it shifts away from the traditional valuing of social science research for the sake of knowledge that has dominated Northern academia (Rosenfield, 1992) toward valuing it for how it can alleviate problems that are felt by communities. Typically, qualitative researchers select research problems on the basis of participation with communities affected by the problem, design their research with affected communities, and translate research findings and social science concepts into language that can be understood by health care practitioners, policymakers, and nongovernmental organizations.

For example, qualitative researchers are documenting ignored social realities such as women's views of their health. One innovative effort to assess the reproductive health needs of rural and sometimes illiterate women as a basis for shaping interventions for improvement was carried out in China. It was decided that the women themselves should create the assessment data. This was achieved by involving 62 peasant women ranging in age from 18 to 57 as photographers of their own everyday activities. They were then included along with community leaders to interpret and discuss what the pictures said about health, work, change, and gender. The results were a self-portrait that was compiled into a photo novella that is carrying the village women's messages to community leaders as well as far beyond their village boundaries, to county-level officials and further (China Yunnan Women's Federation, China Yunnan Women's Reproductive Health and Development Program, & U.S. Western Consortium for Public Health, 1995).

In Peru, public health services are severely compromised by an austerity package designed to control inflation. Newly decentralized municipal health services lack expertise and are seriously underfunded by municipal funding mechanisms. Faculty at the Cayetano Heredia Peruvian University, which houses the country's premier medical, nursing, and midwifery programs, are taking this situation into account while developing strategies for their own development. For example, by upgrading the social science training of their faculty through study fellowships, they are providing, in the long run, for better informed health officials because the Ministry of Health tends to rely upon graduates of this university to fill its top posts. Faculty are also working with government officials to evaluate sex education programs in schools, and regularly involve government health officials in their seminars and workshops on sexual and reproductive health.[7]

The need for social scientists to inform public discussion and health policy is great. In every society, uninformed opinions influence behavior. This is particularly true for silenced topics such as sexuality, domestic violence, and drug abuse. Uninformed policy, media, and public opinion are particularly harmful for women because gender roles in much of the developing world make reproduction an unspoken topic for women. It is hard to undo wrong messages of the past about a health practice. For example, Aníbal Faúndes reminds us that due to the high media profile of the purported high risks of the Dalkon Shield for pelvic inflammatory disease and ectopic pregnancy more than 20 years ago, in much of the world it is still common for women and clinicians to think that all intrauterine devices (IUDs) are unsafe, even though the Dalkon Shield has long been off the market and IUDs are not a risk factor for PID when used in monogamous relationships (Faúndes, 1996). Scientists the world over must play an audible role in correcting the public's and policymakers' misconceptions about safe and healthy practices.

The timing is excellent for researchers to take on this role given that governments, because of a string of recent United Nations conferences in the 1990s, have been primed into consciousness of the need to focus upon social development. Two of these conferences endorsed a reproductive health agenda that can now be used as a reference point by researchers to guide their own qualitative research in health and to justify with policymakers their linking of the research to governmental policy. The Platforms for Action agreed upon by participating governments at both the 1994 International Conference on Population and Development (ICPD) and the 1995 Fourth World Conference on Women (FWCW) created a new research agenda that focuses upon exploring the social, cultural, economic, and political factors that inhibit or enhance reproductive health (United Nations, 1994, 1995).[8] They call for new indicators of program success. For example, instead of counting the number of contraceptives delivered, the new framework would incorporate concepts related to quality of care and client satisfaction; new indicators would go beyond services to capture elements of individual well-being and broader social change such as the empowerment of women. Qualitative research is essential for developing such indicators.

Enhancing the Capacity of Qualitative Research for Informing Health Policy

Capacity enhancement in qualitative research means the process of improving the capabilities of individuals and institutions to increase understanding of the processes and structures of health-illness through research. Its purpose is to establish a self-sustaining environment for a critical mass of transdisciplinary researchers that can replicate their capabilities in future generations. It requires a protracted time-span and a long-term perspective. These scholars need to be an active part of the world scientific community while also conducting research that has clearly recognized national relevance (Barzelatto, J., cited in Willms, 1995, pp. 20-21).

What opportunities should be created to help individuals develop their capacity to carry out sustained analytical efforts that stimulate their students, journalists, and policymakers (Mechanic, 1995)? Focused collaborative thinking is needed to address a bevy of related questions: What would help the individual develop the requisite conceptual, analytic, interpretive, and technical skills, as well as the collaborative and communication skills, that are needed to work in an interdisciplinary group with nonacademics, grassroots organizations, and policymakers? How does one best stimulate and sustain independent thinking? Which academic institutions can be supported with the greatest likelihood of providing self-sustaining intellectual and research environments? What would help link health research to policy formulation? How could the demand for research among policymakers and program planners be created or increased? What are appropriate and effective roles for North-South and South-South partnerships in capacity building in these areas?

We also need to know more about capacity enhancement. How can we know best how successful capacity-building efforts are? Are, for example, measures of process such as people trained, research output, or health outcome adequate? What should be assessed? Should it be the participation of nonacademic partners (community organizations, individuals, policymakers) in the formulation of research questions, and the planning and conduct of health programs? Ideally, capacity enhancement would be an ongoing transsectoral participatory and negotiated process of reflection, action, and learning. Whatever indicators of achievement are selected, they will become incentives for further activities.

The making of a good researcher requires more than graduate education. It requires research infrastructure, working contact with peers, technical backup, and long-term financial commitment (Okanurak, 1994). Trostle (1992) reminds us that

> a sustained research programme requires not only funding opportunities, but also a network of colleagues, a career path, a set of personal and

financial incentives, and a commitment by the state to support or at least tolerate research as a legitimate and valued endeavor. (p. 1322)

It also requires space and support for innovative thinking. Culture plays a large role in defining and therefore limiting what is considered important to study.

For example, cultural norms around the globe constrain researchers as well as parents and educators from confronting sexuality (Boulton & Westherburn, 1990; di Mauro 1995; Laumann, Gagnon, Michael, & Michaels 1994; McKenna, 1996; Zeidenstein & Moore, 1996). In consequence, social science is not adequately informing public discourse concerning sexual relations. Because sexuality underlies many major health challenges that are poorly addressed, such as unwanted pregnancy, early pregnancy, abortion, HIV and STD transmission, sexual abuse/rape, and because in recent years sexuality has become the focus of partisan and religious politics, sexuality research is urgently needed to document ignored realities such as self-esteem and sexuality, sexuality and gender, teen sex, bisexuality, sexual abuse, and heterosexism. Qualitative research is needed to challenge the taboo about discussing sexuality in research and societies, and to challenge false beliefs—such as sex education being linked to increased teen sex, when in fact the opposite is true (Kirby et al., 1994; Sellers, McGraw, & McKinlay, 1994). To the extent that researchers neglect the topic, they help perpetuate the taboo.

Mechanisms for Capacity Enhancement of Qualitative Health Research

A variety of mechanisms are being used to build qualitative research capacity to address health concerns in developing countries. Although faculty at universities in the United States are likely to think first of conducting short courses or consultations abroad as a primary means of achieving this, there are in fact other mechanisms that are equally or even more important because of their potential for generating sustained indigenous development in this area. Other mechanisms include institutional strengthening, individual fellowship programs, journals/periodicals, conferences, and networks.

One strategy that was used extensively in the past by multilateral and private funders was supporting visits by "experts" from resource-rich countries to resource-poor countries. Although this strategy often yielded productive and long-term North-South linkages, it perpetuated an assumption of East/West, North/South difference, and a valuing of one as superior and the other, inferior. There were also cases of "scientific colonialism" (Trostle, 1992), wherein the researcher from the North landed in the South, hired indigenous researchers to complete his or her project, left the country with the data, and published it in a Northern language such as English, with no (or at best token) acknowledgment of the Southern researchers' contributions. This type of relationship becomes intellectual rape when it penetrates, subordinates, and steals the intellectual identity of the country, gets away with it, and gets rewarded for the activity with subsequent grant awards. To avoid this type of outcome, the strategies and mechanisms listed below share a value/goal of enhancing indigenous research capacity.

(1) Institutional strengthening by establishing new programs. Some countries have sufficient academic and/or social science infrastructure to have social scientists capable of undertaking interdisciplinary research projects on key reproductive health issues, and to have launched multidisciplinary advanced degree programs in reproductive health, whereas others have had too few social scientists and too shallow a social science tradition to make graduate education a feasible or appropriate objective. Institutional strengthening in terms of developing new graduate level programs is most feasible in "high infrastructure" countries. Experience suggests that the institutions most likely to be successfully strengthened through the creation of new university programs have shared two characteristics. First, the institution itself was well established in other areas and was committed to supporting the new program, and, second, the universities had a critical mass of qualified and dedicated faculty leadership to develop and sustain the new program. However, even when these two characteristics are present, the start-up costs of new program development are high for participating faculty. By devoting their time and thoughts to curriculum development and student support, faculty tend to let their own research and publications slip, thereby forfeiting (for a time) their own salary increases and promotions to develop the new program, and retarding the generation of knowledge through research.

(2) Individual fellowship programs. Fellowship programs, although costly in time and money, are a time-tested way to develop in-country researcher capacity. Programs that emphasize in-country collaboration have been particularly effective in encouraging new researchers to enter and remain in the research area. For example, one program in China links a national association with an external consultant to design and support research in women's health through a small grants scheme (Chu, 1994).

Another example is multinational. The East African Health and Behaviour Fellowship Program of Harvard Medical School is a collaborative graduate program between Harvard's Department of Social Medicine and the Universities of Dar es Salaam (Tanzania) and Nairobi (Kenya). It has been supported by the Carnegie Corporation since its founding in 1990. Each year, a physician-social scientist pair go from their home countries to Harvard to study research methodologies, medical anthropology, and related conceptual skills, and to develop research proposals that they carry out on their return to their home countries. By focusing upon just two universities in sub-Saharan Africa, the program is working to develop a critical mass of interdisciplinary researchers who can influence faculty colleagues and students through networking and collaborative research. The fellows also help inform the thinking of the Harvard hosts on prevalent public health issues.

(3) Journals/periodicals. Journals are an important mechanism for distributing the best of peer-reviewed research projects and thereby for disseminating new knowledge upon which other scholars can build. For developing country scholars, however, peer-reviewed premier scholarly journals are too often inaccessible. Because much of social science scholarship is published in English, language may be a crucial barrier, discriminating against non-English-speaking scholars and those for whom English is a second or third language. Further, it is rare for developing country scholars to have easy/direct access to well-stocked libraries or to computerized systems that permit low-cost use of the Internet/World Wide Web. Furthermore, little information about the availability of hard-copy books that could be useful as source material gets distributed to developing countries, and purchase is often too expensive due to costs of currency exchange ratios and postage.

Despite these drawbacks, it is important to note that there are some interdisciplinary social science journals that focus upon health. *Health Transition Review* publishes articles reflecting the study of the cultural, social, and behavioral determinants of health, particularly in the Third World. The journal's links with sub-Saharan Africa are especially strong. *Social Science & Medicine* publishes research in areas of common interest to medicine and the sociobehavioral sciences. It accepts articles from a wide variety of disciplines including health, economics, medical anthropology, medical ethics, and public health policy.

(4) Conferences. Given the linguistic, telecommunication, and postal isolation of many developing country scholars, conferences are one of the best ways to overcome their isolation from peers. For example, since 1968, the *Social Science & Medicine* journal editors have hosted biennial international conferences that bring together junior and senior social and biomedical researchers from developing and developed countries to exchange ideas and information across disciplines (not to present formal papers). These meetings fill a gap by providing a forum for the exchange of diverse practical and theoretical perspectives on selected health topics. These and other conferences, whether at the international, regional, or national levels, also foster exchanges of ideas that can help health care practitioners, program planners and coordinators, and policymakers to formulate cross-sectoral responses to pressing health care concerns.

Since 1990, there has been a florescence of regional conferences that bring together health and social scientists, sometimes also with advocates, practitioners, and policymakers. For example, in 1994, a second Asia-Pacific regional Social Science and Medicine Conference brought together groups and individuals from 12 countries with the result that they formally launched the Asia and Pacific Network of the International Forum of Social Sciences in Health (APNET). The APNET has promoted intraregional scholarly collaborative efforts to develop country reports of the teaching of health social sciences resources and of the status of reproductive health, gender, and sexuality. Cross-sectoral collaboration such as this is a powerful way to build coalitions between scientists and social movements. When networking occurs across universities, governments, and nongovernmental agencies, it can also improve the substance of dialogue by providing formal and informal social space in which network members can try out and improve new ideas as well as delicate topics such as gender equity, access to care, and sex education.

(5) Networks in social science and health. Networks serve multiple functions: teaching/learning, peer review, cross-fertilization of thinking, and keeping systems of knowledge open to fresh input. They help provide and develop a regional and international infrastructure to secure health social scientists as a scientific community. A network can achieve depth and diversity of research capability that would not be possible in individual institutions, and also improves members' opportunities for funding. Further, networks can buffer a national institution during a period of political instability. Networking—whether at conferences or workshops, through collaborative research or training programs, or through information exchange via electronic communication—enables discussion of research questions, methods, and findings as well as the usefulness of policy options emanating from them. When professional associations decide that policy should follow from particular research findings, they can effectively inform policymakers' knowledge base and thinking, thereby facilitating the linkage of data to health policy. A variety of types of networks of health and social scientists have emerged in the 1990s. Examples include the following.

The African AIDS Research Network was founded in 1988. It is now a consortium of French- and English-speaking African researchers from 17 countries that provides technical assistance in social science research on AIDS to its members. A membership of some 200 includes junior and senior social scientists and biomedical investigators, many of whom are prominent in national AIDS control committees.

African Medical Anthropologists is a relatively new, regional, discipline-based network aiming to enhance the capacity of researchers' skills as professionals. Skills supported include the ability to generate resources, to collect data effectively, to write cogently, and to disseminate the results of their research to peers as well as to policymakers. Members of the network are recruited as young PhDs from five universities and trained in cohorts of ten.

COHRED, the Council on Health Research for Development, was established in 1993 as an international nongovernmental organization (NGO). Its membership consists of countries, agencies, and organizations, the majority of whom are or are from developing countries. Its objectives are to promote the concept of Essential National Health Research (ENHR), which aims to focus a developing country's comprehensive research resources—academics, researchers, decision makers, NGOs, and communities—in identifying its health and research priorities. One aim is to minimize nonessential research based primarily on researchers' private interests. COHRED encourages multidisciplinary and multisectoral collaboration to ensure that health policies and decisions respond to the actual needs of the public. It is located in the European Office of the United Nations Development Program in Geneva.

HRP, the World Health Organization's Special Programme of Research, Development and Research Training in Human Reproduction, established in 1971-1972, is one of the few multilateral agencies to have played a lead role in social science research capacity building. HRP has a Unit on Social Science Research on Reproductive Health, the objective of which is to provide sound research findings on sociocultural and service-related factors that influence reproductive health and that can inform policy in developing countries. The unit supports research that is proposed and implemented exclusively by developing country scientists who work in local contexts and apply social science research methodology to obtain information directly from persons whose health is the primary focus of concern. The unit launches initiatives on critical and often sensitive topics in reproductive health; the focus of initiatives brings potentially isolated researchers into contact with peers having similar research interests from other countries and regions (Shah & Mundigo, 1996). The review committee also acts as mentors to the scholars, advising them throughout the research process.

IFSSH, the International Forum for Social Sciences in Health, founded in 1992, aims to create and sustain a network of health and social scientists across regional, national, and disciplinary boundaries, and to strengthen activities of common interest among members. Its members are involved in training, research, and policy formation related to health issues. In addition to holding global working conferences, IFSSH facilitates regional initiatives and networks, currently having active regional networks in Africa (SOMA-NET), Arabic Middle East, Asia-Pacific (APNET), Europe, Latin America–the Caribbean, and North America. The international secretariat is currently at the Central University of Venezuela, Caracas (Higgenbotham, 1994, pp. 133-134).

Country Example: Arab Republic of Egypt[9]

The concluding example is from a country where consciousness of the need for qualitative research on health is at an early emergent stage. This example shows how government involvement can be stimulated both from the outside, by foreign funding and technical assistance, and from the inside, by innovative researchers.

The field of social sciences has scarcely developed in the Arab region, and the brightest students enter fields of high prestige such as engineering and medicine. What little social science research is done in health tends to be defined within a medical framework. But since the late 1980s, several mechanisms have emerged that have generated pioneering research in reproductive health, the findings of which can be used to provide evidence to policymakers that women are suffering from reproductive health problems. The mechanisms include support for the development of research centers, short courses, technical assistance from outside the country, external funding, participation in regional and international conferences, and the development of regional networks. Although there are no graduate programs in the social sciences in Egypt, there is the Al Azhar Center for Population Studies and Research, which in the 1990s has come to play a lead role as the only research center engaged in research related to reproductive health. Despite the fragile infrastructure, Egypt has produced some policy-relevant research that uses qualitative approaches, particularly in the previously ignored area of women's reproductive health. Three such studies are described here.

(1) Ministry of Health's National Maternal Mortality Study. The Arab Republic of Egypt's Ministry of Health (1993) undertook a confidential nationwide study of maternal mortality in 1992-1993.[10] This was the first nationwide study on maternal mortality to take place in Egypt. The study found that the maternal mortality ratio was 176

per 100,000 live births, and identified many avoidable factors as contributing to the very high mortality, including delays on the part of the woman and her family in seeking care, and substandard care on the part of the medical professionals. These two factors interact because delays cause complications in management of obstetric cases. However, a very high proportion—71%—of the women who died had attended a medical facility at some time during the events leading to their deaths, pointing to the need to look at the kind of care they needed and received.

(2) *Study of obstetric morbidity in Menoufeya Governorate.* A study of socioeconomic contributors to pregnancy-related morbidity that complemented the Giza Study (described below) on gynecological morbidity was conducted by the Egyptian Fertility Care Society (1995).[11] The Menoufeya study integrated quantitative with qualitative design and methods: It measured prevalence of pregnancy-related conditions and linked them to women's perceptions of the conditions, their health-seeking behavior, and the effects of the conditions upon their lives. It found that the most-reported chronic morbidity (hemorrhoids, 12.5%; genital prolapse, 11.3%; also urinary incontinence, recto-vaginal fistulae, and dyspareunia) often went untreated because the women did not seek medical care. Linked to this study was an anthropology study by Nagla Al Nahal on the life histories of the women who reported the morbidity; the thesis gained visibility by winning the prize for best master's thesis at American University in Cairo.

(3) *The "Giza Study."* The internationally renowned "Giza Study" of gynecological morbidity in Giza, Egypt, is one of several pieces of research produced by the regional Reproductive Health Working Group (RHWG). Under the directorship of Huda Zurayk, a biostatistician/demographer based at the Population Council in Cairo, this interdisciplinary group[12] of researchers from different institutions in the region (which stretches from Morocco to Jordan) developed a conceptual framework that led to the Giza Study as well as to other projects. The framework has three areas of emphasis: reproductive morbidity, quality of care, and women's perceptions of their health. The strength of the framework is that it is holistic and stresses that one part cannot be seen in isolation but must be seen in the context

of the other work (e.g., linking morbidity to quality of care and to women's perceptions).

Anthropologist Hind Khattab began the project with a community study and interviews of 500 women about their experiences of illness related to reproduction; physician Nabil Younis then conducted physical examinations of these women to diagnose the nature and degree of illness. The study found a heavy burden of disease, including reproductive and urinary tract infections, uterine prolapse, and anemia. It also found that the extent of such conditions does not always come to the attention of health care providers, for interrelated reasons concerning communication between the women and physician, quality of care, underuse of services, and the "culture of silence" surrounding these sensitive conditions.

There is a need for the researchers involved in the above studies to consolidate their findings and draw out their service, policy, and ethical implications. For example, several of the studies pointed to preventable factors that contributed to maternal deaths or reproductive morbidity, and raised issues relating to substandard quality of medical care and to underuse of health services.

In addition to support for researchers, activities are needed to enhance the capacity of policymakers, service providers, service planners, and women themselves to realize the importance of research such as this for addressing the health problems that confront them. One notable example of such activity is a recent book titled *Women's Health and Lives*, which was developed by younger and middle-aged women under the auspices of the Cairo Women's Health Collective, with inspiration from the Boston Women's Health Book Collective's classic *Our Bodies, Ourselves*. The book is among the first publications in the Arabic language concerning women's health in Egypt and the Middle East.

The Larger Context of Support for Qualitative Health Research in Egypt

Research projects do not happen in a vacuum. A major stimulus to developing a political consciousness of need for qualitative research in reproductive health came from Egypt's hosting the International Conference on Population and Development (ICPD) in September 1994. The ICPD provided international policymakers as well as

Egyptian hosts' strong incentive and direction for a fundamental shift in approach to "the population problem"—from a focus upon fertility control to a strong endorsement of a comprehensive approach to reproductive health that places women's health and rights at its center. The ICPD also provided an unprecedented arena for interaction between activist and advocacy groups, grassroots nongovernmental organizations, and researchers in Egypt and abroad. Within Egypt, networks of health and social science researchers are growing. Two that bring together qualitative researchers are the Reproductive Health Working Group (RHWG) and the Arab Health and Social Sciences Forum (the Arab Forum).

Researchers in the field of reproductive health in Egypt have been isolated from each other, and there was little cross-fertilization of research across the different disciplines. Younger scholars in particular had few opportunities to exchange ideas and experiences due to the hierarchical nature of many academic institutions. To address these barriers to understanding, in 1987 the Population Council (headquartered in New York) established the regional Reproductive Health Working Group, which is described above for its leadership role in the Giza Study.

There was also a perceived need for an independent forum to debate health issues in the region and to provide a place where socially concerned physicians and health social scientists could debate issues in Arabic in the region. Because of the weakness of the social sciences in the area, particularly in the areas of health and reproductive health, there are few publications in social sciences and health. To meet this need, in 1995 the Arab Forum was established to bring together younger and senior social and health scientists, including a number of social scientists whose research was supported financially and with technical assistance by the Population Council through a Middle East Awards Program.

Conclusion

Ironically, the fact that the political arena is pivotal for effecting change is often clearer to social scientist researchers in developing country contexts, particularly when the government in question has oligarchic or autocratic leanings, than to those in more democratically organized societies such as the United States where each citizen has a right to participate in government, lobbyists abound, and advocacy groups have a strong voice. While outsiders may see the governments of develoing countries as monolithic bureaucracies vested in the interests of the elite, some of those very elite are persons who themselves or whose classmates and other peers are, have been, or will be social science researchers. They know that nothing will happen without the sanction of and push from government, and they know that mch is waiting to be done. Their intimacy with both governing and researching, copupled with their exposure to the immediacy of very large scale social problems that undermine health and quality of life, make it more likely for them than academically oriented social scientists to think about policy from the moment they articulate a research problem and anticipate a research sign. This chapter has argued that they offer qualitative researchers in economically developed countries a vital lesson.

Notes

1. Epithets like *developing countries* and *Third World* are often rightly criticized for implying uniformity in an extremely heterogeneous cluster of countries. I follow widespread practice and use them for lack of equally succinct but more appropriate terminology.

2. For example, from the United States, I think of the work of Paul Farmer, William Foege, Renee C. Fox, Mindy Fullilove, Robert Hahn, Human Rights Watch reports, Dorothy Milio, Dorothy Nelkin, Judith Norsigian, Debra Prothrow-Stith, and Meredeth Turshen, among others.

3. Although outnumbered by nurses, medicine and public health are the health fields that have the strongest voices in Third World health care policy and structures.

4. The situation is, however, improving. In the 1990s, training in reproductive health began to be offered at different degrees of comprehensiveness at the following centers, among others: Center for the Studies of the State and Society (CEDES, Argentina), El Colegio de Mexico (COLMEX, Mexico), Mahidol University (Thailand), State University of Campinas (UNICAMP, Brazil), University of the Philippines, and University of Ibadan (Nigeria).

5. "Reproductive health is a state of complete physical, mental and social well-being and not merely the absence of disease or infirmity, in all matters relating to the reproductive system and to its functions and processes. Reproductive health therefore implies that people are able to have a satisfying and safe sex life and that they have the capability to reproduce and the freedom to decide if, when, and how often to do so. Implicit in this last condition are the right of men and women to be informed and to have to safe, effective, affordable and acceptable methods of family planning of their

choice, as well as other methods of their choice for regulation of fertility which are not against the law, and the right of access to appropriate health-care services that will enable women to go safely through pregnancy and childbirth and provide couples with the best chance of having a healthy infant.

"In line with the above definition of reproductive health, *reproductive health care* is defined as the constellation of methods, techniques and services that contribute to reproductive health and well-being through preventing and solving reproductive health problems. It also includes sexual health, the purpose of which is the enhancement of life and personal relations, and not merely counselling and care related to reproduction and sexually transmitted diseases" (Programme of Action of the International Conference on Population and Development, United Nations, 1994, Chap. VII, sec. 7.2).

6. The DALY counts every year lost due to premature death as one disability-adjusted life year and every year spent sick or incapacitated as a fraction of a DALY, with the value depending on the severity of the disability and the age of the person at its onset. Added across causes and regions, 1.36 billion years were lost in 1990, representing the "global burden of disease" (World Bank, 1993).

7. Although this program is housed in regular teaching departments of the university to ensure its impact on the quality of medical, midwifery, and nursing education, it is coordinated by Dr. Magdalena Chu, Institute of Population Studies.

8. Although originally disseminated by the United Nations, reproduction and dissemination of the documents for both conferences, in print or electronic format, is encouraged.

9. This section was written in collaboration with Jocelyn DeJong, PhD, Program Officer, Human Development and Reproductive Health, The Ford Foundation, Cairo, Egypt.

10. The (British) Overseas Development Association supported Oona Campbell of the London School of Hygiene and Tropical Medicine as consultant to the project. The study was funded by USAID.

11. The study was overseen by Judith Fortney of Family Health International and funded by The Ford Foundation.

12. The FHWG members represent anthropology, demography, obstetrics-gynecology, public health, sociology, and statistics.

References

AbouZahr, C. (1996, June 24-25). *Disability adjusted life years (DALYs) and reproductive health: A critical analysis.* Paper presented at a meeting of the Working Group on Reproductive Health and Family Planning, "Measuring the Achievements and Costs of Reproductive Health Programs," sponsored by the Health and Development Policy Project and the Population Council, Washington, DC.

Alan Guttmacher Institute. (1995). *Hopes and realities: Closing the gap between women's aspirations and their reproductive experiences.* New York: Author.

Arab Republic of Egypt Ministry of Health. (1993). *National Maternal Mortality Study: Findings and conclusions. Egypt 1992-93.* Cairo: Author.

Boulton, M., & Westherburn, P. (1990). *Literature review on bisexuality and HIV transmission.* Geneva: World Health Organization, Global Program on AIDS.

Buse, K. (1994). Spotlight on international organizations: The World Bank. *Health Policy and Planning, 9*(1), 95-99.

China Yunnan Women's Federation, China Yunnan Women's Reproductive Health and Development Program, & U.S. Western Consortium for Public Health. (1995). *Visual voices: 100 photographs of village China by the women of Yunnan Province.* Yunnan: Yunnan People's Publishing House.

Chowdhury, S., Egerö, B., Myntti, C., & Rees, H. (1996). *Sexual and reproductive health: The challenge for research: A discussion paper.* Stockholm: Swedish International Development Cooperation Agency (Sida) and the World Health Organization.

Chu, C. (1994). Reproductive health research in China: The Ford Foundation initiatives. *Acta Tropica, 57*(2-3), 175-184.

di Mauro, D. (1995). *Sexuality research in the United States: An assessment of the social and behavioral sciences.* New York: Social Science Research Council.

Editorial: The World Bank's cure for donor fatigue. (1993). *Lancet, 342*(8863), 63-64.

Editorial: The World Bank, listening and learning. (1996). *Lancet, 347*(8999), 411.

Egyptian Fertility Care Society. (1995). *Study of the prevalence and perception of maternal morbidity in Menoufeya Governorate, Egypt.* Cairo: Author.

Faúndes, A. (1996). Women deserve accurate information. *Network, 16*(2), 4-5.

Gulbenkian Commission. (in press). *Open the social sciences: Report of the Gulbenkian Commission on the Restructuring of the Social Sciences.* Lisbon: Fundaçao Calouste Gulbenkian.

Gupta, J. P., Trakroo, P. L., & Bamezai, G. (Eds.). (1994). *Social dimensions in health: A South East Asia perspective.* New Delhi: National Institute of Health and Family Welfare.

Harcourt, W. (Ed.). (1994). *Feminist perspectives on sustainable development.* London: Zed.

Higgenbotham, N. (1994). Capacity building for health social science: The International Clinical Epidemiology Network (INCLEN) social science program and the International Forum for Social Science in Health (IFSSH). *Acta Tropica, 57*(2-3), 123-138.

Jain, A., & Bruce, J. (1994, February). *A reproductive health approach to the objectives and assessment of family planning programs.* Unpublished paper presented at a USAID Cooperating Agencies meeting, Washington, DC. Compiled by the Robert H. Ebert Program, the Population Council, New York, December.

Kabeer, N. (1994). *Reversed realities: Gender hierarchies in development thought.* New York: Verso.

Kirby, D., Short, L., Collins, J., Rugg, D., Kiolbe, L., Howard, M., Miller, B., Sonenstein, F., & Zabin, L. S. (1994). School-based programs to reduce sexual risk behaviors: A review of effectiveness. *Public Health Reports, 109*(3), 339-361.

Laumann, E. O., Gagnon, J. H., Michael, R. T., & Michaels, S. (1994). *The social organization of sexuality: Sexual practices in the United States.* Chicago: University of Chicago Press.

Lurie, P., Hintzen, P., & Lowe, R. A. (1995). Socioeconomic obstacles to HIV prevention and treatment in developing countries: The roles of the International Monetary Fund and the World Bank. *AIDS, 9,* 539-546.

McKenna, N. (1996). *On the margins: Men who have sex with men and HIV in the developing world.* London: Panos Institute.

Mechanic, D. (1995). Emerging trends in the application of the social sciences to health and medicine. *Social Science & Medicine, 40*(11), 1491-1496.

Okanurak, K. (1994). Strengthening research capability, funding and sustainability: A personal perspective. *Acta Tropica, 57,* 229-237.

Rosenfield, P. L. (1992). The potential of transdisciplinary research for sustaining and extending linkages between the health and social sciences. *Social Science & Medicine, 35*(11), 1343-1357.

Sellers, D. E., McGraw, S. A., & McKinlay, J. B. (1994). Does the promotion and distribution of condoms increase teen sexual activity? Evidence from an HIV prevention program for Latino youth. *Journal of the American Medical Association, 84*(12), 1952-1958.

Shah, I. H., & Mundigo, A. (1966). Social science research. In *HRP Annual Technical Report 1995* (Special Programme of Research, Development and Research Training in Human Reproduction. WHO/HRP/ATR/95/96, pp. 185-198). Geneva: World Health Organization.

Trostle, J. (1992). Research capacity building in international health: Definitions, evaluations and strategies for success. *Social Science & Medicine, 35*, 1321-1324.

United Nations. (1994). *Programme of action of the International Conference on Population and Development* (A/CONF.171/13). New York: Author.

United Nations. (1995). *Beijing Declaration and platform for action*. New York: Department for Policy Coordination and Sustainable Development. (Also in *Women's Studies Quarterly, 34*[1-2], 154-289, 1996).

Willms, D. G. (Ed.). (1995). *Proceedings of the Workshop on Capacity Enhancement for the Social Sciences in Health, October 15-18, 1995* (Huntsville, Canada).

World Bank. (1993). *World development report 1993: Investing in health*. Washington, DC: Author.

Zeidenstein, S., & Moore, K. (Eds.). (1996). *Learning about sexuality: A practical beginning*. New York: Population Council, Inc.

Name Index

Subject Index

African medical anthropologists, 371
Anonymity:
    definition of, 40
    geographic consideration, 51-52
    masking identities, 49-50
    protecting by omitting details, 47-52
    technologies to protect, 47
    threats to, 44-45
Arab Republic of Egypt:
    women's reproductive health,
        373-375
Art encounters, 94-96
Articles:
    authorship guidelines, 31-32
    too lengthy, 21
Artistic forms:
    performance, 98-108
    poetry, 97-98
Asia and Pacific Network of the International Forum of Social Sciences in Health (APNET), 370

Authorship:
    advice regarding, 23-24
    guidelines, 31-32
    intellectual property, 25-26, 29
    manners, 30-31
    order, 25
    student-faculty advisor, 22-24

Biomedical paradigm, 360

Capacity enhancement, 361
    indicators for, 365
    mechanisms for, 367-368
Commentaries, 157
Conferences, 370
    presentation questions, 158
Confidentiality and definition of, 40
    geographic considerations, 51-52
    masking identities, 49-50
    protecting by omitting details, 47-52
    techniques to protect, 47

About the Authors

Judith Albright (MS) is a Clinical Staff Nurse IV and the diabetes educator at Summit Medical Center in Oakland, California. She received her master's degree in the Department of Physiologic Nursing at the University of California, San Francisco. Her research activities include conducting a qualitative study on the dietary habits of elderly, obese people with diabetes, which was published in *Health and Social Care* in 1994. As the chairperson of the Committee on Clinical Inquiry at the medical center, she has worked with Dr. Janice Swanson to increase the utilization of research results in the clinical setting. One of the projects that the committee has recently completed is a study on the readability of patient education materials, which was published in *Applied Nursing Research* in August 1996.

Joan L. Bottorff (RN, PhD) is Associate Professor and National Health Research and Development Program (NHRDP) Health Research Scholar at the School of Nursing, University of British Columbia, Vancouver, Canada. Her research in the fields of health care inter-actions and health promotion has provided her with the opportunity to optimize the use of both qualitative and quantitative research and explore ways in which these methods can be linked. She is on the editorial board for *Qualitative Health Research* and is a reviewer for several journals.

Joyceen S. Boyle (RN, PhD, FAAN) is Chair of the Department of Community Nursing at the Medical College of Georgia, Augusta, Georgia. A graduate of Brigham Young School of Nursing, she holds a master's degree in public health nursing from the University of California at Berkeley and a PhD in nursing from the University of Utah. She is the coeditor of a text titled *Transcultural Concepts in Nursing Care,* now in its second edition. This book received the *American Journal of Nursing* "Book of the Year" award in 1995. Her clinical experiences include community health nursing with high-risk groups from diverse cultures. Her teaching and research endeavors focus on women's health and qualitative research, particularly ethnographic methods. She serves on the editorial review board of six research journals. She has completed field research studies in the People's Republic of China, Guatemala, and the Republic of Iraq. She received the first E. Louise Grant Faculty Scholar Award in the School of Nursing, Medical College of Georgia. This grant funds her current research on African American caregivers for adult children with HIV disease.

Martha Ann Carey (PhD, RN) is an Evaluation Specialist for the Center for Mental Health Services, Substance Abuse and Mental Health Services Administration, U.S. Department of Health and Human Services. Her professional interests involve the development and monitoring of policy-relevant programs of research for health services delivery. Her research interests include managed care, HIV, and women's issues.

Dauna Crooks (RN, DNS) is Assistant Professor in the School of Nursing at McMaster University, Hamilton, Ontario, and holds a joint appointment with the Supportive Cancer Care Research Unit at the Hamilton Regional Cancer Centre. Her research interests include evaluation of health care delivery, supportive care issues for cancer patients, and nursing education issues.

Roberta F. Durham (RN, PhD) is Associate Professor of Nursing in the Department of Nursing at Samuel Merritt College and on staff in the perinatal department at Summit Medical Center. A graduate of the University of Rhode Island, she holds master's and doctoral degrees in nursing from the University of California, San Francisco. Her interests are in the areas of preterm labor and preterm birth prevention for which she uses grounded theory methods to explore women's experiences with high-risk pregnancy. She has published in both substantive and methodological areas.

Judith E. Hupcey (CRNP, EdD) is a Research Associate at The Pennsylvania State University, School of Nursing, working with Dr. Janice Morse. She just completed an NRSA postdoctoral fellowship, sponsored by AHCPR. She has completed research related to primary care nurse practitioners, cardiac patients, and critically ill patients and their families during the ICU experience. Her current research includes social support and the critically ill patient and family, from the critical illness through recovery.

Sally Ambler Hutchinson (RN, PhD, FAAN) is Professor in the College of Nursing, University of Florida Health Science Center, Jacksonville, Florida. She is a Faculty Associate, Center for Gerontological Studies, and Affiliate Professor in the Department of Anthropology. Her NIH-funded research is in the area of psychogerontology: More specifically, she is studying the behavioral symptoms of patients with Alzheimer's dementia. Additional research focuses on nurses and their work and patients with bipolar disorders.

Joy L. Johnson (PhD, RN) is Assistant Professor at the School of Nursing, University of British Columbia, Vancouver, Canada. Having graduated from the University of British Columbia with a BSN, she holds an MN and PhD in nursing from the University of Alberta. Her program of research is directed toward understanding the nature of health behavior and health behavior change, and currently includes a series of qualitative studies that are aimed at increasing our understanding of the health practices of Canadian South Asian women. She has written numerous articles and chapters on health promotion and the application of knowledge in practice and, with Janice Morse, coauthored the book *The Illness Experience: Dimensions of Suffering*.

Juliene G. Lipson (RN, PhD, FAAN) has an MS in psychiatric and community health nursing and a PhD in medical anthropology. She is Professor in the School of Nursing and Medical Anthropology Division, University of California, San Francisco, and teaches international/ cross-cultural and community health nursing at the master's and doctoral levels. She has done research on childbirth- related women's self/help support groups, the health and adjustment of Middle Eastern and Afghan immigrants and refugees to California, and culturally competent nursing care. Recently, she has been interviewing women who experienced pregnancy and childbirth with a physical disability.

Katharyn A. May (RN, DNSc, FAAN) is Professor and Director, School of Nursing, University of British Columbia, Canada. She received her doctorate in nursing science from the University of California, San Francisco, and has held faculty positions at UCSF and Vanderbilt University. She serves as Associate Editor of *Qualitative Health Research* and as a consultant in grounded theory methodology. She has published extensively in the areas of expectant and new fatherhood, and her coauthored maternity nursing texts have twice received the *American Journal of Nursing* "Book of the Year" award. More recently, her research has focused on the impact of high-risk pregnancy on families through a three-year grounded theory project funded by the National Institute of Nursing Research, National Institutes of Health.

Marilyn Merritt-Gray (RN, MN) is Associate Professor in the Faculty of Nursing, University of New Brunswick, Fredericton, New Brunswick, Canada. She is a graduate of the University of New Brunswick (BN) and the University of Washington (MN) and is affiliated with the Muriel McQueen Fergusson Centre for Family Violence Research in New Brunswick. Her clinical and teaching experiences include rural community mental health nursing, community development, acute psychiatric nursing care, and diverse service sector governance activities. Her research interests are resilience, community action, and woman abuse within partner and work relationships.

Janice M. Morse (PhD, anthropology; PhD, nursing; FAAN) was, at the time of preparing this volume, Professor of Nursing and Behavioral Science, The Pennsylvania State University. She is currently Professor, Faculty of Nursing and Director, International Institute of Qualitative Methodology, University of Alberta, and Adjunct Professor, School of Nursing, The Pennsylvania State University. She has an interest in developing qualitative methods and has published on both basic and advanced methods, including *Qualitative Research Methods for Health Professionals* (with Peggy Anne Field) and *Qualitative Health Research* (Sage). This is the third book in this series, following *Qualitative Nursing Research: A Contemporary Dialogue* and *Critical Issues in Qualitative Research*. She is the editor of *Qualitative Health Research*. She is currently funded by NIH, NINR, to conduct a qualitative study to explore the use and meaning of comfort in nursing.

Marjorie A. Muecke (RN, PhD, FAAN) is Program Officer at the Ford Foundation, New York, on leave from her position as Professor of Nursing and Adjunct Professor in the Department of Anthropology and the Department of Health Services at the University of Washington, Seattle. She received a BA in German literature from Mount Holyoke College, South Hadley, Massachusetts, a diploma from the post-bachelor of arts Coordinated Program, Radcliffe College–Massachusetts General Hospital School of Nursing, an MA in child psychiatric nursing from New York University, and an MA and PhD in cultural anthropology from the University of Washington. Her research is based primarily in Thailand and involves a longitudinal study of nonclinical families and the sociocultural construction of gender and health. In the United States, her research focuses on resettled refugees. Prior to joining the Ford Foundation in New York, she consulted to the World Health Organization on community health nursing in Indonesia and to the Ford Foundation on developing applied research in AIDS prevention and women's rights in Thailand.

Judy R. Norris (RN, PhD candidate) is Associate Professor in the Faculty of Nursing, University of Alberta. She has used Readers Theater to disseminate learnings from research and is interested in learning more effective ways for representing the complexity encountered in the study of lived experience.

Margarete J. Sandelowski (PhD, RN, FAAN) is Professor and Chair of the Department of Women's & Children's Health in the School of Nursing at the University of North Carolina at Chapel Hill. She has published extensively in nursing and social science journals and anthologies on the subjects of reproductive technology, technology in nursing, infertility, and qualitative methodology. She is also the author of three books, including two book-length qualitative studies, *Pain, Pleasure, and American Childbirth: From the Twilight Sleep to the Read Method, 1914-1960* (Greenwood Press, 1984) and *With Child in Mind: Studies of the Personal Encounter with Infertility* (University of Pennsylvania Press, 1993), and the latter was awarded the 1994 Eileen Basker Memorial Prize for excellence in scholarship in gender and health from the Medical Anthropology Society of the American Anthropological Association. She edits and contributes to the "Focus on Qualitative Methods" series in *Research in Nursing & Health* and serves as consultant on qualitative methods. She is currently working on a social history of technology in nursing.

Rita Schreiber (DNS) is Assistant Professor, School of Nursing, University of Victoria, British Columbia, Canada. Her research is a direct outgrowth of her many years in practice with women both in depression and recovering from depression.

Phyllis Noerager Stern (DNS, FAAN, NAP) holds the positions of Professor, Department of Family Health, Indiana University School of Nursing, Adjunct Professor, Center for Women's Studies, Indiana University, Purdue University at Indianapolis, and Adjunct Clinical Professor, Department of Community Health, School of Nursing, Medical College of Georgia. She edits the refereed journal, *Health Care for Women International*, and is Council General (CEO) of the International Council on Women's Health Issues. Her research foci are women, health and culture, family survival strategies in crisis situations, and how nurses do their work. She is one of the earliest and most prolific nursing authors on the grounded theory methodology of research.

Janice M. Swanson (RN, PhD, FAAN) is Professor, Department of Nursing, Samuel Merritt College, Oakland. She received her BSN from Wayne State University in Detroit, Michigan, and her MS and PhD from the University of Maryland. She completed a postdoctoral fellowship with the late Anselm Strauss at the University of California, San Francisco. She has coedited three books: *Men's Reproductive Health* with Katherine Forrest, *From Practice to Grounded Theory: Qualitative Research in Nursing* with the late Carole Chenitz, and *Community Health Nursing: Promoting the Health of Aggregates* with Mary Albrecht-Nies. She has published articles in her research area of reproductive and sexual health issues in the community; she is currently studying condom use decision making in Latinas, funded by the National Institutes of Health. She has served as a member of the Nursing Research Study Section, Division of Research Grants, National Institutes of Health. She also serves as a consultant to research teams studying HIV prevention/AIDS in high-risk populations.

Sally Thorne (RN, PhD) is Associate Professor of Nursing at the University of British Columbia School of Nursing, Vancouver, Canada. Her research in the fields of chronic illness experience and health care relationships has provided her with opportunities to challenge existing qualitative approaches and to optimize the use of the research findings. Her recent book *Negotiating Health Care: The Social Context of Chronic Illness* is illustrative of her interest in making the knowledge constructed through qualitative inquiry accessible to a broad audience, ranging from health care consumers and professionals to health policymakers.

Holly Skodol Wilson (RN, PhD, FAAN) is Professor in the Department of Community Health Systems at the University of California, San Francisco, where she also coordinates the Nursing Education minor. She is also Affiliated Professor in the Aging Health Policy Institute and the Women's Health and Healing Programs in the Department of Social and Behavioral Sciences. Her active research focuses on care management for patients who have Alzheimer's dementia and on quality of life assessment and symptom management for HIV/AIDS patients.

Judith Wuest (PhD, RN) is Associate Professor and Director of Graduate Studies in the Faculty of Nursing, University of New Brunswick,

Fredericton, New Brunswick, Canada. She holds degrees from the University of Toronto (BScN), Dalhousie University, Halifax, Nova Scotia (MN), and Wayne State University, Detroit, Michigan (PhD). She is affiliated with the Muriel McQueen Fergusson Centre for Family Violence Research, Fredericton, and is past President of the Canadian Nursing Research Group. Her research interests are in women's health, particularly women's caring and women abuse, using qualitative research methods from a feminist perspective.